T0100233

Building Browser Extensions

Create Modern Extensions for Chrome, Safari, Firefox, and Edge

Matt Frisbie

Foreword by Stefan Aleksic and Louis Vilgo, cofounders of Plasmo

Apress®

Building Browser Extensions: Create Modern Extensions for Chrome, Safari, Firefox, and Edge

Matt Frisbie
California, CA, USA

ISBN-13 (pbk): 978-1-4842-8724-8 ISBN-13 (electronic): 978-1-4842-8725-5
https://doi.org/10.1007/978-1-4842-8725-5

Managing Director, Apress Media LLC: Welmoed Spahr
Acquisitions Editor: Divya Modi
Development Editor: James Markham
Coordinating Editor: Divya Modi

Cover designed by eStudioCalamar

Cover image designed by Pixabay

Distributed to the book trade worldwide by Springer Science+Business Media New York, 1 New York Plaza, Suite 4600, New York, NY 10004-1562, USA. Phone 1-800-SPRINGER, fax (201) 348-4505, e-mail orders-ny@springer-sbm.com, or visit www.springeronline.com. Apress Media, LLC is a California LLC and the sole member (owner) is Springer Science + Business Media Finance Inc (SSBM Finance Inc). SSBM Finance Inc is a **Delaware** corporation.

For information on translations, please e-mail booktranslations@springernature.com; for reprint, paperback, or audio rights, please e-mail bookpermissions@springernature.com.

Apress titles may be purchased in bulk for academic, corporate, or promotional use. eBook versions and licenses are also available for most titles. For more information, reference our Print and eBook Bulk Sales web page at http://www.apress.com/bulk-sales.

Any source code or other supplementary material referenced by the author in this book is available to readers on GitHub via the book's product page, located at https://github.com/Apress/Building-Browser-Extensions-by-Matt-Frisbie. For more detailed information, please visit http://www.apress.com/source-code.

Printed on acid-free paper

To my parents Mona and Patrick and my sister Lauren.
You are all wonderful. I will continue to fill your
bookshelves until you tell me to stop.

To Jordan.
Your unwavering support advances the world
of web development and keeps the corners of our
carpets nice and flat.

Table of Contents

About the Author

Matt Frisbie has worked in web development for over a decade. During that time, he's been a startup co-founder, an engineer at a Big Four tech company, and the first engineer at a Y Combinator startup that would eventually become a billion-dollar company. As a Google software engineer, Matt worked on both the AdSense and Accelerated Mobile Pages (AMP) platforms; his code contributions run on most of the planet's web browsing devices. Prior to this, Matt was the first engineer at DoorDash, where he helped lay the foundation for a company that has become the leader in online food delivery. Matt has written three books, *Professional JavaScript for Web Developers, Angular 2 Cookbook,* and *AngularJS Web Application Development Cookbook,* and recorded two video series, "Introduction to Modern Client-Side Programming" and "Learning AngularJS." He speaks at frontend meetups and webcasts, and is a level 1 sommelier. He majored in Computer Engineering at the University of Illinois Urbana-Champaign. Matt's Twitter handle is @mattfriz.

About the Technical Reviewer

Jeff Friesen is a freelance software developer and educator conversant in multiple operating systems, programming languages, and numerous technologies. He is currently exploring bare metal programming for the Raspberry Pi and developing his own assembler and associating tooling to facilitate the development of a simple Pi-based operating system.

Acknowledgments

I'd like to acknowledge the tremendous work done by editors Divya Modi, Shonmirin P.A., James Markham, and everyone else involved with the book's production. A capable and agile staff does so much to improve the quality of the product. You were all invaluable resources, and it was a pleasure working with you.

I'd also like to thank the book's technical reviewer Jeff Friesen. Technical authors are nothing without this meticulous work behind the scenes, and his contributions were nothing short of outstanding.

Finally, I would like to thank Apress for publishing this book with me. This was my first title where the book was entirely my own concept, and I am thankful that it found a home with such a terrific publisher.

Foreword

We are Stefan and Louis, co-founders of Plasmo. We first started our company building browser extensions for cyber security, experiencing firsthand the many difficulties extension developers face. We quickly realized that the process of building an extension was way too difficult. We decided to open source our framework, and dedicated our company's vision to solving the toughest problems in browser extension development. As of today, our framework is the most popular browser extension SDK worldwide, and our fast-growing extension product suite is used by some of the world's leading extension developers.

A large community soon gathered and shared even more issues blocking their development with us. We were excited to hear that Matt was writing a book on the subject! Extension development is tricky and filled with poor documentation, difficulty getting started, a massive transition from one extension version to another looming, and much more. There has never been a comprehensive guide to extension development, but Matt's book is changing that.

People use browsers for most of their lives. You might use your browser to read the news or find a good breakfast burrito recipe when you wake up. Software engineers might use their browsers to review pull requests and test their front end. Sales representatives use their browsers to send outbound messages to prospective clients on LinkedIn, and security engineers use their browsers to review new phishing alerts. These use cases are different, but each person uses the same tool to do their job.

Browser extensions augment the browser and transform it from a generic tool into a highly specialized one. A sales representative has different needs compared to a security engineer. In a few years, sales representatives and security engineers will have a stack of browser extensions that automate, categorize, and track their work. Some professions have picked up on this faster than others. Ask a high-performing sales representative about browser extensions they have installed, and you might hear a list of more than ten.

Browser extensions are potent but underutilized tools. The lack of know-how and a complete manual such as Matt's book has curbed people's imagination of what their browser could be. As knowledge of building extensions increases, there will be a tremendous appetite for new browser extensions that serve all kinds of niches we have never seen before.

This book encapsulates years of experience and research. It digs deep into critical details you could only find in random forums, obscure documentation, and fragmented source code online. It is everything you need to know about building browser extensions, from a well-rounded beginner-friendly introduction to a comprehensive guide for veterans. We especially love the following chapters:

- Chapter 4, "Browser Extension Architecture," is for adept developers who have yet to work with browser extensions.
- Chapter 6, "Understanding the Implications of Manifest V3," is for developers who need immediate help transitioning their extension to the newer manifest version.
- Chapter 16, "Tooling and Frameworks," is a must-read for developers who want to supercharge their workflow with robust frameworks and DevOps/CI automation to produce enterprise-grade browser extensions.

We can't wait to use your extension one day!

Stefan and Louis
Co-founders of Plasmo

Introduction

The world of browser extensions has far more than meets the eye. Consider the following:

- On average, 40% of Internet users in the United States use an adblocker on any device; overwhelmingly, these adblockers take the form of browser extensions.
- The tech company Honey, whose primary product is a browser extension, was acquired by PayPal in 2020 for $4 billion.
- As of 2021, there were 1.8 million apps in Apple's App Store; the Chrome Web Store has 180,000 extensions.

When I saw there were 0 relevant Amazon search results for "build chrome extension," I nearly fell out of my chair. I knew at once that this book *must* be written.

Building Browser Extensions: Create Modern Extensions for Chrome, Safari, Firefox, and Edge covers all the knowledge you will need to write cross-browser extensions with the latest web development tools. Browser extensions are given access to *extremely* powerful APIs. I believe most developers are blind to that power - and unaware of just how much it is within their reach.

This book is designed to enlighten web developers and illuminate the true potential of the browser extension software platform. It is geared for developers who have experience building websites and can apply their knowledge to a new software domain. This book is not ideal for people new to programming - it would be like an inexperienced cook starting off by learning to make a sauce.

A major barrier to developing browser extensions is the appalling status quo of documentation. The fragmentation between different browsers and different manifest versions turns slogging through the documentation into a mind-numbingly onerous affair. I wrote this book specifically to address this problem. The reader will learn what is possible with the APIs, how they can best be applied, and all the traps to avoid. The book is not intended to *replace* the API documentation, as it is changing all the time. Instead, it is intended to supplement the API documentation; the book has plenty of direct links to the Chrome Developers and MDN sites throughout.

The transition to manifest v3 is upon us, and already it is causing problems. If you are confused about what manifest v3 is, what are its implications, and how best to navigate the ongoing transition, this book is for you. I dedicated an entire chapter to the manifest v2/v3 transition.

The lingua franca of web development is React, and this book gives special attention to the best ways in which you can write a browser extension in React. It also covers all the supplemental tools you'll need along the way, such as Webpack, Parcel, and Plasmo.

Like many developers, I learn by example. I was annoyed that so many APIs listed in the documentation were totally inscrutable. For example, the omnibox API is amazing and incredibly useful, but the documentation on how to use it is *garbage*. I just wanted a simple example to pick apart and play with, and there was nothing to be found. To fill this need, I created a companion extension for the book: *Browser Extension Explorer*. It's an open source browser extension with dozens of interactive demos. Each demo shows how various browser extension pieces and APIs work, and each includes links to the specific source files so you can see how it was built.

You can download *Browser Extension Explorer* from the Chrome Web Store, or find a link to it on the companion website to this book: `https://buildingbrowserextensions.com`.

CHAPTER 1

What Are Browser Extensions?

Browser extensions are strange and powerful parasites. Browser extensions are parasites because they reside in an unusual corner of the world of software: they run on top of web pages yet are totally independent of any website or server. Browser extensions are powerful because they are afforded an unusual degree of agency: some browser extensions can view and modify everything you see in your browser, some can view every HTTP request your browser sends, and others can manage your digital currency wallets. Browser extensions are strange because they can directly antagonize the very companies that support them: uBlock Origin, one of the most popular Google Chrome extensions, exists only to prevent showing the very ads that make up Google's primary revenue channel.

Strange and powerful as they may be, browser extensions are an undoubtedly useful tool. They afford the end user a degree of control over their web browsing experience that is not possible in any other way. The most popular browser extensions have tens of millions of installs, and as of 2022, the Chrome Web Store has over 180,000 extensions published. In recognition of the broad adoption and utility, in 2021 the W3C formed the WebExtensions Community Group to "explore how browser vendors and other interested parties can work together to advance a common browser extension platform."

M. Frisbie, *Building Browser Extensions*, https://doi.org/10.1007/978-1-4842-8725-5_1

Whatever lies ahead for browser extensions, it seems that they will not be going away any time soon.

History of Browser Extensions

Much in the same way that evolutionary biologists learn about modern life forms through the study of transitional fossils, browser extensions can be better understood by examining their software antecedents.

Customizing Software with Plugins

Support for *plugins*, software components that alter the behavior of an existing computer program, was first implemented in the 1970s on the UNIVAC Series 90 mainframe computer (Figure 1-1). EDT, a text editor running on the mainframe's Unisys VS/9 operating system, allowed other programs to "plug in" and access its in-memory buffer, as well as send commands back to it for processing. Granted these abilities, plugin programs were capable of programmatically altering the flow of other programs or invoking text editor commands, tasks that were normally accomplished via direct user input.

Figure 1-1. *UNIVAC Series 90 mainframe computer*

History of Web Browsers

The fundamentals of web browser behavior were a major contributor to the explosive adoption of the Internet. Unlike the conventional software delivery model of distributing executables – binary programs that are difficult to inspect or change – software delivered over HTTP was open source. Anyone who receives an HTML page has the ability to do what they like with it: view the source, modify existing content and styling, or duplicate it and reuse it for their own needs. Good ideas could quickly propagate because it was easy to reverse engineer how a website achieved a feature.

The release of JavaScript in 1995 continued with this idea. Because JavaScript is an interpreted language, scripts delivered to the browser via HTTP were open source. Furthermore, part of JavaScript's usefulness was the Document Object Model (DOM), which allowed scripts to use an API to programmatically inspect and modify what the browser was showing the user. Even decades later, it remains true that every web page in the world can be inspected and modified in JavaScript via the same set of browser APIs.

Native Browser Plugins

At the same time that JavaScript was getting on its feet, software companies were rolling out new ways that software could run in the browser. This software took the form of "browser plugins," which were closed source modules that were able to run programs natively on the host computer from within the browser. Examples of these were Java applets, Adobe Flash, Microsoft Silverlight and ActiveX, and Apple QuickTime. JavaScript at the time was quite slow and feature-limited, so offloading computation to the host system allowed for browsers to utilize more system memory, persistent storage, and graphics APIs that would otherwise be off-limits. Because these plugins lived in a totally different execution context, they were largely sandboxed from the web page around them.

These plugins were adopted out of necessity, but they were replete with problems. Plugins were clunky to install and use, and because they were provided with privileged access to the host system, they introduced lots of browser bugs and security holes. As browsers became more and more capable with HTML5, CSS3, and more fully-featured ECMAScript specifications, these plugins served less of a purpose, and as a result modern browsers have dropped support for them almost entirely.

From Browser Add-ons to Extensions

As early as 1999, Internet Explorer and Firefox supported "add-ons" that were capable of customizing the browser, but these used proprietary integrations and therefore were siloed to a single browser and limited to that vendor's add-on API. It wasn't until September 2009 that the first modern browser extensions became available in Google Chrome. Unlike add-ons for other browsers, these Chrome extensions could be built using HTML, CSS, and JavaScript. They interacted with the browser using a JavaScript extension API, and developers could publish their extensions to the Chrome Web Store.

By June 2012, Chrome passed Internet Explorer as the most popular web browser, and the Chrome Web Store reached 750 million total installs. In the ensuing years, rival browsers began to progressively adopt the APIs and extension model that Google Chrome had pioneered.

The Browser Extension Landscape

In the wake of years of trial and error, the browser extensions of today are a mature software product. They enjoy broad adoption by developers and consumers, have well-defined APIs and documentation, and they can easily reach the end user via a robust app store pipeline. In this section, we'll explore how to think about browser extensions, where users go to install them, and what the different categories of browser extension are.

Comparing Mobile Apps and Browser Extensions

In many respects, modern browser extensions resemble mobile apps. They both explicitly declare which permissions they need from the host system, are restricted by well-defined security models, and utilize a broad collection of APIs to interact with that host. They are both bundled into releases and deployed via a vendor-specific app store. Both mobile app and browser extension releases undergo a review process, and updates are automatically downloaded and installed via the host system.

Whereas mobile apps typically exist as a standalone user interface, extensions usually are built to run atop one or many web pages with a supplementary user interface. Unlike mobile apps, browser extensions do not necessarily have a user interface; many popular browser extensions are nothing more than a piece of JavaScript that runs in the background to execute a handler upon some event.

Browser Extension Stores

All major browsers offer a store where extensions can be published and downloaded:

- Google Chrome extensions can be installed from the Chrome Web Store (`https://chrome.google.com/webstore`). This extension store is the largest and most popular.
- Safari extensions can only be downloaded from the Apple App Store.
- Mozilla Firefox extensions can be installed from the Add-ons marketplace (`https://addons.mozilla.org/`). Notably, Firefox is the only browser that allows for extensions to be used on both desktop and mobile devices.
- Microsoft Edge extensions can be installed from the Edge Add-ons marketplace (`https://microsoftedge.microsoft.com/addons/Microsoft-Edge-Extensions-Home`). The Edge browser's recent adoption of the Chromium rendering engine means that Chrome Web Store extensions can be installed in the Edge browser by enabling the "Allow extensions from other stores" setting.
- Opera extensions can be downloaded from the Opera Addons marketplace (`https://addons.opera.com/`). Like the Edge browser, Opera is a Chromium-based browser and can be configured to install extensions from the Chrome Web Store.

Types of Browser Extensions

Because of the broad API at their disposal, developers are capable of building browser extensions able to perform a remarkable range of tasks. However, just as Unix programs are expected to "do one thing and do it well," browser extensions are generally geared toward being smaller and more targeted in their purview.

Ad and Tracking Blockers

Easily the most common extension type, ad and tracking blockers serve a very simple purpose: to block unwanted content. Modern web pages are constructed from a cascade of requests for individual pieces of content. Most of these requests are for essential pieces of content like CSS and JavaScript to render the page, but many are for scripts that render ads, collect analytics, or track the user.

The core strategy these blocking extensions utilize is simple. When installed, a blocking extension is granted the ability to inspect and manage all HTTP requests a page makes. The extension also comes bundled with a list of URL domains and regular expressions that are known to serve ads or tracking content. As each page request goes out, the extension checks it against the list, and kills the request if there is a match.

From the page's perspective, it will appear that the request simply failed - something that is completely normal and expected when sending requests to a remote resource. From the user's perspective, the web page will *usually* be correctly rendered with only the ads and tracking scripts teased out. From the ad or tracker server's perspective, they have no idea that the user ever visited the page, since the outgoing request never reaches the server.

Of course, this sort of extension is problematic for entities that depend on the blocked content to generate information or revenue. In response, the ad and tracker industries have begun to roll out countermeasures to address the widespread use of blocker extensions. Some pages now will only render their content if the ad and tracker scripts load; they assume that a failed request is *always* because a blocking extension killed the request. Some ad and tracking servers serve their scripts using "CNAME cloaking," where the ad or tracking script request pretends to be regular content loaded from the page's domain. Furthermore, Google Chrome is using its dominant extension market share to champion a transition to a new manifest format, manifest v3, that will severely reduce the ability of extensions to effectively block ad and tracker requests.

Note The APIs used by extensions to manage network requests are covered more in the *Networking* chapter. The transition to manifest v3 is covered in depth in the *Extension Manifests* chapter.

Password Managers

Extensions can manage a JavaScript execution environment that is completely separated from any web page. This sandboxed environment is ideally suited to load and store secret information, where it can be securely passed to and from web pages on demand. Password managers leverage this to record username/password combinations, save them locally or remotely, and type them in for the user.

A password manager extension allows the user to log in to the password manager service inside a sandboxed extension interface. Once credentialed, they will load the user's encrypted passwords from a remote server and decrypt them locally. With the passwords now available in memory, the extension manager is granted permissions that allow it to effectively manage a user's passwords:

- View and manage the page DOM to automatically detect username and password inputs, type in usernames and passwords, and render additional content on the page to manage user credentials

- View and manage outgoing requests to automatically detect requests that contain user credentials

Perhaps the most important aspect of using password managers is their inherent ability to almost completely prevent any phishing attempts. Password managers can accurately associate a user's credentials with the domains upon which they should be used. For example, a user's credentials on `realsite.com` should only ever be filled when the browser is on `realsite.com`. Suppose the user receives a phishing email and is tricked to click on a link that takes them to `fakesite.com` (pretending to be `realsite.com`). Even though `fakesite.com` may appear to the user to be an exact replica of `realsite.com`. the password manager extension sees the URL is not `realsite.com`, and it will decline to fill the credentials. Of course, this doesn't prevent the user from entering their password manually, but nevertheless the URL matching feature is a robust point of defense against this type of attack.

Smart Writing Management Tools

Extensions can be granted full access to the page DOM, and as a result they are capable of viewing and managing page content - including text inputs and their text content. Browser extensions that listen for keyboard events and clicks are afforded a real-time feed of exactly what the user is typing. This text content can be piped through to any number of text management tools, such as spell checkers, grammar checkers, and smart writing assistants. These extensions can then style the text and insert popup boxes into the page that provide the user an on-demand interactive interface to manage the smart text management tools alongside the actual HTML input fields.

Accessibility Tools

The primary way to consume content on the Internet is via text, and not everyone has an easy time reading a computer screen. Just as smart writing management extensions can read and change input text, accessibility extensions can take the existing page text and format it in a way to make it more accessible to the user. This can take the form of automatically translating page text, piping the page text to screen reading software, reformatting the page text to make it more legible (by increasing size, contrast, or choosing alternate fonts), or by offering quick access to a dictionary.

Content and Link Aggregators

Plenty of web users find the need to quickly and easily save web page URLs or partial content of those pages. Aggregator extensions can add in a user interface to quickly grab URLs or portions of page HTML and save them, either locally or on a third-party server. Extensions also have access to the Bookmark API, allowing them to view and manage the browser's bookmarked sites.

Tab Management Tools

Browser extensions have access to an extensive tab management API, allowing them to perform a wide range of tab-centric actions that otherwise would need to be accomplished directly by the user. Custom new tab behavior, reordering existing tabs, discarding stale tabs, and quickly accessing commonly used tabs are just a few of the possible features these types of extensions provide.

Screen Recording Tools

Not only are browser extensions capable of viewing the page DOM, they are also able to make use of HTML5 APIs to *literally* see what your browser page looks like. These are useful for tools like screen recording, screen sharing, and capturing screenshots.

Note Extensions that use these HTML5 APIs still require the user to explicitly give permission. Permission-gated APIs such as the Screen Capture API will still generate a browser dialog box asking the user to grant access when a browser extension requests it.

Integrations for Software Platforms

Plenty of software platforms with a public API have seen fit to publish browser extensions that can directly connect to that API. This is especially useful when the content sent to those APIs is drawn from a web page the user is currently viewing. Sending content to remote file storage, automated access to a user's calendar, and accessing a third-party note-taking API are just a few of the ways that browser extensions use tight integration with a web page to improve user experience.

Digital Currency Wallets

The increasingly popular world of digital currencies brings along with it a new way that users must manage payments. The details vary between platforms and currencies, but the tasks that digital currency users must perform generally fall into one of the following buckets:

- **The user must read a long string of characters presented to them.** This might be a cryptocurrency address that they wish to send funds to or receive funds from. These strings are usually dozens of random characters, so typing or writing them down without making a mistake is impractical.

- **The user must perform a handshake with a platform.** This takes different forms depending on the technology involved, but digital currency platforms will often support some form of "connection" with your wallet that allows for payments to be sent or actions to be signed or explicitly authorized.

Browser extensions are well-suited for both tasks. Their ability to automatically read page content means long character strings become trivial to manage. Furthermore, their separate execution context is a very secure place for developers to host a digital wallet.

Developer Tools

Modern web development could not have happened without developer browser extensions. In the early days of the web, developers were desperate for ways to more easily debug the websites they were developing. One of the earliest solutions to this was a Firefox addon released in 2006 called Firebug, which allowed developers to view and tease apart the web page they were currently viewing (Figure 1-2). This greatly simplified their debug process for HTML, JavaScript, and CSS, which without the addon would incur a patchwork mess of using print statements and viewing the raw page source.

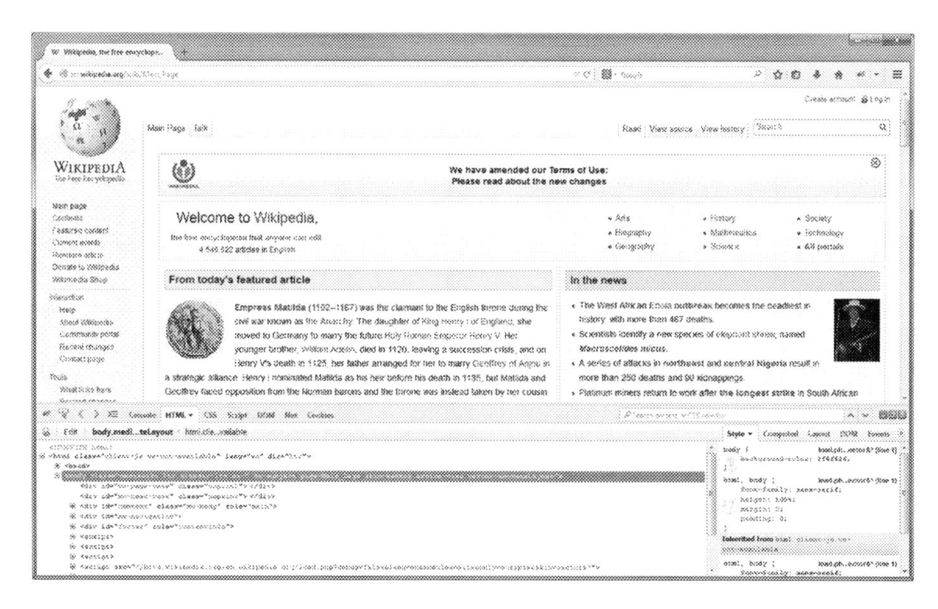

***Figure 1-2.** Firebug user interface*

Browsers quickly caught on that there was incredible demand for this sort of tooling, and they began to roll out native versions of debuggers that matched the feature set of Firebug. Having become redundant, the Firebug extension was shut down in 2017.

With the mass adoption of single page applications like React, demand for developer tooling has followed in turn. The native browser debugger is not well-suited for debugging these sorts of applications, as the logic and architecture governing how the page renders is sequestered in large blobs of third-party JavaScript that is very difficult to debug.

To address this issue, many teams that work on these single page application frameworks also release a companion browser extension. The browser extension is intimately familiar with the internals of how a specific single page application behaves and is equipped with a broad toolkit that allows the developer to peer into the framework and understand what it is doing. This affords developers a much richer insight into what is happening on the page – and more importantly, how to fix it.

Furthermore, browser extensions have evolved to support direct integration into the browser's developer tools. Extensions can insert a custom *devtools page* into the browser's debug interface, interact with the inspected page, and debug network requests. They also have access to a custom DevTools API. The React Developer Tools user interface embedded inside the browser's developer tools is shown in Figure 1-3.

Figure 1-3. *React Developer Tools user interface*

Summary

Browser extensions have sneakily become an essential component of modern computing. From the humble of beginnings of the mainframe computer, they have evolved over decades into a veritable Swiss Army Knife for the modern browser.

The power of browser extensions is acutely expressed in the broad range of tooling that they enable. From powerful security and privacy tools like ad blockers and password managers, to a suite of tools for in-browser writing, to a broad set of single page application developer tools, browser extensions enable and augment more of the modern web experience than most people might realize.

The next chapter will explore all the different pieces that compose a browser extension.

Credits

Figure 1-1: `https://commons.wikimedia.org/wiki/File:Univac9060.jpg`
Source: United States Navy

Figure 1-2: `https://commons.wikimedia.org/wiki/File:Firebug_extension_screenshot.png`
Source: Article: Wikipedia contributors Firebug: Firebug contributors screenshot: SteveSims, CC BY-SA 3.0, via Wikimedia Commons

CHAPTER 2

Fundamental Elements of Browser Extensions

As with most software platforms, browser extensions can be conceptually divided into a handful of discrete pieces. Developers new to the world of browser extensions may find the idiosyncrasies of these pieces tricky to internalize, as some of the behavior is redundant or not intuitive. Understanding how the pieces of browser extensions fit together is critical for becoming an expert at browser extension development.

Note This chapter will individually cover each piece of browser extensions at a high level and without diving into too much code. Subsequent chapters will probe each of these pieces in depth.

The Browser Model

Before exploring the various elements of browser extensions, let's first begin by reviewing the default behavior of a browser. Consider the following diagram of a web browser with an open tab (Figure 2-1).

M. Frisbie, *Building Browser Extensions*, https://doi.org/10.1007/978-1-4842-8725-5_2

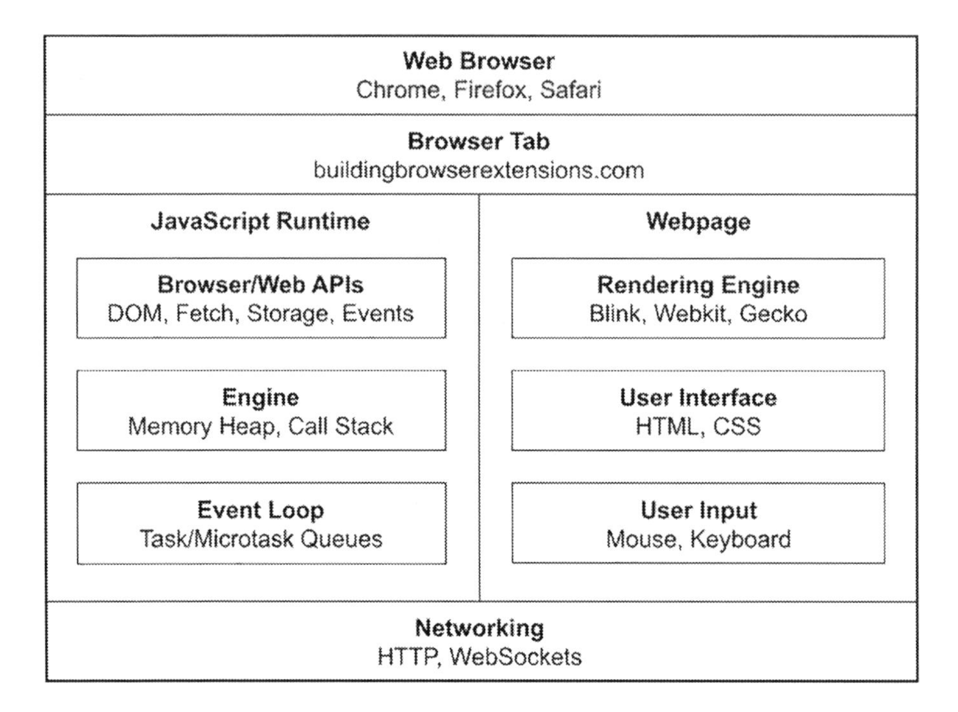

Figure 2-1. *Simplified model of the web browser*

Note A basic understanding of how a web page is rendered, how JavaScript executes, and how the browser performs network requests is a prerequisite for browser extension development. If these topics are unfamiliar to you, an excellent list of resources can be found at `https://developer.mozilla.org/en-US/docs/Web/Guide/Introduction_to_Web_development`

This diagram illustrates the high-level concepts at play when a web browser has a single tab directed to a URL. The web page renders in the browser's primary user interface and has its own JavaScript runtime. Both the web page itself and the scripts within it make subsequent network requests after the initial HTML loads: the page head will load assets like CSS, images, and additional scripts, and the scripts can execute additional requests to load assets and send and receive data.

Browser Tabs

Let's extend the previous diagram to show when multiple tabs are open in a browser (Figure 2-2).

<table>
<tr><td colspan="4">Web Browser
Chrome, Firefox, Safari</td></tr>
<tr><td colspan="2">Browser Tab
buildingbrowserextensions.com</td><td colspan="2">Browser Tab
apress.com</td></tr>
<tr><td>JavaScript Runtime</td><td>Webpage</td><td>JavaScript Runtime</td><td>Webpage</td></tr>
<tr><td colspan="4">Networking
HTTP, WebSockets</td></tr>
</table>

Figure 2-2. *Web browser with multiple tabs*

Browsers effectively sandbox different tabs, providing each with their own document object, JavaScript runtime, memory, and depending on the browser, their own system thread and process. Of course, there are a myriad of critical considerations when it comes to matching origins. Although each tab will be afforded separate runtimes, two separate tabs with matching origins are able to share resources. To name a few

- Cookies
- LocalStorage
- IndexedDB

- Shared Workers
- Service Workers
- HTTP Cache

Same-Origin Policy

Origins are also a consideration when applying the Same-Origin Policy (SOP). In brief, the SOP is a set of security policies implemented by all browsers that control access to data between web applications. When two web applications have different origins, the browser automatically applies a set of restrictions to protect potentially sensitive information from an untrusted origin. Web developers typically encounter the SOP in three places: when sending network requests to foreign origins, when executing scripts from a different origin, and when accessing storage APIs from different origins.

The Browser Extension Model

From the perspective of the web page, browser extensions can be thought of as an invisible supplemental entity. They execute JavaScript in their own runtime, they render pages in their own sandboxed contexts, and they have access to their own separate set of APIs. The web page will have no idea browser extensions are installed or what it they are doing.

Note Content scripts are an important exception to this, as they allow for both the web page and the extension to access the DOM and some shared resources, but as you will see in the *Content Scripts* chapter, they are subjected to some extension-specific sandboxing of their own.

Consider the diagram of a browser with an extension installed as in Figure 2-3.

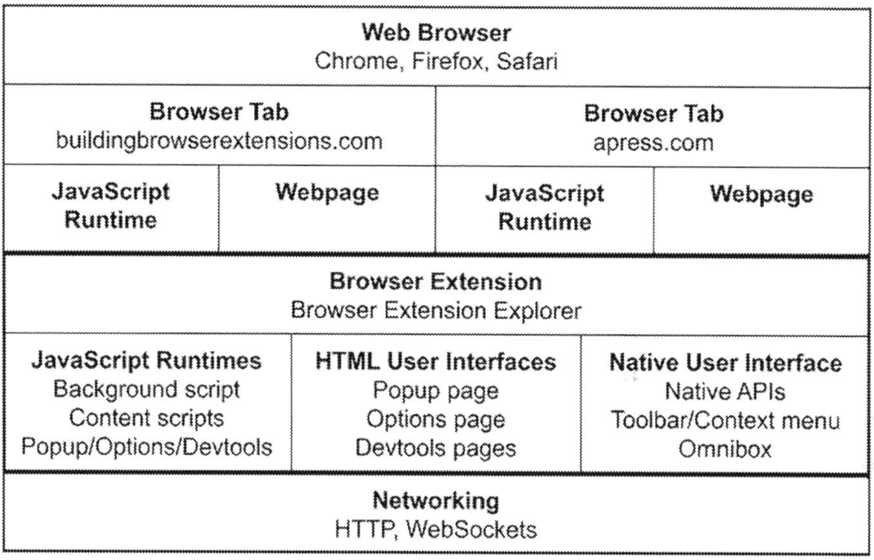

Web Browser
Chrome, Firefox, Safari

Browser Tab
buildingbrowserextensions.com
JavaScript Runtime | **Webpage**

Browser Tab
apress.com
JavaScript Runtime | **Webpage**

Browser Extension
Browser Extension Explorer

JavaScript Runtimes
Background script
Content scripts
Popup/Options/Devtools

HTML User Interfaces
Popup page
Options page
Devtools pages

Native User Interface
Native APIs
Toolbar/Context menu
Omnibox

Networking
HTTP, WebSockets

Figure 2-3. *Web browser with multiple tabs and an extension installed*

Let's examine each of the important concepts shown in this diagram.

Independent JavaScript Pages and Runtimes

Once installed, browser extensions can offer multiple custom HTML user interfaces in several places: the popup page, the options page, and the devtools pages. These pages behave like normal web pages in nearly every way:

- Each page is rendered in the same way as a normal web page, with load events and a conventional document object.

- Each page is provided a dedicated native browser container and completely separated from all other web pages.
- Each interface is provided its own JavaScript runtime.

Background scripts and content scripts are provided their own runtime, but they do not exist as a standalone user interface.

Note The details of popup, options, devtools, background script, and content script are covered later in this chapter.

Native APIs and User Interfaces

Browser extensions have access to a suite of native browser APIs that allow them to control the behavior, appearance, and data of the browser. Some examples

- Tabs API
- Bookmarks API
- Downloads API
- Browser History API
- Browsing Data API

Note These APIs will be covered in depth in the *Extension and Browser APIs* chapter.

Furthermore, browser extensions are afforded several ways to integrate with the browser user interface itself. This includes the ability to manage how the toolbar icon appears and behaves, specifying behavior for the URL bar omnibox interface, and defining what should appear in the extension context menu when it is opened.

Tab and Domain Access

Browser extensions are not restricted to a single domain or tab - they live in the browser itself. When given the proper permissions, browser extensions are capable of interacting with multiple tabs on multiple domains. This means that a browser extension is able to inspect and manage a portion or the entirety of a browser's open pages.

Browser extensions are also not required to use a web page at all. Extensions are adequately equipped to exist as standalone pieces of software that live only in the browser itself. Of course, some aspects of browser extensions like content scripts and devtools interfaces are only useful when manipulating web pages.

Observing and Intercepting Network Requests

Normally, network requests dispatched from a web page are handed off directly to the browser. Browser extensions can be given permission to act as a network request shim, where requests dispatched to the page will be preprocessed by the extension before being passed off to the browser. This means that the extension can add rules for conditionally modifying requests, or even blocking them outright. It also means that the extension can see a stream of traffic in an out of the page in real time.

Note The mechanics of modifying network requests are being significantly changed between manifest v2 and v3. This is covered in depth in the *Networking* chapter.

Elements of Browser Extensions

The previous section covered browser extensions as a holistic entity. This is useful when trying to get a grasp on the concept as a whole. However, as alluded to in the introduction to this chapter, browser extensions exist as a collection of semi-independent elements. This section will examine each of these elements at a high level.

Extension Manifest

The manifest is the rulebook for the browser extension. Every extension is required to provide this manifest as JSON data in a `manifest.json` file. Some examples of what is contained in the manifest

- Public information such as the extension name, description, semantic version, icons, and author
- Pointers to entrypoint files for background scripts, popup pages, options pages, devtools pages, and content scripts
- Requirements and configurations the extension needs to properly operate, such as permissions, content security policies, cross-origin policies, and minimum browser versions
- Pattern-match rule sets for managing network requests, enabled domains, and resources the extension wishes to inject into the page via content script
- Miscellaneous extension-specific options like enabling offline and incognito and keyboard shortcuts

Note The specifics of how to write a `manifest.json` file can be found in the *Extension Manifests* chapter.

Manifest v2 and v3

The world of browser extensions is currently in a transitional period between two versions of the `manifest.json` file: version 2 (v2) and version 3 (v3). The new manifest v3 significantly alters how extensions execute, and it changes the APIs that they can access. Google Chrome is spearheading the transition to manifest v3; due to their market dominance, other browser vendors are for the most part following in turn.

The transition to manifest v3 will be a major theme in this book. The changes it makes are highly controversial in the browser extension developer community, and they broadly impact a number of extremely popular browser extensions.

Background Scripts

The primary purpose of background scripts is to handle browser events. These events might be extension lifecycle events such as an install or uninstall, or they might be browser events like navigating to a web page or adding a new bookmark. Background scripts can be defined in JavaScript files, or as a single HTML file that runs the background scripts via one or more `<script>` tags in a headless page.

Tip Most simple browser extensions are adequately served by a single background script.

Although background scripts are provided their own JavaScript runtime, they do not exist in isolation. They can access the WebExtensions APIs and therefore are capable of performing actions such as exchanging messages with other parts of the extension, exchanging messages with other extensions, or programmatically injecting content scripts into a page.

Background scripts undergo a significant transformation between manifest v2 and manifest v3. In manifest v2, the background script had the option of being either "persistent," meaning the background script is initialized exactly once and lives in memory until the browser is closed, or nonpersistent, where the background script exists as an "event page" that is initialized on demand whenever a relevant browser event occurs. In manifest v3, background scripts exist as service workers, which largely replicate the behavior of the manifest v2 nonpersistent background scripts.

Note The *Background Scripts* chapter includes more details on background scripts.

The Popup Page

The popup page is a native browser container that browser extensions can use to display a custom user interface. The popup page behaves as a dialog box that "pops" over the web page when the user clicks the extension toolbar button. The popup page will always appear directly below the toolbar. Because it can be quickly accessed and can show over any web page, the popup page typically contains content that users need easy access to. An example of a popup page is shown in Figure 2-4.

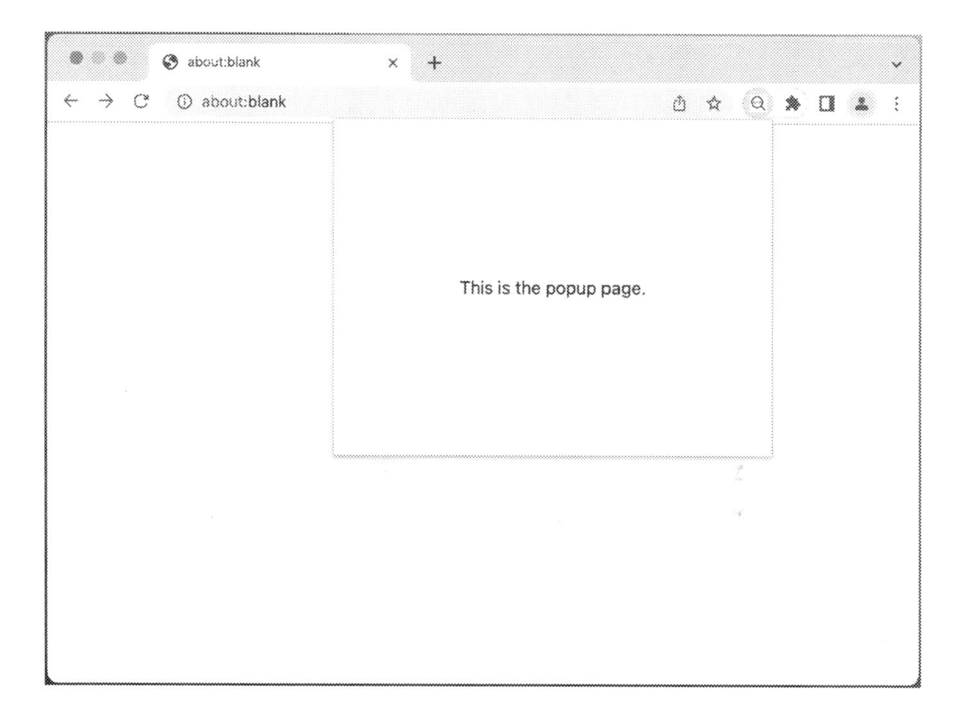

Figure 2-4. *Simple popup page*

Popup pages are rendered just like regular web pages, but their dialog-like nature means they are disposable: the popup will be freshly rendered each time the popup is opened, and unloaded when the popup is closed. Like background scripts, popup pages can access the WebExtensions API, meaning they have the same set of capabilities.

Note The popup page cannot be opened programmatically, it must be triggered by a toolbar click or similar privileged browser action. This is to prevent extensions from abusing this ability and frequently or opportunistically opening their popup pages, which would be problematic for the user experience.

The Options Page

The options page is a native browser container that browser extensions can use to display a custom user interface. The options page behaves as a standalone web page that opens when the user clicks "Options" in the extension toolbar context menu. An example of opening an options page is shown in Figures 2-5 and 2-6.

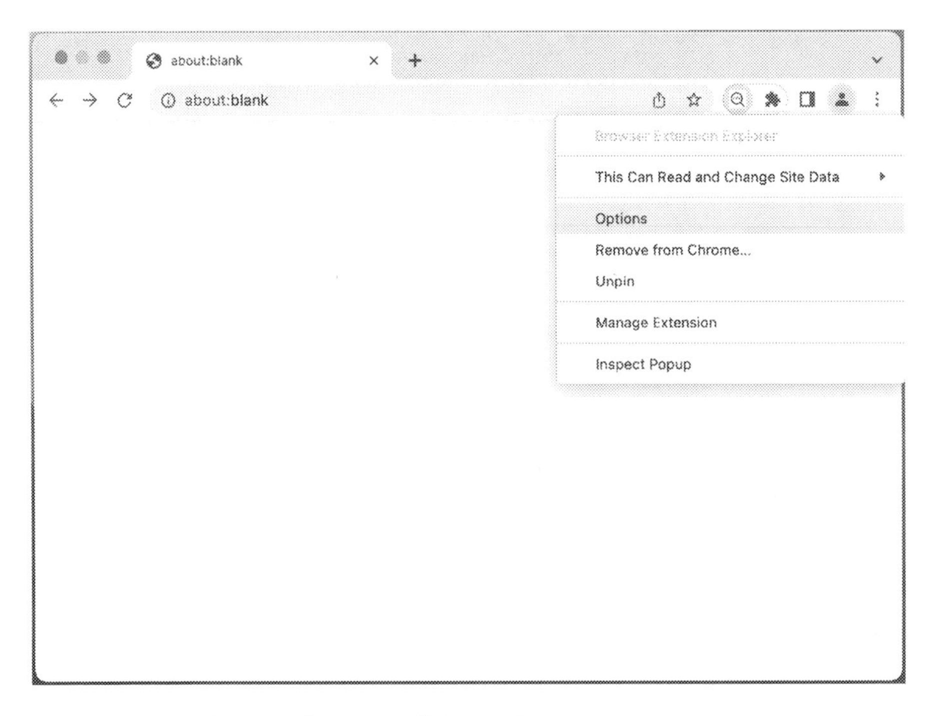

***Figure 2-5.** Selecting "Options" from the extension context menu*

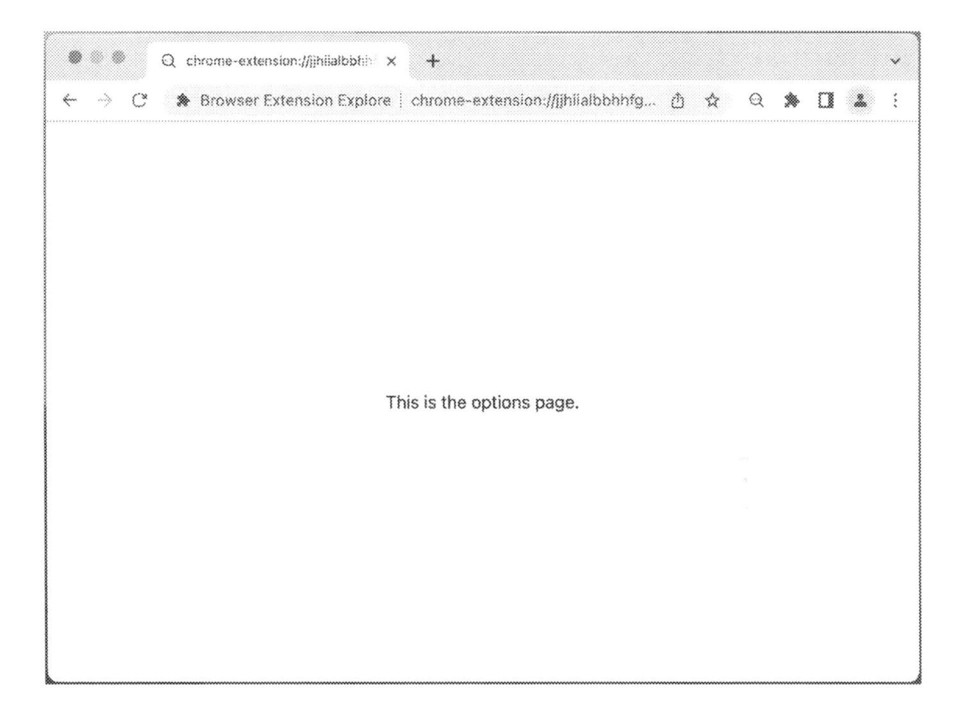

Figure 2-6. *Simple options page*

The "options" name is misleading: this page is not restricted to just showing options for the extension. Like the popup page, this is a fully featured web page with access to the WebExtensions API, meaning you are capable of using it as a full web application.

Note Refer to the *Popup and Options Pages* chapter for more details on how these pages work and how to use them.

Content Scripts

The term *content script* broadly refers to any content that is injected into a web page. JavaScript can either be injected declaratively in the manifest, or programmatically from an extension page or background script via the WebExtensions API. This content can be JavaScript, CSS, or both. The JavaScript is sandboxed in its own separate runtime, meaning it cannot read JavaScript variables or properties in the primary web page runtime, but it still shares access to the same DOM as the web page itself. This means that content scripts are fully capable of reading and writing the page, enabling things like in-page widgets or full integration with the web page.

Content scripts have limited access to the WebExtensions API, so they are incapable of many actions that are possible in the popup page, options page, or background script. They can, however, exchanges messages with other extension elements like background scripts. Therefore, content scripts can still indirectly use the WebExtensions API by delegating actions to a background script.

Note Refer to the *Content Scripts* chapter for more details on how content scripts work and how to use them.

Devtools Panels and Sidebars

Devtools panel and sidebar pages are native browser containers that browser extensions can use to display a custom user interface. The devtools interfaces behave as panes nested in the native browser's developer tools when the user selects their corresponding tabs in the developer tools interface, shown in Figures 2-7 and 2-8.

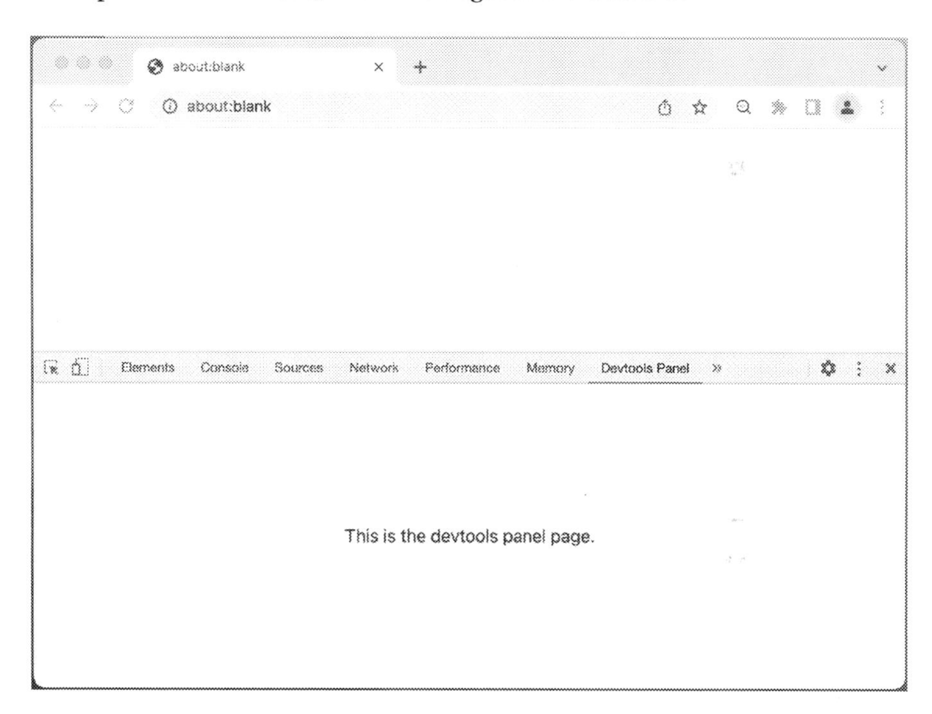

Figure 2-7. *Simple devtools panel page*

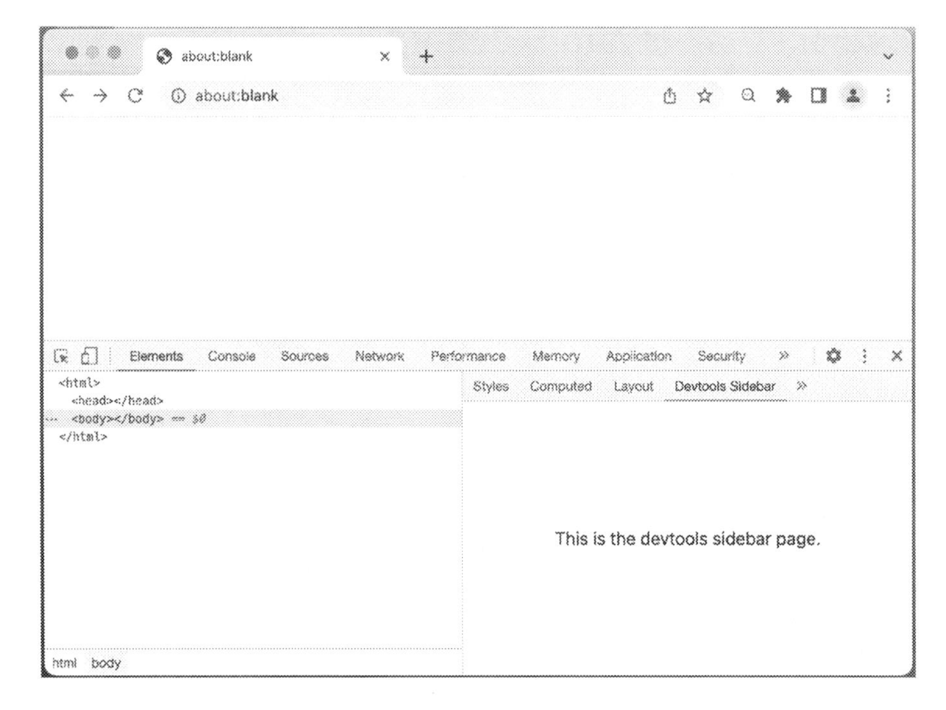

Figure 2-8. *Simple devtools sidebar page*

Like the popup page, this is a fully featured web page, but like content scripts, it has limited access to the WebExtensions API. However, it is provided access to the additional Devtools API that can be used to perform actions like inspecting the page and observing the page's network traffic.

Note Refer to the *Devtools Pages* chapter for more details on how these pages work and how to use them.

Extension Elements in Action

To aid in understanding how all these elements fit together, let's examine how these pieces fit into a handful of popular browser extensions. Based on what we know about how the various elements of browser extensions behave, we can understand how the extension is accomplishing these user interfaces even without having access to the codebases.

Honey

Honey is a browser extension that can detect when the user is checking out on an ecommerce website and automatically apply coupon codes (Figure 2-9).

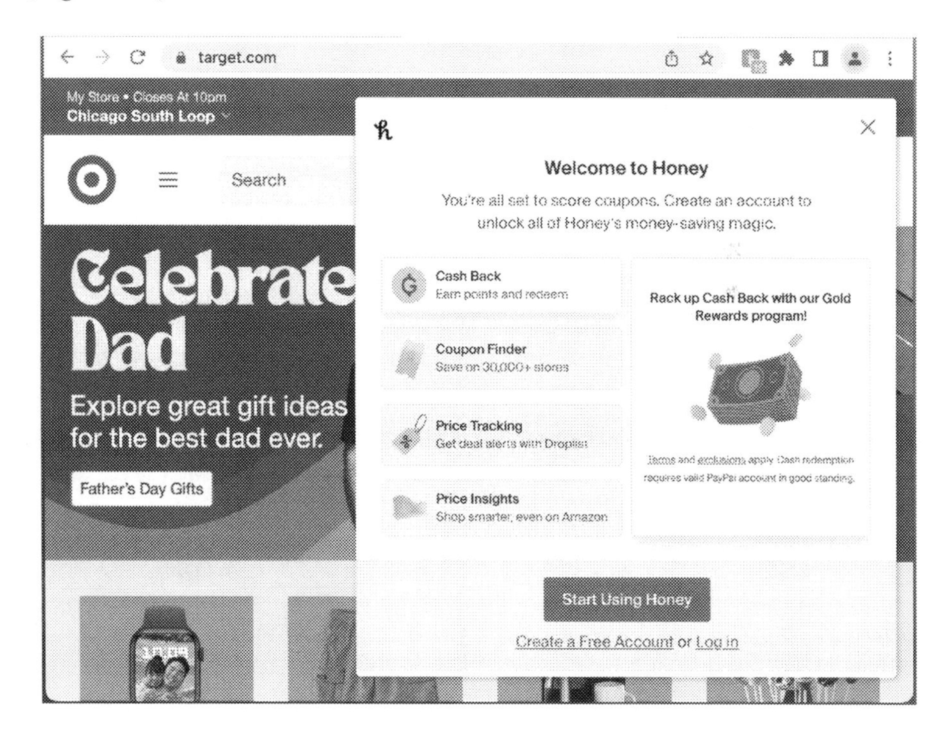

***Figure 2-9.** Honey browser extension showing content script widget and toolbar icon with badge*

Here, Honey is rendering a widget over the page using a content script. It also uses a content script to programmatically submit coupon codes when the user is in the checkout flow.

Furthermore, note that the toolbar icon is displaying a badge containing "15," which is Honey telling us there are 15 possible coupon codes to try on this domain. Honey knows this because it can assess what domain the user is visiting and checking that against the Honey database of matching coupon codes. The extension is then able to use its ability to dynamically set what the toolbar icon shows and render the Honey logo with the "15" badge (Figure 2-10).

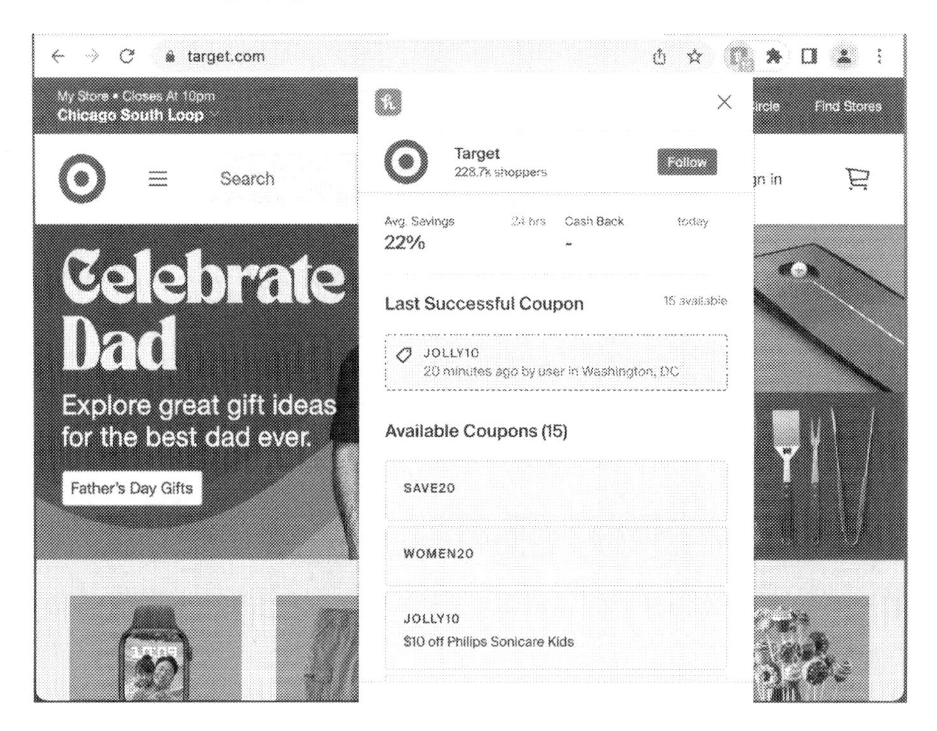

Figure 2-10. *Honey browser extension showing the popup page*

The above screenshot shows the popup view in Honey. Honey does not rely on this as a primary user interface, as it is not possible to programmatically open the popup window. The extension needs to automatically display content to the user when it detects that it can submit coupon codes, and the extension relies on widgets powered by content scripts to accomplish this.

LastPass

LastPass is a browser extension that can securely store and autofill a user's passwords, as well as record new passwords when they are submitted (Figure 2-11).

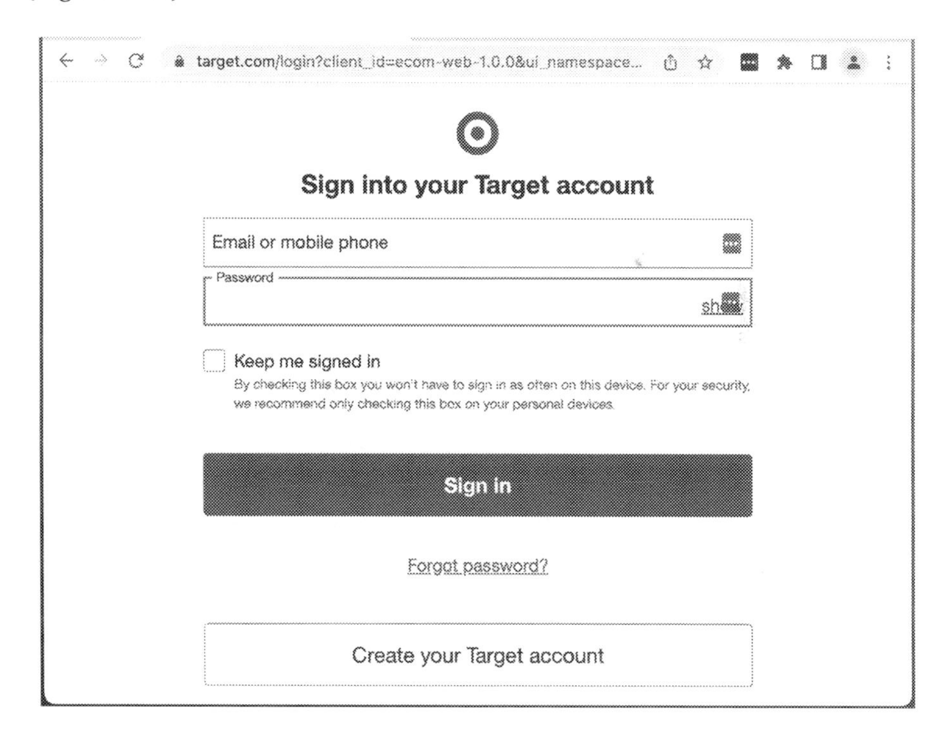

***Figure 2-11.** LastPass browser extension with content script widget buttons*

LastPass uses a content script to find and fill authentication form fields, as well as to render widgets for managing passwords from within the form fields. LastPass also watches traffic in and out of the browser for requests that set or update passwords and records the request payload in your encrypted account credential list (Figure 2-12).

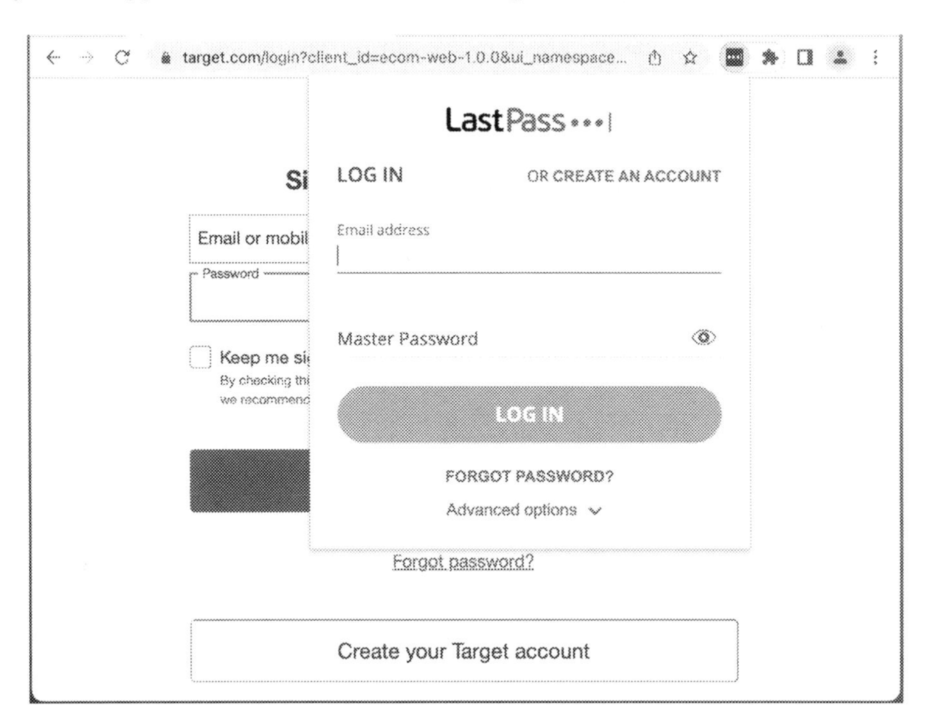

Figure 2-12. *LastPass browser extension showing popup page*

Of course, form detection will never be perfect, so LastPass offers all the same password utilities from the popup window to account for scenarios where the content script widget does not render (Figure 2-13).

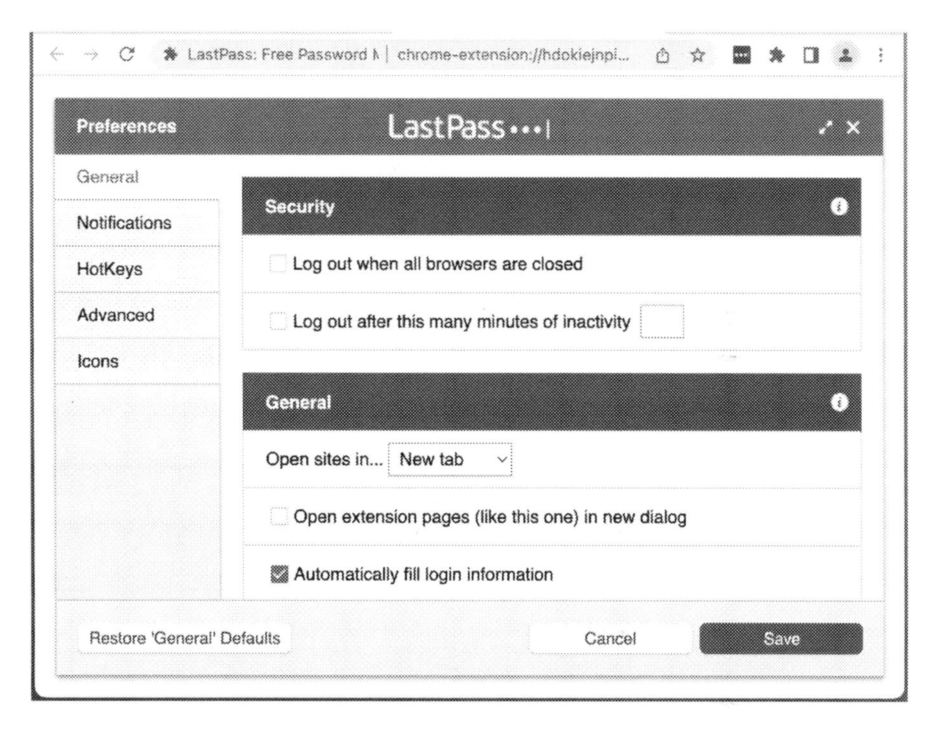

***Figure 2-13.** LastPass browser extension showing options page*

In addition to managing passwords, LastPass has a broad suite of security tools and allows for intricate customization of its behavior. The browser extension exposes these settings in the extension options page, shown above.

Grammarly

Grammarly is a browser extension that observes the text a user types into the browser and automatically offers suggestions on how to fix or improve it (Figures 2-14 and 2-15).

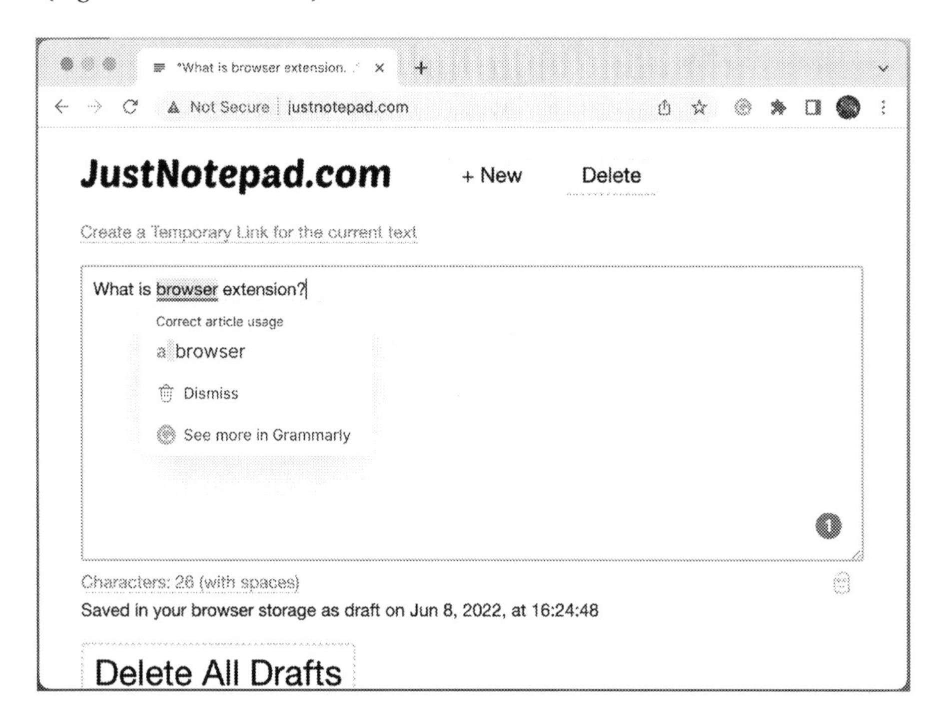

Figure 2-14. *Grammarly browser extension showing the content script widget*

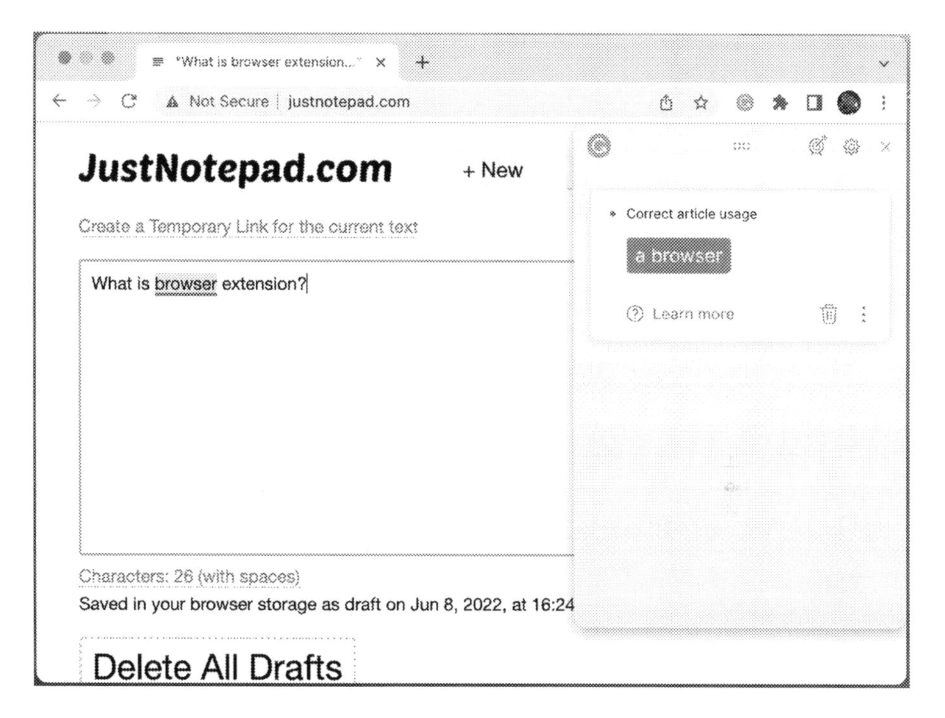

***Figure 2-15.** Grammarly browser extension showing the collated content script widget*

Similar to how LastPass detects authentication form fields, Grammarly uses a content script to intelligently detect when the user is typing content into the page, parses that content, and renders suggestions on top of that content. The extension is also able to collate all active suggestions into the unified content script widget (Figure 2-16).

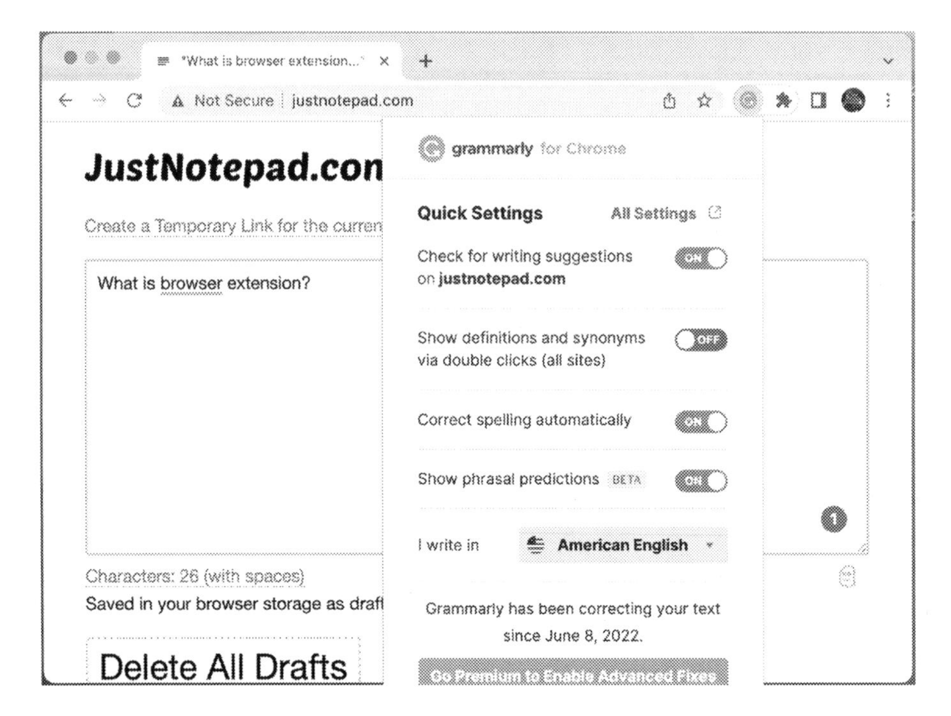

Figure 2-16. *Grammarly browser extension showing the content script widget*

Grammarly also offers toggles for extension settings in the popup page.

React Developer Tools

React Developer Tools is a browser extension that allows the user to understand how a React application is rendering in the page (Figure 2-17).

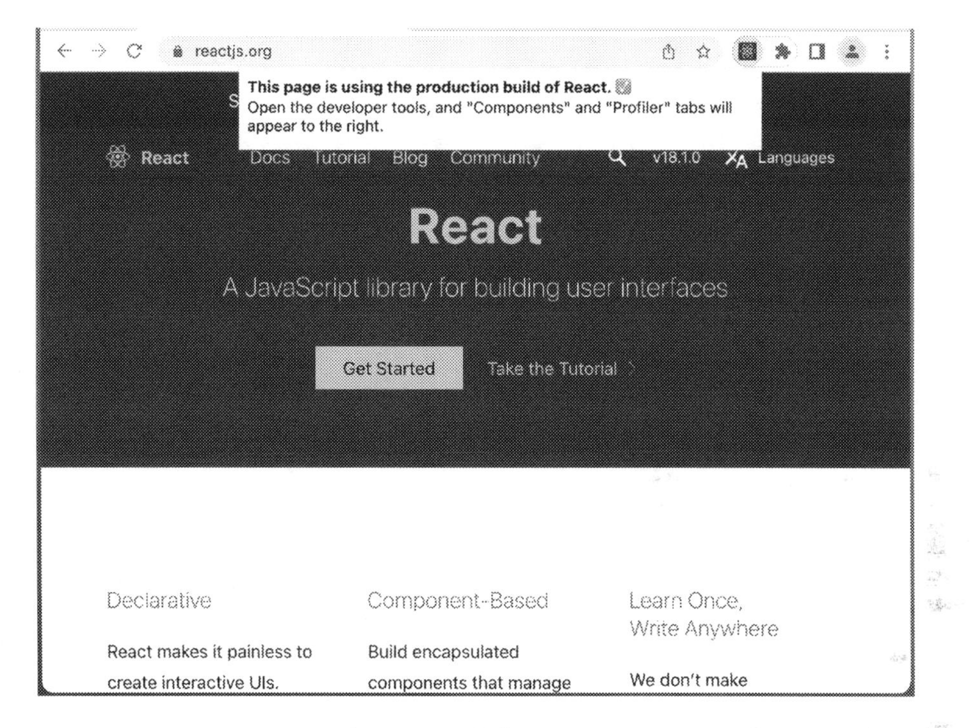

Figure 2-17. *React Developer Tools browser extension showing the popup widget*

The browser extension can analyze the web page to detect if it is a React application. If it is, the toolbar icon will indicate as much, and the popup page informs the user what type of React application is present (Figure 2-18).

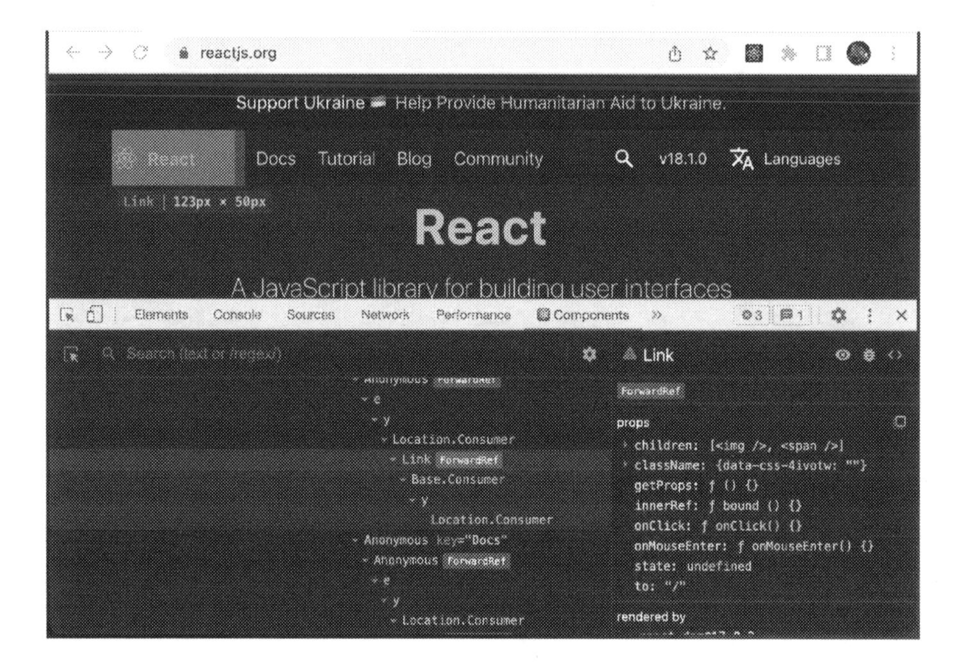

***Figure 2-18.** React Developer Tools browser extension showing a devtools panel page with element highlighted*

The extension uses the Devtools API to create a custom panel in the browser's developer tools interface. It parses the page content and unpacks it into a browseable component tree inside the panel page.

Summary

As the name suggests, browser extensions are more of an extension of the browser rather than the page. The WebExtensions API allows extensions to perform actions that web pages cannot normally accomplish.

Browser extensions are composed of a collection of elements. The only required element is the manifest. Optional elements include background scripts, the popup page, the options page, devtools pages, and content scripts.

The next chapter will take you through a crash course covering how to build and install a basic browser extension.

CHAPTER 3

Browser Extension Crash Course

Chapters later in this book will cover various aspects of browser extensions in great detail. This chapter, on the other hand, will guide you through the quickest way to get up and running with browser extensions. The crash course will cover building a trivial browser extension from scratch. It will *not* use any third-party libraries or dependencies, just vanilla HTML, CSS, and JavaScript.

This chapter is geared toward developers that have never built an extension before; however, even if you are already somewhat comfortable with extension development, this chapter may yet prove useful as it touches upon some corners of the domain that you may not have experimented with before.

Note For the sake of simplicity, the crash course will only focus on developing a manifest v3 browser extension for Google Chrome. Creating a manifest v2 browser extension, or supporting other browsers, requires steps that are not covered in this crash course.

M. Frisbie, *Building Browser Extensions*, https://doi.org/10.1007/978-1-4842-8725-5_3

Creating the Manifest

As described in the previous chapter, the extension manifest primarily defines the following:

1. What the extension is allowed to do
2. Where its files are located

Begin by creating a new empty directory named `extension-crash-course`. All the files we create in this crash course will be created inside it:

```
extension-crash-course/
└─ manifest.json
```

Inside this directory, let's create the simplest possible `manifest.json` file. The file structure is shown here:

manifest.json

```
{
  "name": "Extension Crash Course",
  "description": "Browser extension created from scratch",
  "version": "1.0",
  "manifest_version": 3
}
```

These fields define the formal browser extension name string `Extension Crash Course`, and the description string `Browser extension created from scratch`. These strings will be reflected both within the browser itself when the extension is installed, as well as in the Chrome Web Store when the extension is published. Also defined in this file is the semantic version `1.0`, indicating the version of the extension package. It also defines the manifest version string `3`, indicating to the browser how the `manifest.json` file should be parsed.

Minimum Viable Extension

Besides the manifest file, all elements of browser extensions are optional for use. Therefore, this lone `manifest.json` file with its small amount of boilerplate is the minimum viable browser extension. The extension has no features or user interfaces, and it incurs effectively zero browser overhead. It is essentially the browser extension equivalent of a NOOP instruction. Nevertheless, Google Chrome will happily install this single file as a new browser extension just as it would any other.

Installing Your Extension

The fastest way to install and test your extension is to load it into Google Chrome by enabling extension developer mode. This mode can be enabled on your browser's Chrome Extensions page. There are two ways to reach this page:

- **⋮ > More Tools > Extensions (Figure 3-1)**
- Navigate your browser to `chrome://extensions`

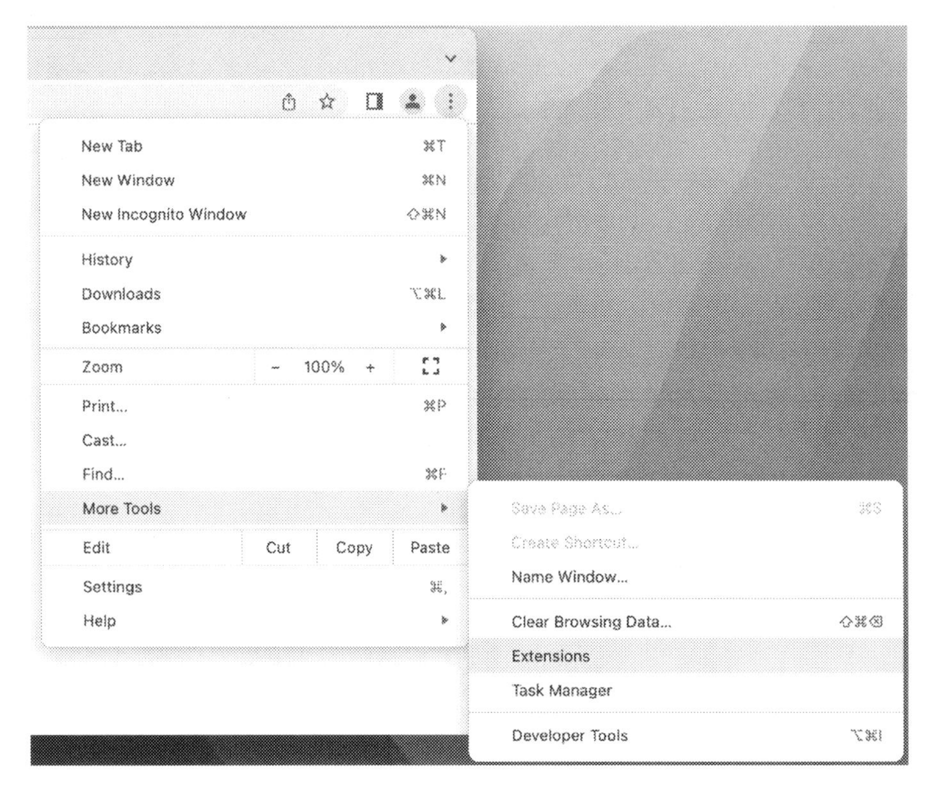

***Figure 3-1.** Opening the Chrome Extensions page via browser menu*

The default behavior of Google Chrome is to disallow loading extensions from the local filesystem. To enable this behavior, on the Chrome Extensions page, you will need to enable the *Developer mode* toggle, shown in Figures 3-2 and 3-3.

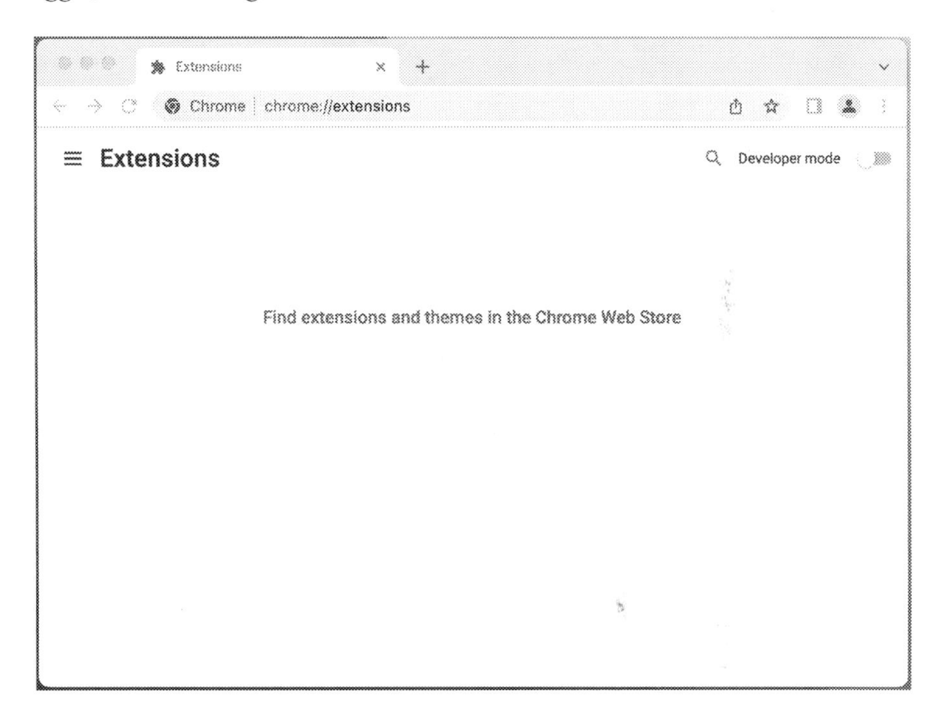

Figure 3-2. *The Chrome Extensions page with Developer mode disabled*

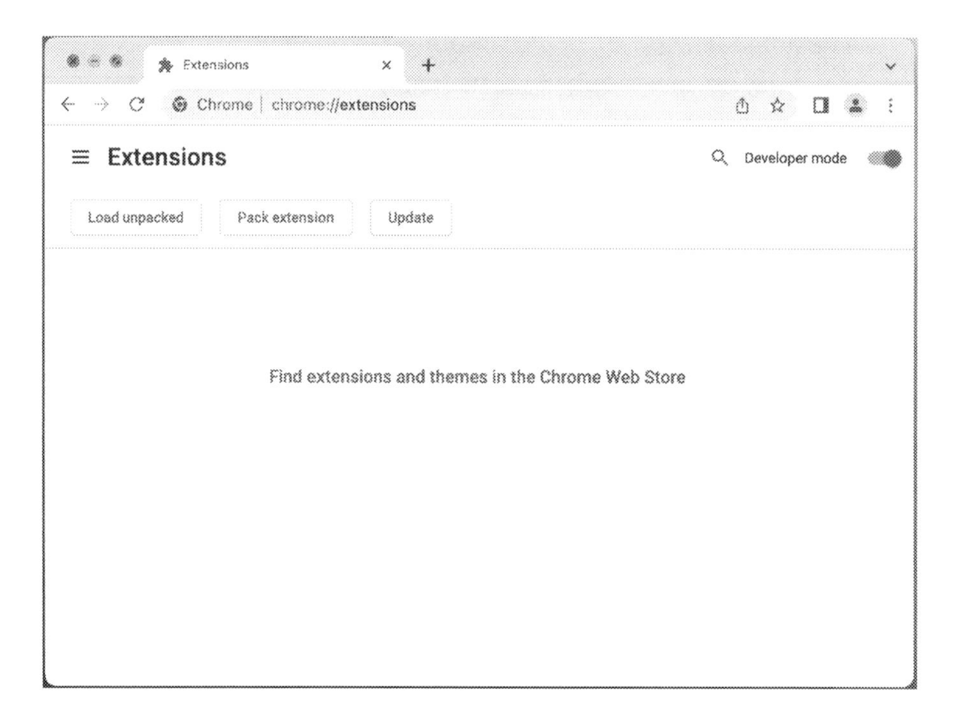

Figure 3-3. *The Chrome Extensions page with Developer mode enabled*

With Developer mode enabled, you can then load the extension by clicking "Load unpacked" and selecting the `extension-crash-course` directory that contains `manifest.json` (Figure 3-4).

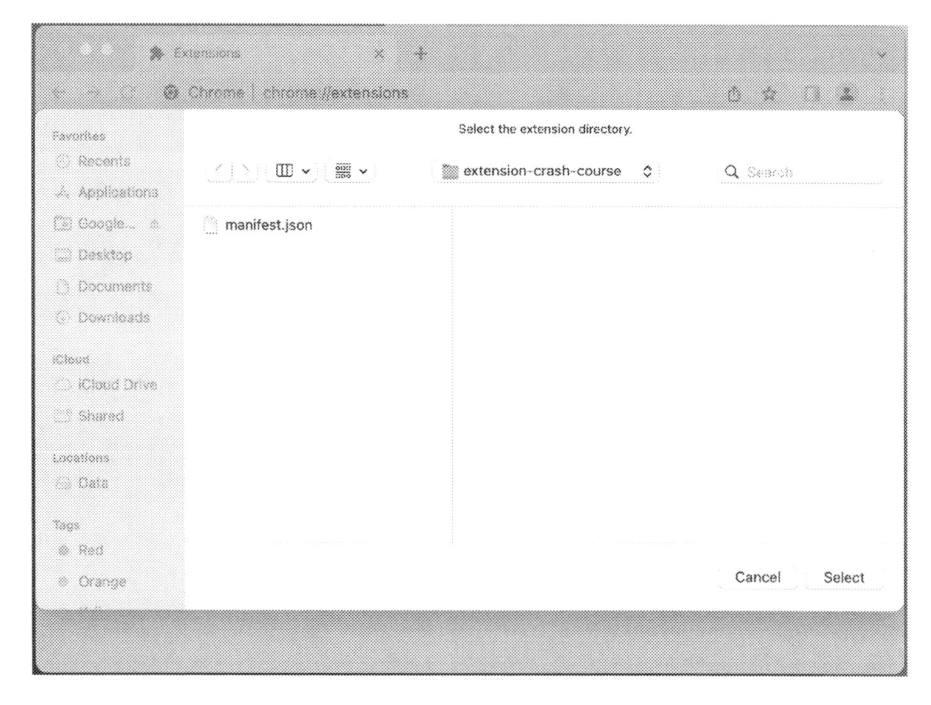

***Figure 3-4.** Selecting the directory to load the unpacked extension*

After selecting the directory, your extension will be installed in the browser and the Chrome Extensions page will reflect this by adding a card for the new extension (Figure 3-5).

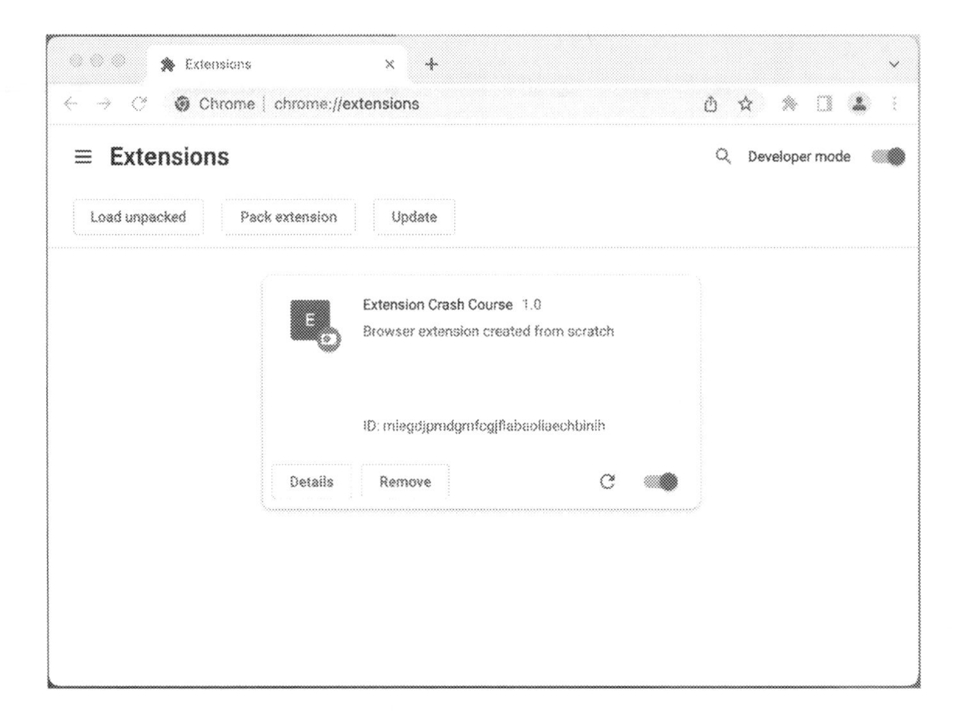

Figure 3-5. *Google Chrome with the crash course extension newly installed*

Note For ease of access, you should pin the extension toolbar icon so that it always displays. Click on the puzzle piece extension icon, and then click the pin button.

Reloading Your Extension

When making changes to extension code, understanding when those changes should appear can be difficult. Different parts of extensions will be reloaded at different times. Furthermore, multiple tabs and windows mean that you may have multiple versions of an extension running at the same time!

There are several different points at which portions of the extension are reloaded:

- An **extension reload** obtains a new copy of `manifest.json`, updates the background service worker, and closes any stale popups and options pages that are open. This is required when the `manifest.json` changes.
- An **extension page reload** is a page refresh of any page that uses the extension protocol `chrome-extension://`. This is required to reflect changes in HTML, JS, CSS, and images in popup and options pages.
- A **web page reload** is a page refresh of any web page that has content scripts injected. This is required to reflect changes in the injected content scripts.
- A **devtools reload** is closing and opening the browser's developer tools interface. This is required to reflect changes in devtools pages.

There are three ways to force an extension reload:

- Uninstall and reinstall the extension
- Click the reload icon ↻ in the corresponding card on the Chrome Extensions page
- Programmatically reload the extension using `chrome.runtime.reload()` or `chrome.management.setEnabled()`

Note Programmatically reloading the extension is covered more in the *Extension Development and Deployment* chapter.

When sending messages using the WebExtensions API, you will occasionally see an error similar to the following:

```
Uncaught (in promise) Error: Could not establish connection.
Receiving end does not exist.
```

Browsers understand that different versions of extensions can be running at the same time, and so they explicitly disallow sending messages between extension parts of different versions. Seeing this error typically indicates that a part of your extension needs to be reloaded.

Note For the purposes of this crash course, reloading the extension *and* the extension page will be sufficient to reflect any changes you have made.

Adding a Background Script

Next, let's add a simple background script and verify that it is running. In the same directory as `manifest.json`, create a `background.js` file:

```
extension-crash-course/
├─ manifest.json
└─ background.js
```

The file content is shown below:

background.js

```
console.log('Hello from the background script!');
```

The manifest doesn't know this file exists, so let's update it so it loads this script file as a background service worker:

manifest.json

```
{
  "name": "Extension Crash Course",
  "description": "Browser extension created from scratch",
  "version": "1.0",
  "manifest_version": 3,
  "background": {
    "service_worker": "background.js"
  }
}
```

After reloading the extension, you will notice that the card on the Chrome Extensions page shows a link to the service worker (Figure 3-6):

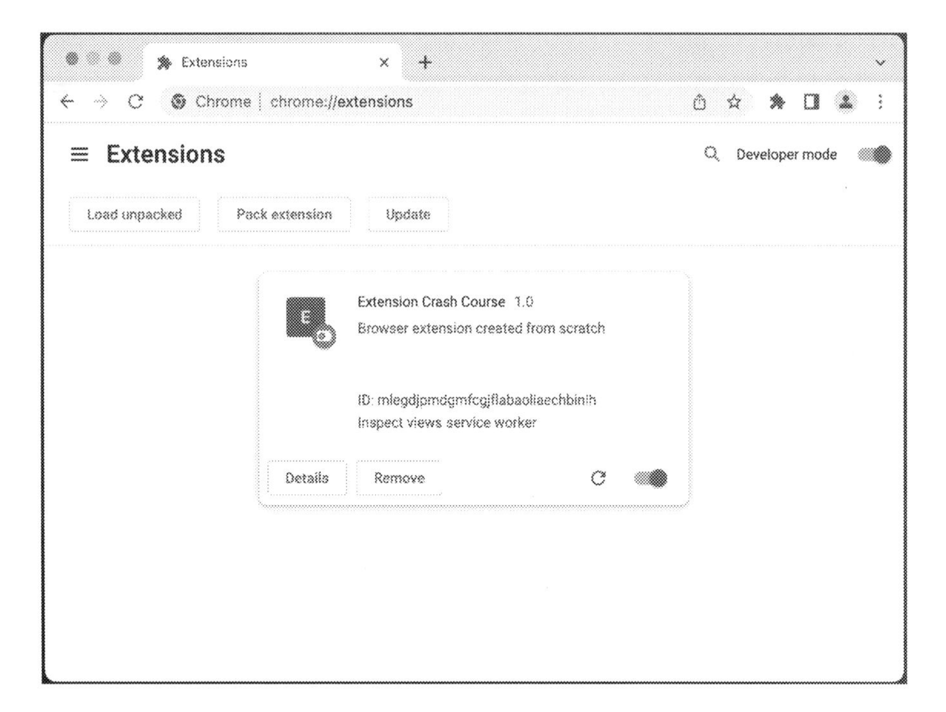

Figure 3-6. *Extensions with a link to the service worker*

This link will open a developer tools console for the background service worker, where you will see the output of the `console.log` (Figure 3-7).

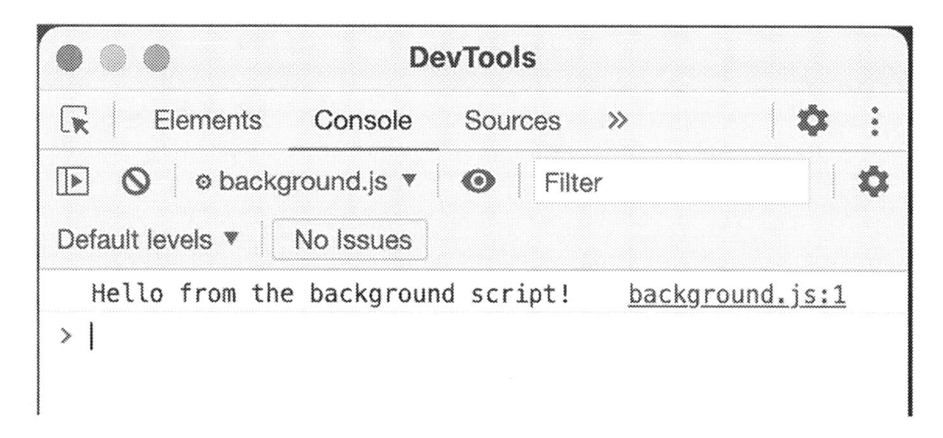

Figure 3-7. *Console for the background service worker*

Now that the background script is working properly, let's configure it to log event messages it receives via the WebExtensions API:

background.js

```
console.log('Hello from the background script!');

chrome.runtime.onMessage.addListener((msg) => {
  console.log(msg.text);
});
```

Note This listener won't print anything until a message is sent from elsewhere in the browser.

You'll note that the card in the Chrome Extension page may show the service worker as *inactive* after a period of time. In the interest of freeing unused system resources, Google Chrome decided that the service worker was idle and automatically unloaded it. The worker is reloaded when needed again, such as when an extension message is sent.

Note Unloading and reloading service workers is an important concept. It will be covered further in the *Background Scripts* chapter.

Adding a Popup Page

Next, let's add the first user interface to the extension. Create a new popup directory in the same directory as `manifest.json`. Inside the new directory, create three new files: `popup.html`, `popup.css`, and `popup.js`:

```
extension-crash-course/
├─ manifest.json
├─ background.js
└─ popup/
   ├─ popup.html
   ├─ popup.css
   └─ popup.js
```

The file contents are shown below:

popup/popup.html

```
<!DOCTYPE html>
<html>
  <head>
    <link href="popup.css" rel="stylesheet" />
  </head>
  <body>
    <h1>This is the popup page!</h1>

    <script src="popup.js"></script>
  </body>
</html>
```

popup/popup.css

```
body {
  width: 400px;
  margin: 2rem;
}
```

popup/popup.js

```
console.log('Hello from the popup!');
```

The manifest needs to be told when to render this HTML, so let's update it so it opens the popup page when the toolbar icon is clicked:

manifest.json

```
{
  "name": "Extension Crash Course",
  "description": "Browser extension created from scratch",
  "version": "1.0",
  "manifest_version": 3,
  "background": {
    "service_worker": "background.js"
  },
  "action": {
    "default_popup": "popup/popup.html"
  }
}
```

After reloading the extension, click the toolbar extension icon to open the popup page (Figure 3-8).

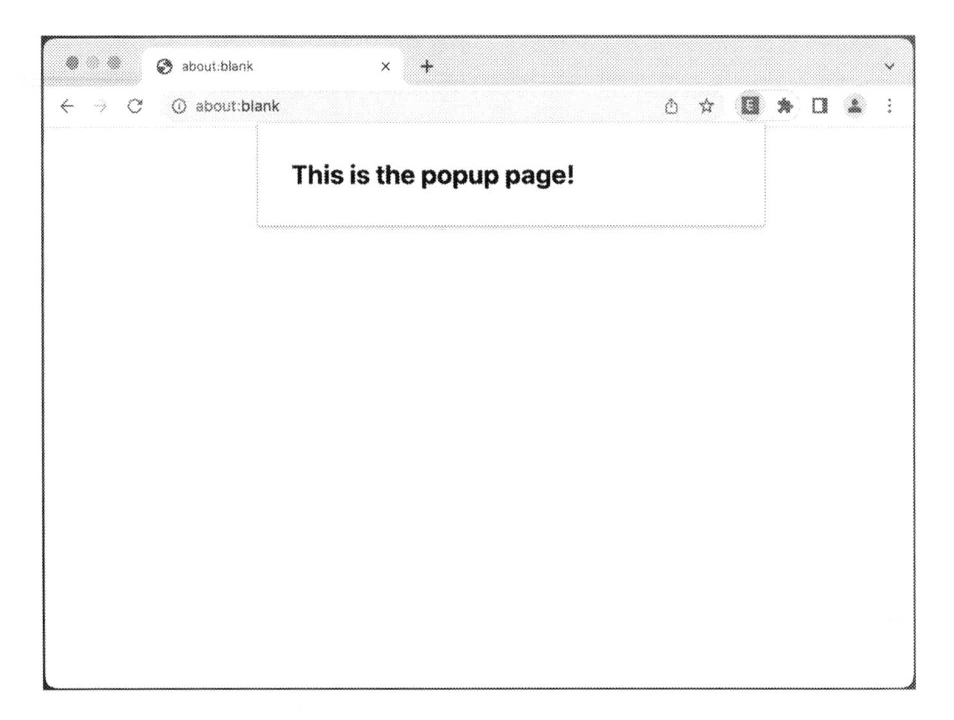

Figure 3-8. *Opened popup page*

Note Because you have not defined an extension icon, Google Chrome will automatically generate one from the name of the extension. As shown here, the default is the first letter of the extension name, E, on a gray background.

Next, let's send a message from the popup to the background script. Update the following files:

popup/popup.html

```
<!DOCTYPE html>
<html>
  <head>
```

```
    <link href="popup.css" rel="stylesheet" />
  </head>
  <body>
    <h1>This is the popup page!</h1>

    <button id="btn">Send popup message</button>

    <script src="popup.js"></script>
  </body>
</html>
```

popup/popup.js

```
console.log('Hello from the popup!');

document.querySelector("#btn").
addEventListener('click', () => {
  chrome.runtime.sendMessage({ text: "Popup" });
});

chrome.runtime.onMessage.addListener((msg) => {
  document.body.innerHTML += `<div>${msg.text}</div>`;
});
```

This new code adds a button to the popup that sends a message to the rest of the extension. It also adds a listener for incoming messages. Reload the extension, click the new button in the popup, and inspect the background script to see the message logged (Figure 3-9).

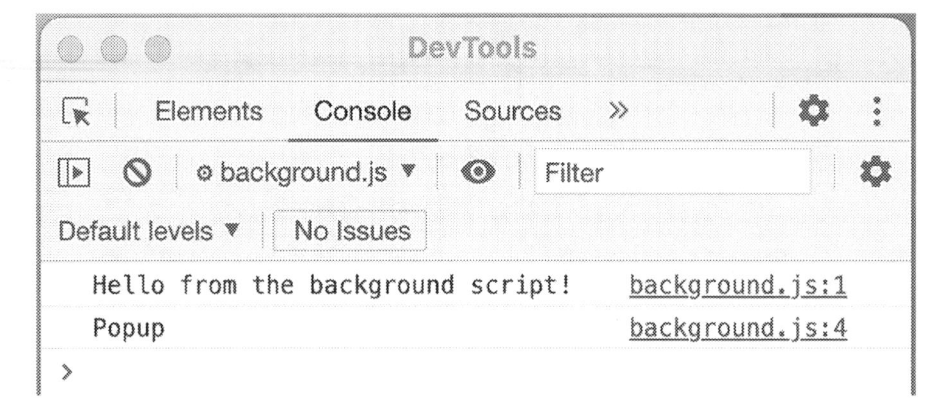

***Figure 3-9.** Background script logs the message from the popup page*

Note that, even though we set a listener for messages in the popup page, it did not handle an incoming message. Although the extension message infrastructure works as a broadcast, the source that sends the message will not also receive it.

Adding an Options Page

Next, let's add an options page with a similar structure to the popup page:

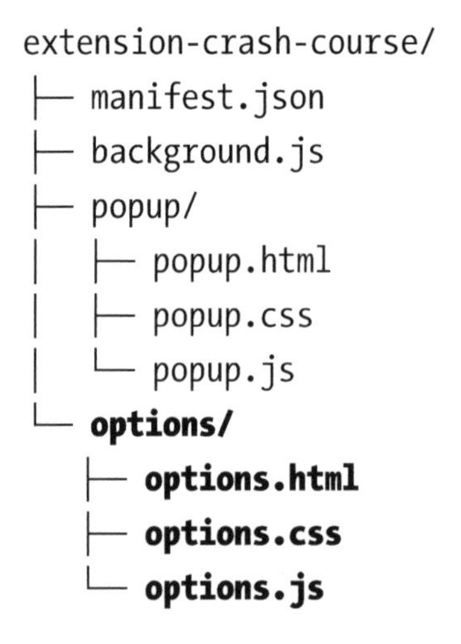

```
extension-crash-course/
├── manifest.json
├── background.js
├── popup/
│   ├── popup.html
│   ├── popup.css
│   └── popup.js
└── options/
    ├── options.html
    ├── options.css
    └── options.js
```

The file contents are shown below:

options/options.html

```
<!DOCTYPE html>
<html>
  <head>
    <link href="options.css" rel="stylesheet" />
  </head>
  <body>
    <h1>This is the options page!</h1>

    <button id="btn">Send options message</button>

    <script src="options.js"></script>
  </body>
</html>
```

options/options.css

```
body {
  margin: 2rem;
}
```

options/options.js

```
console.log('Hello from options!');

document.querySelector("#btn").
addEventListener('click', () => {
  chrome.runtime.sendMessage({ text: "Options" });
});

chrome.runtime.onMessage.addListener((msg) => {
  document.body.innerHTML += `<div>${msg.text}</div>`;
});
```

The manifest needs to configured to use this HTML as the options page:

manifest.json

```
{
  "name": "Extension Crash Course",
  "description": "Browser extension created from scratch",
  "version": "1.0",
  "manifest_version": 3,
  "background": {
    "service_worker": "background.js"
  },
  "action": {
    "default_popup": "popup/popup.html"
  },
  "options_page": "options/options.html"
}
```

Reload the extension, and open the extension options page by right clicking on the toolbar icon and selecting "Options" (Figure 3-10).

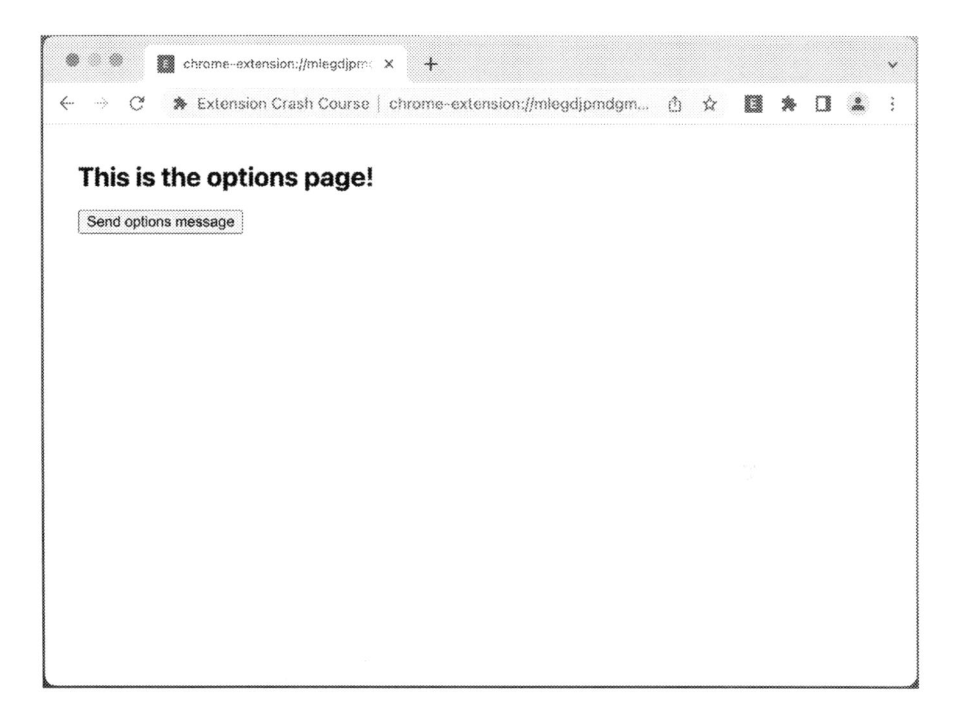

Figure 3-10. *Extension options page*

To test the messaging system between extension components, open the popup page and click its button. The message handler on the options page will add the message into the page (Figure 3-11).

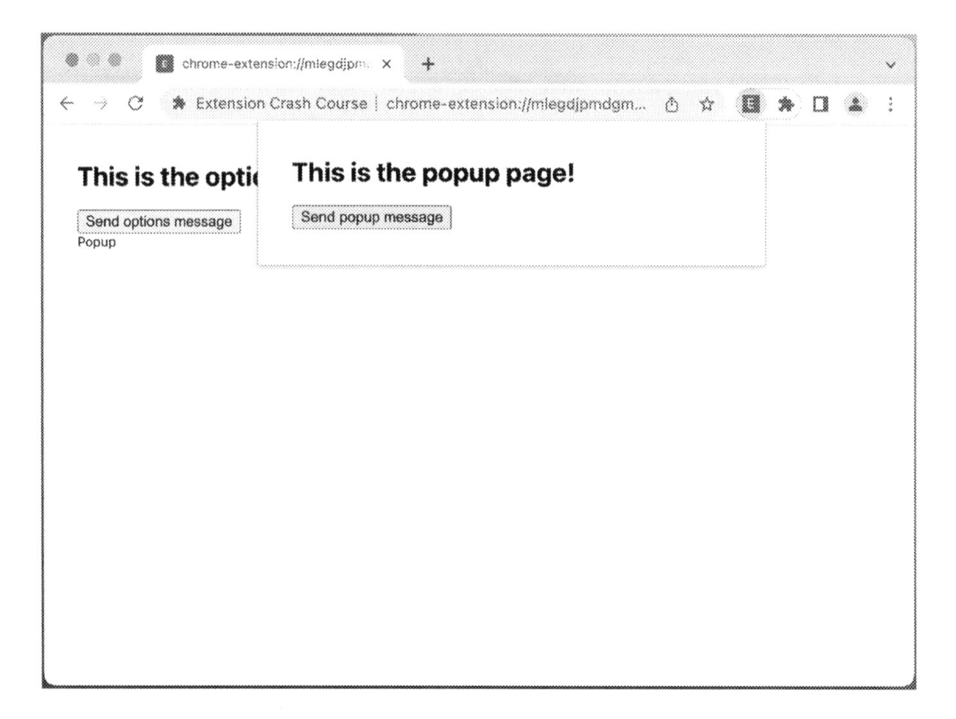

Figure 3-11. *Extension options page with popup message*

Adding a Content Script

Next, let's create some content scripts that add similar behavior to the options and popup pages:

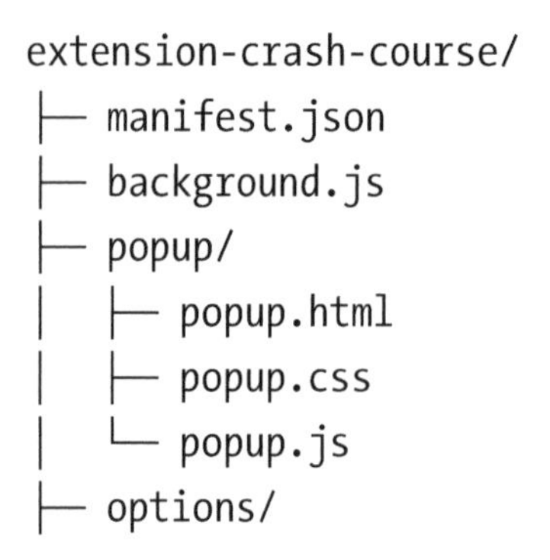

```
extension-crash-course/
├── manifest.json
├── background.js
├── popup/
│   ├── popup.html
│   ├── popup.css
│   └── popup.js
├── options/
```

```
|   ├─ options.html
|   ├─ options.css
|   └─ options.js
└─ content-scripts/
    ├─ content-script.css
    └─ content-script.js
```

The content scripts will add a styled custom container into the page:

content-scripts/content-script.css

```
#container {
  position: absolute;
  background-color: gray;
  color: white;
  padding: 2rem;
  top: 0;
  left: 0;
}
```

content-scripts/content-script.js

```
console.log('Hello from content script!');

document.body.innerHTML += `
<div id="container">
  <h1>This is the content script!</h1>
  <button id="btn">Send content script message</button>
</div>
`;

document.querySelector("#btn").
addEventListener('click', () => {
  chrome.runtime.sendMessage({ text: "Content script" });
});
```

```
chrome.runtime.onMessage.addListener((msg) => {
  document.querySelector('#container').innerHTML +=
`<div>${msg.text}</div>`;
});
```

Configure the manifest to inject these content scripts into all valid web pages:

manifest.json

```
{
  "name": "Extension Crash Course",
  "description": "Browser extension created from scratch",
  "version": "1.0",
  "manifest_version": 3,
  "background": {
    "service_worker": "background.js"
  },
  "action": {
    "default_popup": "popup/popup.html"
  },
  "options_page": "options/options.html",
  "content_scripts": [
    {
      "matches": ["<all_urls>"],
      "css": ["content-scripts/content-script.css"],
      "js": ["content-scripts/content-script.js"]
    }
  ]
}
```

Open a real web page such as `https://blank.org` to see the content script render (Figure 3-12):

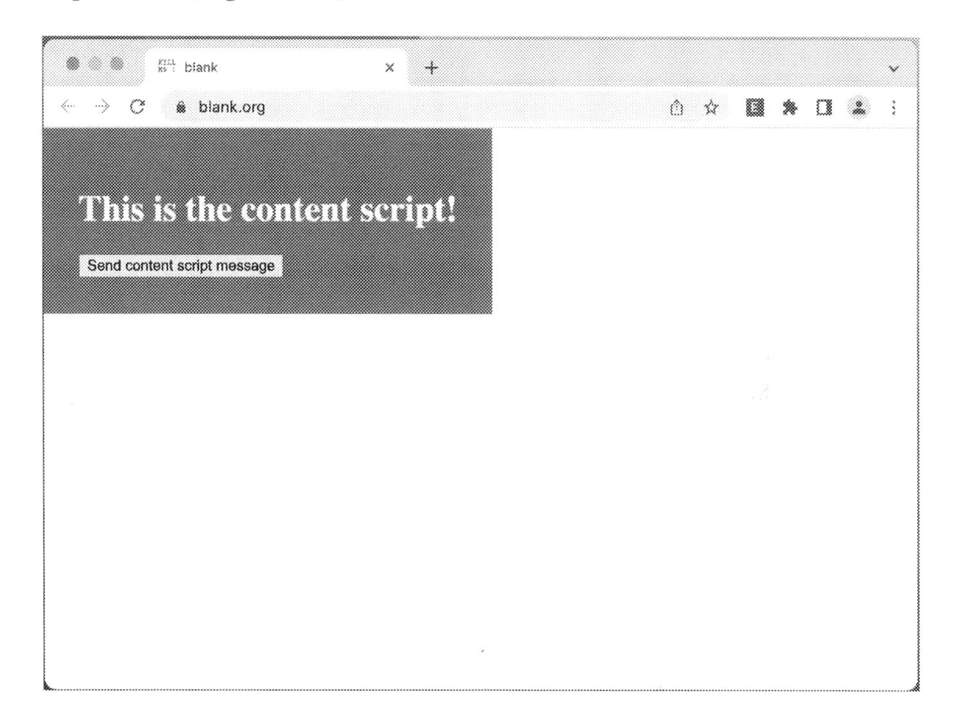

Figure 3-12. *Content script running on web page*

In this state, you will be able to click the content script button and have the messages show up in the extension views, such as on the options page.

Working with Multiple Tabs

After experimenting with the extension in this state, you will discover that the messages can be successfully sent from the content scripts to the other parts of the extension, but messages are *not* received in the content script.

This is because content scripts are inherently bound to the browser's tab model. There may be many tabs open all running the same content script, so there must be consideration as to which content script instances should receive the message. To send a message to a content script, the WebExtensions API allows you to individually target tabs. Update the popup script to the following:

popup/popup.js

```
console.log('Hello from the popup!');

document.querySelector("#btn").
addEventListener('click', () => {
  chrome.runtime.sendMessage({ text: "Popup" });

  chrome.tabs.query({
    active: true,
    currentWindow: true
  }, (tabs) => {
    chrome.tabs.sendMessage(
      tabs[0]?.id,
      { text: "Popup" }
    );
  });
});

chrome.runtime.onMessage.addListener((msg) => {
  document.body.innerHTML += `<div>${msg.text}</div>`;
});
```

After reloading the extension, you should now see that messages sent from the popup page's button will show up in the content script view, but *only* on the active tab.

Tip Before continuing, experiment with the extension in its current state. Open multiple tabs, multiple browser windows, multiple popups in different windows, and send messages from different locations to see where they do or do not show up. The results may surprise you. This will be an instructive lesson on how the broadcast messaging model works for extensions.

Adding a Devtools Panel

Next, let's add a panel to the Chrome developer tools. Create the following files:

```
extension-crash-course/
├── manifest.json
├── background.js
├── popup/
│   ├── popup.html
│   ├── popup.css
│   └── popup.js
├── options/
│   ├── options.html
│   ├── options.css
│   └── options.js
├── content-scripts/
│   ├── content-script.css
│   └── content-script.js
└── devtools/
    ├── devtools.html
    ├── devtools.js
    ├── devtools_panel.html
    └── devtools_panel.js
```

Adding devtools interfaces is slightly different from other extension interfaces. The extension is provided a top-level headless page that uses the WebExtensions API in a script to insert custom developer tools interfaces. The files should appear as follows:

devtools/devtools.html

```
<!DOCTYPE html>
<html>
  <body>
    <script src="devtools.js"></script>
  </body>
</html>
```

devtools/devtools.js

```
chrome.devtools.panels.create(
  "Devtools Panel",
  "",
  "/devtools/devtools_panel.html"
);
```

Next, configure the devtools panel to log the URL of all outgoing network activity from the page using the Devtools API:

devtools/devtools_panel.html

```
<!DOCTYPE html>
<html>
  <body>
    <h1>This is the devtools panel!</h1>

    <script src="devtools_panel.js"></script>
  </body>
</html>
```

devtools/devtools_panel.js

```
console.log("Hello from the devtools panel!");

chrome.devtools.network.onRequestFinished.addListener(
  (request) => {
    document.body.innerHTML +=
      `<div>${request.request.url}</div>`;
  }
);
```

Finally, update the manifest to use the devtools headless page:

manifest.json

```
{
  "name": "Extension Crash Course",
  "description": "Browser extension created from scratch",
  "version": "1.0",
  "manifest_version": 3,
  "background": {
    "service_worker": "background.js"
  },
  "action": {
    "default_popup": "popup/popup.html"
  },
  "options_page": "options/options.html",
  "devtools_page": "devtools/devtools.html",
  "content_scripts": [
    {
      "matches": ["<all_urls>"],
      "css": ["content-scripts/content-script.css"],
      "js": ["content-scripts/content-script.js"]
    }
  ]
}
```

You'll need to reload the extension as well as close and reopen any open developer tools windows to see the changes. Visiting any web page will log its traffic (Figure 3-13).

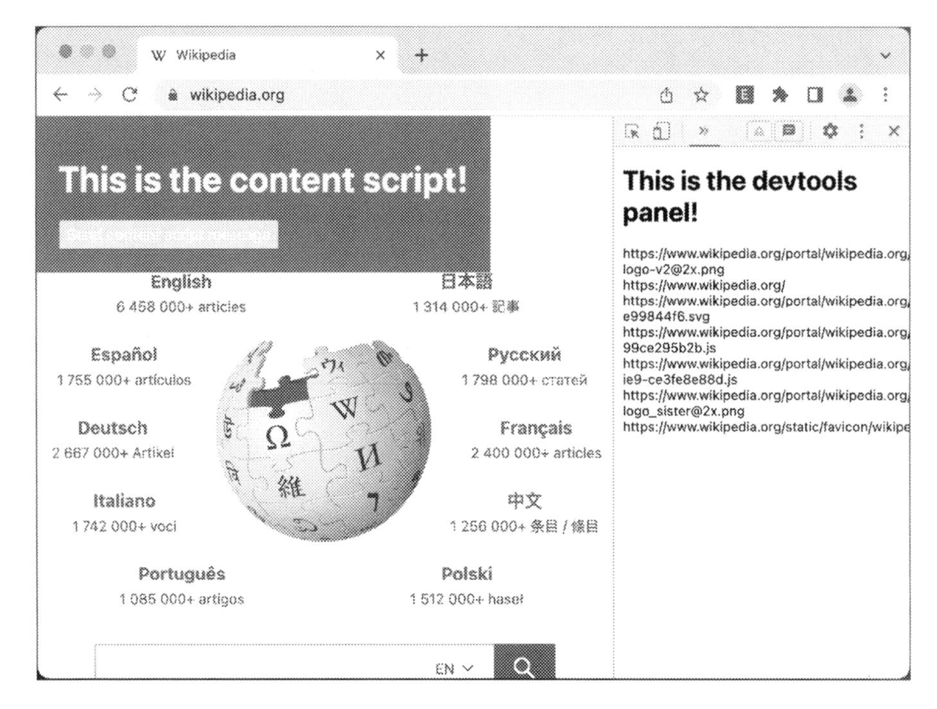

Figure 3-13. *Devtools panel logging network traffic*

Summary

In this chapter, you were guided through the process of creating a simple Chrome extension. The purpose of this crash course was to provide step-by-step instructions on how to create an extension that touched all the different user interface elements that browser extensions can use. After completing the crash course, you should have a good understanding of how various user interfaces are produced from their source code, as well as how a manifest should be laid out to achieve these ends.

You should also have a very basic understanding of how the WebExtensions API can be used. This crash course only touched upon a handful of basic methods, but it gives you an initial concept for all the various ways that browser extensions can manipulate the browser to achieve their ends.

The next chapter will explore the architecture of browser extensions, including how files are organized and how the various elements behave inside the browser.

CHAPTER 4

Browser Extension Architecture

Understanding how the various elements of browser extensions work is important, but even more important is understanding how they work together. The architecture of browser extensions is unusual and multifaceted:

- They lack centralization and instead are formed by a network of distributed elements: background scripts, content scripts, popup and options pages, and devtools pages.
- They can manage the complex browser page infrastructure that spans across multiple windows and tabs. Because content scripts can run on multiple pages and are independently loaded, they require special considerations such as a multiplexed communication channel and update version control.

M. Frisbie, *Building Browser Extensions*, https://doi.org/10.1007/978-1-4842-8725-5_4

- They can offer a web page-based user interface in the popup page, options pages, devtools pages, and content scripts. They can also directly integrate with the native browser chrome with features such as keyboard shortcuts, omniboxes, and desktop notifications.

Note This chapter is a high-level overview covering how the pieces connect and interact. The APIs and other specific details are primarily covered later in this book.

Architecture Overview

The browser extension architecture can be more easily understood visually. Consider the following diagram displaying how all the pieces of browser extensions fit together (Figure 4-1).

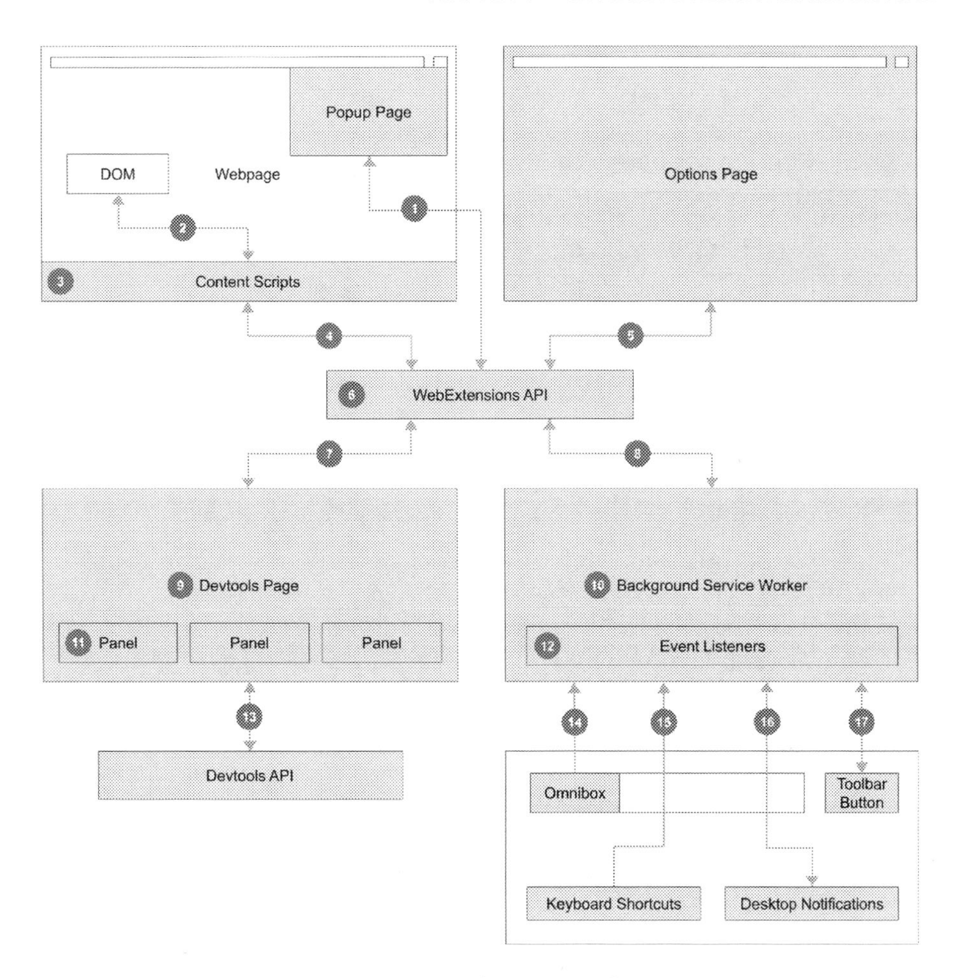

***Figure 4-1.** Browser extension architecture diagram*

Let's unpack the various elements and connections displayed here, identified in the above diagram by number:

1. Popup pages can use the WebExtensions API to perform tasks like reading/writing data to the storage API, sending messages to the background page, or triggering behavior in the active tab's content script.

2. Content scripts can view and manipulate the host web page DOM as well as listen for DOM events.

3. Content scripts are injected directly into web pages and executed in a sandboxed JavaScript runtime. Each tab with a permitted scheme (`http://`, `https://`, `ftp://`, `file:///`) is eligible to have content scripts injected.

4. Content scripts can use WebExtensions API to perform tasks like sending and receiving instructions from the background script, as well as exporting information from the page DOM. Content scripts on a single tab or subset of tabs can be targeted via `chrome.tabs.query()`.

5. In a similar fashion to popup pages, options pages interact with the rest of the extension via the WebExtensions API.

6. The WebExtensions API is the connective tissue for any web extension. It allows for bidirectional messaging between any two elements, as well as access to a shared storage API. The extensions messaging protocol is a broadcast format, meaning that any other part of the extension can listen to all messages being sent.

7. Devtools pages are only able to use a limited subset of the WebExtensions API.

8. Background service workers can manage the rest of the extension via the WebExtensions API. This includes dispatching messages to another part of the extension when an API event handler is triggered.

9. The devtools page is initialized each time the developer tools interface is opened, and torn down when it is closed. It is primarily used to initialize child elements such as panels. Devtools pages are headless web pages.

10. The background service worker is the nerve center of the extension. It is frequently used to handle events, dispatch messages, and perform authentication duties. The background service worker has the useful property of being a singleton; for any number of tabs or windows, only one service worker will ever be running.

11. Using the Devtools API, a devtools page can generate multiple child pages that render natively inside the browser's devtools interface. These child pages take the form of panels and sidebars.

12. The background service worker is the only element of a browser extension that can reliably handle browser events. Elements of extensions like options pages, popup pages, content scripts, and devtools pages are transient and therefore may miss events when they are not running.

13. Devtools pages are granted access to a supplementary Devtools API which enables methods for creating child views, and inspecting and debugging web pages.

14. The Omnibox can be enabled and configured in the manifest. When a special keyword is typed into the URL bar, a special search-like interface displays. This interface will dispatch omnibox events with the search bar's contents to the extension, thereby allowing the extension to offer search engine-style behavior.

15. Keyboard shortcuts can be enabled to either trigger native behavior like opening the popup page, or to trigger a custom command event.

16. Native desktop notifications can be displayed programmatically. The notifications will also trigger click and close events.

17. The native toolbar icon can perform in one of two ways: it can trigger the popup page, or it can fire an extension click event.

Plurality, Lifecycles, and Updates

Some critical considerations when developing browser extensions are how many of each element can exist at any given time, the fashion in which these elements are created and destroyed, and how they handle updates to the extension.

Background Service Worker

The background service worker is the only extension element that guarantees singleton behavior irrespective of the number of extension pages, windows, or tabs open. The service worker is torn down when the browser detects the service worker is idle and restarted on demand (e.g., when the browser detects an incoming event with a handler). The browser will restart the service worker when the extension is updated.

Note For more details on how background service workers behave, refer to the *Background Scripts* chapter.

Popup and Options Pages

Browsers will ensure that only one popup page is ever opened per window. However, if multiple windows are open, each window can independently open a popup. Popup pages are transient: they initialize when the popup interface expands and torn down immediately when the popup interface closes. The browser will forcibly close all open popups when the extension is updated.

There is no limit to the number of options pages that are opened. However, if you set the manifest option `options_ui.open_in_tab` to `false`, the browser will ensure that only one modal options page is open per window. Options pages, in both modal and tab forms, have a normal web page lifecycle. The browser will forcibly close all open options pages when the extension is updated.

Note For more details on how popup and options pages behave, refer to the *Popup and Options Pages* chapter.

Devtools Pages

The devtools page is rendered exactly once each time the browser's devtools interface is opened. Therefore, because there can be only one developer tools interface per window, there can be exactly one devtools page per window. This page and the child pages it creates, consisting of panels and sidebars, will persist as long as the developer tools interface is opened. Importantly, these developer tools pages will not be affected when the extension is updated and so they are susceptible to becoming stale.

Note For more details on how devtools pages behave, refer to the *Devtools Pages* chapter.

Content Scripts

Content scripts will be injected into web pages in a manner defined by the extension manifest. Furthermore, multiple content scripts can be injected into a single web page. For an extension with M content scripts defined, and a browser with N tabs open, the total number of content scripts running at any given time is bounded by M x N. Content scripts can be injected into the page upon different pageload events, but all of these are approximately when the page is initially loaded. They behave identically to regular web page scripts and will execute in the same fashion. Importantly, content scripts will not be affected when the extension is updated and so they are susceptible to becoming stale.

Note For more details on how content scripts behave, refer to the *Content Scripts* chapter.

Browser Extension File Server

When an extension is installed, the browser will enable the extension's files to be accessible via a simple file server. To explore this, let's use a simple extension that can be used to demonstrate some extension file server concepts. The file structure is as follows:

Example 4-1a. manifest.json

```
{
  "name": "MVX",
  "version": "0.0.1",
  "manifest_version": 3,
  "background": {
    "service_worker": "background.js",
    "type": "module"
  },
  "content_scripts": [
    {
      "matches": ["<all_urls>"],
      "js": ["content-script.js"]
    }
  ],
  "web_accessible_resources": [
    {
      "resources": ["fetch-page.js"],
      "matches": ["<all_urls>"]
    }
  ]
}
```

Example 4-1b. background.js

```
import "./fetch-page.js";

console.log("background.js");
```

Example 4-1c. content-script.js

```
console.log("content-script.js");

import(chrome.runtime.getURL("fetch-page.js"));

const el = document.createElement("script");
el.src = chrome.runtime.getURL("fetch-page.js");
document.body.appendChild(el);
```

Example 4-1d. fetch-page.js

```
console.log("fetch-page.js");

fetch(chrome.runtime.getURL("extra.html"));
```

Example 4-1e. extra.html

```
<!DOCTYPE html>
<html>
  <body>
    <h1>Extra Page</h1>

    <script src="fetch-page.js"></script>
  </body>
</html>
```

Take a minute to examine what this extension is doing. Some things to note

- The extension will inject `content-script.js` on all web pages.
- The manifest designates `fetch-page.js` as a web accessible resource and is accessible by all web pages.
- `content-script.js` attempts to load `fetch-page.js` in two different ways: via dynamic `import`, and via dynamic `<script>` loading.
- `fetch-page.js` sends a network request for the `extra.html` file. This file will be loaded and executed in multiple locations in the extension, with different results.

To understand how the extension file server works, we'll unpack this extension one file at a time. Begin by loading the extension in Google Chrome and inspecting the background service worker console output by clicking the *service worker* link in the extension card (Figure 4-2).

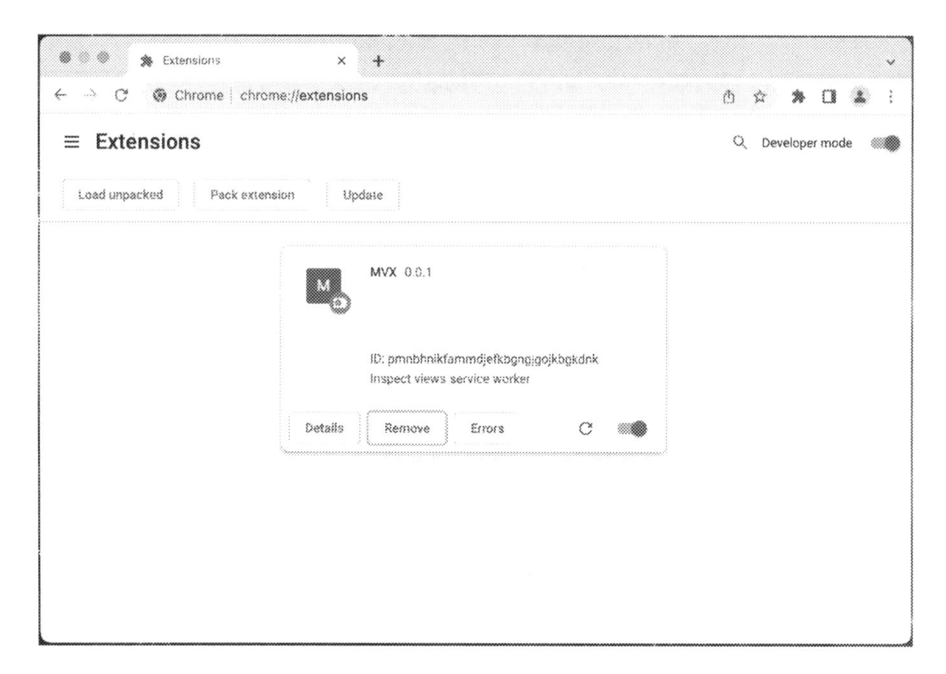

Figure 4-2. *Clicking the service worker link will open the background console output*

The background service worker console output will appear as in Figure 4-3.

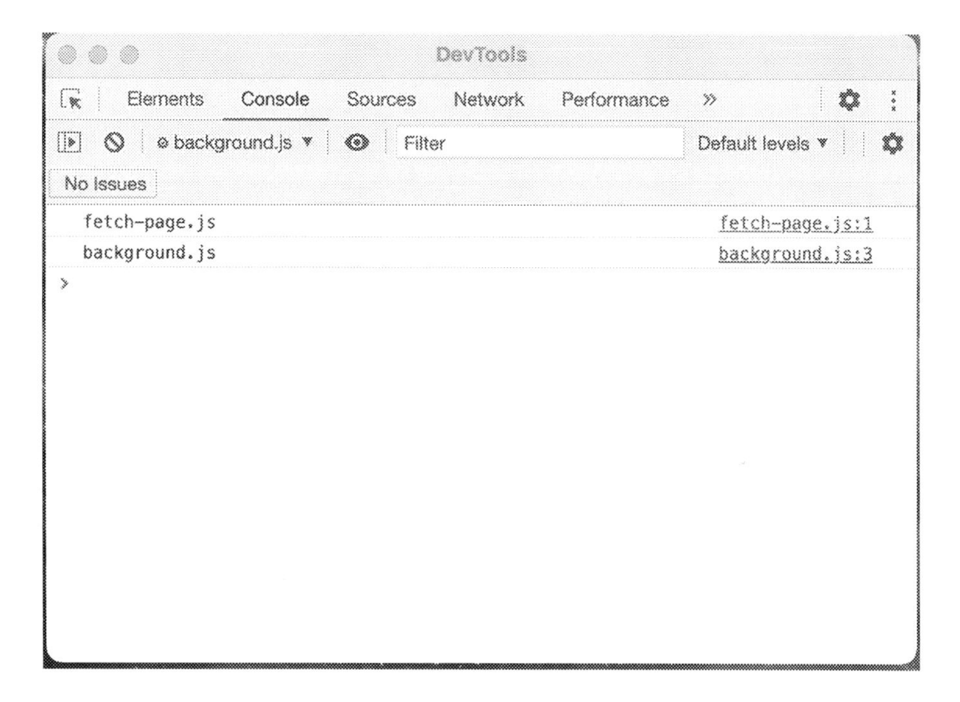

***Figure 4-3.** The background console output*

This indicates that the background script was able to successfully import and execute the `fetch-page.js` script. Let's look to the *Network* tab to see how this occurred (Figure 4-4).

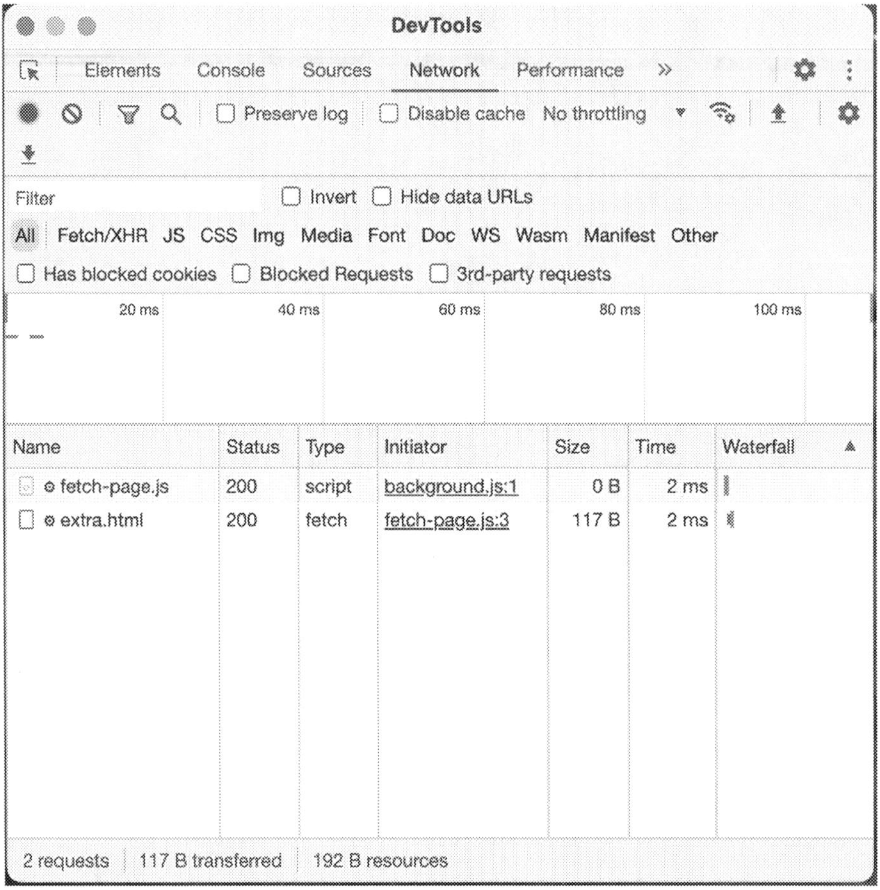

Figure 4-4. *The background network activity log*

Reload the extension to trigger these network requests. You will see two successful network requests: one for the imported JS file and one for the fetched HTML file. Inspecting the JS request reveals the following (Figure 4-5).

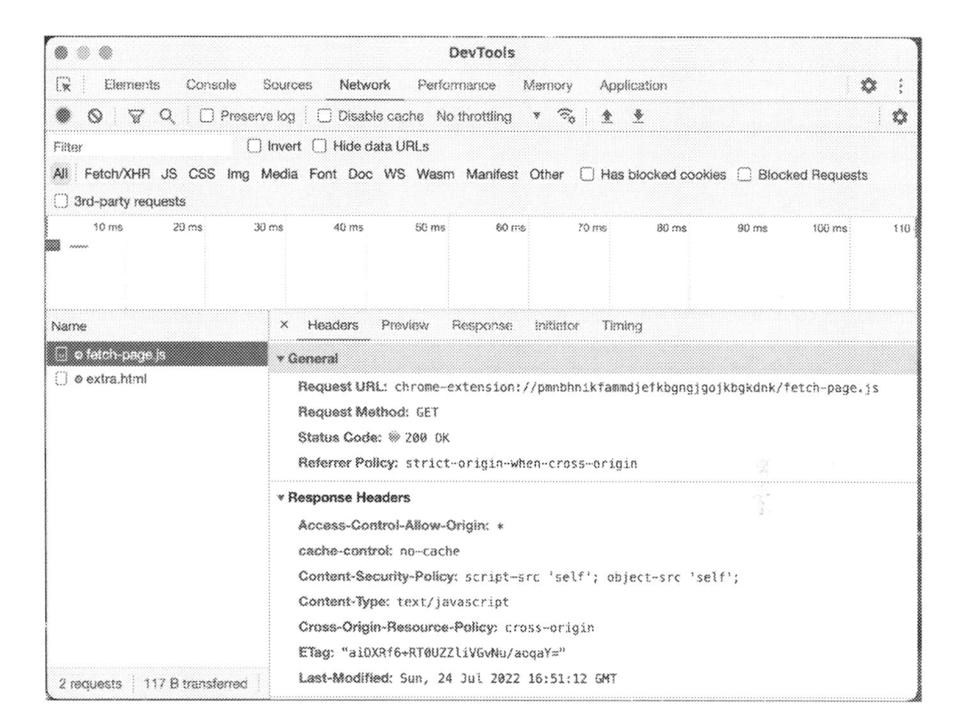

Figure 4-5. *The `fetch-page.js` request*

This network request successfully sends a GET request to the extension file server, and the file server returns a 200. Note the URL beginning with the `chrome-extension://` protocol. Let's unpack the parts of this URL:

- **chrome-extension:**// is the URL protocol, which indicates to Google Chrome that the request should be routed to the browser's installed extensions. The protocol differs between browsers: Mozilla Firefox uses `moz-extension://`, Microsoft Edge uses `extension://`, Opera uses `opera://`.
- **pmnbhnikfammdjefkbgngjgojkbgkdnk** is the extension ID. Your extension's ID will be different. This ID is used to uniquely identify this instance of the extension both inside the browser as well as when published in the extension marketplace. The ID format

will vary slightly between browsers: for example, Google Chrome uses an unbroken string of lowercase letters, whereas Mozilla Firefox uses a v4 UUID.

- **fetch-page.js** is the URL path. This will exactly match the file path inside the extension directory.

Next, examine the `extra.html` request (Figure 4-6).

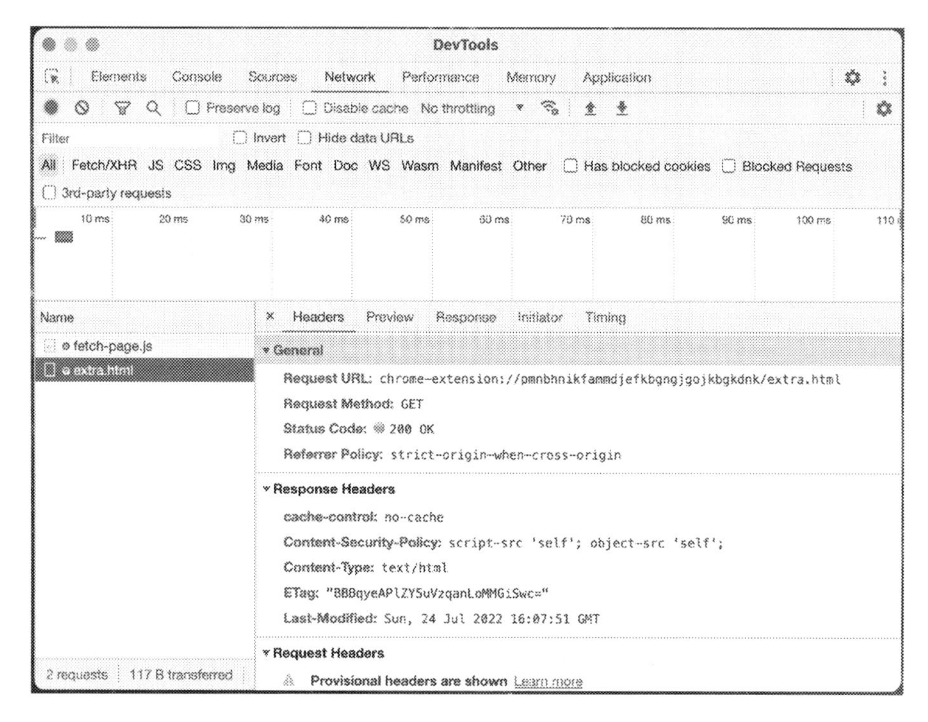

***Figure 4-6.** The `extra.html` request*

Compare the two requests and note the presence or absence of the `Access-Control-Allow-Origin` and `Cross-Origin-Resource-Policy` headers. These are automatically added because `fetch-page.js` is listed under `web_accessible_resources`. Compare this to the request for `extra.html`: you will notice these headers are absent, as `extra.html` is not listed as a web accessible resource.

Note You also will notice that `extra.html` is not referenced directly or indirectly anywhere in the manifest, and yet the extension file server is perfectly happy to return the file. When sending requests from an extension context (background, popup, extension protocol), requests for *any* file in the extension will return that file successfully.

Next, let's copy the URL of the `extra.html` request (yours will differ from the screenshot above) and open it in a new browser tab. Open the developer tools once the page is loaded (Figure 4-7).

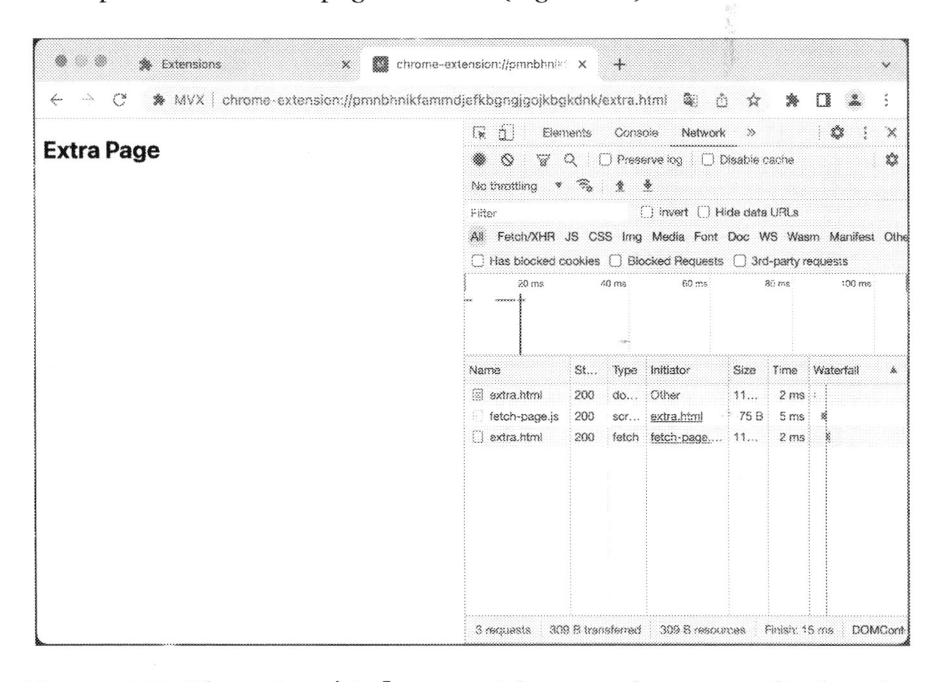

Figure 4-7. The `extra.html` page with network requests displayed

Tip An easy way of accomplishing this is to right click on the network request and select "Open in new tab."

The browser is loading `extra.html` from the extension file server, rendering it as a normal web page, and successfully loading the `<script>` and executing its payload (which performs a duplicate fetch of `extra.html`). There are some critical takeaways to note here:

- Because it can load and render any file included in the extension, browser extensions can have an unlimited number of web pages, including ones that are not explicitly referenced by the manifest.
- The special `chrome-extension://` protocol routes requests to the file server. Pages rendered in this way can use the WebExtensions API in their scripts, as well as send requests for any file in the extension directory.

This behavior is drastically different when compared to content script execution. Note that the manifest is configured to inject the content script on any web page, so next direct your browser to an inert test site such as `blank.org` and view the console output (Figure 4-8).

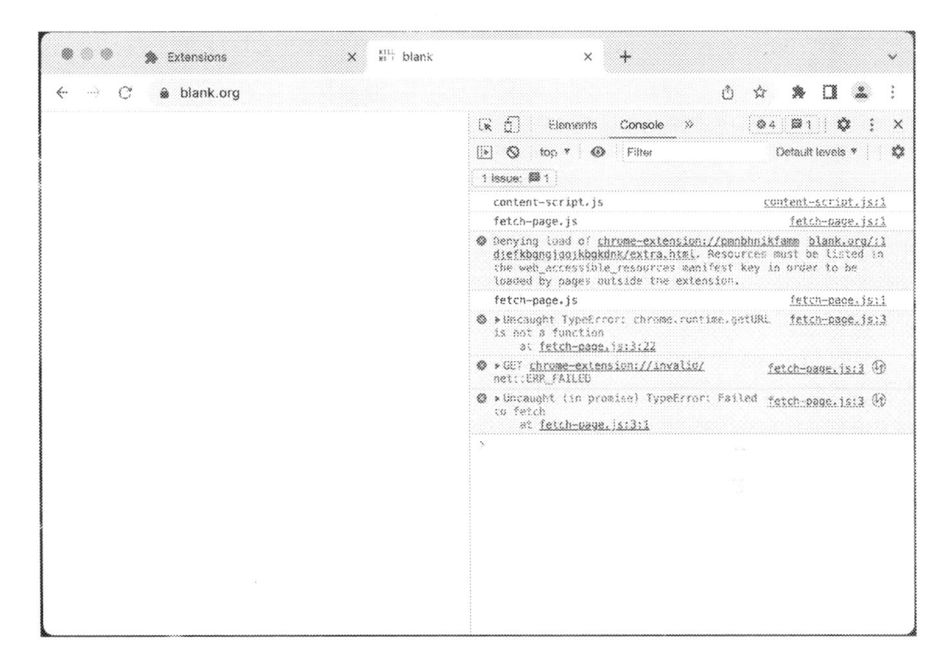

Figure 4-8. *The console output from the extension's content scripts*

First off, note that the content script is *not* being served via network request. Rather than being loaded from the extension file server, the browser is injecting it into the page directly.

Observe that the content script is attempting to fetch the JS file in two different ways, and each throws an error for a different reason:

- The first attempt dynamically imports the `fetch-page.js` file and executes it. The dynamic import succeeds because `fetch-page.js` is a web accessible resource. However, because this is executing inside a content script, it cannot load the HTML file since it is *not* made accessible under `web_accessible_resources`. This throws a `Denying load` error.

- The second attempt creates a `<script>` element to load the `fetch-page.js` file and execute it. The script load succeeds because `fetch-page.js` is a web accessible resource. However, the execution context of the loaded script is not granted access to the WebExtensions API, and therefore the attempt to use `chrome.runtime.getURL` throws a `TypeError`.

Although content scripts still can access the extension file server, its access is considerably more restricted.

Tip The extension file server is a flexible way to make your extension behave more like a web page with multiple views and routing, but the request routing does not support basic features like redirects or custom 404 pages.

Sandboxed Pages

In manifest v3, the values allowed in the Content Security Policy (CSP) is considerably more limited when compared to v2. It newly disallows the following in extension pages:

- Inline scripts
- Remotely loaded code
- `eval()`
- User-provided scripts

To use these tools, you must run an extension page in a sandbox. Doing so will allow the page to use the disallowed features listed above, but at a cost - the page will lose all access to the WebExtensions APIs.

Note Unless specified, the default sandbox content security policy is `sandbox allow-scripts allow-forms allow-popups allow-modals; script-src 'self' 'unsafe-inline' 'unsafe-eval'; child-src 'self';`

The following example defines the popup page as a sandboxed page. When opening the popup page, the inline script will execute the `eval()` without issue:

Example 4-2a. manifest.json

```
{
  "name": "MVX",
  "version": "0.0.1",
  "manifest_version": 3,
  "action": {
    "default_popup": "popup.html"
  },
  "sandbox": {
    "pages": ["popup.html"]
  }
}
```

Example 4-2b. popup.html

```
<!DOCTYPE html>
<html>
  <body>
    <h1>Popup</h1>

    <script>
      eval(`document.body.innerHTML += '<div>Foobar</div>'`);
```

```
    </script>
  </body>
</html>
```

Summary

In this chapter, you were presented with an overview of how all the elements of a browser extension work in concert. With this knowledge, you should now be able to analyze how a given extension moves information around and makes API calls. This chapter also equips you to more effectively be able to plan for how to take an idea for a browser extension and turn it into actual code. You should also have a good understanding of how the browser extension file server can deliver files in various ways, as well as the tradeoffs involved when declaring a sandboxed page.

The next chapter will cover all the fields that can appear in an extension manifest as well as how each field's definition can control the behavior of an extension.

CHAPTER 5

The Extension Manifest

The extension manifest is the blueprint of the browser extension. Broadly speaking, it is a config file containing a collection of key-value pairs that dictate what the extension can do and in what fashion.

The content of a manifest differs between manifest versions and browsers. Not all properties can be used by all browsers; some browsers will partially support a property, or even not support it at all. Between manifest v2 to manifest v3, new properties are added, others are removed; and some change in how they are defined.

MDN offers a very good table of manifest property support here: `https://developer.mozilla.org/en-US/docs/Mozilla/Add-ons/WebExtensions/manifest.json#browser_compatibility`.

Note This chapter omits a handful of manifest properties which are either not widely supported by most web browsers (such as `theme` and `theme_experiment`), or are completely undocumented (such as `natively_connectable`).

M. Frisbie, *Building Browser Extensions*, https://doi.org/10.1007/978-1-4842-8725-5_5

The Manifest File

The extension manifest is defined in a single `manifest.json` file that lives in the root directory of the extension. This is the only file that is required for a browser extension to be considered valid:

```
simple-extension-directory/
└── manifest.json
```

Note This file is a standard JSON file, with the notable exception that `//`-style comments are allowed. If your text editor is using a standard JSON linter, it may indicate that comments are not allowed in `manifest.json` – ignore this error. All browsers and extension stores allow comments in the manifest.

The JSON file contains a single object with a large number of required and optional properties that configure how the extension behaves. There are only three required properties:

- `manifest_version`, which indicates to the browser how the manifest should be interpreted. This has a large number of implications on the behavior of the extension.
- `version`, which declares the version number of the extension. This is used by extension stores for differentiating between releases.
- `name`, which declares the name of the extension. This is used by both the browser as well as extension stores as the top-line identifier of the extension.

Therefore, the simplest possible manifest would be the following:

manifest.json

```
{
  "name": "MVP Extension",
  "version": "1.0",
  "manifest_version": 3
}
```

Supporting Different Locales

Several manifest properties define strings and textual images that are visible to the user. In situations where the extension needs to support multiple languages based on the user's locale, hardcoding these values is not appropriate. To account for this, the manifest supports loading strings from message files based on the user's locale.

To add locale support, message files must be added to a `_locales` directory. This directory contains one directory for each locale you wish to support. Inside each of these subdirectories, a single `messages.json` file defines the localized strings. The manifest can then automatically load these strings with the special `__MSG_messagename__` identifier.

The following example shows a simple manifest that supports English and French locales:

```
localized-extension-directory/
├── manifest.json
└── _locales/
    ├── en/
    │   └── messages.json
    └── fr/
        └── messages.json
```

The manifest file would be written as follows:

manifest.json

```
{
  "name": "__MSG_extensionName__",
  "version": "1.0",
  "manifest_version": 3,
  "default_locale": "en",
}
```

When using locales, the `default_locale` property is required in your manifest. The required formatting of the `messages.json` files is shown below:

_locales/en/messages.json

```
{
  "extensionName": {
    "message": "Hello world!"
  }
}
```

_locales/fr/messages.json

```
{
  "extensionName": {
    "message": "Bonjour le monde!"
  }
}
```

Note Locales and internationalization is a broad and deep subject. Refer to `https://developer.mozilla.org/en-US/docs/Mozilla/Add-ons/WebExtensions/Internationalization` for additional details on locale placeholders, additional message properties, and more.

Note The WebExtensions i18n API and extension CSS files can also use locale strings from these `messages.json` files. Refer to the *Extension and Browser APIs* chapter for details.

Match Patterns and Globs

Several properties in the manifest can use match patterns and globs to specify multiple URLs or files at once.

File Path Match Patterns

Properties such as `web_accessible_resources` can use match patterns to select single files or entire directories. As is the case with all file paths in the manifest file, they are resolved with respect to the root directory of the extension. The syntax allows for the use of * wildcards to match zero to many characters. The following are some examples of valid file match patterns:

- `"/*"` selects all files
- `"/foo/*"` selects all files in the `foo` directory
- `"/foo/*.png"` selects all PNG files in the `foo` directory
- `"/foo/bar.png"` selects a single PNG file in the `foo` directory

URL Match Patterns

Properties such as `content_scripts` can use match patterns to whitelist single URLs or entire web origins. The syntax allows for the use of * wildcards to match zero to many characters. The following are some examples of valid URL match patterns:

- `"<all_urls>"` selects all URLs with a protocol of `http://`, `https://`, `ws://`, `wss://`, `ftp://`, `data://`, or `file://`
- `"https://*/*"` selects all URLs with a `https://` protocol
- `"*://example.com/*"` selects all URLs with an `example.com` origin
- `"https://example.com/foo/*"` selects all `example.com` URLs with a `foo/` path prefix
- `"https://example.com/foo/bar"` selects a single URL

Note For specific details on the rules for match patterns, refer to `https://developer.chrome.com/docs/extensions/mv3/match_patterns/`.

URL Globs

Properties such as `content_scripts` can use globs to add additional filtering to URL match patterns. Globs are an extension of URL match patterns; their syntax allows for the use of * wildcards to match zero to many characters, as well as ? to match exactly one character:

- "*://example.com/*" selects all URLs with an example.com origin
- "*://example.???/*" selects all URLs with an example. origin followed by a three-character TLD, such as example.com, example.org and example.gov

---

Note For specific details on the rules for globs, refer to https://developer.chrome.com/docs/extensions/mv3/content_scripts/#matchAndGlob

---

Manifest Properties

This section contains a comprehensive list of manifest properties and how their values should be defined. Many of these properties are linked to additional browser permissions or parts of the WebExtensions API; each section will direct you to the portion of the book detailing the interplay of the manifest property value, required permissions, and the involved APIs.

If you wish to inspect the browser source code involved with parsing manifest properties, use the following resources:

- Chromium manifests: https://chromium.googlesource.com/chromium/src/+/main/chrome/common/extensions/api/_manifest_features.json
- Firefox manifests: https://searchfox.org/mozilla-central/source/browser/components/extensions/schemas

Tip To experiment with these properties in a real extension, you can add them to the "MVP Extension" `manifest.json` defined at the beginning of the chapter. (Many of these properties require supplemental APIs, permissions, and files to work.) Recall that each change to the manifest requires an extension reload.

action

This property defines an object containing values which dictate the behavior and appearance of the extension icon in the browser toolbar (Figure 5-1). This is the manifest v3 replacement for the `browser_action` and `page_action` properties in manifest v2.

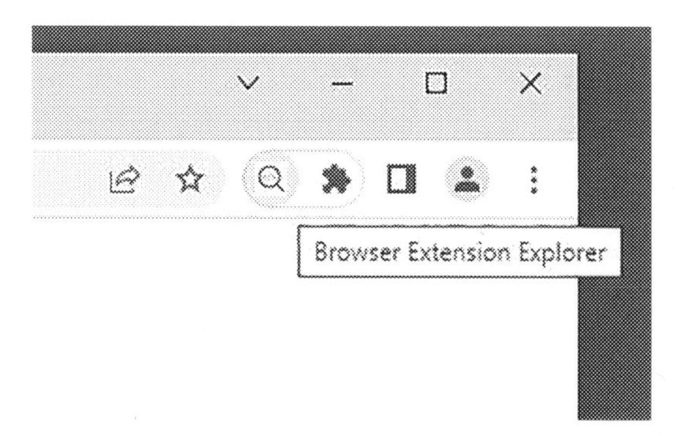

Figure 5-1. *The extension toolbar icon with hover title revealed*

Note This property can be only used in manifest v3. If writing for manifest v2, use `browser_action`.

The property with is shown below with a fully defined example value:

action property in manifest.json

```
{
  ...
  "action": {
    "default_icon": {
      "16": "icons/icon-16.png",
      "32": "icons/icon-32.png",
      "64": "icons/icon-64.png"
    },
    "default_popup": "popup/popup.html",
    "default_title": "Building Browser Extensions",
    "browser_style": true,
    "theme_icons": [
      {
        "light": "icons/icon-16-light.png",
        "dark": "icons/icon-16.png",
        "size": 16
      },
      {
        "light": "icons/icon-32-light.png",
        "dark": "icons/icon-32.png",
        "size": 32
      }
    ]
  },
  ...
}
```

The `action` object allows for the following properties:

default_icon

This property tells the browser where to locate icons for the toolbar via relative paths to image files. There are two ways to define this property: either provide PNG or JPEG image icons and allow the browser to intelligently select which icon it would prefer, or provide a single vector image.

Providing one or multiple image icons allows the browser to decide which icon is best for the current hardware configuration. (For example, an Apple Retina display prefers an icon with twice the resolution.) Providing icons of 16x16px, 32x32px, and 64x64px is sufficient to cover all possible cases. The following is an example of how this property can be used:

Example value for default_icon with sized images

```
{
  ...
  "action": {
    "default_icon": {
      "16": "icons/icon-16.png",
      "32": "icons/icon-32.png",
      "64": "icons/icon-64.png"
    },
    ...
  },
  ...
}
```

If you wish to provide a vector instead, the browser only needs a single vector file to account for all rendering configurations:

Example value for default_icon with vector image

```
{
  ...
  "action": {
```

```
    "default_icon": "icons/icon.svg"
    ...
  },
  ...
}
```

default_popup

This property tells the browser where to locate the HTML file that should render as a popup when the extension's toolbar icon is clicked. This can also be set or changed via the WebExtension API's `chrome.action.setPopup()` method. The following is an example of how this property can be used:

Example value for default_popup

```
{
  ...
  "action": {
    "default_popup": "components/popup/popup.html"
    ...
  },
  ...
}
```

Note If this property is not defined, no popup page will appear when the extension's toolbar icon is clicked. Instead, the browser will dispatch a click event in any background scripts (if they exist).

---

default_title

This property tells the browser the text that should render as a tooltip when the extension's toolbar icon is hovered over. This can also be set or changed via the WebExtension API's `chrome.action.setTitle()` method. The following is an example of how this property can be used:

Example value for default_title

```
{
  ...
  "action": {
    "default_title": "Open Explorer menu"
    ...
  },
  ...
}
```

Note If this property is not defined, the browser will use the extension `name` property as the hover text.

---

browser_style

(Firefox only) This property is a boolean that tells the browser if it should inject a stylesheet in the popup to style it consistently with the browser. These stylesheets can be viewed in any Firefox browser at `chrome://browser/content/extension.css`, or `chrome://browser/content/extension-mac.css` on macOS. The property defaults to `false`. The following is an example of how this property can be used:

Example value for browser_style

```
{
  ...
  "action": {
    "browser_style": true
    ...
  },
  ...
}
```

theme_icons

(Firefox only) This property allows you to define alternate icons based on the current active Firefox theme. It effectively extends the behavior of `default_icon`. The following is an example of how this property can be used:

Example value for theme_icons

```
{
  ...
  "action": {
    ...,
    "theme_icons": [
      {
        "light": "icons/icon-16-light.png",
        "dark": "icons/icon-16.png",
        "size": 16
      },
      {
        "light": "icons/icon-32-light.png",
        "dark": "icons/icon-32.png",
        "size": 32
      }
```

```
    ],
    ...
  },
  ...
}
```

author

This property provides an author name for display in the browser. The following is an example of how this property can be used:

Example value for author

```
{
  ...
  "author": "Matt Frisbie"
  ...
}
```

Note If the `developer.name` property is defined, it will override this value.

---

automation

(Chromium browsers only) This property allows developers to access the accessibility tree for the browser. This property is only needed in cases where the extension is directly targeting assistive devices. Per MDN, "Browsers create an accessibility tree based on the DOM tree, which is used by platform-specific Accessibility APIs to provide a representation that can be understood by assistive technologies, such as screen readers."

Note Technologies supporting accessibility are out of the scope of this book. For details on using this API, refer to `https://developer.chrome.com/docs/extensions/reference/automation/` and `https://developer.mozilla.org/en-US/docs/Glossary/Accessibility_tree`.

background

This property allows you to define what file or files will be used for the background script. This property is used in both manifest v2 and v3, but the value of the property has significant differences between the two versions.

Manifest v2 background scripts

One way of creating background scripts in manifest v2 was to provide references to one or more script files in a `scripts` array. These scripts are loaded in their array order. They are loaded in a headless web page and will have access to a window object and the DOM. The following is an example of how to provide background scripts in this fashion:

Example value for background scripts

```
{
  ...
  "background": {
    "scripts": [
      "scripts/background-1.js",
      "scripts/background-2.js"
    ]
  },
  ...
}
```

Manifest v2 background page

Another way of creating background scripts in manifest v2 was to provide a page reference to a single HTML file with `<script>` tags that load the background script files. This page is rendered as a headless web page, and therefore these scripts are loaded in whatever order the browser's JavaScript engine performs. The following is an example of how to provide background scripts in this fashion:

Example value for background page

```
{
  ...
  "background": {
    "page": "background.html"
  },
  ...
}
```

This strategy has several advantages. It allows the user to use import statements by adding `type="module"`, as well as to add content to the HTML headless page.

Manifest v2 persistent pages and event pages

In addition to defining how background scripts should be loaded, the background property also allows you to define how the scripts should execute via the boolean `persistent` property. The default value is `true`:

- When `persistent` is `true`, a persistent background page is created. It is kept in memory at all times. It starts up when the extension is loaded or the browser is launched, and it lasts until the extension is unloaded or the browser is closed.

- When `persistent` is `false`, a nonpersistent background page is created. Sometimes referred to as an "event page," this background script can be unloaded and reloaded whenever the browser decides it is idle.

The following is an example of how to provide background scripts in this fashion:

Example value for persistent background page

```
{
  ...
  "background": {
    "page": "background.html",
    "persistent": true

  },
  ...
}
```

Manifest v3 service worker

In manifest v3, the options for creating a background script are much more limited. Because persistent pages in manifest v2 had the potential to consume too many system resources, all background scripts for manifest v3 must execute as a service worker. The closest analog of this in manifest v2 is a single script event page.

Example value for background service worker

```
{
  ...
  "background": {
    "service_worker": "scripts/background.js"
```

```
  },
  ...
}
```

In order to enable using `import` statements in the background script, `"type": "module"` can be added:

Example value for background service worker with a module script

```
{
  ...
  "background": {
    "service_worker": "scripts/background.js",
    "type": "module",
  },
  ...
}
```

Note Refer to the *Background Scripts* chapter for details on setting up background scripts.

---

browser_action

(Manifest v2 only) The `browser_action` property was replaced by `action` in manifest v3. The property values and behaviors are effectively identical. If using manifest v2, refer to the `action` property for details on how to assign a value for this property.

Note This property is an artifact of extension tooling for older browser versions. `browser_action` and `page_action` are redundant in all modern browsers. As a result, these properties have been merged into the `action` property, which is identical in format and behavior.

---

browser_specific_settings

This property defines values that are relevant only to certain browsers. It is rare to have the need to use this property at all. The property takes the form of an object with keys that allocate values to particular browser vendors. Common keys are edge, gecko, and `safari`, which correspond to browsers matching those vendors/engines. The following is an example of how this property can be used:

Example value for browser_specific_settings

```
{
  ...
  "browser_specific_settings": {
    "edge": {
      "browser_action_next_to_addressbar": false
    },
    "gecko": {
      "id": "owner@example.com",
      "strict_min_version": "51.0",
      "strict_max_version": "62.*",
      "update_url": "https://example.com/updates.json"
    },
```

```
    "safari": {
      "strict_min_version": "21",
      "strict_max_version": "28"
    }
  },
  ...
}
```

Note Google Chrome does not support this key.

---

chrome_settings_overrides

This property allows the extension to override the default settings for certain browser interfaces. Its value is an object with the following optional properties:

- `homepage` overrides the default homepage of the browser
- `search_provider` defines a new search provider to add to the browser
- `startup_pages` overrides the default start pages of the browser. This is only supported in Chromium browsers

The browser will indicate that these settings are applied in the extension management interface (Figure 5-2).

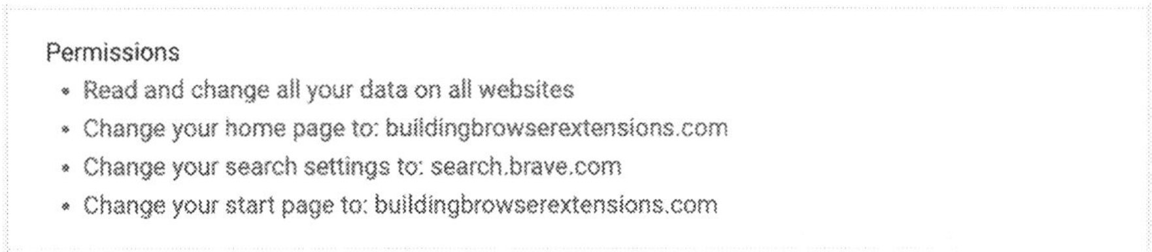

Permissions

- Read and change all your data on all websites
- Change your home page to: buildingbrowserextensions.com
- Change your search settings to: search.brave.com
- Change your start page to: buildingbrowserextensions.com

Figure 5-2. *Google Chrome's extension management interface showing the permissions for an extension with applied settings overrides*

Custom Homepage

The browser homepage is the URL that the browser directs the user to when they click the "home" button in their browser (Figure 5-3). All major browsers no longer display a home button by default, but it can be easily enabled in the browser's settings menu. The homepage URL can be overridden as follows:

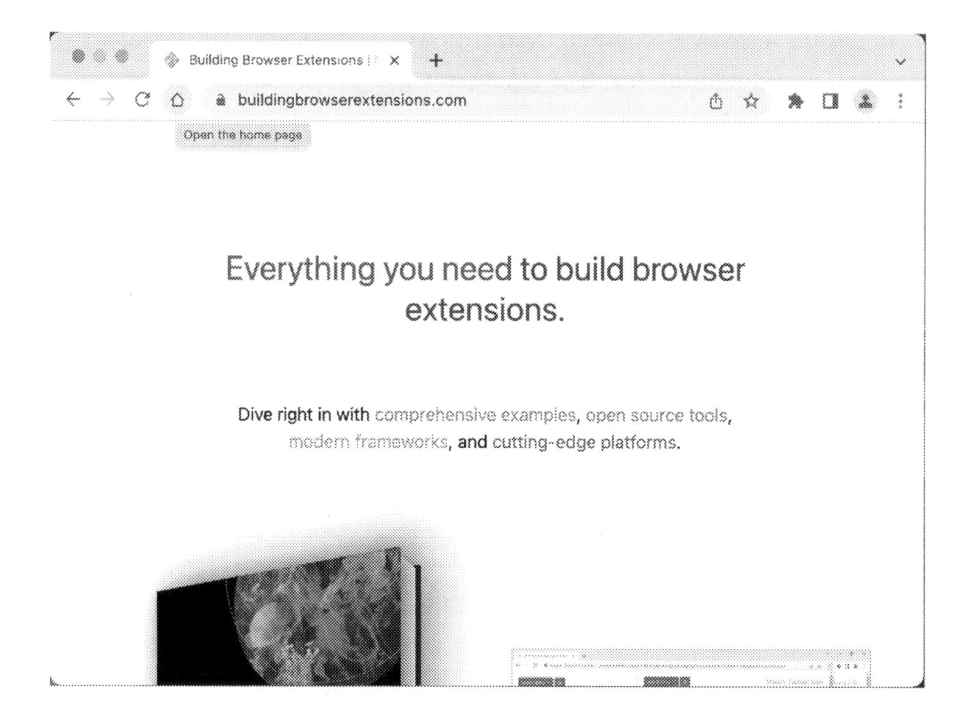

Figure 5-3. *Google Chrome with homepage button enabled and showing the result of clicking the homepage button*

Example value for overriding homepage

```
{
  ...
  "chrome_settings_overrides": {
    "homepage": "https://www.buildingbrowserextensions.com"
  },
  ...
}
```

Custom Search Engine

The search provider decides where to send queries typed into the browser's address bar. Extensions can access the query string via `searchTerms`, interpolate it into a URL of choice, and dispatch that URL (Figures 5-4, 5-5, 5-6, 5-7).

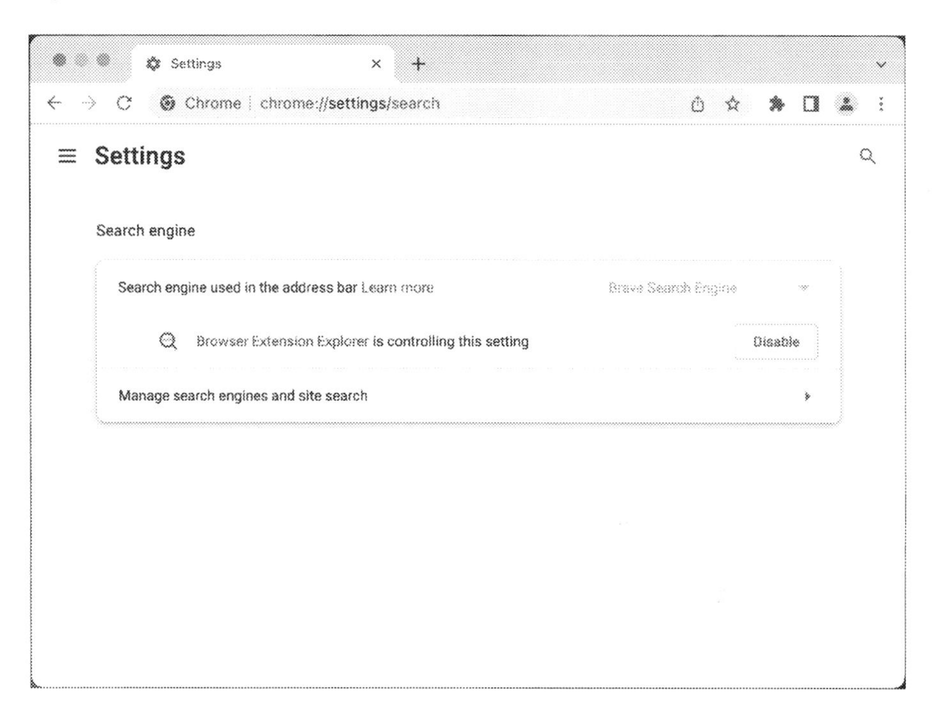

Figure 5-4. *Chrome settings page indicating an extension is controlling the default search engine*

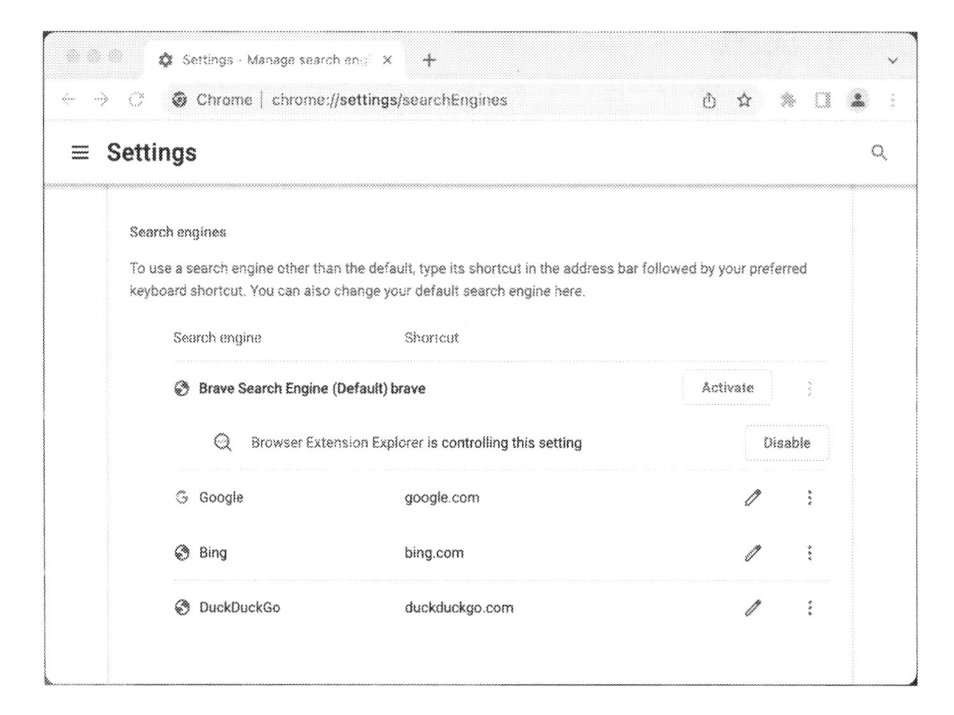

***Figure 5-5.** Chrome search engine settings showing an extension controlling the default engine*

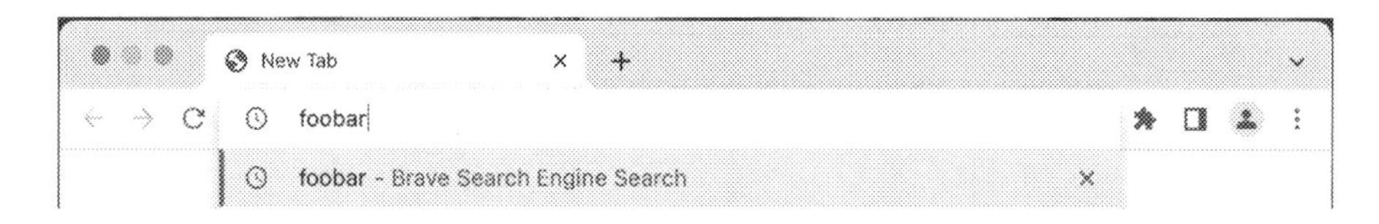

***Figure 5-6.** Typing in a search query into the address bar shows it being routed to the custom search engine*

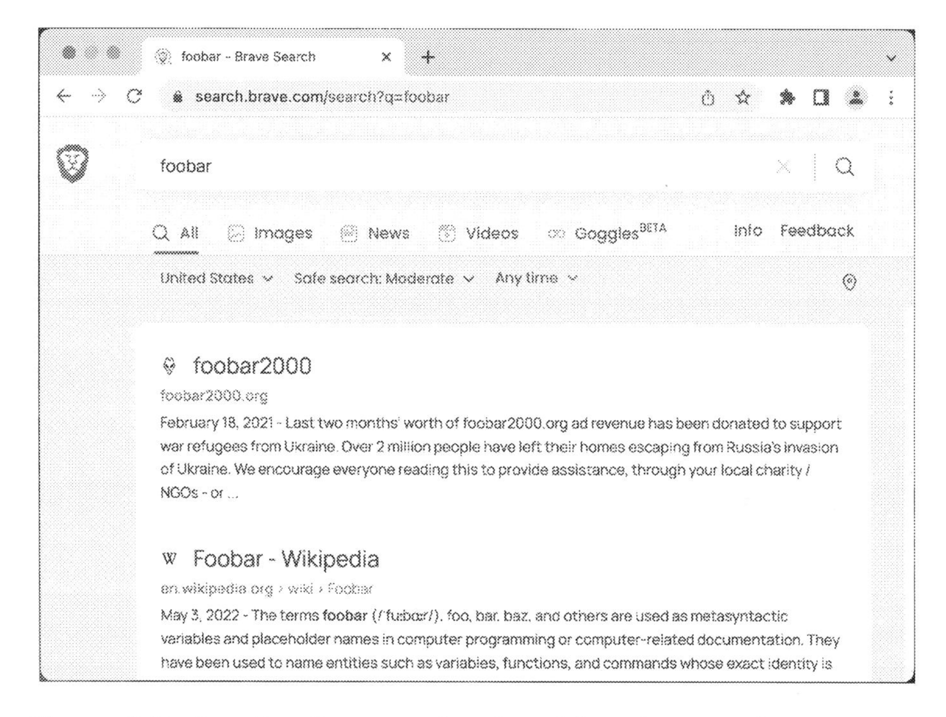

***Figure 5-7.** Results after executing the address bar search*

Note The browser's search engine settings are initialized early in the browser startup. You may need to reboot your browser entirely to see these manifest changes take effect.

The search engine can be overridden as follows:

Example value for overriding search_provider

```
{
  ...
  "chrome_settings_overrides": {
    "search_provider": {
      "name": "Brave Search Engine",
```

```
      "search_url": "https://search.brave.com/
      search?q={searchTerms}",
      "encoding": "UTF-8",
      "is_default": true
    }
  } ...
}
```

The search_provider object can also define the following supplementary properties:

- alternate_urls
- favicon_url
- image_url
- image_url_post_params
- instant_url
- instant_url_post_params
- keyword
- prepopulated_id
- search_url_post_params
- suggest_url
- suggest_url_post_params

Note Support and documentation of these supplementary properties is limited – your mileage may vary. For details, refer to https://developer.mozilla.org/en-US/docs/Mozilla/Add-ons/WebExtensions/manifest.json/chrome_settings_overrides.

Custom Startup Page

(Chromium browsers only) The startup page is the page that opens when the browser program initially starts up. An extension can set the startup page by providing an array containing exactly one URL (Figure 5-8). The startup page URL can be overridden as follows:

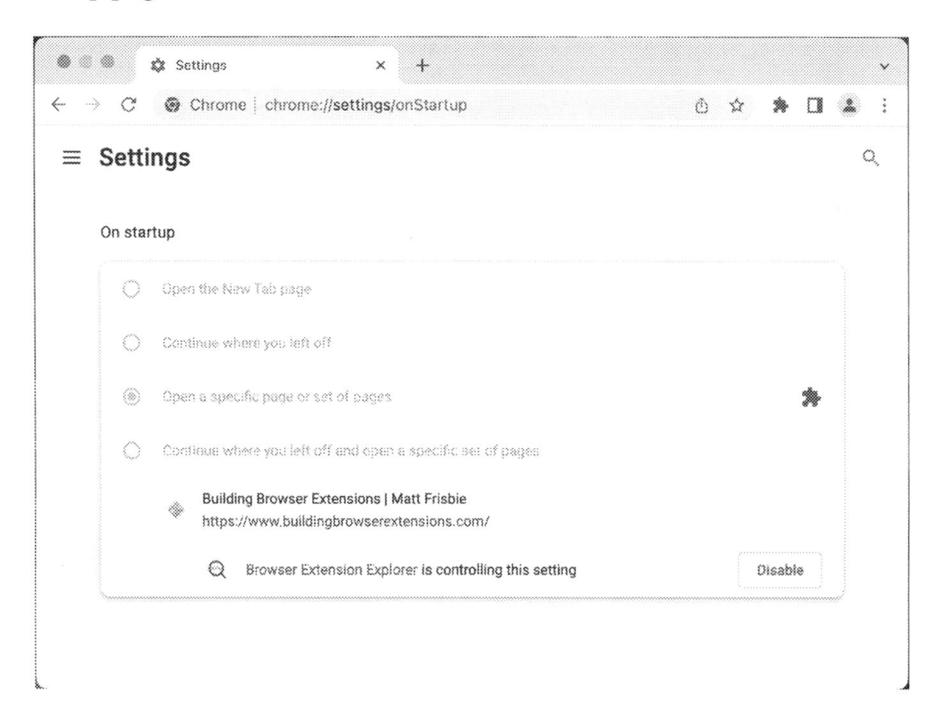

Figure 5-8. *Chrome settings displaying the overridden startup page*

Example value for overriding startup page

```
{
  ...
  "chrome_settings_overrides": {
    "startup_pages": [
      https://www.buildingbrowserextensions.com
    ]
```

```
  },
  ...
}
```

Note The `chrome_` prefix is unrelated to browser compatibility. This property is at least partially supported by Chromium browsers and Firefox.

---

chrome_url_overrides

This property allows the extension to override the default page for certain browser interfaces. Each extension may override exactly one of the following browser pages:

- History page
- Bookmarks page
- New Tab page

The `chrome_url_overrides` value should be an object with only one of the following properties: `history`, `bookmarks`, `newtab`. The following is an example of how this property can be used:

Example value for chrome_url_overrides

```
{
  ...
  "chrome_url_overrides": {
    "newtab": "components/newtab/newtab.html"
  },
  ...
}
```

Note The `chrome_` prefix is unrelated to browser compatibility. This property is at least partially supported by Chromium browsers and Firefox.

commands

This property is used to map keyboard commands to perform various tasks in your extension. An example of this is opening and closing the extension popup when the user presses `Ctrl+Shift+F`. Whereas mapping multi-key commands in JavaScript involves setting listeners for `keydown` or similar events, the `commands` property allows you to natively map multi-key keyboard commands using a simple and intuitive syntax. You can define two types of commands: shortcuts, which associate a keyboard command with a predefined set of native browser behaviors, or custom commands, which associate a keyboard command with a special event that can be handled via the WebExtensions API.

Command Syntax

All commands have the same syntax. Each takes the form of an object with two properties: a `suggested_key` object, which defines the multi-key shortcuts that should invoke the command, and a `description` string, which will appear in the extension keyboard shortcut management UI. The following is an example of how to define a shortcut for a generic `foobar` command:

Example value for a generic foobar command

```
{
  ...
"commands": {
```

```
    "foobar": {
      "suggested_key": {
        "default": "Ctrl+Shift+F"
      },
      "description": "Run 'foobar' on the current page."
    }, ...
}
```

Once the extension is loaded, the browser will reflect this shortcut in its keyboard shortcut management UI (Figure 5-9).

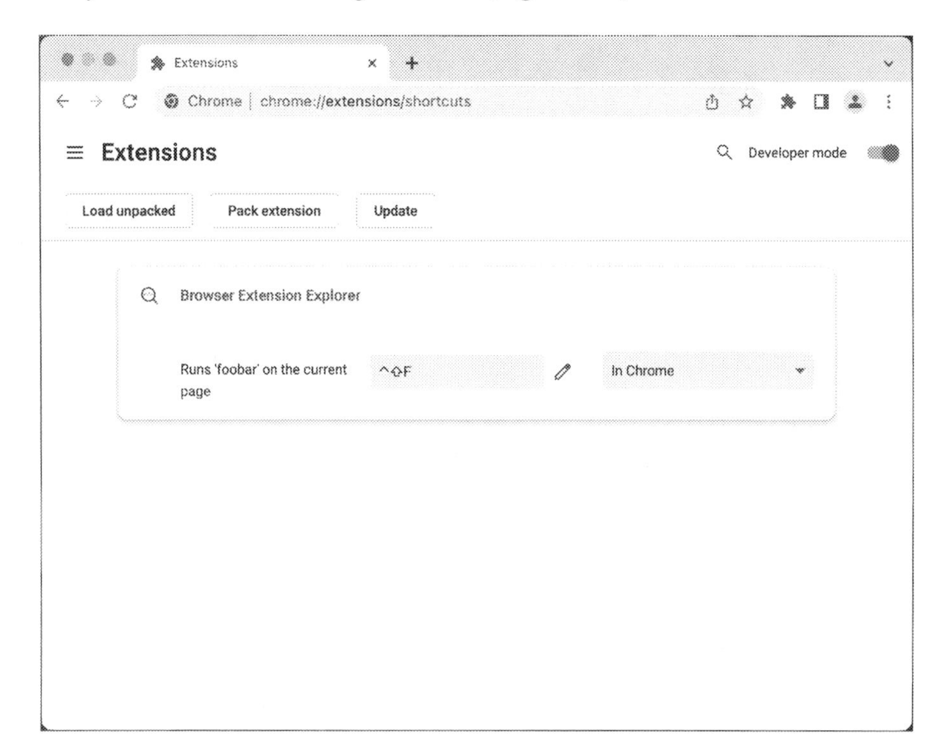

Figure 5-9. *Chrome shortcuts page showing the registered extension command shortcut*

Note The shortcuts list is available at `chrome://extensions/shortcuts` in Chromium browsers and in the `about:addons` interface in Firefox.

Defining Key Shortcuts

When a key shortcut is defined, the browser will watch for the specified key combination and execute the matching command when they are pressed. The following key identifiers are available for use:

- Alphanumeric Keys: `A-Z` and `0-9`
- General Keys: `Comma`, `Period`, `Home`, `End`, `PageUp`, `PageDown`, `Space`, `Insert`, `Delete`
- Function Keys: `F1-F12`
- Arrow Keys: `Up`, `Down`, `Left`, `Right`
- Media Keys: `MediaNextTrack`, `MediaPlayPause`, `MediaPrevTrack`, `MediaStop`
- Modifier Keys: `Ctrl`, `Alt`, `Shift`, `MacCtrl` (macOS only), `Command` (macOS only), `Search` (ChromeOS only)

Key shortcuts have the following restrictions:

- Key shortcuts cannot overlap with default browser key combinations. For example, `Ctrl+R` is already mapped by the browser to reload the page and therefore is unavailable for use by extension commands.
- Key shortcuts must consist of either two or three keys.
- Key shortcuts must include either `Ctrl` (or `MacCtrl` on MacOS) or `Alt` but not both.

The shortcut is defined as a string with the key identifiers concatenated by +. Some examples of valid key shortcuts

- `Ctrl+Shift+F`
- `Alt+Q`
- `MacCtrl+Shift+F12`
- `Alt+MediaPlayPause`

Multi-browser Support

The `suggested_key` object at minimum should define a `default` key shortcut. To support different operating systems, the following properties can additionally be defined:

- `mac`
- `linux`
- `windows`
- `chromeos`
- `android`
- `ios`

If these values are provided and match the host OS, the browser will automatically select them instead of the default value.

Reserved Commands

The browser will give some command names special treatment:

- In manifest v3, `_execute_action` will act as a click on the extension toolbar button.
- In manifest v2, `_execute_page_action` will act as a click on the extension page action button.

- In manifest v2, `_execute_browser_action` will act as a click on the extension browser action button.
- In Firefox and manifest v2, `_execute_sidebar_action` will open the extension's sidebar.

The following command would open the popup when the user uses the `Ctrl+Shift+F` shortcut:

Example value for a reserved _execute_action command

```
{
  ...
  "commands": {
    "_execute_action": {
      "suggested_key": {
        "default": "Ctrl+Shift+F"
      }
    }
  },
  ...
}
```

Note When these reserved commands execute, the browser will not fire the `onCommand()` method.

Custom Commands

For all command identifiers that do not match the reserved commands, the key shortcut will dispatch a command event to all listeners of `command.onCommand()`.

Example value for a generic foobar command

```
{
  ...
  "commands": {
    "foobar": {
      "suggested_key": {
        "default": "Ctrl+Shift+F"
      },
      "description": "Run 'foobar' on the current page."
    }
  },
  ...
}
```

The foobar command from above would be handled as follows:

```
chrome.commands.onCommand.addListener((command) => {
  console.log(`Command: ${command}`); // Command: foobar
});
```

Global Commands

By default, when the browser is not focused on the device, keyboard shortcuts will not dispatch any extension commands. Chromium browsers support an optional `global` property for commands which allows commands which use only shortcuts matching `Ctrl+Shift+[0..9]` to be triggered even when the browser does not have focus. The following is an example of this:

Example value for a global foobar command

```
{
  ...
  "commands": {
    "foobar": {
```

```
    "suggested_key": {
      "default": "Ctrl+Shift+O"
    },
    "description": "Run 'foobar' on the current page.",
    "global": true
  }, ...
}
```

Note For details on using the commands API, refer to the *Extension and Browser APIs* chapter.

---

content_capabilities

This property is obsolete and should not be used. Before the release of the Clipboard API and the Persistent Storage API, it was useful for granting extensions the ability to access the clipboard or unlimited storage. With access to these new APIs, this property is no longer needed.

content_scripts

This property defines which files should be injected as content scripts, where to inject them, and in what fashion. Its value is an array of objects, each of which defines a separate set of content scripts and rules for those scripts. Each object contains the following:

- The `matches` property must contain an array of one or more URL matchers. Each URL that matches these URL matchers will have the scripts injected. This property is required.

- The `js` and `css` properties each contain an array of one or more files that should be injected as content scripts when the page URL is a match. One or both should be defined.
- The `run_at` property defines when the content scripts are to be injected. This can be either `document_start`, `document_end`, or `document_idle`. The default value is `document_idle`.
  - `document_start` injects the scripts when `document.readyState === "loading"`
  - `document_end` injects the scripts when `document.readyState === "interactive"`
  - `document_idle` injects the scripts when `document.readyState === "complete"`
- You can optionally subject the URL to three additional filters, evaluated as follows:
  - The `include_globs` property can be defined as a whitelist of URL globs. If provided, the content scripts will *only* be injected if the URL matches this glob array.
  - The `exclude_matches` property can be defined as a blacklist of URL matchers. If provided, the content scripts will *only* be injected if the URL *does not match* this matchers array.
  - The `exclude_globs` property can be defined as a blacklist of URL globs. If provided, the content scripts will *only* be injected if the URL *does not match* this glob array.

- The `match_about_blank` property enables the content script to be injected on the `about:blank` or `about:srcdoc` URLs.
- The `all_frames` property enables the content script to be injected into nested frames.

The following is an example of how this property can be used:

Example value for content_scripts

```
{
  ...
  "content_scripts": [
    {
      "matches": [
        "*://example.com/*"
      ],
      "include_globs": [
        "*archive*"
      ],
      "exclude_matches": [
        "*://example.com/experimental/*"
      ],
      "exclude_globs": [
        "*?display=legacy*"
      ],
      "js": [
        "scripts/content-script.js"
      ],
      "css": [
        "styles/content-script.css"
      ],
      "run_at": "document_end",
```

```
      "match_about_blank": true,
      "all_frames": true
    }
  ],
  ...
}
```

Tip The `match_about_blank` key has some very interesting background: `https://stackoverflow.com/questions/41408936`

Note For additional details on content scripts, refer to the *Content Scripts* chapter.

content_security_policy

This property defines the content security policies (CSP) of the extension. This property was significantly altered between manifest v2 and v3, including in structure and in allowed values.

Manifest v2 content security policy

The manifest v2 `content_security_policy` property was a string that set the CSP values for the entire application. Manifest v2 was very relaxed about CSP restrictions: it freely allowed for script execution such as `eval()` which had the potential to open up security holes. The following is an example of how this property can be used in manifest v2:

Example value for content_security_policy in manifest v2

```
{
  ...
```

```
  "content_security_policy": "script-src 'self' 'unsafe-eval'
  https://example.com; object-src 'self'",
  ...
}
```

Manifest v3 content security policy

Manifest v3 considerably changes the `content_security_policy` format. The property is now an object, with two possible keys:

- `extension_pages` defines the CSP for all non-sandboxed extension pages
- `sandbox` defines the CSP for all sandboxed extension pages

Furthermore, manifest v3 in Chromium browsers disallows some CSP values in non-sandboxed extension pages to prevent insecure operations like `eval()` and third-party script execution. The following is an example of how this property can be used in manifest v3:

Example value for content_security_policy in manifest v3

```
{
  ...
  "content_security_policy": {
    "extension_pages": "script-src 'self'",
    "sandbox": "script-src 'self' https://example.com; object-
    src 'self'"
  },
  ...
}
```

Note Details of extension content security policy definition is covered in the Extension Architecture chapter. For details on manifest v3 CSP restrictions, refer to `https://developer.chrome.com/docs/extensions/mv3/intro/mv3-migration/#content-security-policy`

converted_from_user_script

This property was used as part of Google's supported transition from userscripts in 2016. Its purpose was so that Chrome Apps, which shared APIs with web extensions, could direct their users to a replacement Progressive Web Application via a `installReplacementWebApp()` method. No modern extensions will have a use for this property.

Note Read more about the transition from Chrome Apps here: `https://developer.chrome.com/docs/apps/migration/`.

cross_origin_embedder_policy

(Chromium browsers only, manifest v3 only) This property defines the Cross-Origin-Embedder-Policy (COEP) header value for requests to the extension's origin. Because the extension behaves in many ways like a web server, it can be vulnerable to the same origin-based security issues that web servers are. If you wish to enable features that are only accessible with cross-origin isolation, this property is used to set the COEP header value to behave in such a manner. This property must be set in conjunction with the `cross_origin_opener_policy` property to enable cross-origin isolation.

The property contains an object with a single `value` property. The following is an example of how this property can be used to enable cross-origin isolation:

Example value for cross_origin_embedder_policy

```
{
  ...
  "cross_origin_embedder_policy": {
    "value": "require-corp"
  },
  ...
}
```

Note Cross-origin isolation is an important subject outside the scope of this book. For an excellent blog post on it, visit `https://web.dev/coop-coep/`.

---

cross_origin_opener_policy

(Chromium browsers only, manifest v3 only) This property defines the Cross-Origin-Opener-Policy (COOP) header value for requests to the extension's origin. Because the extension behaves in many ways like a web server, it can be vulnerable to the same origin-based security issues that web servers are. If you wish to enable features that are only accessible with cross-origin isolation, this property is used to set the COOP header value to behave in such a manner. This property must be set in conjunction with the `cross_origin_embedder_policy` property to enable cross-origin isolation.

The property contains an object with a single `value` property. The following is an example of how this property can be used to enable cross-origin isolation:

Example value for cross_origin_opener_policy

```
{
  ...
  "cross_origin_opener_policy": {
    "value": "same-origin"
  },
  ...
}
```

Note Cross-origin isolation is an important subject outside the scope of this book. For an excellent blog post on it, visit `https://web.dev/coop-coep/`.

---

declarative_net_request

(Manifest v3 and Chromium browsers only) This property defines the rulesets to be used for the Declarative Net Request API. The value is an object with a single `rule_resources` key, which defines an array of all the ruleset objects provided in the extension. Each ruleset object must define a unique `id` string, an `enabled` boolean controlling if the browser should use the ruleset, and `path` string with relative path to the ruleset JSON file. The following is an example of how this property can be used:

Example value for declarative_net_request

```
{
  ...
```

```
  "declarative_net_request": {
    "rule_resources" : [
      {
        "id": "ruleset_1",
        "enabled": true,
        "path": "ruleset_1.json"
      }, {
        "id": "ruleset_2",
        "enabled": false,
        "path": "ruleset_1.json"
      }
    ]
  },
  ...
}
```

Note For details on the Declarative Net Request API, ruleset definition, and permissions for `declarative_net_request`, refer to the *Networking* chapter.

---

default_locale

This property defines the default locale string. The property must be present if and only if there is a `_locales` directory as described in the locales section earlier in this chapter. The following is an example of how this property can be used:

Example value for default_locale

```
{
  ...
```

```
  "default_locale": "en",
  ...
}
```

description

This property defines the formal description of the extension. This value is displayed in the browser as well as in the extension marketplaces. The following is an example of how this property can be used:

Example value for description

```
{
  ...
  "description": "A collection of browser extension examples",
  ...
}
```

developer

This property defines an object containing an author name and/or extension homepage URL for display in the browser. Both the `name` and `url` properties are optional. The following is an example of how this property can be used:

Example value for developer

```
{
  ...
  "developer": {
    "name": "Matt Frisbie",
    "url": "https://www.buildingbrowserextensions.com"
  },
  ...
}
```

Note If the `developer` properties are defined, they will override the `author` and `homepage_url` properties.

devtools_page

This property tells the browser where to locate the HTML file that should be used as the entrypoint to your extension's developer tools content. This page is used to bootstrap the developer utilities, but it renders as a headless page. The following is an example of how this property can be used:

Example value for devtools_page

```
{
  ...
  "devtools_page": "components/devtools/devtools.html",
  ...
}
```

Note Refer to the *Devtools Pages* chapter for details on setting up custom developer tools interfaces.

differential_fingerprint

This property is an internal key used by the Chrome Web Store for extension update distribution. You should not set this property in any circumstance.

Note The Chrome Web Store generates the property when sending out a differential extension update. The property uniquely identifies only the files that changed in the new version of that extension. The key is automatically stripped out when the extension is installed.

---

event_rules

(Chromium browsers only) This property is deprecated; it defines rules that can modify in-flight network requests using `declarativeWebRequest` or take actions depending on the page content – all without requiring permission to read the page's content using `declarativeContent`. `declarativeWebRequest` is deprecated in favor of `declarativeNetRequest`, so this property should not be used.

externally_connectable

This property defines which foreign extensions or web pages can interact with this extension via `runtime.connect()` or `runtime.sendMessage()`. If not defined, the default behavior is to allow all foreign extensions to communicate via these methods, but to disallow all web pages from communicating via these methods. The property value is an object which can define the following:

- If the `ids` array is defined, only extensions with matching IDs are allowed to connect. This array accepts a * wildcard to allow all extensions.
- If the `matches` array is defined, only web pages with matching URLs will be allowed to connect.

- If the `accepts_tls_channel_id` property is set to `true`, messages will include the TLS channel ID in the outgoing message to identify the originating frame.

The following is an example of how this property can be used:

Example value for externally_connectable

```
{
  ...
  "externally_connectable": {
    "ids": [
      "allowmeabcdefabcdefabcdefabcdefa"
    ],
    "matches": [
      "https://*.example.com/*"
    ],
    "accepts_tls_channel_id": true
  },
  ...
}
```

file_browser_handlers

(Manifest v3 and Chrome/Chrome OS only) This property defines an array containing file browser handler objects that can extend the Chrome OS file browser. This is only applicable on Chrome OS devices. The following is an example of how this property can be used:

Example value for file_browser_handlers

```
{
  ...
  "file_browser_handlers": [
    {
```

```
      "id": "upload",
      "default_title": "Save File",
      "file_filters": [
        "filesystem:*.*",
      ]
    }
  ],
  ...
}
```

Note The Chrome OS file browser handler is out of the scope of this book. For documentation, refer to `https://developer.chrome.com/docs/extensions/reference/fileBrowserHandler/`.

---

file_system_provider_capabilities

(Manifest v3 and Chrome/Chrome OS only) This property defines an object containing properties that govern how the extension can interact with the host device's filesystem via the File System Provider API. This is only applicable on Chrome OS devices. The following is an example of how this property can be used:

Example value for file_system_provider_capabilities

```
{
  ...
  "file_system_provider_capabilities": {
    "configurable": true,
    "watchable": false,
    "multiple_mounts": true,
```

```
    "source": "network"
  },
  ...
}
```

Note The Chrome OS file manager and filesystem are out of the scope of this book. For documentation, refer to `https://developer.chrome.com/docs/extensions/reference/fileSystemProvider/`.

homepage_url

This property provides an extension homepage URL for display in the browser. The following is an example of how this property can be used:

Example value for homepage_url

```
{
  ...
  "homepage_url": "https://www.buildingbrowserextensions.com"
  ...
}
```

Note If the `developer.url` property is defined, it will override this value. This is not supported in Chrome or Safari.

host_permissions

(Manifest v3 only) This property defines the host match patterns that the extension requires to run. If the web page matches one or more patterns in this list, the extension will have the ability to read or modify host data, such as `cookies`, `webRequest`, and `tabs.executeScript`. The following is an example of how this property can be used:

Example value for host_permissions

```
{
  ...
  "host_permissions": [
    "*://developer.mozilla.org/*",
    "*://developer.chrome.com/*"
  ],
  ...
}
```

Importantly, the `host_permissions` values are unrelated to the `content_scripts` pattern matchers. Pattern matchers that control which pages should have content scripts injected are defined inside the `content_scripts` property.

Note Refer to the *Permissions* chapter for details on extension permissions.

---

icons

This property defines an object containing values which dictate the extension's primary icon. This icon is used both during installation as well as in various extension marketplaces. At minimum, you should define a 128x128 raster image (JPEG, PNG, BMP, or ICO image). If you wish to support all marketplaces and browsers, you should define four PNG images with dimensions 16x16, 32x32, 48x48, and 128x128.

The following is an example of how this property can be used:

Example value for icons

```
{
  ...
  "icons": {
    "16": "assets/icons/icon-16.png",
    "32": " assets/icons/icon-32.png",
    "48": " assets/icons/icon-48.png",
    "128": " assets/icons/icon-128.png"
  },
  ...
}
```

Note SVG files are not supported for this property.

---

incognito

This property allows you to define how the extension can interact with private browsing windows. The following is an example of how this property can be used:

Example value for incognito

```
{
  ...
  "incognito": "spanning"
  ...
}
```

The `incognito` property can have one of three values:

- `spanning` allows the extension to treat both private and non-private pages in the same manner. It can differentiate between the two via the `chrome.windows.getLastFocused()` method. This value is the default.
- `split` will partition the extension into two separate parts: one part handles private pages, one part handles non-private pages. These parts behave as two separate extension instances.
- `not_allowed` disables the extension on private browsing.

Note Support for this property is fragmented between browsers, refer to `https://developer.chrome.com/docs/extensions/mv2/manifest/incognito/` and `https://developer.mozilla.org/en-US/docs/Mozilla/Add-ons/WebExtensions/manifest.json/incognito` for details.

---

key

(Chromium browsers only) This property explicitly defines for the browser what the 32-character extension ID should be. If key is not provided, the browser will automatically generate it for you.

Example value for key

```
{
  ...
  "key": "hdokiejnpivrijdhajhdlcegeplioahd"
  ...
}
```

Note This is only needed in the rare circumstance where you wish to explicitly define the extension ID for local development at load time. This value is not used when deploying to a web store.

---

manifest_version

This property defines which indicates to the browser how the manifest should be interpreted. As described earlier in the chapter, this integer has significant implications for how the overall manifest file must be structured. The following is an example of how this property can be used:

Example value for manifest_version

```
{
  ...
  "manifest_version": 3
  ...
}
```

Note Some browsers like Firefox are still in the process of rolling out support for manifest v3, but other browsers like Chrome are actively phasing out support for manifest v2. Your application will need to generate multiple `manifest.json` files to support multiple marketplaces.

---

minimum_chrome_version

(Chromium browsers only) This property defines the minimum version of Chrome required for the extension. Non-Chromium browsers will ignore this property. The following is an example of how this property can be used:

Example value for minimum_chrome_version

```
{
  ...
  "minimum_chrome_version": "90"
  ...
}
```

nacl_modules

This property was used for Native Client support (NaCl), its use is deprecated.

Note Native Client was a sandbox for running compiled C and C++ code in the browser efficiently and securely, independent of the user's operating system. It was deprecated in 2020 and support ended in June 2021.

---

name

This property defines the formal name of the extension. This value is displayed in the browser as well as in the extension marketplaces. This name should not exceed 45 characters. The following is an example of how this property can be used:

Example value for name

```
{
  ...
  "name": "Building Browser Extensions",
  ...
}
```

oauth2

(Chromium browsers only) This property is used to register your extension as an OAuth2 client. Its value is an object with the OAuth2 client ID and scopes:

Example value for optional_permissions

```
{
  ...
  "oauth2": {
    "client_id": "oAuthClientID.apps.googleusercontent.com",
    "scopes": [
      "https://www.googleapis.com/auth/contacts.readonly"
    ],
  },
  ...
}
```

Note Refer to the *Extension and Browser APIs* chapter for details on setting up authentication for your extension.

---

offline_enabled

This property is deprecated and should not be used. In legacy codebases, it indicated if the extension was expected to work offline.

omnibox

This property enables the browser's native omnibox interface by defining its entry keyword. The value is an object containing a single `keyword` property. The following is an example of how this property can be used:

Example value for omnibox

```
{
  ...
  "omnibox": {
    "keyword": "bbx",
  },
  ...
}
```

Suppose a user has an extension installed with the omnibox configuration shown above. The omnibox interface works as follows:

1. The user focuses on the empty browser address bar.
2. The user types `bbx` followed by a space.
3. The browser opens the omnibox interface (Figure 5-10).

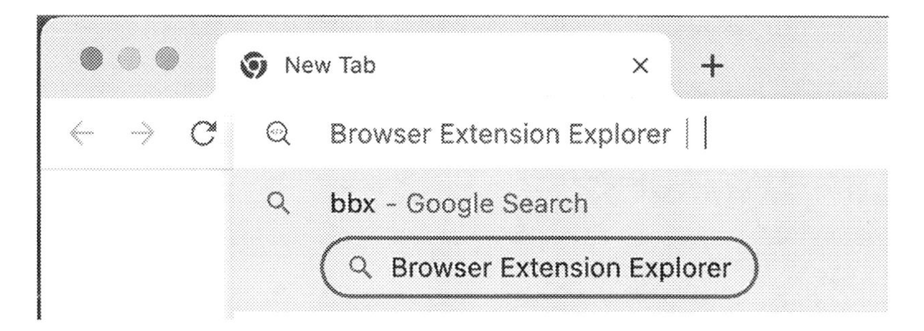

Figure 5-10. *The omnibox interface*

Note The extension can control the omnibox behavior with the Omnibox API. This is covered in depth in the *Extension and Browser APIs* chapter.

---

optional_host_permissions

(Manifest v3 and Chromium only) This property defines the host match patterns that the extension does not explicitly require to run, but that the user can opt into. The match pattern behavior and syntax are identical to `host_permissions`. The permission granting user interface is identical to `optional_permissions`.

optional_permissions

This property defines the permissions that the extension does not require to run correctly, but that it can prompt the user for access at runtime. This property is often used to add extension permissions in subsequent releases without requiring that all users grant access to a new permission. Not all permission types are eligible to appear in this array. The following is an example of how this property can be used:

Example value for optional_permissions

```
{
  ...
  "optional_permissions": [
    "cookies",
    "history",
    "notifications"
  ],
  ...
}
```

Note Refer to the *Permissions* chapter for details on extension permissions.

---

options_page

This is a deprecated property. Use `options_ui` instead.

options_ui

This property tells the browser where to locate the HTML file that should render as the options page when opened either programmatically, by URL, or via the toolbar context menu. It is an object that typically only contains a single `page` property, but also supports additional properties in some browsers. The following is an example of how this property can be used:

Example value for options_ui

```
{
  ...
```

```
  "options_ui": {
    "page": "components/options/options.html"
  },
  ...
}
```

browser_style

(Firefox only) This property is a boolean that tells the browser if it should inject a stylesheet in the options page to style it consistently with the browser. These stylesheets can be viewed in any Firefox browser at `chrome://browser/content/extension.css`, or `chrome://browser/content/extension-mac.css` on macOS. The property defaults to `false`. The following is an example of how this property can be used:

Example value for browser_style

```
{
  ...
  "options_ui": {
    "page": "components/options/options.html",
    "browser_style": true,
  },
  ...
}
```

open_in_tab

(Firefox only) This property is a boolean that tells the browser if it should open the options page in a normal browser tab, rather than in an embedded options page (Figure 5-11). The property defaults to `true`.

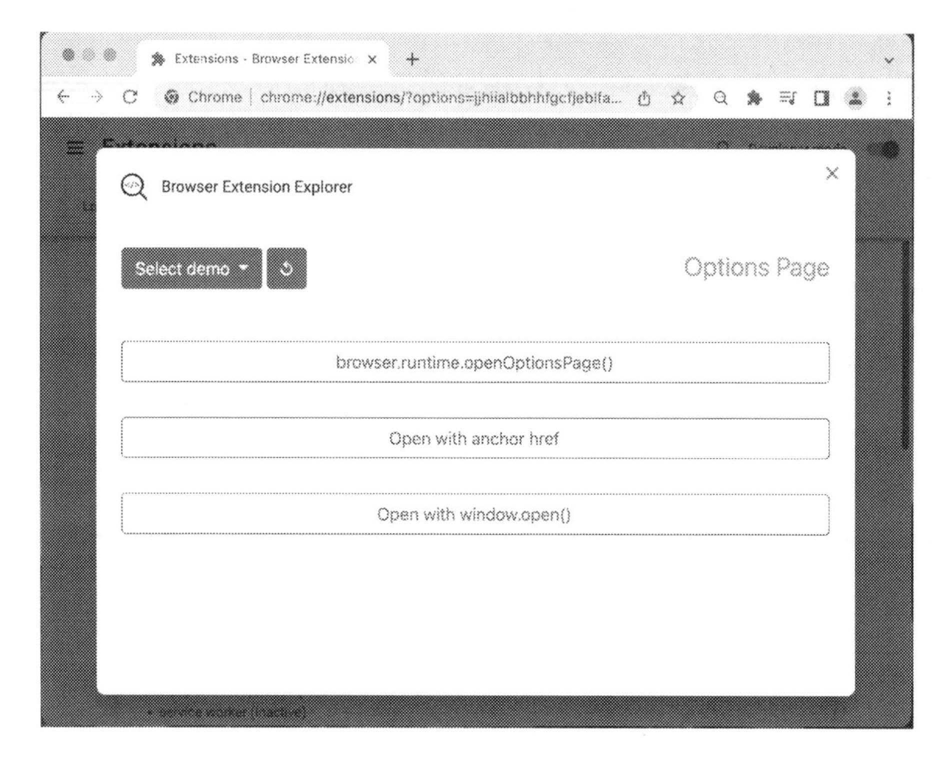

***Figure 5-11.** An embedded options interface*

The following is an example of how this property can be used:

Example value for options_ui

```
{
  ...
  "options_ui": {
    "page": "components/options/options.html",
    "open_in_tab": false,
  },
  ...
}
```

page_action

(Manifest v2 only) The page_action property was replaced by action in manifest v3. The property values and behaviors are effectively identical. If using manifest v2, refer to the action property for details on how to assign a value for this property.

Note This property is an artifact of extension tooling for older browser versions. browser_action and page_action are redundant in all modern browsers. As a result, these properties have been merged into the action property, which is identical in format and behavior.

---

permissions

This property defines the permissions that the extension requires to run correctly. All permission types are eligible to appear in this array. Upon installation and updates, all additions to this array will require that users explicitly grant access to the newly added permission in a popup dialog. The following is an example of how this property can be used:

Example value for permissions

```
{
  ...
  "permissions": [
    "activeTab",
    "declarativeNetRequest",
    "geolocation"
  ],
  ...
}
```

In manifest v2, the permissions array also included URL pattern matchers that are now defined in the `host_permissions` property. Modern extensions should now be placing URL pattern matchers only in the `host_permissions` or `optional_host_permissions` properties.

Note Refer to the *Permissions* chapter for details on extension permissions.

---

platforms

This property was used for Native Client support (NaCl), its use is deprecated.

Note Native Client was a sandbox for running compiled C and C++ code in the browser efficiently and securely, independent of the user's operating system. It was deprecated in 2020 and support ended in June 2021.

---

replacement_web_app

This property was used as part of Google's supported transition from Chrome Apps in 2016. Its purpose was so that Chrome Apps, which shared APIs with web extensions, could direct their users to a replacement Progressive Web Application via a `installReplacementWebApp()` method. No modern extensions will have a use for this property.

Note Read more about the transition from Chrome Apps here: `https://developer.chrome.com/docs/apps/migration/`.

---

requirements

(Chromium browsers only) This property defines the browser technologies required by the extension. If a user's device does not meet the requirements, the Chrome Web Store will inform them that their device lacks the needed technology to run the extension. Currently, the only actively supported property is "3D." The following is an example of how this property can be used:

Example value for requirements

```
{
  ...
  "requirements": {
    "3D": {
      "features": [
        "webgl"
      ]
    }
  },
  ...
}
```

sandbox

(Chromium browsers only) This property defines which pages should render in sandbox mode. Its value is an object with a single page array containing paths to each file that should render in sandbox mode. The following is an example of how this property can be used:

Example value for sandbox

```
{
  ...
```

```
  "sandbox": {
    "pages": [
      "components/popup/popup.html",
      "components/options/options.html",
    ]
  },
  ...
}
```

Note For additional details on sandboxing pages, refer to the *Extension Architecture* chapter.

---

short_name

This property defines the secondary name of the extension that will be used in contexts where the `name` property is too long. This name should not exceed 12 characters. If this is not provided, the browser will simply truncate the `name` property. The following is an example of how this property can be used:

Example value for short_name

```
{
  ...
  "short_name": "BBX",
  ...
}
```

storage

This property specifies the schema file for managed storage, which is involved with the `storage.managed` API. The following is an example of how this property can be used:

Example value for storage

```
{
  ...
  "storage": {
    "managed_schema": "schema.json"
  },
  ...
}
```

Note Browsers handle managed storage differently. Refer to the *Extension and Browser APIs* chapter for more details.

---

system_indicator

This property is deprecated and should not be used.

Note Refer to `https://bugs.chromium.org/p/chromium/issues/detail?id=142450` for a history of this property.

---

tts_engine

(Chromium browsers only) This property is used to declare all the voices and voice configurations the extension wishes to use for the browser's text-to-speech engine. The following is an example of how this property can be used:

Example value for tts_engine

```
{
  ...
  "tts_engine": {
    "voices": [
      {
        "voice_name": "Alice",
        "lang": "en-US",
        "event_types": ["start", "marker", "end"]
      },
      {
        "voice_name": "Pat",
        "lang": "en-US",
        "event_types": ["end"]
      }
    ]
  },
  ...
}
```

Note For details on Chrome's text-to-speech API, refer to `https://developer.chrome.com/docs/extensions/reference/ttsEngine/`.

---

update_url

(Chromium browsers only) This property defines the URL from which the browser should request updates. It is only used for Chrome extensions that are not hosted on the Chrome Web Store. The following is an example of how this property can be used:

Example value for update_url

```
{
  ...
  "update_url": "https://example.com/updates.xml",
  ...
}
```

Note Refer to the *Extension Development and Deployment* chapter for details on self-hosting extensions.

---

version

This property defines the formal version number of the extension. It is used to both uniquely identify different releases of your extension, as well as to determine ordinality of those releases.

Browsers set different requirements for this value; for example, the Chrome version validator is more restrictive than Firefox. For simplicity and cross-browser compatibility, it is strongly recommended that you conform to the semantic versioning standards described at `https://semver.org/`. The following is an example of how this property can be used:

Example value for version

```
{
  ...
  "version": "1.5.0"
  ...
}
```

Note Using the `MAJOR.MINOR`, `MAJOR.MINOR.PATCH`, or `MAJOR.MINOR.PATCH.BUILD` are all acceptable version formats that all browsers will accept.

---

version_name

This property defines a descriptor for the extension version. It allows you to add in handles like `beta` or `rc1` that offer additional information about the release but do not conform to the browser's extension version validators. The following is an example of how this property can be used:

Example value for version_name

```
{
  ...
  "version_name": "1.5.0 beta"
  ...
}
```

web_accessible_resources

This property defines which files in the extension can be accessed outside the extension, either the web page or another extension. Any files that are part of the extension are eligible to be listed here, but this property is intended to allow for JS, CSS, HTML, and image files in the extension to be added into the page or a foreign extension. The property is used in both manifest v2 and v3, but the manifest v3 specification adds extra controls for managing an access control list for each resource.

Manifest v2

The manifest v2 version of `web_accessible_resources` is very simple: simply an array of pattern strings. If a resource matched this pattern string, web pages or remote extensions were granted read access. The following is an example of how this property can be used:

Example value for manifest v2 web_accessible_resources

```
{
  ...
  "web_accessible_resources": [
    "scripts/widget.js",
    "assets/images/*"
  ]
  ...
}
```

Manifest v3

Manifest v3 extends this property to allow for control of which origins or extensions have access to certain assets, as well as the option to enable dynamic resource URLs. The new format is an array of objects with the following properties:

- `resources` is the list of patterns that match files in the extension. This is equivalent to the full `web_accessible_resources` property in manifest v2. This property is required

- `matches` and `extension_ids` control where the resources list is accessible. Exactly one of these properties must be defined. `matches` is an array of patterns that match web page origins eligible to access the resource list. `extension_ids` is an array of extension IDs eligible to access the resource list.
- `use_dynamic_url` is a boolean that, when `true`, will instruct the browser to rotate the URL of the resources each session. This property defaults to `false`. Because extension IDs are static throughout the lifetime of that extension, any resource by default will have the same URL between releases. Enabling this property makes the URL of that resource unpredictable.

Summary

In this chapter, you were guided through what a manifest does and how to create one. The chapter took you through all possible manifest properties, what they do, how they should be defined, what APIs they work with, and which browsers can use them. When you come across a manifest property, you should be able to refer to the relevant section in this chapter to quickly decipher what that property is doing.

The next chapter will cover the transition from manifest v2 to v3. It explores the differences between the two versions and how it will affect the world of browser extensions.

CHAPTER 6

Understanding the Implications of Manifest V3

The world of browser extensions is undergoing a major transformation. Google Chrome is spearheading a transition that changes how extensions work and what they are capable of doing, and the rest of the major browsers are likely to follow suit. Some of these changes are controversial, as they have significant implications for many very popular chrome extensions. The changes are embodied within a refashioning in how the `manifest.json` is written (by defining a new `manifest_version` 3); thus, these changes are commonly referred to as "manifest v3."

Note The transition is far from over, and many details of where the ecosystem will end up remain to be finalized. This chapter will mostly cover information and examples that are certain.

M. Frisbie, *Building Browser Extensions*, https://doi.org/10.1007/978-1-4842-8725-5_6

Motivation for Manifest V3

All the major changes contained in manifest v3 can be grouped into a handful of motivations: security, performance, privacy and transparency, and revenue.

Security

Manifest v2 allowed extensions to execute JavaScript that was loaded from remote URLs or provided by the user. This was judged to be problematic, as a malicious script executing with access to extension APIs and permissions could cause a lot of damage. To address this security hole, manifest v3 restricts extensions to only be able to execute scripts which are included in the extension package itself.

Performance

Several manifest v2 features had the potential to introduce performance problems in the browser.

Migration to DeclarativeNetRequest

The manifest v2 webRequest API allowed developers to run JavaScript at different points in the lifecycle of a network request. When used in the extreme, extensions that managed *all* network traffic on *all* pages would therefore execute blocking JavaScript for every single network request that the browser makes.

Manifest v3 addresses this by moving the blocking scripts into a static set of declarative rules for how to manage network traffic (block, redirect, etc.). The browser loads these static rules and natively executes them as needed, thereby eliminating the need to run extra JavaScript for each network request.

Migration to Service Workers

Background scripts in manifest v2 were capable of being "persistent," meaning the script would never terminate. The implication of this was that each extension with a persistent background script would introduce an extra JavaScript runtime that the browser must manage.

Manifest v3 addresses this by migrating background scripts to run as service workers. These service workers will automatically spin up on demand in response to observed browser events and terminate when there is no activity to free up system resources.

Note The removal of persistent background scripts is highly controversial and causes problems for extensions which require the use of long-lived entities such as websockets. Read on in this chapter for strategies to address these issues.

Privacy and Transparency

Like mobile apps, browser extensions require permission from users before they are allowed to perform all but the most basic of tasks. Many permissions, once granted, provide unfiltered access to sensitive information such as page content, cookies, and browsing activity. Manifest v3 alters the manifest permissions structure and introduces increased control and visibility into which permissions an extension is using.

Revenue

It is no secret that many tech giants rely heavily on revenue from web advertisements. Some of the most popular browser extensions are "ad blockers," extensions which are exceptionally adept at preventing users from seeing ads and eliminating any potential for ad revenue. Despite the dominance of mobile web traffic, desktop web traffic continues to be a significant slice of all web traffic - and a large percentage of this slice uses ad blockers.

The companies that lose this ad revenue to ad blockers are the same ones that support the browser extension APIs and browser extension marketplaces that power these ad blockers. To resolve this conflict, manifest v3 takes aim at the extension APIs that ad blockers rely upon. The changes in manifest v3 don't entirely wipe out the ability to block ads, but it is significantly diminished.

Implications of Background Service Workers

In manifest v2, background scripts could be defined as either a *persistent script* or an *event page*. The persistent script was initialized and kept alive for the entire time that the browser remained open. This allowed the background script to run in parallel with the page, perform work in the top level of the script, open long-lived network connections like websockets, listen for incoming events from external sources, and perform tasks at short intervals, all without the threat of the script being terminated. Extensions that did not have a need for this persistent script state could elect to instead run their background script as an event page. The browser would run the background script to initialize listeners for browser events and then suspend the background script when it was deemed to be idle. When a browser event with a handler was fired, the event page would wake up and run the handler.

Manifest v3 discards the duality of persistent scripts and event pages in favor of *service workers*. In many ways, the background service worker is analogous to an event page. Even so, background scripts in manifest v2 and manifest v3 have several crucial differences:

DOM

In manifest v2, background scripts were created as a headless browser page, including full access to a DOM. In manifest v3, the service worker cannot access the DOM or any DOM APIs. However, it still has access to the OffscreenCanvas API.

XMLHttpRequest

In manifest v2, background scripts were able to make network requests using `XMLHttpRequest`. In manifest v3, because all background scripts are service workers, network requests must be made via `fetch()`.

Timer API

In manifest v2, a persistent script could use a timer API method like `setTimeout()` or `setInterval()` in the top level of the script and have the handler reliably execute. The following is an example of a timeout handler which would reliably run in a persistent manifest v2 extension with a persistent background:

Timer which will reliably run in a persistent background script in manifest v2

```
// Log message after 5 minute delay
setTimeout(() => console.log("5 minutes is up!"), 5 * 60
* 1000);
```

In manifest v3, because there is no option to require persistence, these handlers may not reliably execute. The browser does not factor in these timer handlers into its decision about if a service worker is idle. When the browser decides to stop an idle service worker, these timer handlers will be silently canceled. In the above example, the log statement would never print if the service worker was stopped prior to the handler execution.

The recommended substitute is to use the extension Alarms API. These methods are similar to the timer API methods in that they can fire timed events, but these events *will* wake the service worker and execute the handler. The following example reworks the above example so that it will function properly in a manifest v3 service worker:

Alarm which will reliably run in a background service worker in manifest v3

```
// Schedule an alarm event to be fired in 5 minutes
chrome.alarms.create({ delayInMinutes: 5 });

// Set a handler for alarm events
chrome.alarms.onAlarm.addListener(() => console.log("5 minutes
is up!"));
```

In this reworked example, the service worker will wake up for the alarm event. Therefore, it is guaranteed that the handler will run as expected. When comparing these two strategies, you will notice that the Alarms API is a poor substitute for higher frequency events.

Note The Alarms API is covered in the *Extension and Browser APIs* chapter. Refer to the *Background Scripts* chapter for strategies to address high-frequency timers.

Event Handlers

Because service workers are expected to start and stop on a regular basis, the background script must be organized in a particular fashion to ensure correct behavior. Keep the following behavior in mind when writing your service worker:

- Service worker listeners are always terminated when the service worker stops.
- Service worker listeners are always added when the service worker starts.
- When a service worker starts in response to an event, that event will be dispatched to the service worker immediately after it starts.

When writing a background service worker, you should assume that an event may be fired immediately after you set the handler. As a result, event handlers must be registered *in the first turn of the event loop*. The following is an example of a handler which is not registered in the first turn of the event loop, and therefore may miss click events dispatched when the service worker restarts:

Event handler registration which may not handle all events correctly

```
// Bad
setTimeout(
  () => chrome.action.onClicked.addListener(() => console.
  log("click")),
  10
);
```

The following is an example of a handler which is registered in the first turn of the event loop, and therefore will correctly handle events dispatched when the service worker restarts:

Event handler registration which will handle all events correctly

```
// Good
chrome.action.onClicked.addListener(
  () => console.log("click"));
```

Tip The rule of thumb is to always register events at the top level of the background script.

Service Worker Persistence

In manifest v2, a persistent background script would be initialized upon installation or browser startup and run uninterrupted until the browser was closed or the extension was uninstalled. In manifest v3, service workers are stopped when the browser detects they are idle.

Consider the following extension, which sets a timer in the background service worker to measure how long it stays alive:

background.js which logs to console until the service worker is shut down

```
const t0 = performance.now();

setInterval(() => {
  const t1 = performance.now();
  console.log(`Alive for ${Math.round((t1 - t0) / 1e3)}s`);
}, 1e3);
```

Tip In Google Chrome, if you visit `chrome://serviceworker-internals/?devtools` you will find the Service Worker Internals interface, which allows you to monitor the real-time status of your service workers as well as their console output. Unlike the browser inspector interface, which may prevent the browser from recognizing a service worker as idle, this tool will allow the service workers to go idle and be stopped.

The following screenshots show this extension service worker in the RUNNING and STOPPED states (Figures 6-1 and 6-2):

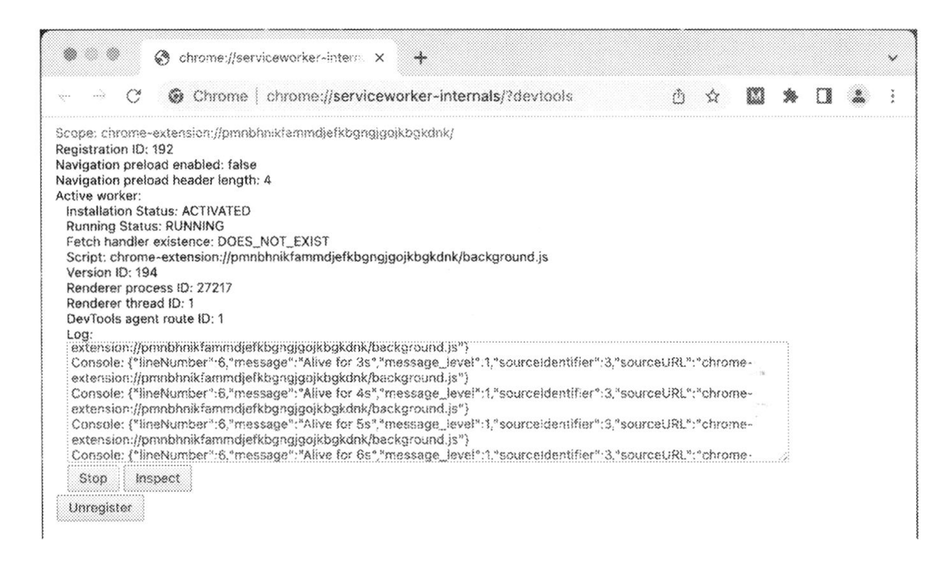

Figure 6-1. *The background service worker in the RUNNING state*

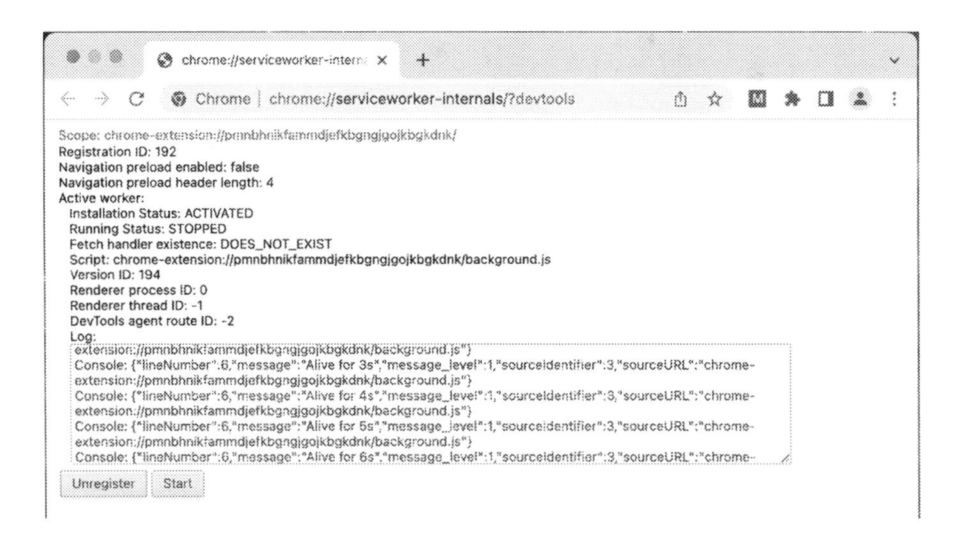

Figure 6-2. *The background service worker in the STOPPED state*

Even with the interval timer, the browser will consider this script idle. Typically, you will see the timer log for 30 seconds before the browser stops the service worker.

Open long-lived connections like extension messaging ports or websockets will delay the shutdown of the service worker, but Chrome will still stop the service worker after 5 minutes and sever the connections. Therefore, manifest v3 extensions should be organized as to avoid relying on long-lived connections from the background script.

Note This particular aspect of service workers is extremely controversial. In many cases, long-lived connections in the background script are required for the extension to work properly. There are a handful of tricks to force the service worker to stay running. For more details, refer to the *Background Scripts* chapter.

Global State and Storage

Manifest v2 extensions commonly relied on global state in the background script when using persistent scripts. The following is an example of a simple background script that counts action button clicks:

Example 6-1a. manifest.json for manifest v2 example

```
{
  "name": "MVX",
  "version": "0.0.1",
  "manifest_version": 2,
  "background": {
    "scripts": ["background.js"],
    "persistent": true
```

```
  },
  "browser_action": {}
}
```

Example 6-1b. background.js for manifest v2 example

```
let count = 0;

chrome.browserAction.onClicked.addListener(() => {
  console.log(`Clicked ${++count} times`);
});
```

Because the count variable is in a persistent global scope, the extension can access it in perpetuity with no problems. However, consider this example when it is converted to manifest v3:

Example 6-2a. manifest.json for manifest v3 example

```
{
  "name": "MVX",
  "version": "0.0.1",
  "manifest_version": 3,
  "background": {
    "service_worker": "background.js"
  },
  "action": {}
}
```

Example 6-2b. background.js for manifest v3 example

```
let count = 0;

chrome.action.onClicked.addListener(() => {
  console.log(`Clicked ${++count} times`);
});
```

This will work correctly until the service worker stops. At that time, the global variable will reset, as any variables in the global scope are lost. The recommended solution is to use the Storage API, which will persist through service worker stops and starts. The following code shows this example refactored to use this API:

Example 6-3a. Refactored manifest.json for manifest v3 example

```
{
  "name": "MVX",
  "version": "0.0.1",
  "manifest_version": 3,
  "background": {
    "service_worker": "background.js"
  },
  "action": {},
  "permissions": ["storage"]
}
```

Example 6-3b. Refactored background.js for manifest v3 example

```
chrome.action.onClicked.addListener(() => {
  chrome.storage.local.get(["count"], ({ count = 0 }) => {
    console.log(`Clicked ${++count} times`);

    chrome.storage.local.set({ count });
  });
});
```

Note For more details on the Storage API, refer to the *Extension and Browser APIs* chapter.

Audio and Video

Service workers are not able to play or capture media streams in the browser. To use these media APIs, a chrome extension page or a content script must be used.

Implications of Content Security Policy Restrictions

In manifest v2, extensions were allowed to load scripts from remote origins, run user-provided scripts, and run scripts inline in the browser. In manifest v3, these are explicitly forbidden. It is still possible to make use of these in a sandboxed page, but these sandboxed scripts cannot access extension APIs.

The following popup page shows three instances of scripts that will throw runtime errors when loaded in a manifest v3 extension:

popup.js with forbitten eval()

```
// eval() is not allowed
eval(`console.log('foobar');`);
```

popup.html with forbidden scripts

```
<!DOCTYPE html>
<html>
  <body>
    <h1>Popup</h1>

    <!-- Inline scripts not allowed -->
    <script>
      console.log("foobar");
    </script>
```

```
    <script src="popup.js"></script>

    <!-- Loading from remote origin not allowed -->
    <script
      src="https://code.jquery.com/jquery-3.6.0.js"
      integrity="sha256-H+K7U5CnXl1h5ywQfKtSj8PCmoN9aaq30gDh27X
      c0jk="
      crossorigin="anonymous"
    ></script>
  </body>
</html>
```

For manifest v3 extensions, the principle is simple: all JavaScript that runs in the extension must be loaded along with the extension. If your extension needs to use third-party libraries, you must include static copies of those libraries in your extension payload. Developers that build their extensions with tools such as Webpack will not have to worry about doing this, as the libraries are already bundled and included.

Note With all these script techniques disabled, in manifest v3 it is no longer possible for extension users to supply their own scripts at runtime to run in any extension. As a result, this change breaks all userscript extensions like Greasemonkey and Tampermonkey.

Implications of DeclarativeNetRequest

The change from `webRequest` to `declarativeNetRequest` isn't strictly part of manifest v3, but the transition is occurring simultaneously, and its impact is just as significant. With `webRequest`, the browser intercepts and routes network traffic to the extension, and the extension programmatically manipulates each request in JavaScript. The DeclarativeNetRequest API inverts this paradigm: the extension defines a set of rules to instruct the browser on how to handle each network request, and the browser performs the request manipulation.

For example, the following manifest v2 extension uses a simple URL matcher to block the Google logo from loading:

Example 6-4a. manifest.json for manifest v2 google logo blocker

```
{
  "name": "MVX",
  "version": "0.0.1",
  "manifest_version": 2,
  "background": {
    "scripts": ["background.js"]
  },
  "permissions": [
    "webRequest",
    "webRequestBlocking",
    "<all_urls>"
  ]
}
```

Example 6-4b. background.js for manifest v2 google logo blocker

```
chrome.webRequest.onBeforeRequest.addListener(
  () => {
    return { cancel: true };
  },
  { urls: ["*://*.google.com/logos/*"] },
  ["blocking"]
);
```

This extension will kill all requests for network requests matching `*://*.google.com/logos/*`. Load the extension and visit `google.com` to test.

This behavior can be replicated in manifest v3 as follows:

Example 6-5a. manifest.json for manifest v3 Google logo blocker

```
{
  "name": "MVX",
  "version": "0.0.1",
  "manifest_version": 3,
  "permissions": ["declarativeNetRequest"],
  "host_permissions": ["<all_urls>"],
  "declarative_net_request": {
    "rule_resources": [
      {
        "id": "ruleset_1",
        "enabled": true,
        "path": "rules.json"
      }
    ]
  }
}
```

Example 6-5b. rules.json for manifest v3 Google logo blocker

```
[
  {
    "id": 1,
    "priority": 1,
    "action": { "type": "block" },
    "condition": {
      "urlFilter": "*.google.com/logos/*",
```

```
      "resourceTypes": ["image"]
    }
  }
]
```

Note Details on networking can be found in the *Networking* chapter.

Load google.com again to test the logo blocker (Figure 6-3).

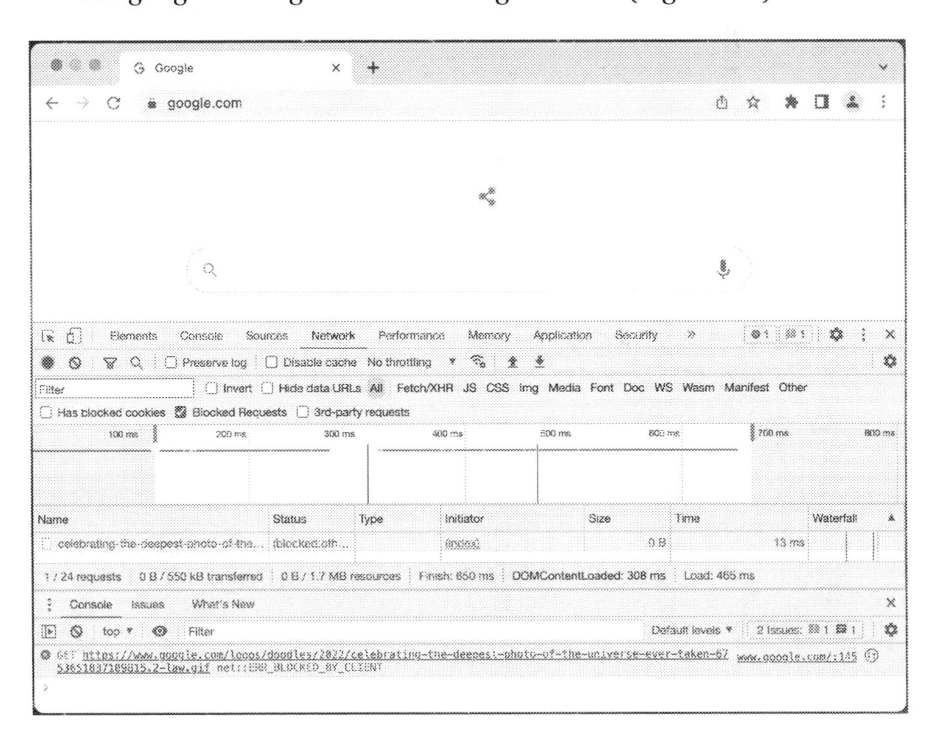

Figure 6-3. *google.com with the request for the logo blocked*

The DeclarativeNetRequest API imposes some problematic limitations on ad blockers. Google Chrome enforces a *global static rule limit*, meaning that all extensions installed in a browser each contribute toward a combined sum of rules. At the time that this book was written that total was 150,000, although the number may continue to fluctuate based on community feedback. This may seem to be a generous number – but considering that uBlock Origin alone defines on the order of 100,000 rules, this limit will quickly be reached.

Furthermore, the request matching capabilities of `declarativeNetRequest` are painfully limited when compared to what `webRequest` could offer: blocking requests based on payload size, disabling of JavaScript execution through the injection of CSP directives, and stripping cookie headers from outgoing requests. Because of these limitations, some browsers like Firefox appear to be positioning themselves to preserve the features of `webRequest` in manifest v3.

Note For further reading on how manifest v3 affects ad blockers, refer to the following threads:

`https://github.com/uBlockOrigin/uBlock-issues/issues/338`

`https://bugs.chromium.org/p/chromium/issues/detail?id=896897`

Summary

The changeover from manifest v2 to manifest v3 has major implications for the browser extension ecosystem. The most dramatic changes are service workers and `declarativeNetRequest`, both of which have broad implications for how extensions behave. With these changes, extensions become more secure and performant, but at the same time it appears that some valuable features are being killed entirely.

The next chapter will explore background scripts. It will cover in depth how they work, how best to build them, and how they behave as the nerve center of browser extension.

CHAPTER 7

Background Scripts

Browser extension developers often find the need to execute JavaScript in the background of a browser. Background scripts, as their name suggests, are the answer to this problem: they are a separate JavaScript runtime that can communicate with all the different pieces of the extension, add handlers for many different browser events, and operate without dependence on any web page or extension user interface.

Note This chapter will focus on the manifest v3 implementation of background scripts as service workers. Manifest v2 featured background pages, which were considerably more useful. However, Google Chrome is phasing out support for them, so I do not recommend building a browser extension that explicitly relies on manifest v2 background pages.

Web Page Service Workers vs. Extension Service Workers

A common point of confusion for web developers new to browser extensions is the nature of background service workers. Although many web developers have experience dealing with service workers in the content of building web pages, the nature of service workers in extensions has some notable differences.

M. Frisbie, *Building Browser Extensions*, https://doi.org/10.1007/978-1-4842-8725-5_7

Compare the following two examples, a simple web page service worker and a simple browser extension service worker:

Web page service worker

```
// Establish a cache name
const cacheName = cache_v1';

// Assets to precache
const precachedAssets = [
  '/img1.jpg',
  '/img2.jpg',
  '/img3.jpg'
];

self.addEventListener('install', (event) => {
  // Precache assets on install
  event.waitUntil(caches.open(cacheName).then((cache) => {
    return cache.addAll(precachedAssets);
  }));
});

self.addEventListener('fetch', (event) => {
  // Test for precached assets match
  const url = new URL(event.request.url);
  const isPrecachedRequest =
      precachedAssets.includes(url.pathname);

  if (isPrecachedRequest) {
    // Grab the precached asset from the cache
    event.respondWith(caches.open(cacheName).then((cache) => {
      return cache.match(event.request.url);
    }));
```

```
  } else {
    // Go to the network
    return;
  }
});
```

This simple web page service worker defines a cache for some images. On an install event, it preloads the images into the cache. When it sees a fetch event matching the URL for one of those images, it intercepts the request and returns the value from the cache.

Extension service worker

```
// This will run on an install or update
chrome.runtime.onInstalled.addListener(() => {
  console.log(Installed or updated!');
});

// This will run when a bookmark is created.
chrome.bookmarks.onCreated.addListener(() => {
  console.log('Created a new bookmark!');
});

const filter = {
  url: [
    {
      urlMatches: 'https://www.example.com/',
    },
  ],
};

// This will run when the example site is visited
chrome.webNavigation.onCompleted.addListener(() => {
  console.log("Loaded the example site!");
}, filter);
```

This simple extension service worker sets listeners for the `runtime.onInstalled`, `bookmark.onCreated`, and `webNavigation.onCompleted` events. Each handler prints a log statement to the console when those events are fired.

Similarities

The W3C specification for service workers begins with the following high-level characterization:

> *The core of this specification is a worker that wakes to receive events.*

In this respect, a web page service worker and an extension service worker are serving the same purpose. What's more, the distinction between a "web page" service worker and an "extension" service worker only describes how the service worker is deployed in that context; the underlying service worker platform remains unchanged.

When comparing the two examples from above, you may have noticed the following:

- Both service worker scripts are largely composed of event handlers being assigned in the top level of the script.
- Both service workers are listening for some form of an installation event.
- Both service workers can access network requests occurring in the browser.

These similarities underscore many of the similarities between the two. With these code similarities in mind, let's explore the ways that these service worker contexts are alike.

Single Occupancy

For both web page service workers and extension service workers, there will only ever be a single service worker per script. When installing updates to service workers, the browser will carefully swap out old service workers for new ones while ensuring there is only ever a single service worker active at any given time.

This is critically important in both contexts: multiple service workers would cause complete chaos with caching, network interception, and event handling.

Installation and Lifecycle

All service workers are installed exactly once, and subsequently may become idle and eventually terminated. The browser will decide when to wake the service worker, usually because of an event being fired, and the service worker script will re-execute each time.

Although the concept of an "installed" event has different meanings for web pages and extensions, the use of these handlers remains unchanged. The developer should expect that the service worker script will be executed an unlimited number of times, but the installed handler will execute only once and therefore should be utilized to perform setup work that should not be duplicated.

Top-Level Event Handling

Because the service worker is expected to undergo a repetitive cycle of becoming idle, being terminated, and being re-activated, service worker script structures must account for this. Events that are fired by the browser and passed to the service worker must have handlers added in the first turn of the event loop - otherwise there is a risk of missing the event. The reason for this is that service workers are often woken in direct response to an event being fired. The browser will wake the service worker, execute one turn of the event loop, and then fire the queued event in the service worker. If the handler for that event is not present at the end of that turn, the event may pass through unhandled.

Async Messaging

Because all service workers are strictly asynchronous, both must use a form of asynchronous messaging to communicate with other parts of the browser.

- For web page service workers, this takes the form of `postMessage()` or the MessageChannel API.
- For browser extensions, this takes the form of `runtime.sendMessage()`, `tabs.sendMessage()`, `runtime.connect()`, or `tabs.connect()`.

Differences

Although web page service workers and extension service workers use the same underlying platform, they differ in a handful of important ways.

Registration

Web page service workers must be registered from a page-level script. An example of this is shown below:

Example web page service worker registration

```
if ('serviceWorker' in navigator) {
  navigator.serviceWorker.register('/sw.js')
  .then((registration) => {
    registration.addEventListener('updatefound', () => {
      console.log('A new service worker is being installed:');
    });
```

```
  })
  .catch((error) => {
    console.error(`Service worker registration failed:
    ${error}`);
  });
} else {
  console.error('Service workers are not supported.');
}
```

For extension service workers, the only step needed to register a service worker is to specify the `background.service_worker` script in the manifest. Web page service worker registration includes the `installing`/`waiting`/`active` states that are not meaningful for extension service workers.

Note For additional information on web page service workers, refer to `https://developer.mozilla.org/en-US/docs/Web/API/Service_Worker_API`.

Purpose

The most important difference between web page service workers and extension service workers is their primary purpose. Web page service workers are equipped to act as a cache, and this is their most common use case. They're able to conditionally intercept network requests and return cached content. Service workers can also be used to build progressive web applications (PWAs), web pages that emulate app behavior with installation, offline capabilities, and server-sent push notifications.

Because browser extension scripts are assets and all served from the browser, there is no longer a need to cache these resources, as they are not being loaded from a remote server. Furthermore, interfaces such as popup pages and options pages are perfectly capable of operating normally offline without the use of a background service worker. Instead, extension service workers are primarily tasked with handling the wide range of events that are fired by the browser and the WebExtensions API.

Note For the remainder of this chapter, an extension service worker will be simply referred to as a "service worker."

Manifest v2 vs. Manifest v3

Manifest v3 transformed background scripts considerably. Manifest v2 background scripts were treated as *background pages*: JavaScript that executed in a headless web page. These background pages were also capable of running indefinitely, meaning they were suitable for managing long-running operations and web requests. In manifest v3, background scripts now execute as *service workers*. These workers are more lightweight, but they are diminished in a number of important ways.

Scripts vs. Service Workers

In manifest v2, the manifest background value could be passed an array of scripts:

Manifest v2 manifest.json

```
{
  "manifest_version": 2,
  ...
  "background": {
    "scripts": ["bg1.js", "bg2.js", "bg3.js"]
  }
  ...
}
```

These scripts were loaded in the order they appeared in the array, and all executed inside the same background page. In manifest v3, the background script is a single service worker:

Manifest v3 manifest.json

```
{
  "manifest_version": 3,
  ...
  "background": {
    "service_worker": "bg.js"
  }
  ...
}
```

JavaScript Imports

In manifest v2, the only way to use a JavaScript `import` was to use the `background.page` property and to use script tags in the background page HTML:

manifest.json enabling a background HTML page

```
{
  "manifest_version": 2,
  ...
  "background": {
    "page": "bg.html"
  }
  ...
}
```

bg.html

```
<html>
```

```
  <body>
    <!-- imports allowed in this JS file -->
    <script type="module" src="bg.js"></script>
  </body>
</html>
```

In manifest v3, you can simply set the `background.module` property to `"module,"` shown here:

Manifest v3 manifest.json allowing for the `import` keyword

```
{
  "manifest_version": 3,
  ...
  "background": {
    "service_worker": "bg.js",
    "type": "module"
  }
  ...
}
```

No Access to DOM and Limited Global APIs

In manifest v2, background pages are effectively headless web pages with full access to a DOM and a web page global object. In manifest v3, service workers have no access to a DOM and the global object is the `ServiceWorkerGlobalScope`, which is missing many of the APIs available in the web page global object. This has some important implications:

- **No access to the `document` object.** The DOM and all its associated methods are no longer available. This also means the background service worker can no longer create and cache assets.

- **No ability to render content for display in other contexts.** Rendering content in the headless page was useful in some situations, but this is no longer possible. Partial workarounds include using a third-party library like `jsdom` or using the OffscreenCanvas API.
- **No access to the `window` object.** This means that methods like `window.open()` are no longer available.
- **No ability to play or capture media directly in a service worker.** Doing so is still possible, but it requires a host active content script or an extension view to grant access to the media APIs.
- **No access to localStorage, sessionStorage, cookies.**
- **No ability to use XMLHttpRequest.** `fetch()` should be used.

Note Losing access to the window object is especially problematic when attempting to authenticate from the service worker, as third-party authentication libraries frequently rely on opening a new window for the OAuth flow. Refer to the *Networking* chapter for more coverage on authentication.

Nonpersistent

Manifest v2 allowed for background pages to be "persistent," which effectively meant they would run indefinitely as long as the host browser program was open. In manifest v3, this ability is removed. This has several implications:

- **`setTimeout()` and `setInterval()` will no longer reliably execute.** These methods are still available. However, if the service worker terminates before the scheduled function executes, it will silently be skipped. The `chrome.alarms` API replaces some of this functionality, but it cannot be used for time intervals less than a minute.
- **Long-running queries and websockets may be killed.** The service worker will ignore open network connections when determining if a service worker is idle, meaning that these connections may be severed if the service worker terminates while the connections are still active.

Tip There are some tricks later on in this chapter that can extend the life of a service worker.

No Shutdown Event

Manifest v2 allowed the developer to add handler for `runtime.onSuspend` and `runtime.onSuspendCanceled` events. This gave the extension opportunity to do some clean up. In manifest v3, service workers have no handler for a shutdown event, meaning that service worker scripts must eagerly perform tasks with the expectation that a shutdown could occur at any time.

No Programmatic Background Access

In manifest v2, it was possible to access the background window object from an extension interface in the foreground using `chrome.extension.getBackgroundPage()`. In manifest v3, this ability has been removed.

Working with Background Scripts

Let's begin by creating a simple browser extension with a background script. This is accomplished by defining the `background.service_worker` property in the manifest:

Example 7-1a. manifest.json

```
{
  "name": "MVX",
  "version": "0.0.1",
  "manifest_version": 3,
  "background": {
    "service_worker": "background.js"
  }
}
```

Example 7-1b. background.js

```
console.log("Initialized background script!");

chrome.runtime.onInstalled.addListener((object) => {
  console.log("Installed background script!");
});
```

This simple background script logs to the console, sets an install handler, and exits.

Inspecting Background Service Workers

After installing this extension in your browser, your extension management page will show a new card for the extension that includes a *service worker* link (Figure 7-1).

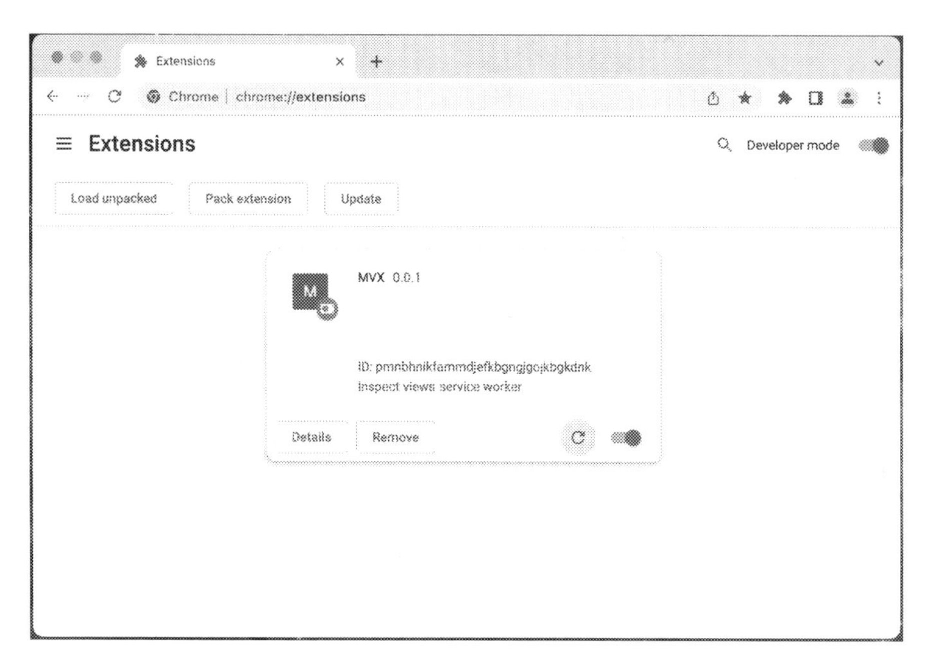

Figure 7-1. *The installed extension with background service worker*

You can inspect the background script by clicking the *service worker* link (Figure 7-2).

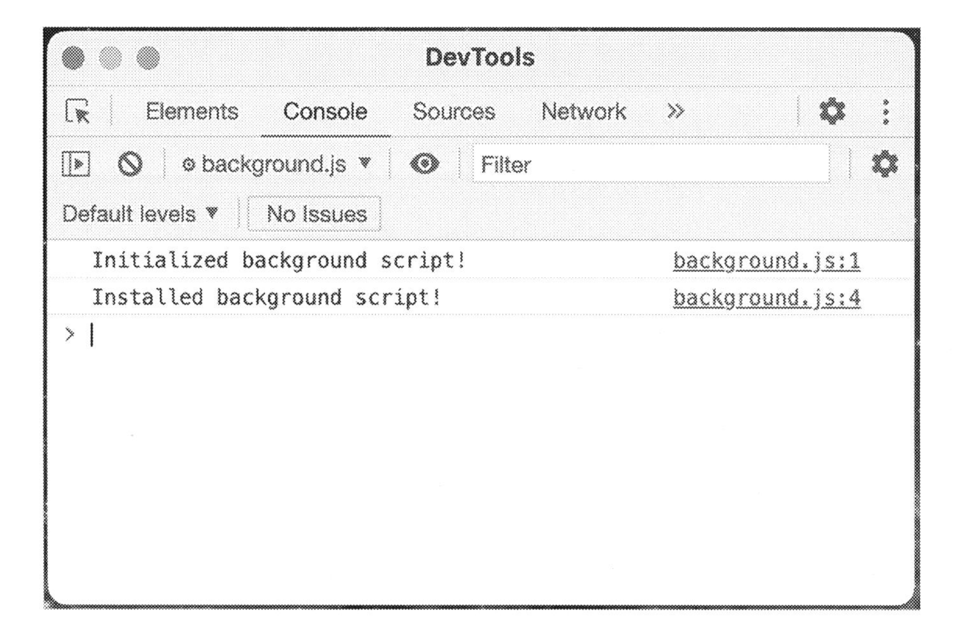

***Figure 7-2.** The console output of the background service worker*

Note This devtools interface is very useful for inspecting and debugging your service worker, but keep in mind that leaving this window open will prevent the browser from suspending the service worker. Unintentionally leaving a devtools window open can cause unexpected extension behavior when attempting to reload or debug background scripts.

To view the state of all service workers in the browser without interfering with their normal lifecycle, navigate your browser to `chrome://serviceworker-internals/`, shown in Figure 7-3.

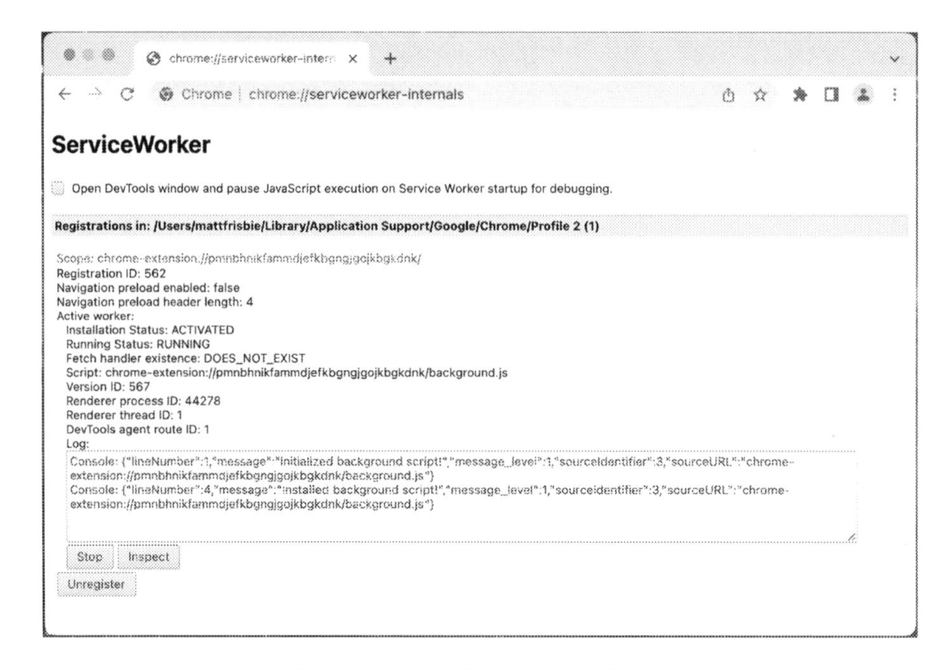

Figure 7-3. *Chrome's service worker internals page*

Note This page will show *all* service workers your browser has installed – not just for extensions. Recall that the browser does not make a distinction between a web page service worker and an extension service worker.

Service Worker Errors

Note For this section, you must begin with the extension installed as shown in Example 7-1 *and* all devtools windows closed.

Modify the background script as shown here:

Example 7-2. background.js

```
console.log("Initialized background script!");

chrome.runtime.onInstalled.addListener((object) => {
  console.log("Installed background script!");
});

throw new Error("foo");
```

Once the background script is saved, click the reload button in the extension card. You will see the service worker immediately becomes inactive and an *Errors* button appears (Figure 7-4).

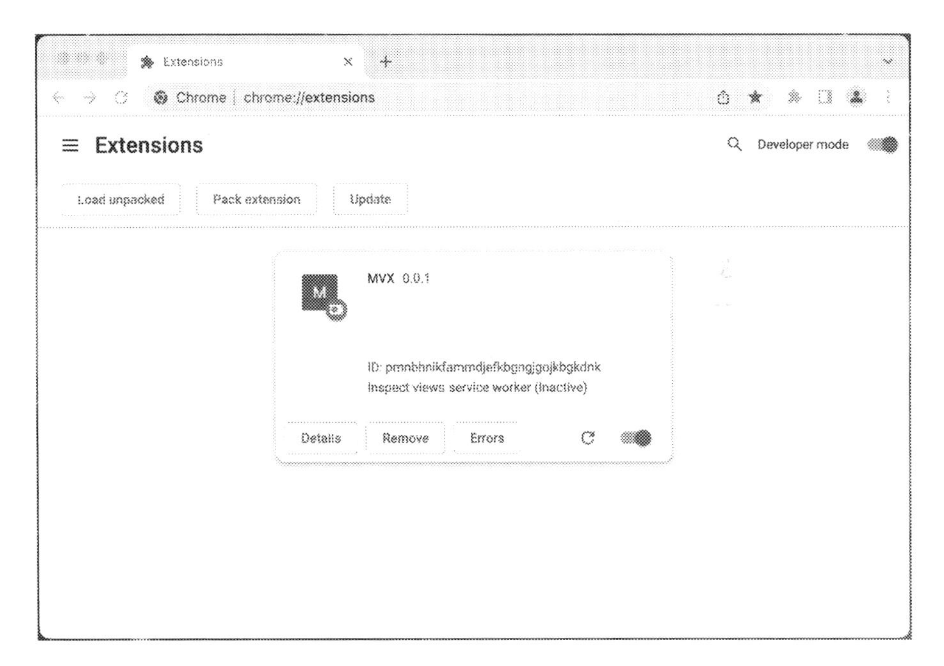

Figure 7-4. *The extension Errors button appears*

Click the Errors button to reveal the error view (Figure 7-5).

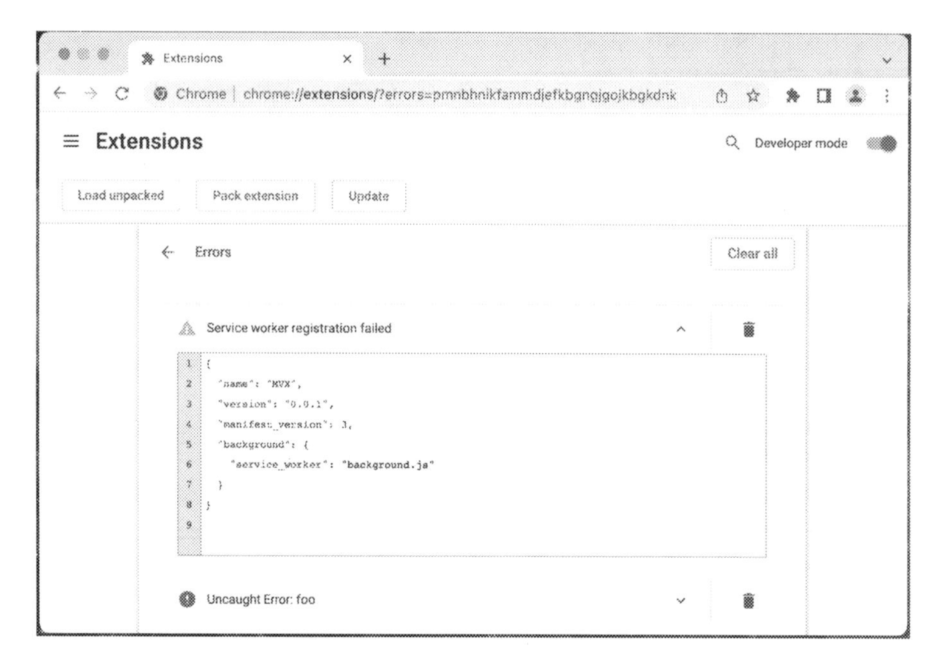

Figure 7-5. *The extension error view*

You will see the expected "foo" error readout at the bottom, but also that the browser is telling us that the service worker failed to register. This is very important: **when a service worker throws an error in the first turn of the event loop, the service worker will fail to register.**

Note The errors page is especially useful in situations where the background script fails to register. When registration fails, since the service worker does not exist, you will not be able to inspect the error output of the service worker. Instead, the errors page will contain the error readout to assist in debugging.

Service Worker Termination

Note For this section, you must keep all devtools windows closed to allow the service worker to become idle.

Install the following extension:

Example 7-3a. manifest.json

```
{
  "name": "MVX",
  "version": "0.0.1",
  "manifest_version": 3,
  "action": {},
  "background": {
    "service_worker": "background.js"
  }
}
```

Example 7-3b. background.js

```
console.log("Initialized background script!");

chrome.runtime.onInstalled.addListener((object) => {
  console.log("Installed background script!");
});

chrome.action.onClicked.addListener(() => {
  console.log("Clicked toolbar icon!");
});

let elapsed = 0;
setInterval(() => console.log(`${++elapsed}s`), 1000);
```

This background script will log to the console every 1000ms until the service worker is terminated. (Recall that `setInterval()` will not prevent a service worker from becoming idle.) It will also log to the console whenever the toolbar icon is clicked.

After reloading the extension, open the `chrome://serviceworker-internals` page to observe the log output. The browser sees that this extension is not actively doing work, and therefore is considered to be *idle*. After approximately 30 seconds, you will see the browser stop the service worker (Figure 7-6).

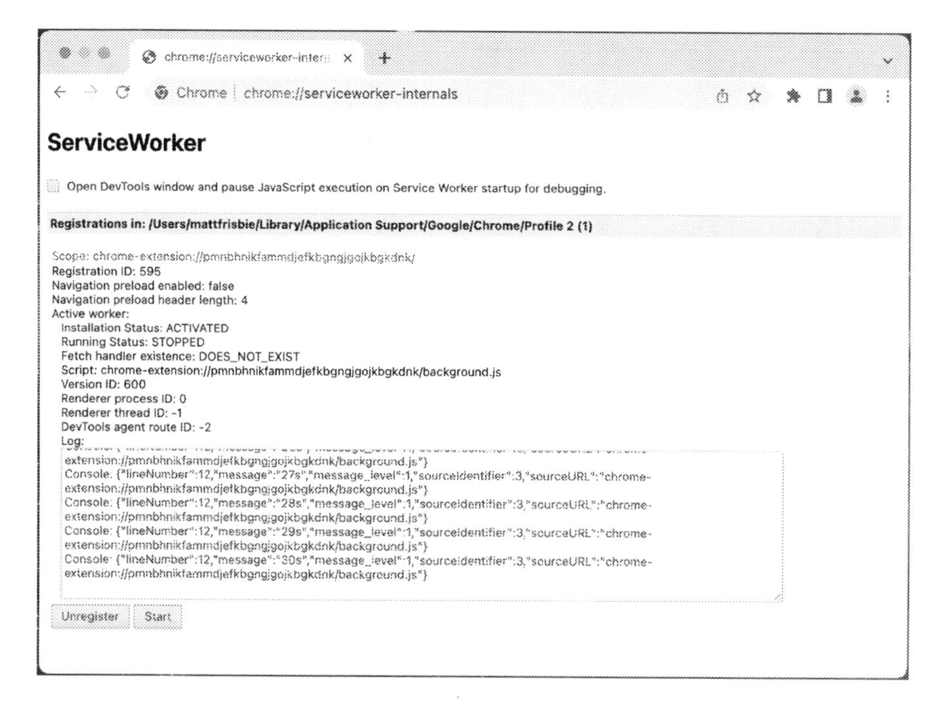

Figure 7-6. *The browser stops the service worker after being idle for 30 seconds*

The extension management page will also reflect this (Figure 7-7).

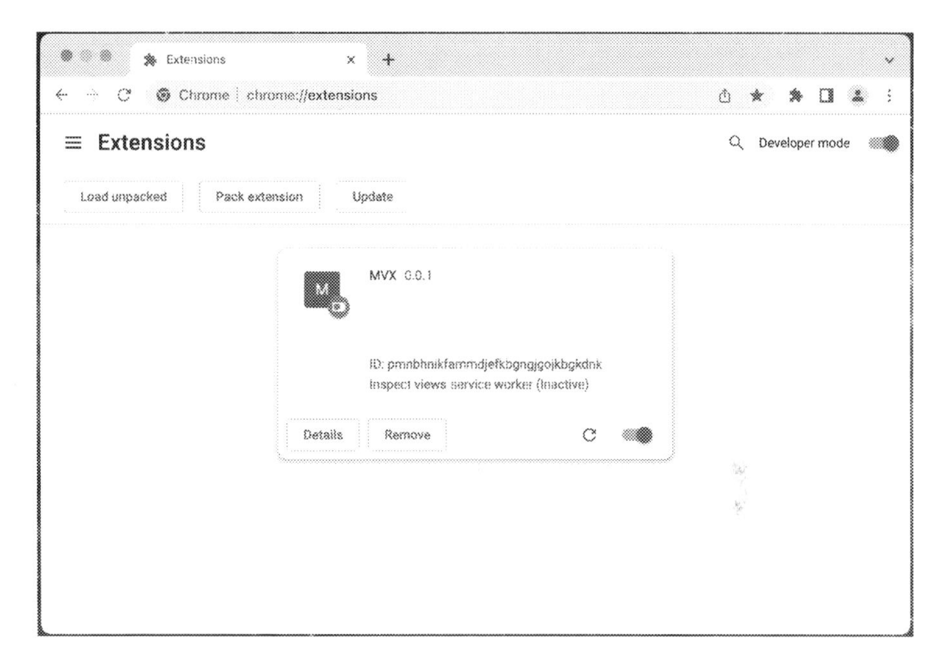

***Figure 7-7.** The inactive service worker as shown on the extension management page*

Because you set a handler for the `action.onClicked`, the browser will wake the service worker, rerun the script, and restart the counter once you click the toolbar icon.

Note Carefully observe the console output after clicking the toolbar icon button. You will notice that the global state in the service worker has been reset.

Common Patterns

In this section, we will explore a handful of patterns that background service workers are frequently used for.

Event Handler

The WebExtensions API allows the browser to send a huge range of different events into the extension to be handled. Since the API is accessible in content scripts, popups, options pages, and background scripts, these events can technically be handled in any of these places. However, since content scripts, popups, and options pages are ephemeral, only the background script *guarantees* that the event will be handled.

The following example extension sets up a background script to handle a myriad of different API events:

Example 7-4a. manifest.json

```
{
  "name": "MVX",
  "version": "0.0.1",
  "manifest_version": 3,
  "background": {
    "service_worker": "background.js"
  },
  "permissions": ["alarms", "tabs"],
  "action": {},
  "commands": {
    "foobar": {
      "suggested_key": {
        "default": "Ctrl+Shift+J",
        "mac": "MacCtrl+Shift+J"
      },
      "description": "Perform foobar action"
    }
  }
}
```

Example 7-4b. background.json

```
// Logs when the extension is installed
chrome.runtime.onInstalled.addListener(() => {
  console.log("Installed background!");
});

chrome.alarms.create("My alarm", { periodInMinutes: 1 });

// Logs every minute
chrome.alarms.onAlarm.addListener((alarmInfo) => {
  console.log(`Alarm fired: ${alarmInfo.name}`);
});

// Logs when the tab state changes
chrome.tabs.onUpdated.addListener(() => {
  console.log("Tabs updated");
});

// Logs when Ctrl+Shift+J is typed
chrome.commands.onCommand.addListener((command) => {
  console.log(`Command: ${command}`);
});

// Logs when the toolbar icon is clicked
chrome.action.onClicked.addListener(() => {
  console.log(`Clicked toolbar icon`);
});
```

Of course, this code could be transplanted into a popup script as-is. However, the events would *only* be handled if the popup was open. Placing handlers in the background script guarantees that the handlers will execute.

If the service worker is terminated, the browser will restart the service worker, run one turn of the event loop to set all the handlers, and only then will it fire all the events inside the service worker. In this way, you can guarantee event handling by assigning handlers at the top level.

Secret Management and Authentication

Extensions frequently need to manage authentication and secret values apart from untrusted web pages. This is especially true in situations where a content script needs to communicate with a server. Sending the request from the content script will usually not work, as the content script's network requests are still bound by the host page's cross-origin restrictions. Furthermore, collecting credentials or storing the authentication secrets in the content script is a *terrible* idea, as the page's DOM and storage APIs are shared by the host page:

- If a content script were to place a JSON Web Token (JWT) into `localStorage`, the host page's JavaScript could access that JWT.
- If a content script collects credentials in `<input>` tags in the host page, the host page is capable of reading the values out of those HTML elements.

The following is an example of a secure authentication flow:

1. Collect the user's credentials in a trusted user interface, such as a popup page or options page. (Anything with the host `chrome-extension://my-extension-id` or similar).
2. Authenticate with the credentials from the trusted page.
3. Store the authentication token with the `chrome.storage` API

After performing these steps, your background service worker can access this authentication token and send authenticated requests to the remote server. A content script can indirectly send authenticated requests via a message relay:

1. Content script uses extension message API to send a message to the background indicating the type of authenticated request it wishes to send
2. Background script accesses the authentication token from storage and sends the authenticated request
3. When the request returns, the background script collects the response and sends it back up to the requesting content script
4. Content script receives the response payload via the extension message API

This strategy is advantageous for several reasons:

- The content script never has to collect credentials
- The content script never has to store secrets
- The content script is no longer bound by the host page's cross-origin restrictions

Message Hub

Any piece of an extension can use the extension messaging API, but the background script is the only entity that guarantees the message will be heard. Furthermore, it also guarantees that the message will be received exactly once. In this way, it is often useful for an array of content scripts to all connect to a single background service worker and use it as a message hub. The following example extension will create a message port on each page that is opened and repeatedly send messages to the background.

Install the extension, open several tabs of `https://example.com`, and inspect the logs of the pages and the background service worker to observe the background independently communicating with each page.

Example 7-5a. manifest.json

```
{
  "name": "MVX",
  "version": "0.0.1",
  "manifest_version": 3,
  "background": {
    "service_worker": "background.js",
    "type": "module"
  },
  "content_scripts": [
    {
      "matches": ["<all_urls>"],
      "css": [],
      "js": ["content-script.js"]
    }
  ]
}
```

Example 7-5b. background.js

```
// Messages include information about the sender
chrome.runtime.onMessage.addListener((request, sender,
sendResponse) => {
  // This handler will fire for all runtime.sendMessage
  payloads.
  // Use a value in the payload to filter.
  if (request.type === "getCurrentTabId") {
    // Send the tab's ID back to the content script
```

```
    sendResponse({ currentTabId: sender.tab.id });
  }
});

// This will fire when the content script
// calls runtime.connect()
chrome.runtime.onConnect.addListener((port) => {
  console.log(`Connected to ${port.name}`);

  // Messages sent from the content script
  port.onMessage.addListener((msg) => {
    console.log(port.name, msg);

    // Subtract 1 and send value back up to content script
    port.postMessage({ value: msg.value - 1 });
  });
});
```

Example 7-5c. content-script.js

```
function initializeCountdown(currentTabId) {
  // This will fire the runtime.onConnect event
  // in the background
  const port = chrome.runtime.connect({
    name: `Tab ${currentTabId}`,
  });

  // Messages sent from the service worker
  port.onMessage.addListener((msg) => {
    console.log(port.name, msg);

    // Keep passing the value to the background while > 0
    if (msg.value > 0) {
      port.postMessage({ value: msg.value });
```

```
    }
  });

  // Start a countdown sequence every 1000ms
  setInterval(() => {
    const value = Math.floor(Math.random() * 10) + 1;

    console.log(`New countdown sequence: ${value}`);

    // Send the inital postMessage in the sequence
    port.postMessage({ value });
  }, 1000);
}

// Send a call/response message to the background
// to determine current tab's ID
chrome.runtime.sendMessage(
  // Providing a type allows the background to filter
  // incoming messages
  { type: "getCurrentTabId" },
  // Background can reply to this message with the tab ID
  (response) => initializeCountdown(response.currentTabId)
);
```

Storage Manager

For extensions that need to store large amounts of data, the background service worker can make use of IndexedDB. Popups, options pages, and content scripts can all use the messaging API to read and write to IndexedDB. The advantage of using the background as the IndexedDB manager is versioning: the browser guarantees one background service worker per extension at any time, so any IndexedDB migrations you need to run can safely execute inside the service worker without risking a versioning conflict.

Injecting Scripts

Background service workers can programmatically inject content scripts into the page. This is very useful when you need to inject a content script conditionally or asynchronously. The following example injects a small content script when the toolbar icon button is clicked:

Example 7-6a. manifest.json

```
{
  "name": "MVX",
  "version": "0.0.1",
  "manifest_version": 3,
  "background": {
    "service_worker": "background.js",
    "type": "module"
  },
  "action": {},
  "permissions": ["activeTab", "scripting"]
}
```

Example 7-6b. background.js

```
function wipeOutPage() {
  document.body.innerHTML = "";
}

chrome.action.onClicked.addListener((tab) => {
  chrome.scripting.executeScript({
    target: { tabId: tab.id },
    func: wipeOutPage,
  });
});
```

Note Refer to the *Content Scripts* chapter for more details on this.

Sniffing Web Traffic

The background service worker can track the pages the user is visiting and conditionally perform logic based on the details of that page. The following example logs the URL on every page visited, and logs a special message only on a specific URL:

Example 7-7a. manifest.json

```
{
  "name": "MVX",
  "version": "0.0.1",
  "manifest_version": 3,
  "background": {
    "service_worker": "background.js",
    "type": "module"
  },
  "action": {},
  "permissions": ["webNavigation"]
}
```

Example 7-7b. background.js

```
const filter = {
  url: [
    {
      urlMatches: "https://www.example.com/",
    },
  ],
};
```

```
chrome.webNavigation.onCompleted.addListener(() => {
  console.log("Visited the special site!");
}, filter);

chrome.webNavigation.onDOMContentLoaded.
addListener((details) => {
  console.log(`Loaded ${details.url}!`);
});
```

Installed/Updated Events

Developers often need to run a piece of code only when the extension is updated or installed. The `runtime.onInstalled` event should be used for this purpose. It is capable of differentiating between install events and different update events via the `reason` property. The following background script identifies when each install reason will execute:

background.js

```
console.log("This will run each time the service worker starts");

chrome.runtime.onInstalled.addListener((details) => {
  switch (details.reason) {
    case chrome.runtime.OnInstalledReason.INSTALL:
      console.log("This runs when the extension is newly
      installed.");
      break;
    case chrome.runtime.OnInstalledReason.CHROME_UPDATE:
      console.log("This runs when a chrome chrome update
      installs.");
      break;
    case chrome.runtime.OnInstalledReason.SHARED_MODULE_UPDATE:
      console.log("This runs when a shared module update
      installs.");
```

```
      break;
    case chrome.runtime.OnInstalledReason.UPDATE:
      console.log("This runs when an extension update
      installs.");
      break;
    default:
      break;
  }
});
```

Opening Tabs

Content script can't open extension URLs, but they can delegate the opening to the background script. The following example adds two buttons to the page: one will fail to open the extension URL indirectly, and one sends a message to the background script to open the URL.

Example 7-8a. manifest.json

```
{
  "name": "MVX",
  "version": "0.0.1",
  "manifest_version": 3,
  "background": {
    "service_worker": "background.js",
    "type": "module"
  },
  "content_scripts": [
    {
      "matches": ["<all_urls>"],
      "css": [],
      "js": ["content-script.js"]
```

```
    }
  ],
  "permissions": ["tabs"]
}
```

Example 7-8b. background.js

```
chrome.runtime.onMessage.addListener((msg) => {
  chrome.tabs.create({ url: msg.url });
});
```

Example 7-8c. content-script.js

```
const root = document.createElement("div");
root.innerHTML = `
<div style="position:fixed;top:0;left:0">
    <button id="direct-open">THIS WILL NOT WORK</button>
    <button id="indirect-open">THIS WILL WORK</button>
</div>
`;

document.body.appendChild(root);

const url = chrome.runtime.getURL("foobar.html");

document.querySelector("#direct-open").
addEventListener("click", () => {
  window.open(url);
});

document.querySelector("#indirect-open").
addEventListener("click", () => {
  chrome.runtime.sendMessage({ url });
});
```

Example 7-8d. foobar.html

```
<!DOCTYPE html>
<html>
  <body>
    <h1>Foobar</h1>
  </body>
</html>
```

Forcing Service Worker Persistence

As described earlier in the chapter, service workers are designed to shut down frequently. For most extension developers, this is not an issue, as their needs can be adequately met by the service worker form factor. For the handful of situations where a persistent background script is *absolutely essential,* there are no officially supported remedies. However, there are some unofficial strategies that can prolong the life of your service worker.

Implementation

All the forced persistence workarounds all rely on the same overall strategy. When an extension message port is opened between a content script and the background, the browser will not terminate the service worker for 5 minutes. There does not need to be any message passing going on, the port just needs to remain open. Once these 5 minutes are up, the browser may decide the service worker is idle and terminate it. If, however, a new port is connected before 5 minutes is up, the browser will restart the 5-minute timer. If the extension continually re-opens new ports, the background service worker can theoretically remain active indefinitely.

Stack overflow user wOxxOm has an excellent writeup about this here: `https://stackoverflow.com/questions/66618136/persistent-service-worker-in-chrome-extension#answer-66618269`. One of their demos is adapted below:

Example 7-9a. manifest.json

```
{
  "name": "MVX",
  "version": "0.0.1",
  "manifest_version": 3,
  "background": {
    "service_worker": "background.js",
    "type": "module"
  },
  "permissions": ["scripting"],
  "host_permissions": ["<all_urls>"]
}
```

Example 7-9b. background.js

```
let lifeline;

// Disconnect and reconnect
function keepAliveForced() {
  lifeline?.disconnect();
  lifeline = null;
  keepAlive();
}

async function keepAlive() {
  if (lifeline) {
    return;
  }
```

```
  // Locate any eligible tab and connect to it
  for (const tab of await chrome.tabs.query({})) {
    try {
      await chrome.scripting.executeScript({
        target: { tabId: tab.id },
        function: () => chrome.runtime.connect({
          name: "KEEPALIVE"
        }),
      });

      return;
    } catch (e) {}
  }
}

chrome.runtime.onConnect.addListener((port) => {
  if (port.name == "KEEPALIVE") {
    lifeline = port;

    // Refresh the connection after 1 minute
    setTimeout(keepAliveForced, 6e4);
    port.onDisconnect.addListener(keepAliveForced);
  }
});

// Any tab change means reconnecting may be required
chrome.tabs.onUpdated.addListener((tabId, info, tab) => {
  if (info.url && /^(file|https?):/.test(info.url)) {
    keepAlive();
  }
});
```

```
keepAlive();

let age = 0;
setInterval(() => console.log(`Age: ${++age}s`), 1000);
```

To see this working:

- Install the extension and ensure all devtools windows are closed.
- Have at least one tab open that has a protocol of `http://`, `https://`, or `file://`
- Open the `chrome://serviceworker-internals` page. You will see the extension continue to log to the console indefinitely.

Drawbacks and Limitations

The main issue with this strategy is that it relies on a content script on the other end to complete the connection. If, for example, the user only has tabs open with `chrome://` protocols, the background script will have no eligible tab to connect to, and the service worker will not connect and eventually terminate. One solution to this issue is to force open an eligible tab using `tabs.create()`, but this may degrade the user's experience as they will see a new tab magically be created by the extension unexpectedly.

Warning Overall, this solution is a bit of a clever hack. At the time of publication, it does appear to force the service worker to persist indefinitely, but there is no guarantee that Chrome or any other browsers will continue to behave this way into the future. Your mileage may vary!

Summary

In this chapter, you learned all about how extension code can run in the background in the browser. You were shown the similarities and differences between service workers that run in a web page vs. in an extension, as well as all the important changes between background scripts in manifest v2 and v3. Next, we went through all the basics of inspecting and debugging background scripts. Finally, you were shown a variety of common patterns that developers use in background scripts, as well as a clever strategy for extending the lifetime of a service worker.

In the next chapter, you will learn about the two primary user interface components of extensions: the popup and options pages.

CHAPTER 8

Popup and Options Pages

Brower extensions almost always need to allow the user to control some aspect of its behavior via a user interface. The popup and options pages are the bread-and-butter extension components that should be used for this need. Content scripts can also be used to offer an in-page user interface, but there are important tradeoffs and complications when doing so.

Note Refer to the *Content Scripts* chapter for coverage on these tradeoffs.

Popup Pages

As its name suggests, the popup page is a web page that renders inside a container that "pops up" over the browser's web page. It is completely controlled by the browser extension and guaranteed to overlay the browser's current web page (Figure 8-1).

M. Frisbie, *Building Browser Extensions*, https://doi.org/10.1007/978-1-4842-8725-5_8

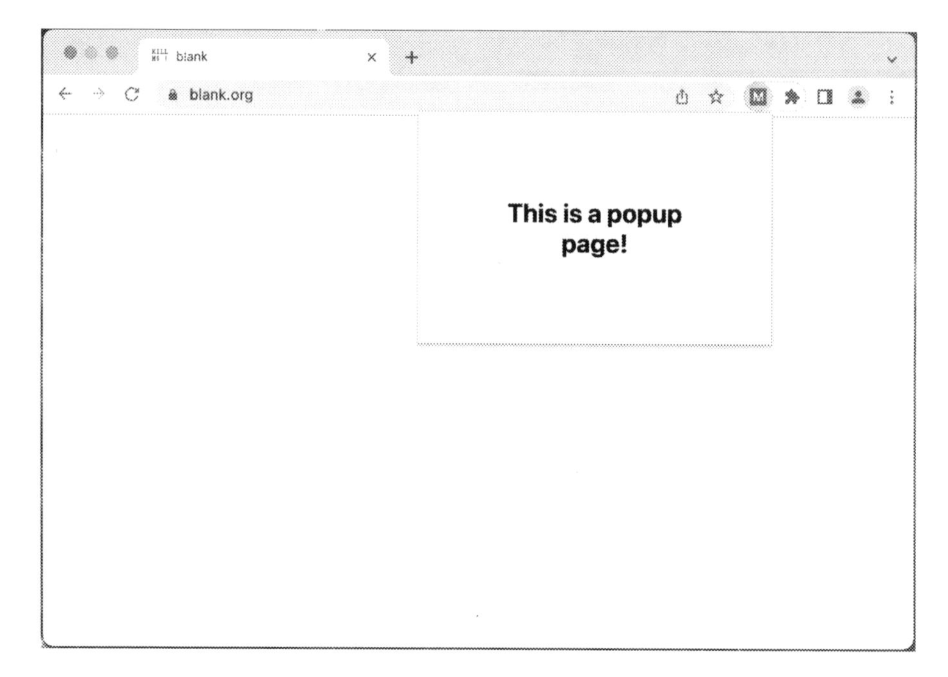

Figure 8-1. *A simple popup page*

Popup Page Properties

The popup page container can be thought of as a simple browser tab without any browser chrome: no URL bar, no browser controls, etc. In nearly every other respect, the popup page is like any other web page. The following demo extension demonstrates some basic properties of popup pages (Figure 8-2):

Example 8-1a. manifest.json

```
{
  "name": "MVX",
  "version": "0.0.1",
  "manifest_version": 3,
  "action": {
```

```
    "default_popup": "popup.html"
  }
}
```

Example 8-1b. popup.html

```
<!DOCTYPE html>
<html>
  <head>
    <link href="popup.css" rel="stylesheet" />
  </head>
  <body>
    <h1>This is a popup page!</h1>
    <div id="url"></div>
    <div id="xid"></div>
    <a href="popup.js">popup.js</a>

    <script src="popup.js"></script>
  </body>
</html>
```

Example 8-1c. popup.js

```
document.querySelector("#url").innerHTML = `
<pre>Page URL: ${window.location.href}</pre>
`;

document.querySelector("#xid").innerHTML = `
<pre>Extension ID: ${chrome.runtime.id}</pre>
`;
```

Example 8-1d. popup.css

```
body {
    text-align: center;
```

```
    min-width: 20rem;
    padding: 4rem;
}
```

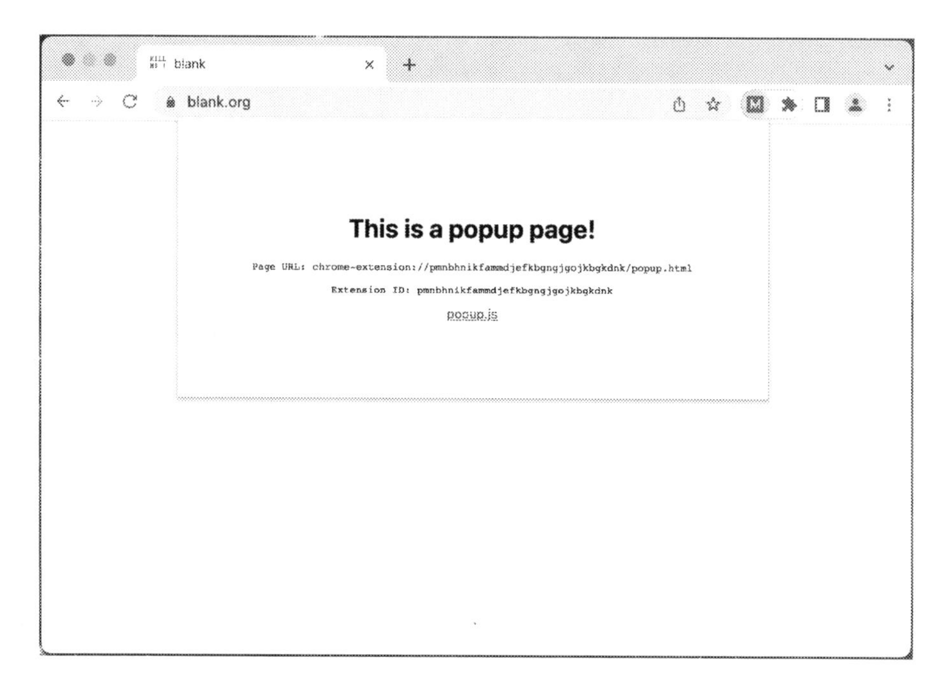

Figure 8-2. *The opened popup page of the demo extension*

In `manifest.json`, the popup page is declared by specifying the path to the popup HTML file via the `action.default_popup` value. As described in the *Extension Manifest* chapter, the `action` dictionary defines how the toolbar icon button appears and behaves:

- If the `action` dictionary is defined with a `default_popup` value, clicking that button will open the popup.
- If the `action` dictionary is defined *without* a `default_popup` value, clicking the toolbar icon button will instead call the `chrome.action.onClicked()` handler wherever it is defined.

The popup container will be sized to fit the content of the popup page, but browsers will handle the sizing rules slightly differently. For example, Google Chrome sets no upper bound on the maximum size of the popup, allowing it to even expand larger than the browser window itself. Conversely, Mozilla Firefox limits the popup to be no larger than 800px by 600px.

Tip To handle these variable popup size limits, you should either make the popup page responsive or limit the amount of content that appears inside the popup.

Because the popup page is served from the browser's extension protocol – in Google Chrome, `chrome-extension://` – the page's JavaScript has access to the WebExtensions API. The popup page is not restricted from navigating to other URLs, so clicking the link to `popup.js` will successfully navigate the popup page to a new URL.

More advanced extensions will often build multi-view single page applications inside the popup page. These extensions should use the HTML page that the manifest specifies as a popup as the equivalent of a web page's `index.html` entrypoint.

Opening and Closing Popup Pages

Popup pages are intended to show only after an explicit user action. Browsers intentionally prevent you from programmatically opening a popup page to prevent extensions from spamming the user with page overlays. Therefore, there are essentially two ways of opening the popup page:

- Clicking the toolbar icon button when the manifest has `action.default_popup` defined

- Entering the key shortcut defined in the manifest's `commands._execute_action` when `action.default_popup` is defined

---

Note There is a `chrome.action.openPopup()` method listen in extension documentation, but at the time this book was written this method is still not supported. When support is eventually rolled out, it will still only be usable directly after an eligible user interaction; therefore, programmatic popup page opening will remain effectively disallowed.

Once the popup is open, there are many more ways to trigger a close. From popup page's perspective, closing the popup is identical to a tab being closed. The following actions will trigger a popup close:

- Clicking the toolbar icon button when the popup is already open
- Clicking outside the opened popup window *and* inside the same browser window
- Calling `window.close()` from inside the popup JavaScript
- Using the escape key

Note Importantly, clicks outside the browser window will *not* close the popup. This behavior allows you to open one popup page per window. It also means must assume the user can have multiple popup pages open simultaneously.

Changing the Popup Page

You are able to change the popup page via the WebExtensions API. Any changes made will persist through browser sessions. The following snippet demonstrates how to change the popup page:

```
chrome.action.setPopup({
  popup: chrome.runtime.getURL("new-popup.html")
});
```

Detecting Popup State

Browser extensions implicitly keep track of active window objects that are controlled by the extension. The `chrome.extension.getViews()` method provides access to this list, and you are able to provide a `type` to filter only the popup views, shown here:

```
// Returns an array of window objects
chrome.extension.getViews({ type: "popup" });
```

If you wish to detect if a view is being rendered inside a popup, you can perform a simple check against the `window` object:

```
const popups = chrome.extension.getViews({ type: "popup" });

console.log(`Inside a popup: ${popups.includes(window)}`);
```

Suggested Use

When developing popup pages, you should follow these strategies:

- Popup pages are best used for user interfaces that the user needs to access quickly without losing the context of the current page that they are on.
- As some browsers will restrict the page dimensions of the popup page, a good rule of thumb is that the interface should contain approximately as much content as a phone app.
- Because popup pages will be closed and re-opened quickly, the popup page should efficiently render and not rely on long-running operations that may need to terminate early.
- When you need the popup page be stateful or load data, it should aggressively utilize a caching strategy to avoid any UX slowdowns.
- In situations where you need more screen real estate, a popup page can offer links or buttons that will open the options page or other views in a separate browser tab.

Options Pages

The options page is a web page that renders in one of two ways: as a standalone tab, or inside a modal container over the browser's extension manager page (Figures 8-3 and 8-4). It is completely controlled by the browser extension.

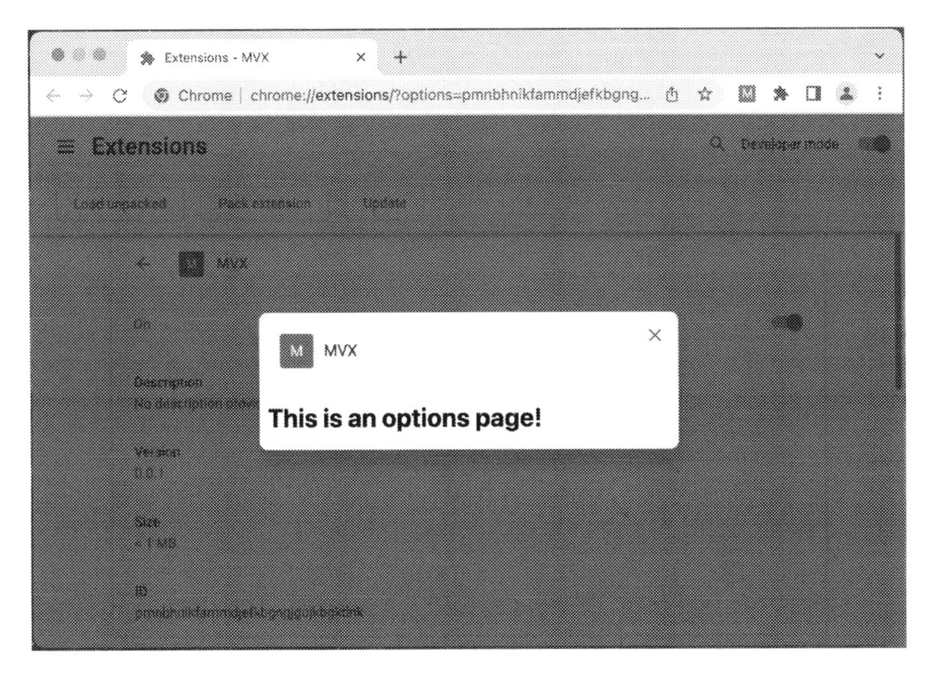

***Figure 8-3.** The options page rendered inside the extension manager page modal*

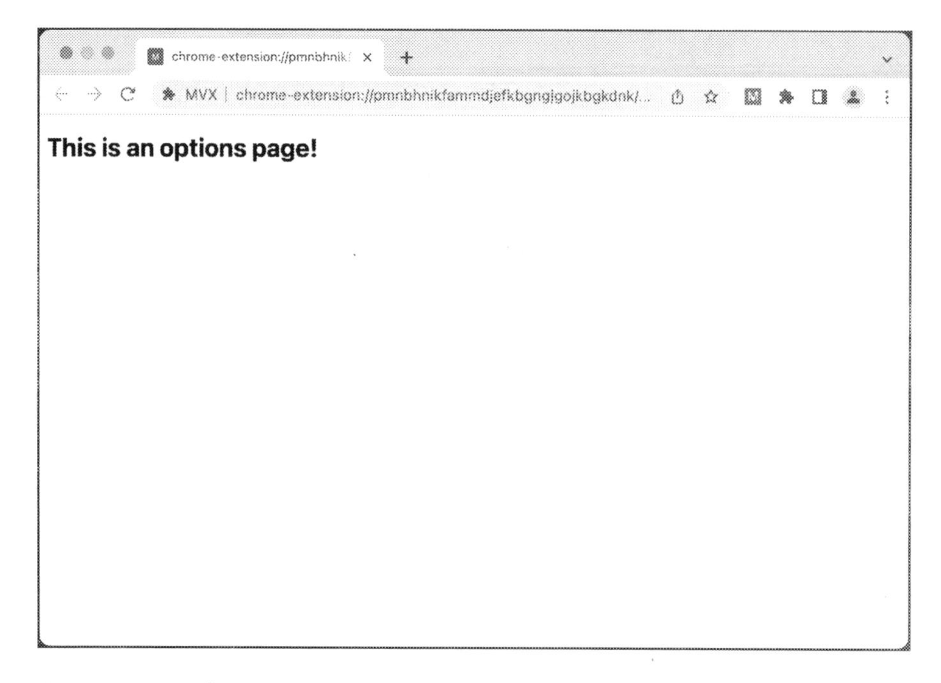

Figure 8-4. *The options page rendered in a tab*

Options Page Properties

When opened in a tab, the options page is like any other web page. When opened as a modal, the options modal container can be thought of as a simple browser tab without any browser chrome: no URL bar, no browser controls, etc. The following demo extension demonstrates some basic properties of options pages:

Example 8-2a. manifest.json

```
{
  "name": "MVX",
  "version": "0.0.1",
  "manifest_version": 3,
  "action": {
```

```
    "default_popup": "popup.html"
  },
  "options_ui": {
    "open_in_tab": false,
    "page": "options.html"
  }
}
```

Example 8-2b. popup.html

```
<!DOCTYPE html>
<html>
  <body>
    <h1>Popup</h1>
    <button id="opts">Options</button>
    <a href="options.html" target="_blank">options.html</a>

    <script src="popup.js"></script>
  </body>
</html>
```

Example 8-2c. popup.js

```
document.querySelector("#opts").addEventListener(
  "click",
  () => chrome.runtime.openOptionsPage());
```

Example 8-2d. options.html

```
<!DOCTYPE html>
<html>
  <body>
    <h1>Options</h1>
```

```
    <a href="options.js">options.js</a>
  </body>
</html>
```

In `manifest.json`, the options page is declared by specifying the path to the options HTML file via the `options_ui.page` value. The options page default rendering can occur in one of two ways:

- If `options_ui.open_in_tab` is `false`, the options page by default will open in a browser tab.
- If `options_ui.open_in_tab` is `true`, the options page by default will open in a modal over the browser's extension manager page.

If opened as a modal, the options container will be sized to fit the content of the options page. The options page can specify body dimensions to grow or shrink as needed.

Because the options page is served from the browser's extension protocol – in Google Chrome, `chrome-extension://` – the page's JavaScript has access to the WebExtensions API. In both tab and modal mode, the options page is not restricted from navigating to other URLs, so clicking the link to `options.js` will successfully navigate the options page to a new URL.

More advanced extensions will often build multi-view single page applications inside the options page. These extensions should use the HTML page that the manifest specifies as options as the equivalent of a web page's `index.html` entrypoint.

Opening and Closing Options Pages

There are several ways to open the options page, and unlike the popup, the options page *can* be opened programmatically. The following actions will open the options page, and will always respect the `options_ui.open_in_tab` value:

- Right clicking the toolbar icon button and selecting *Options*
- Call `chrome.runtime.openOptionsPage()`

When the options page is opened in a tab, it closes like a standard web page. When opened as a modal, the following actions will trigger an options close:

- Clicking the X button inside the options page modal
- Calling `window.close()` from inside the options JavaScript
- Using the `escape` key when viewing the options modal
- Closing the extension manager tab

Note The "options page" designation refers mainly to the stems from the browser's ability to access the page via context menu item or WebExtensions API method. Once opened as a tab, the options page is no different than any other extension HTML file opened via the extension protocol URL.

Detecting Options Pages

When options pages are opened as a tab, they are treated as any other tab and therefore can be detected via `chrome.extension.getViews()` or `tabs.query()`. However, when opened as a modal, the options page will have the following limitations:

- `chrome.tabs.query()` will not return the options page

- The `chrome.tabs.onCreated` and `chrome.tabs.onUpdated` events will not fire when the modal is opened or changes
- The modal options page cannot be sent messages via `chrome.tabs.connect()` or `chrome.tabs.sendMessage()`
- `chrome.extension.getViews({ type: "tab" })` will not return the modal options window. Note that `chrome.extension.getViews()` will still include the modal options window.

Suggested Use

When developing options pages, you should follow these strategies:

- Options pages are best used for user interfaces that contain controls for how the extension behaves.
- The options page has no restrictions on content. However, since a very common path to accessing it is to right click on the toolbar icon and select "Options," the options page should probably resemble a page with which to control extension options.
- There isn't much of an upside to using the modal version of the extension page. Users are likely not familiar with the extension management interface, so displaying a modal view over it could be confusing. I recommend sticking to using the tab version.

Content Script Restrictions

One tricky and important behavior to note is that programmatic access to options pages (and any other extension URLs) is forbidden. Consider the following example extension, which has a popup page with four buttons, each of which attempts to open the options page in a different way:

Example 8-3a. manifest.json

```
{
  "name": "MVX",
  "version": "0.0.1",
  "manifest_version": 3,
  "action": {
    "default_popup": "popup.html"
  },
  "options_ui": {
    "open_in_tab": true,
    "page": "options.html"
  },
  "permissions": ["scripting"],
  "host_permissions": ["<all_urls>"]
}
```

Example 8-3b. popup.html

```
<!DOCTYPE html>
<html>
  <body>
    <h1>Popup</h1>

    <button id="popup-api">Popup API</button>
    <button id="popup-url">Popup URL</button>
    <button id="cs-api">Content Script API</button>
```

```
    <button id="cs-url">Content Script URL</button>

    <script src="popup.js"></script>
  </body>
</html>
```

Example 8-3c. popup.js

```
function openOptionsWithUrl() {
  window.open(chrome.runtime.getURL("options.html"));
}

function openOptionsWithApi() {
  chrome.runtime.openOptionsPage();
}

async function sendFnToActiveTab(fn) {
  let [tab] = await chrome.tabs.query({
    active: true,
    currentWindow: true,
  });

  chrome.scripting.executeScript({
    target: { tabId: tab.id },
    function: fn,
  });
}

document.querySelector("#popup-api").addEventListener(
  "click",
  () => openOptionsWithApi());

document.querySelector("#popup-url").addEventListener(
  "click",
  () => openOptionsWithUrl());
```

```
document.querySelector("#cs-api").addEventListener(
  "click",
  () => sendFnToActiveTab(openOptionsWithApi));

document.querySelector("#cs-url").addEventListener(
  "click", () => sendFnToActiveTab(openOptionsWithUrl));
```

Example 8-3d. options.html

```
<!DOCTYPE html>
<html>
  <body>
    <h1>Options</h1>
  </body>
</html>
```

Note The content script buttons must be used with a valid active tab such as `https://blank.org`.

The popup page's four buttons each offer one of the four combinations of popup origin or content script origin, and API open or URL open. Initially, nothing here should appear out of the order. When you click the two popup buttons, the options page will correctly open without incident.

However, after clicking each of the content script buttons, the options page will not correctly open and you will see the errors shown in Figures 8-5 and 8-6.

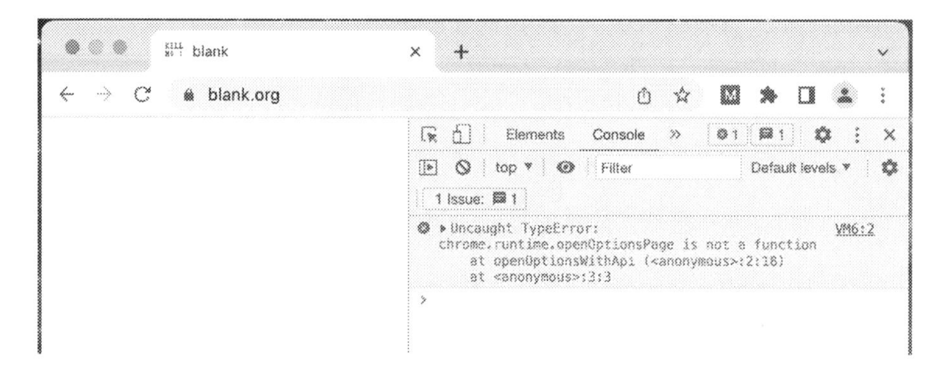

***Figure 8-5.** The error shown after clicking the Content Script API button*

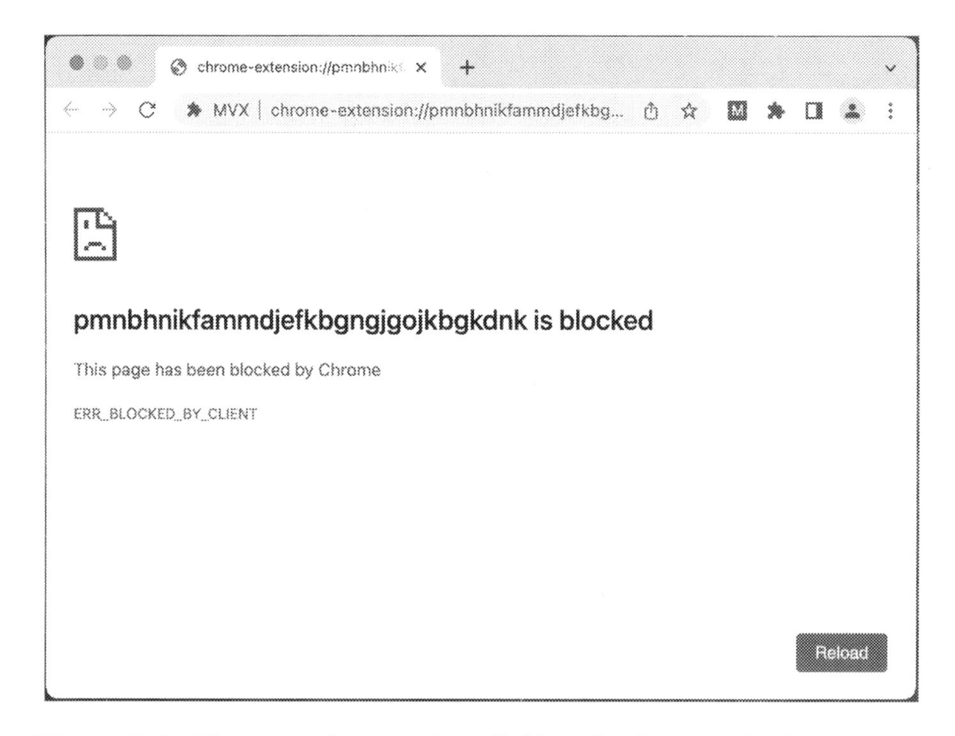

***Figure 8-6.** The error shown after clicking the Content Script URL button*

The browser prevents the content script from programmatically opening the options page. In the content script, the API method is simply removed, and the extension URL is prevented from accessing the extension's fileserver.

The reason for this is presumably security related. The potential for content scripts to abuse their ability to kick the user into a new tab is too great, so content scripts are restricted from doing so.

Summary

In this chapter, you learned about the two major building user interface building blocks of browser extensions: popup pages and options pages. The chapter took you through the details of how each one operates inside the browser, how they can fit into the user flow, and the advantages and disadvantages of using each one.

In the next chapter, you will learn about how content scripts can complement and enhance popup and options pages, as well as enable an entirely new extension domain in which to architect user interfaces.

CHAPTER 9

Content Scripts

Contents scripts are one of the most powerful tools available in browser extensions. They allow you to inject JavaScript and CSS into any web page and modify it with almost no restrictions. The injected content can be as simple as a few visual tweaks, or as complicated as entire single page application frameworks. Extensions can also use them for nonuser interface reasons: content scripts can read and modify the page DOM, as well as send network requests as the authenticated user.

Introduction to Content Scripts

The most common way that content scripts are used is by declarative injection via the manifest. The manifest specifies the files that should be injected, and the domains in which they should be injected, and the browser will inject them into the page. Injected JavaScript is analogous to dynamically inserting a `<script>` tag into the page, and injected CSS is analogous to dynamically inserting a `<link>` tag into the page. The following example demonstrates an extension that will inject JS and CSS into all web pages:

Example 9-1a. manifest.json

```
{
  "name": "MVX",
  "version": "0.0.1",
```


M. Frisbie, *Building Browser Extensions*, https://doi.org/10.1007/978-1-4842-8725-5_9

```
  "manifest_version": 3,
  "content_scripts": [
    {
      "matches": ["<all_urls>"],
      "css": ["content-script.css"],
      "js": ["content-script.js"]
    }
  ],
  "permissions": []
}
```

Example 9-1b. content-script.js

```
console.log(window.jQuery);

document.body.innerHTML = "Hello, world!";
```

Example 9-1c. content-script.css

```
body {
    background-color: red !important;
}
```

Injecting CSS

Injecting CSS content scripts into a host page is relatively straightforward. If the URL is a match, the script will be injected as though it were listed as an extra `<link>` element. Install the previous example extension and visit any website to see the CSS injection result (Figure 9-1).

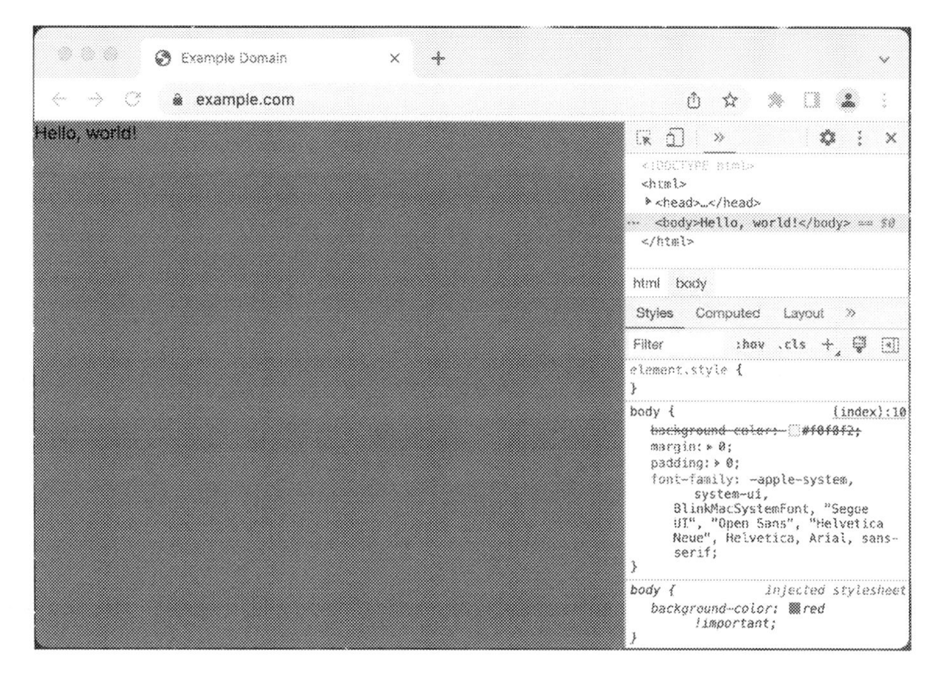

***Figure 9-1.** example.com with the content script's CSS applied*

There are a few things to notice here:

- The content scripts are only projected into the page. You will not see actual `<script>` or `<link>` tags added.
- The injected CSS specificity is less than the page's CSS, so using `!important` is often necessary.

Content Script Isolation

Next, navigate to `jquery.com` (or any other website that loads the jQuery library) (Figure 9-2).

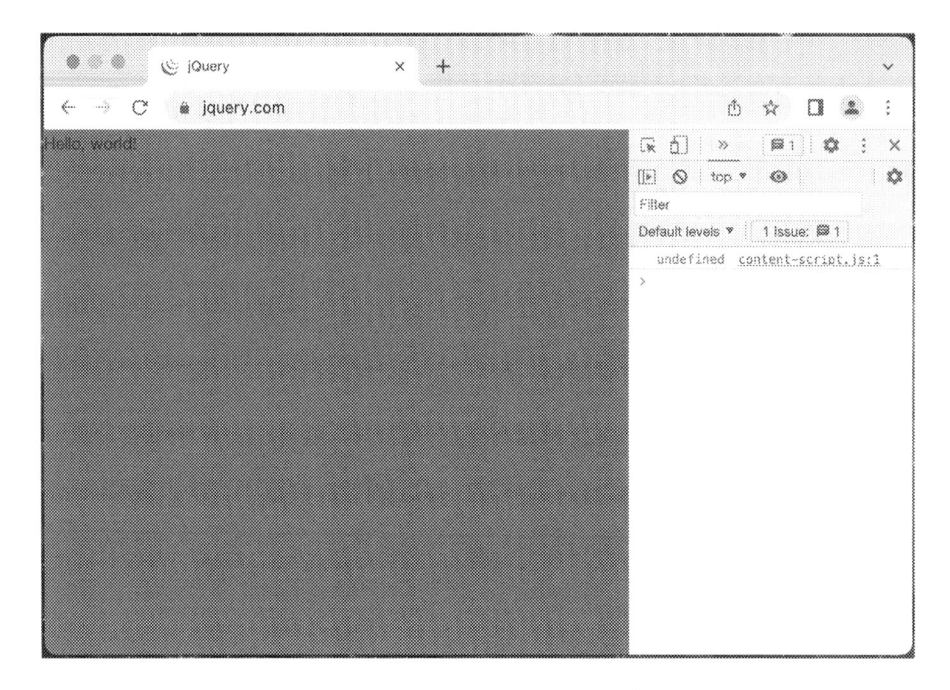

Figure 9-2. *jquery.com with the content script's log output*

When the jQuery JavaScript library is loaded on `jquery.com`, the `jQuery` property is defined on the `window` object, but the content script is unable to see this property. However, in the developer tools, `window.jQuery` will be defined. This is due to the content script's runtime isolation.

Content script JavaScript executes in a separate runtime in parallel to the host page. Neither runtime can access the other's variables, and each has its own event loop, global scope, and task queue. However, both can access APIs that interact with the same objects: for example, the DOM, `localStorage`, `sessionStorage`, `IndexedDB`, `cookieStore`, etc. Suppose the host page defines a variable in the global scope. The content script has no way of accessing its value. However, if the host page were to write that variable into `localStorage`, the content script's `localStorage` API would have access to that value!

Shared access to the DOM is particularly interesting. One immediately useful feature is the ability of a content script to add, modify, or remove DOM nodes from the host page. For example, if you wanted to wipe out all the CSS styling on all web pages, you could use the following example extension:

Example 9-2a. manifest.json

```
{
  "name": "MVX",
  "version": "0.0.1",
  "manifest_version": 3,
  "content_scripts": [
    {
      "matches": ["<all_urls>"],
      "css": [],
      "js": ["content-script.js"]
    }
  ],
  "permissions": []
}
```

Example 9-2b. content-script.js

```
for (const el of document.querySelectorAll("style")) {
  el.parentElement.removeChild(el);
}

for (const el of document.querySelectorAll('link[rel=
"stylesheet"]')) {
  el.parentElement.removeChild(el);
}
```

```
for (const el of document.querySelectorAll("[style]")) {
  el.removeAttribute("style");
}
```

Load this extension and navigate to any web page. You will notice that all the CSS styling will be completely stripped out.

Note This will not affect CSS styling that is added by JavaScript after the content script runs. One trivial solution might be to wrap this script in a `setInterval()`, but then there may be performance considerations to take into account with all the extra `querySelectorAll` expressions being evaluated. This sort of page management is what makes content scripts so tricky to get right.

Page Automation

Although a content script cannot access event handlers, it can dispatch events on shared DOM nodes. Event handlers that the host page assigned in the host JavaScript context will be called by events dispatched from the content script JavaScript context. The following example demonstrates this by automating a search on `Wikipedia.org`.

Example 9-3a. manifest.json

```
{
  "name": "MVX",
  "version": "0.0.1",
  "manifest_version": 3,
  "content_scripts": [
    {
      "matches": ["https://*.wikipedia.org/*"],
```

```
      "css": [],
      "js": ["content-script.js"]
    }
  ],
  "permissions": []
}
```

Example 9-3b. content-script.js

```
// Wait a few seconds so the user
// can see the query being entered
setTimeout(() => {
  document.querySelector("#searchInput").value = "javascript";
}, 2000);

setTimeout(() => {
  document.querySelector('button[type="submit"]').click();
}, 3000);
```

After loading this extension, visit `https://wikipedia.org`. You will see the extension set a value in the input field and click the search button, and you will be taken to the page on JavaScript.

If you wanted to make the text entry more realistic, you could adjust the background script to the following:

content-script.js

```
const typedValue = "javascript";
const input = document.querySelector("#searchInput");
const form = document.querySelector("#search-form");

function typeOrSubmit(idx = 0) {
  const char = typedValue[idx];

  if (!char) {
    setTimeout(() => form.submit(), 500);
```

```
  } else {
    input.value = input.value + char;

    setTimeout(() => typeOrSubmit(++idx), 100);
  }
}

if (input && form) {
  setTimeout(() => {
    input.focus();

    typeOrSubmit();
  }, 2000);
}
```

Reload the extension and the Wikipedia page. The content script will progressively type out the search term. Also note here that the content script is submitting the form directly, not just clicking the search button.

This touches upon an important concept to keep in mind when writing content scripts: you are at the mercy of the host page. In the above example, we are using selectors defined by the host page to locate the elements we want to interact with. If the host page changes these selectors even a small amount, the content script will break. Furthermore, note that the content scripts are using built-in event dispatching methods like `click()`, `focus()`, and `submit()`. These are handy because they are succinct and partially allow you the ability to avoid dispatching events manually.

Sometimes, dispatching events manually is required. A content script can't see which elements have event handlers attached, but the developer can find this information out ahead of time using the `getEventListeners()` method. For example, on `https://wikipedia.org`, you can use this method to find all the event listeners on the "Read Wikipedia in your language" button (Figure 9-3).

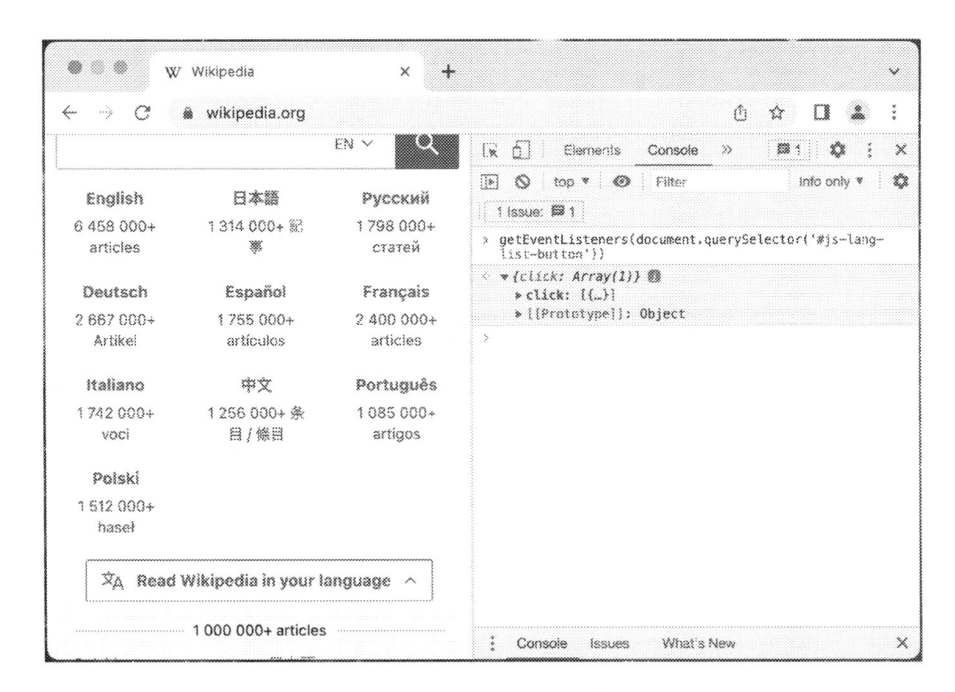

Figure 9-3. *The result of getEventListeners()*

We see here there is an event listener set by the host page. We can then check what this handler is doing by just dispatching a test click event in the developer console – and you should see it toggle the language menu. To automate the opening of this menu, we could certainly call `click()` in the content script, but for the sake of this example let's instead open the menu by manually dispatching a click event:

content-script.js

```
setTimeout(() => {
  const el = document.querySelector("#js-lang-list-button");

  // Scroll down to the button so we can see the click work
  el.scrollIntoView();

  el.dispatchEvent(new Event("click"));
}, 2000);
```

Reload the extension and the Wikipedia page. You should see the content script scroll the page down and automatically open the language menu.

Logging and Errors

Console messages and errors produced by a content script will show up in the host page's developer console (Figure 9-4).

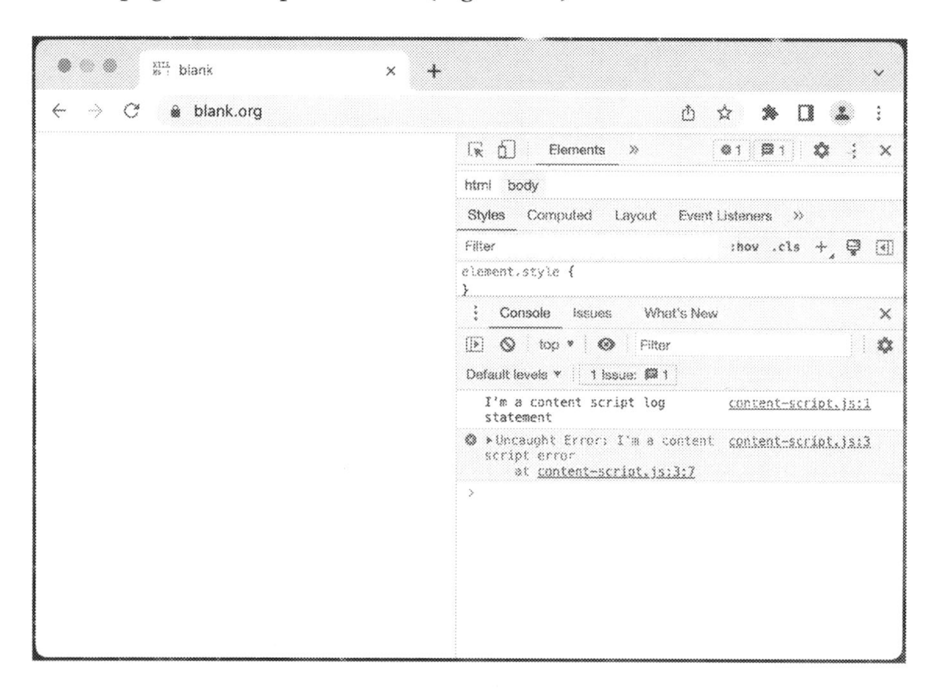

***Figure 9-4.** Console messages and errors from a content script*

Because uncaught errors thrown in the content script are still part of the extension context, these error messages will also surface in the extension's error view (Figure 9-5).

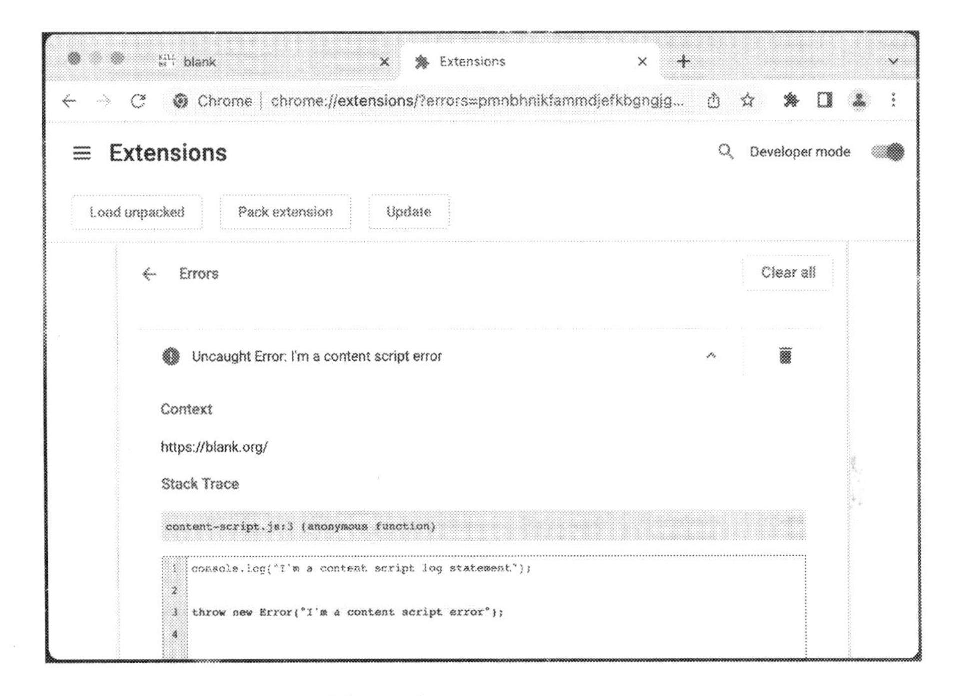

Figure 9-5. *Errors visible in the extension error view*

Extension API Access

Unlike popups and options pages, content scripts can only access a limited portion of the WebExtensions API:

- `chrome.i18n.*`
- `chrome.storage.*`
- `chrome.runtime.connect`
- `chrome.runtime.getManifest`
- `chrome.runtime.getURL`
- `chrome.runtime.id`

- `chrome.runtime.onConnect`
- `chrome.runtime.onMessage`
- `chrome.runtime.sendMessage`

If you require other parts of the API, you can delegate to the background service worker by sending a message to trigger a remote procedure call. The background service worker can use the full API and send back the result if needed.

One unusual aspect of content scripts is, although they can use `runtime.getURL()`, they are prevented from opening tabs of extension URLs. The tab will open, but the page will not render and instead show a browser error. Content scripts run in an untrusted environment, and therefore using `<a href>` or `window.open(chrome-extension://...)` to access extension pages would necessarily mean that the host pages could open those URLs too. As shown in the *Background Scripts* chapter, the solution to this is to send a message to the background directing it to open a new tab with the desired URL.

Modules and Code Splitting

As any experienced developer knows, modern JavaScript makes heavy use of ES6 modules and the `import` keyword. Because the top-level content script is not a module, and there is currently no way to define it as a module, it cannot have static imports. Fortunately, there are a handful of straightforward solutions.

Bundling

Most extension development is done using sophisticated build tools like Parcel, Webpack, or Plasmo, and these are usually configured to smush the entire content script code graph into a single file, thereby eliminating the need for using imports in the top-level content script. Traditional web applications have more of a need for lazy loading, since from a performance perspective loading data from a remote server is expensive. Since browser extensions are exclusively served from the extension file server on the local device, there is a negligible penalty for bundling the entire content script into a gigantic monolithic script.

Dynamic Imports

Content scripts may not be able to use static imports, but they are perfectly happy using dynamic imports and loading a secondary module that *can* use static imports. Doing so requires an additional network request to the extension file server, but this penalty is negligible and therefore acceptable.

Of course, any static or dynamic `import` in a content script will generate a network request for that module. Therefore, to allow these modules to be imported, they must be listed as under `web_accessible_resources`. This is demonstrated in the following example extension, which performs a dynamic import. Load the extension and inspect the console output:

Example 9-4a. manifest.json

```
{
  "name": "MVX",
  "version": "0.0.1",
  "manifest_version": 3,
  "content_scripts": [
    {
      "matches": ["<all_urls>"],
      "css": [],
      "js": ["content-script.js"]
    }
  ],
```

```
  "permissions": [],
  "web_accessible_resources": [
    {
      "resources": ["*.js"],
      "matches": ["<all_urls>"]
    }
  ]
}
```

Example 9-4b. content-script.js

```
const url = chrome.runtime.getURL("foo.js");

import(url).then((fooModule) => {
  fooModule.bar();
});
```

Example 9-4c. foo.js

```
import apiTest from "./api-test.js";

export function bar() {
  console.log("Called bar!");
}

console.log("Loaded foo module!");
apiTest();
```

Example 9-4d. api-test.js

```
export default function () {
  // You will only see this method present if
  // the script has access to the WebExtensions API
  console.log("Can access API:", !!chrome.runtime.getURL);
}
```

The result is shown in Figure 9-6.

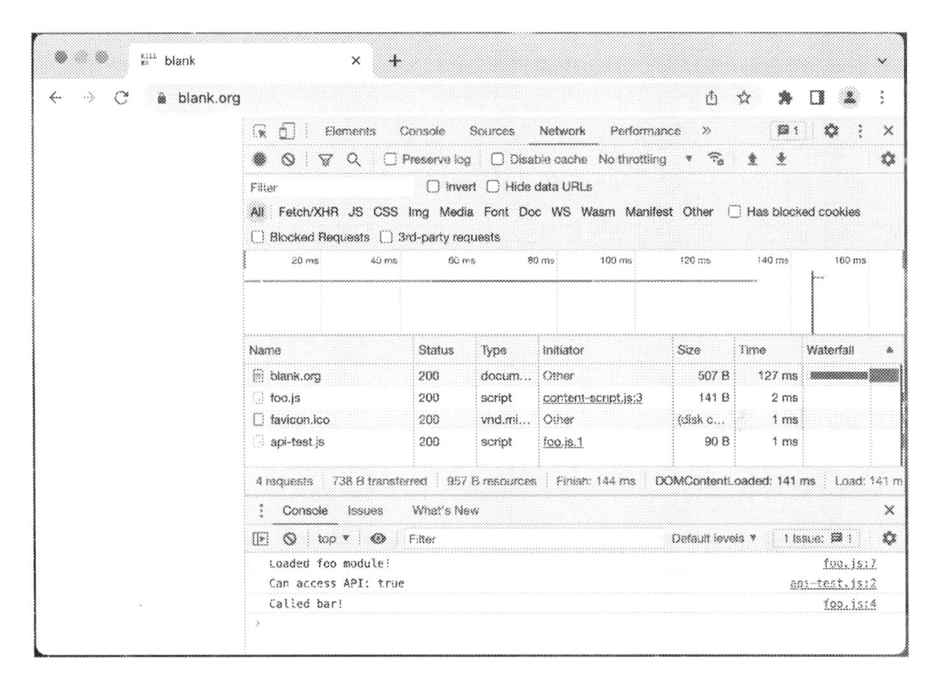

***Figure 9-6.** Dynamic module import network requests and console output*

There are a few things to note here:

- As expected, both the static and dynamic `import` incurred network requests for the module files.
- The imported module retains access to the WebExtensions API and can import other modules.
- Because it's a dynamic import, you can call methods on the imported module from the returned module object.

Dynamic Script Tags

It is also possible to load modules in a similar fashion by dynamically creating a `<script type="module">` in the page. Change the previous example extension to match the following:

Example 9-5. content-script.js

```
const url = chrome.runtime.getURL("foo.js");

const script = document.createElement("script");
script.setAttribute("type", "module");
script.setAttribute("src", url);
document.head.appendChild(script);
```

Reload the extension and you will see the screen shown in Figure 9-7.

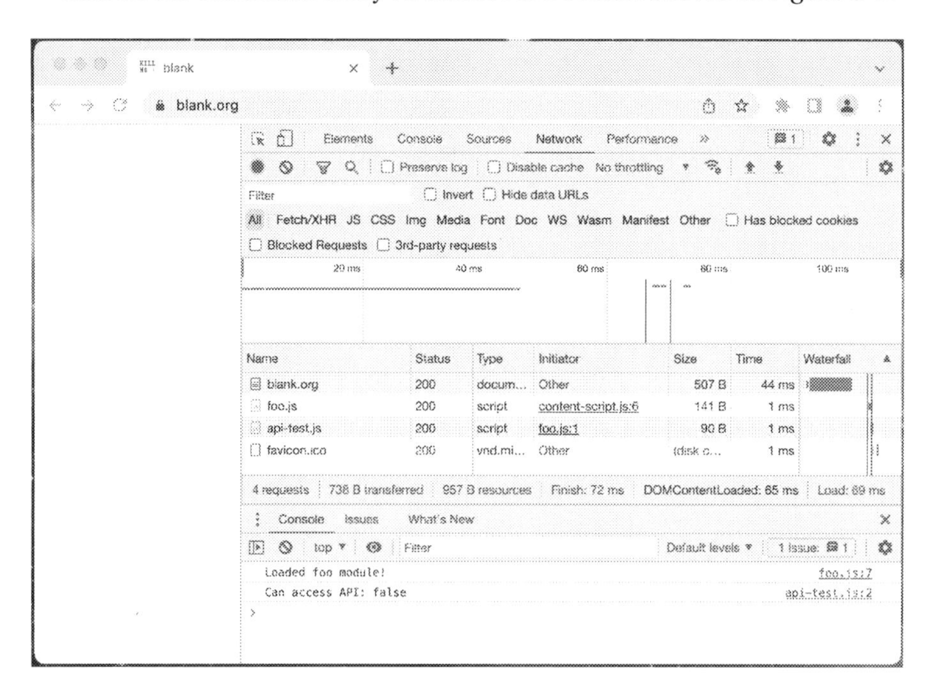

Figure 9-7. *Dynamic script tag network requests and console output*

There are a few things to note here:

- Dynamically created script tags lose access to the WebExtensions API.
- Because this isn't using the `import` keyword, we are unable to use specific exports from the module.

You may encounter some special situations where dynamic script tag creation is useful, but overall it is less useful than using dynamic imports.

Specialized Content Script Properties

Content scripts can be further customized to control when the script is injected, which URL paths it should or should not inject on, and whether or not it should inject in special URLs like `about:blank`. The following properties are available:

- `run_at`
- `match_about_blank`
- `match_origin_as_fallback`
- `exclude_matches`
- `include_globs`
- `exclude_globs`
- `all_frames`

Their behavior is detailed in the *Extension Manifests* chapter.

Programmatic Injection

The manifest is not the only way to inject content scripts. It is also possible to programmatically inject JavaScript and CSS into the page using the `chrome.scripting` API. Consider the following example that injects both JS and CSS after the toolbar icon is clicked:

Example 9-6a. manifest.json

```
{
  "name": "MVX",
  "version": "0.0.1",
  "manifest_version": 3,
  "background": {
    "service_worker": "background.js",
    "type": "module"
  },
  "permissions": ["scripting", "activeTab"],
  "action": {}
}
```

Example 9-6b. background.js

```
chrome.action.onClicked.addListener((tab) => {
  const target = {
    tabId: tab.id,
  };

  chrome.scripting.executeScript({
    target,
    func: () => {
      document.body.innerHTML = `Hello, world!`;
    },
  });
```

```
  chrome.scripting.insertCSS({
    target,
    css: `body { background-color: red !important; }`,
  });
});
```

As shown here, the `chrome.scripting` API can be used to easily inject JavaScript and CSS into the page on an ad-hoc basis. The mechanism by which the function is passed into the page is somewhat unusual: it is effectively calling `func.toString()`, and then evaluating that string in the context of the page.

Instead of passing in functions and strings, it is also possible to provide file references. The following example behaves identically to the previous one:

Example 9-7a. manifest.json

```
{
  "name": "MVX",
  "version": "0.0.1",
  "manifest_version": 3,
  "background": {
    "service_worker": "background.js",
    "type": "module"
  },
  "permissions": ["scripting", "activeTab"],
  "action": {}
}
```

Example 9-7b. background.js

```
chrome.action.onClicked.addListener((tab) => {
  const target = {
    tabId: tab.id,
  };

  chrome.scripting.executeScript({
    target,
    files: ["content-script.js"],
  });

  chrome.scripting.insertCSS({
    target,
    files: ["content-script.css"],
  });
});
```

Example 9-7c. content-script.js

```
document.body.innerHTML = `Hello, world!`;
```

Example 9-7d. content-script.css

```
body {
  background-color: red !important;
}
```

Importantly, no function closure is captured during serialization; any outside variables references are lost. Instead, variables can be serialized and curried into the function via an `args` property. The following example demonstrates this:

Example 9-8. background.js

```
const outerVar = "foobar";

function wipeOutPage(bg) {
  // Record the typeof inside the content script
  const cs = typeof outerVar;
  document.body.innerHTML = `${bg} -> ${cs}`;
}

const css = `
body {
    background-color: red !important;
}`;

chrome.action.onClicked.addListener((tab) => {
  const target = {
    tabId: tab.id,
  };

  // Record the typeof inside the background
  const backgroundTypeof = typeof outerVar;

  chrome.scripting.executeScript({
    target,
    func: wipeOutPage,
    // This array of values will be curried
    // into `func` (similar to Array.apply)
    args: [backgroundTypeof]
  });

  chrome.scripting.insertCSS({
    target,
    css,
  });
});
```

Reload this extension. You will see that the page content is `string -> undefined`. This indicates that the variable reference has been lost when the function is evaluated in the page.

Note It was formerly possible to pass in a function string to `executeScript()`. In manifest v3 this is no longer possible, as this would enable arbitrary code execution

---

It is also possible to register and unregister declarative content scripts on the fly. This is analogous to updating the manifest `content_scripts` property. Since this is modifying the declarative injection list, the scripts will not be injected until the next pageload. The following example is an extension which toggles the declarative injection when the toolbar icon is clicked.

Example 9-9a. manifest.json

```
{
  "name": "MVX",
  "version": "0.0.1",
  "manifest_version": 3,
  "background": {
    "service_worker": "background.js",
    "type": "module"
  },
  "permissions": ["scripting", "activeTab"],
  "action": {}
}
```

Example 9-9b. background.js

```
const id = "1";

chrome.action.onClicked.addListener(async () => {
  const activeScripts = await chrome.scripting.
  getRegisteredContentScripts();

  // Toggle the content script
  if (activeScripts.find((x) => x.id === id)) {
    chrome.scripting.unregisterContentScripts({
      ids: [id],
    });
    console.log("Unregistered content script");
  } else {
    chrome.scripting.registerContentScripts([
      {
        id,
        matches: ["<all_urls>"],
        js: ["content-script.js"],
        css: ["content-script.css"],
      },
    ]);
    console.log("Registered content script");
  }
});
```

Example 9-9c. content-script.js

```
document.body.innerHTML = "Hello, world!";
```

Example 9-9d. content-script.css

```
body {
    background-color: red !important;
}
```

Summary

In this chapter, you learn about how content scripts allow you to exert almost total control over host web pages. Although they have limited access to the WebExtensions API, content scripts can coordinate with the background service worker to add profoundly powerful enhancements to the user's browser experience. Finally, you were shown how content scripts can be dynamically added and removed from the page.

In the next chapter, you will learn how to build custom devtools pages into your browser's developer tools interface. You will also learn how to use the custom devtools APIs that are only accessible from an extension's devtools pages.

CHAPTER 10

Devtools Pages

Modern browsers offer developers a rich suite off developer tools for debugging, profiling, and inspecting web pages. Browser extensions are able to supplement these tools by providing custom interfaces that live inside the developer tools interface and can access special developer tools APIs.

Web developers are the intended audience for devtools pages, so consumer facing extensions will likely not need to make use of them. In general, browser extensions will only need devtools pages if they wish to use the Devtools API to inspect or profile the web page.

Note There are two separate concepts in this chapter with similar names: "devtools pages" and "developer tools". The term "developer tools" refers to the browser's native interface that is opened by right clicking on a web page and selecting "Inspect". The term "devtools pages" are extra interfaces added inside the developer tools. Browser extensions use the Devtools API to add these extra interfaces.

M. Frisbie, *Building Browser Extensions*, https://doi.org/10.1007/978-1-4842-8725-5_10

Introduction to Devtools Pages

The browser's developer tools is a special interface that is granted total control and transparency over the active web page (Figure 10-1). It is fully capable of inspecting and managing the HTML, adding and modifying the page, and sniffing all network traffic. It is not restricted by cross origin rules, and so it is totally capable of inspecting web pages frames from any origin. Its JavaScript debugger can pause execution and lay bare the entire memory model of a JavaScript runtime.

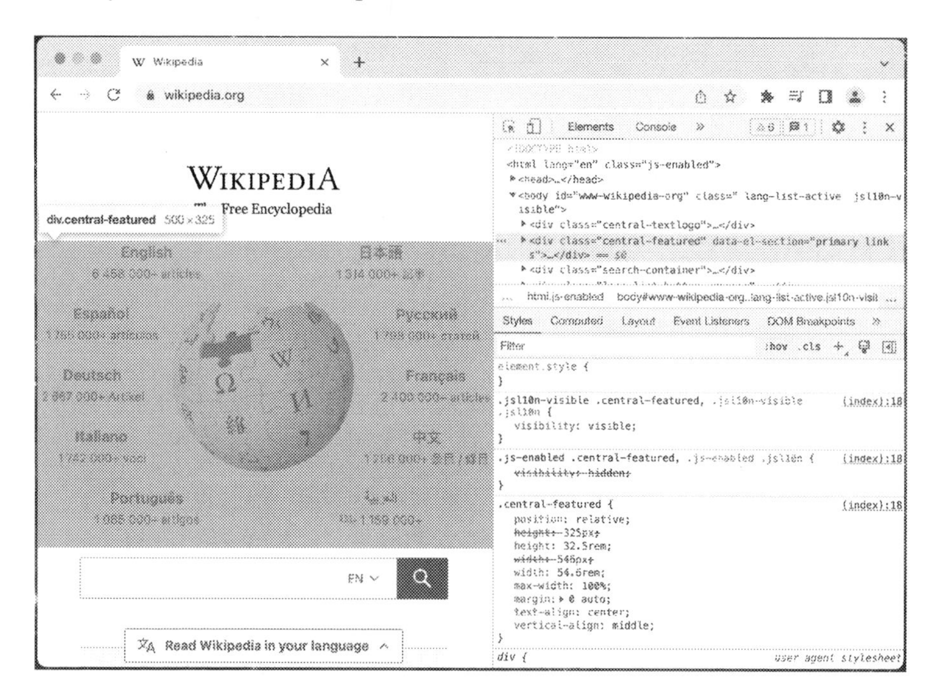

***Figure 10-1.** wikipedia.org with the Google Chrome developer tools opened to the Elements tab*

The developer tools interface is complicated and information dense, so it relies on a hierarchical tabbed interface to break up these views into discrete pieces. Browser extensions can augment this developer tools interface by adding additional tabs. These added tabs are like any other extension-controlled user interface.

Creating a devtools Page

Browser extensions use an unusual strategy for adding extra interfaces to the browser's developer tools. A browser extension has the option to define the devtools_page property inside the manifest. The HTML page referenced will render as a headless page each time the browser's developer tools is opened. This headless page has a single purpose: it will load and execute scripts that use the Devtools API to insert additional interfaces.

The names can be confusing, so it's best to learn by example. Here is a simple extension that provides a devtools page that does nothing:

Example 10-1a. manifest.json

```
{
  "name": "MVX",
  "version": "0.0.1",
  "manifest_version": 3,
  "devtools_page": "devtools.html"
}
```

Example 10-1b. devtools.html

```
<!DOCTYPE html>
<html>
  <body>
    <script src="devtools.js"></script>
  </body>
</html>
```

Example 10-1c. devtools.js

```
// Use this script to access the Devtools API
```

Don't worry about loading this extension, it doesn't do anything yet.

Note The headless devtools page only runs each time the developer tools opens. This means that, when you make changes to the added panels, they will not re-render even if the extension is updated or the page is reloaded. When making updates to devtools pages, you must close and reopen the devtools interface or reload the updated devtools frames.

Adding panels and sidebars

Browser extensions can add two types of interfaces to the developer tools: panels and sidebars. They appear in different places inside the developer tools, but otherwise they behave identically. Both panels and sidebars have access to the same limited subset of the WebExtensions API as content scripts. Additionally, they are allowed to access the Devtools API.

Note Most browser extension interfaces like popups and options pages are created declaratively: the manifest specifies an HTML file path as an entrypoint, and the browser understands how to interpret that and automatically incorporate the new interface. Conversely, devtools pages are created imperatively: to create an interface, you must call methods from the Devtools API and pass in an HTML file path.

Adding a Panel

To add a new panel to the developer tools, use the `chrome.devtools.panels.create()` method. Modify the previous example as follows:

Example 10-2a. foo_panel.html

```
<!DOCTYPE html>
<html>
  <body>
    <h1>I'm the foo panel!</h1>
  </body>
</html>
```

Example 10-2b. devtools.js

```
chrome.devtools.panels.create("Demo Devtools",
                              "",
                              "foo_panel.html");
```

The `create()` method takes a title, an icon URL (here it is left blank), and a panel HTML file. With this extension loaded, close and reopen the developer tools and look to your panel menu. You will notice there is a new option called "Demo Devtools" (Figure 10-2).

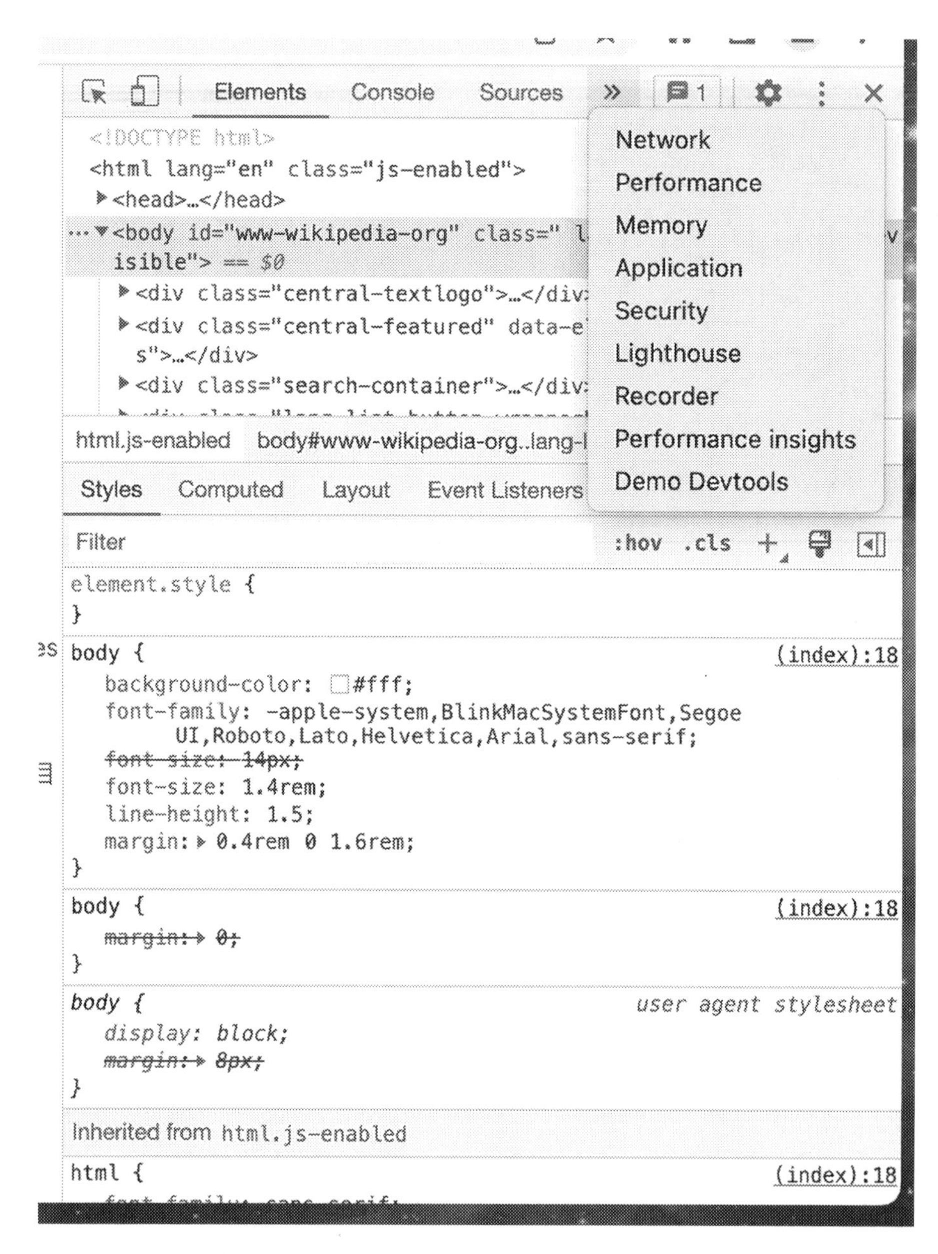

***Figure 10-2.** The added devtools panel*

Click this option to reveal the new panel (Figure 10-3).

Figure 10-3. *The newly added Demo Devtools panel revealed*

Adding a Sidebar

Sidebars are slightly different from panels. Whereas a panel is a top-level interface in the developer tools, sidebars are interfaces that live alongside one of several existing interfaces inside devtools. Currently, there are two interfaces that you can add sidebars to:

- Elements
- Sources

Adding a sidebar is somewhat convoluted. You must call `createSidebarPane()` on the corresponding property for that interface: `elements` or `sources`. The callback for this method is passed the new sidebar pane as an argument, which you can use to add your custom page via the `setPage()` method.

The following example modifies the previous extension to instead add two sidebars: one to the elements interface, and one to the sources interface:

Example 10-3a. devtools.js

```
chrome.devtools.panels.sources.createSidebarPane(
  "Demo Sources Sidebar",
  (sidebar) => {
    sidebar.setPage("sources_sidebar.html");
  }
);

chrome.devtools.panels.elements.createSidebarPane(
  "Demo Elements Sidebar",
  (sidebar) => {
    sidebar.setPage("elements_sidebar.html");
  }
);
```

Example 10-3b. elements_sidebar.html

```
<!DOCTYPE html>
<html>
  <body>
    <h1>I'm the elements sidebar!</h1>
  </body>
</html>
```

Example 10-3c. sources_sidebar.html

```
<!DOCTYPE html>
<html>
  <body>
    <h1>I'm the sources sidebar!</h1>
  </body>
</html>
```

Install this extension, and reopen the developer tools. In the *Elements* and *Sources* tabs, you will see a new child option (Figures 10-4, 10-5, 10-6, and 10-7).

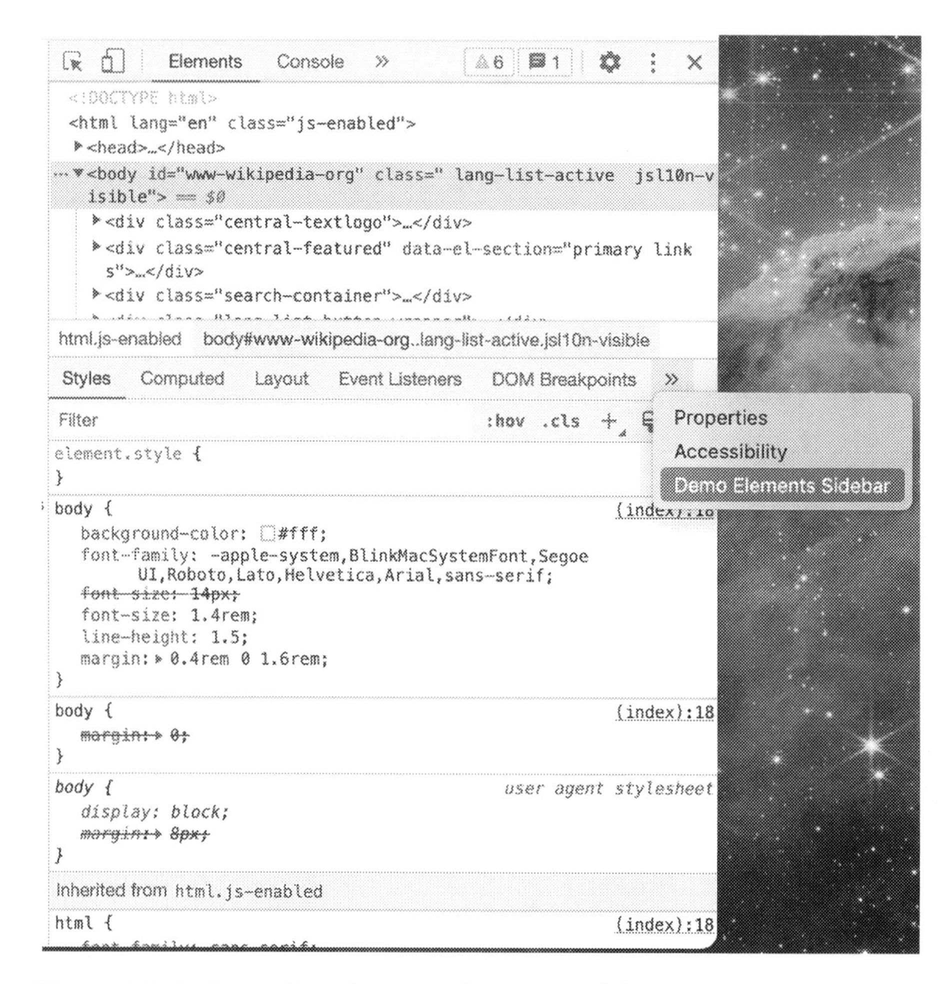

Figure 10-4. *Revealing the new elements sidebar option*

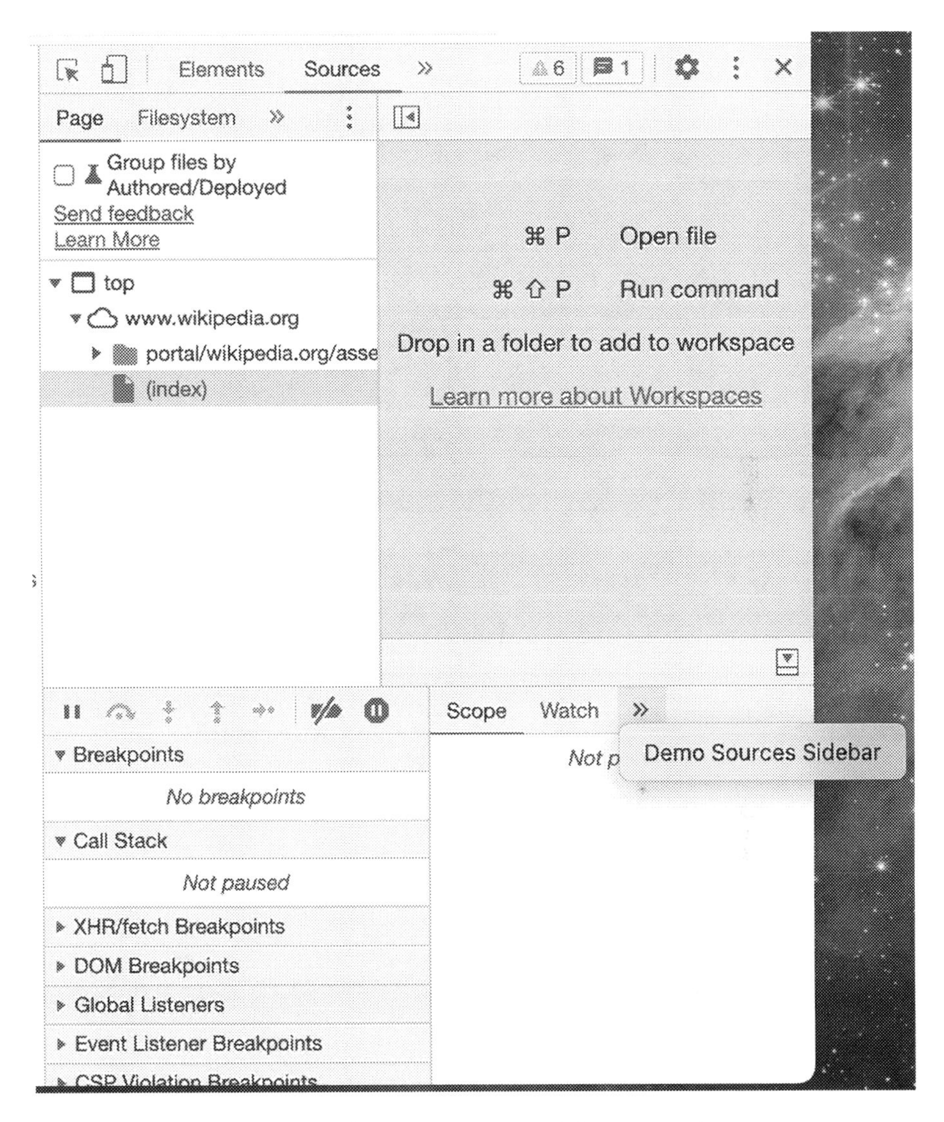

Figure 10-5. *Revealing the new sources sidebar option*

Figure 10-6. *Viewing the new elements sidebar option*

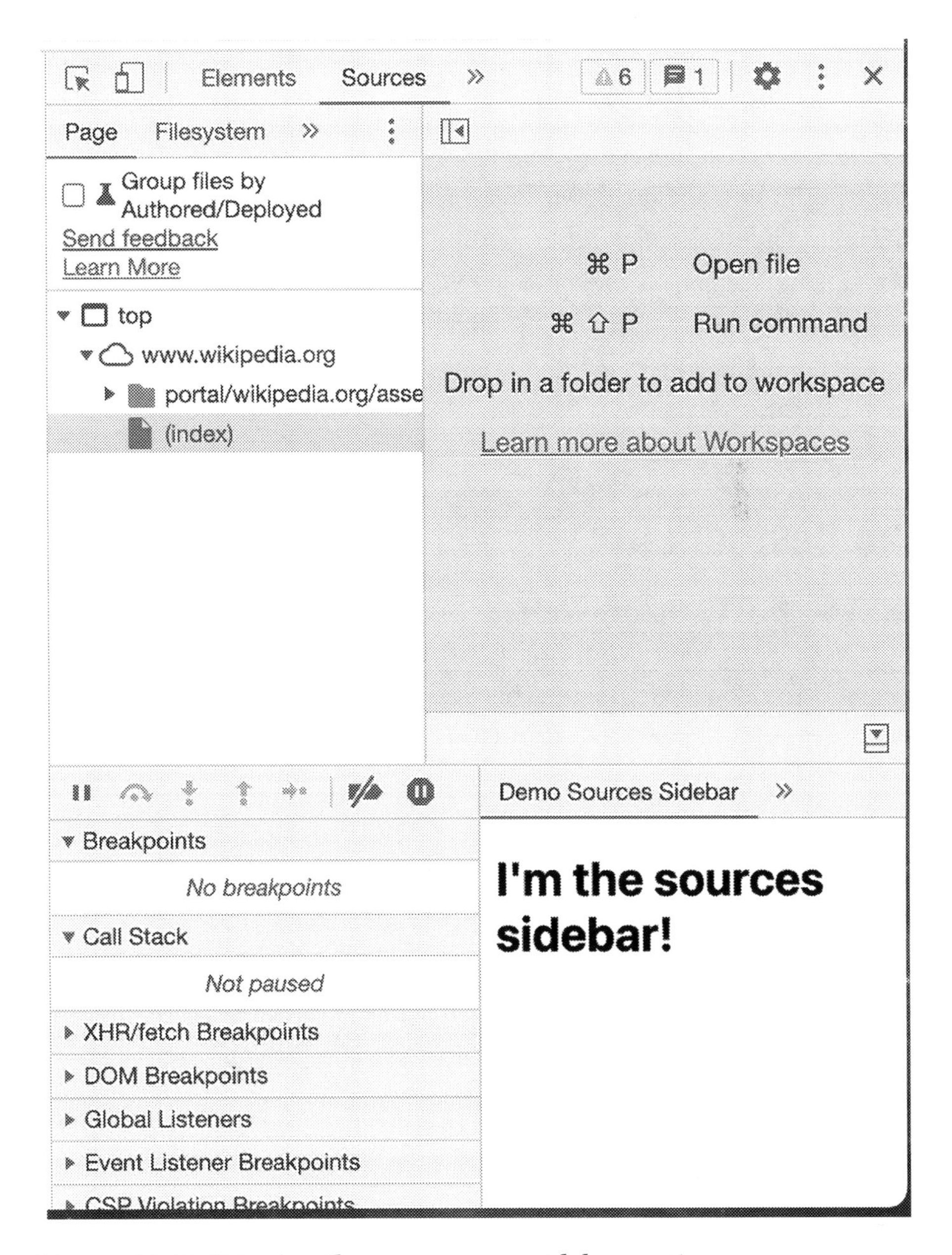

Figure 10-7. *Viewing the new sources sidebar option*

Click these options to view the new sidebar interfaces:

Of course, these views don't do anything useful yet. In the next section, we will cover the special methods these views can access.

Note The panel and sidebar views will re-render the HTML page each time the tab is opened. For example, if you were to click into your custom panel, click over to the Elements tab, and click back over to the original panel, it will have rendered two separate times. Keep this in mind should you need to preserve state.

The Devtools API

The Devtools API is an add-on to the WebExtensions API and only available to extension views inside the developer tools interface. The API contains the following four namespaces:

- `chrome.devtools.panels` is used to programmatically add custom panels and sidebars to the developer tools. These methods are typically called from the headless devtools page that is rendered when the developer tools interface is opened.
- `chrome.devtools.network` is used to sniff the network traffic in this page. It is similar to the `webNavigation` API, but the devtools version records traffic in the HTTP Archive format (HAR).
- `chrome.devtools.inspectedWindow` is used to inspect the current web page in ways that the normal WebExtensions API cannot. It can evaluate JavaScript expressions in the context of the page as well as view a list of resources (such as a document, script, or image) that the current web page is using.

- `chrome.devtools.recorder` is used to customize the developer tools Recorder panel. At the time this book was written, this API was in preview and only supported exporting recorder data.

Note Google Chrome and other chromium-based browsers will fully support the Devtools API. Other browsers like Safari and Firefox may not support these APIs fully.

Sniffing network traffic

Most web developers will be very familiar with the developer tools Network panel. This panel shows extremely detailed real-time information about the active web page's outgoing network requests. A browser extension can tap into this same feed with the Devtools API. The API allows you to access a log of recorded network requests, as well as add handlers for some network request lifecycle events.

The API will provide information about network requests in the HTTP Archive (HAR) format. A truncated example of the HAR format for a GET request to `wikipedia.org` is shown below:

Example HAR data for wikipedia.org GET request

```
{
  "_initiator": {
    "type": "other"
  },
  "_priority": "VeryHigh",
  "_resourceType": "document",
  "cache": {},
  "connection": "769999",
  "pageref": "page_2",
```

```
  "request": {
    "method": "GET",
    "url": "https://www.wikipedia.org/",
    "httpVersion": "http/2.0",
    "headers": [
      {
        "name": ":method",
        "value": "GET"
      },
      {
        "name": ":path",
        "value": "/"
      },
      {
        "name": ":scheme",
        "value": "https"
      },
      ...
    ],
    "queryString": [],
    "cookies": [
      ...
    ],
    "headersSize": -1,
    "bodySize": 0
  },
  "response": {
    "status": 304,
    "statusText": "",
    "httpVersion": "http/2.0",
    "headers": [
```

```
    {
      "name": "content-encoding",
      "value": "gzip"
    },
    {
      "name": "content-type",
      "value": "text/html"
    },
    ...
  ],
  "cookies": [],
  "content": {
    "size": 75189,
    "mimeType": "text/html"
  },
  "redirectURL": "",
  "headersSize": -1,
  "bodySize": 0,
  "_transferSize": 1145,
  "_error": null
},
"serverIPAddress": "208.80.154.224",
"startedDateTime": "2022-08-24T15:28:35.006Z",
"time": 45.61999998986721,
"timings": {
  "blocked": 3.410000022381544,
  "dns": -1,
  "ssl": -1,
  "connect": -1,
  "send": 0.2370000000000001,
  "wait": 41.07399999056011,
```

```
    "receive": 0.8989999769255519,
    "_blocked_queueing": 1.8070000223815441
  }
}
```

For developers who have spent lots of time in the Network panel, you will quickly recognize this as the JSON data dump of all the information displayed in the panel.

The Devtools API only has one method and two events for you to use, but this is sufficient for you to be able to architect your own version of a network inspector. The following example creates a very simple custom network panel:

Example 10-4a. manifest.json

```
{
  "name": "MVX",
  "version": "0.0.1",
  "manifest_version": 3,
  "devtools_page": "devtools.html"
}
```

Example 10-4b. devtools.html

```
<!DOCTYPE html>
<html>
  <body>
    <script src="devtools.js"></script>
  </body>
</html>
```

Example 10-4c. devtools.js

```
chrome.devtools.panels.create("Devtools Traffic", "", "traffic_
panel.html");
```

Example 10-4d. traffic_panel.html

```
<!DOCTYPE html>
<html>
  <head>
    <script src="traffic_panel.js" defer></script>
  </head>
  <body></body>
</html>
```

Example 10-4e. traffic_panel.js

```
function logRequest(har) {
  document.body.innerHTML += `
  <div>
    ${har.request.method} ${har.request.url}
    (${har.response.status})
  </div>`;
}

// One-time call to acquire all the requests accumulated
// so far. This allows you to navigate between
// devtools panels without losing the traffic log.
chrome.devtools.network.getHAR((harLog) => {
  for (let har in harLog.entries) {
    logRequest(har);
  }
});
```

```
// Fires each time the top-level webpage changes URL
chrome.devtools.network.onNavigated.addListener((url) => {
  document.body.innerHTML += `<hr><h1>${url}</h1><hr>`;
});

// Fired each time anything in the webpage
// makes a network request
chrome.devtools.network.onRequestFinished.addListener(
  (har) => logRequest(har));
```

Load this extension, open the developer tools, and select the new “Devtools Traffic” panel. Navigate to any web page and you will see all the requests dump out into this panel, as shown in Figure 10-8.

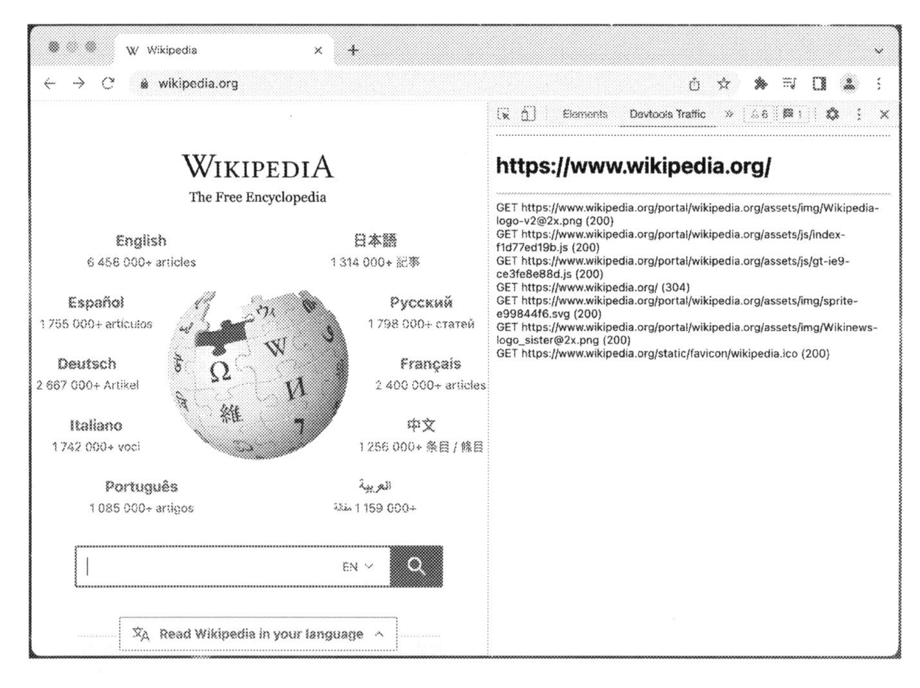

***Figure 10-8.** Custom network panel showing traffic coming from wikipedia.org*

Inspecting the Page

The Devtools API allows you to run JavaScript expressions in the context of the web page using the `eval()` method. This method is very similar to `scripting.executeScript()`: you provide a piece of JavaScript in the local devtools context, it is passed up and evaluated in the remote web page context, and a serializable value can be returned. However, unlike the `scripting.executeScript()` method, `eval()` also provides access to the JavaScript state of the page. Additionally, `eval()` uses string expressions, whereas `executeScript` uses a function object or file reference.

In the *Content Scripts* chapter, we examined how a content script was unable to access the JavaScript state of the host page with an example showing how an injected script could not see the host page's global `jQuery` object. Using the Devtools API, it is now possible to see and interact with the host page's JavaScript state. This behavior is demonstrated in the following example:

Example 10-5a. manifest.json

```
{
  "name": "MVX",
  "version": "0.0.1",
  "manifest_version": 3,
  "devtools_page": "devtools.html"
}
```

Example 10-5b. devtools.html

```
<!DOCTYPE html>
<html>
  <body>
    <script src="devtools.js"></script>
  </body>
</html>
```

Example 10-5c. devtools.js

```
chrome.devtools.panels.create("Devtools Inspector", "",
"inspect_panel.html");
```

Example 10-5d. inspect_panel.html

```
<!DOCTYPE html>
<html>
  <head>
    <script src="inspect_panel.js" defer></script>
  </head>
  <body>
    <button id="check">CHECK FOR JQUERY</button>
  </body>
</html>
```

Example 10-5e. inspect_panel.js

```
document.querySelector("#check").
addEventListener("click", () => {
  chrome.devtools.inspectedWindow.eval(
    `({
      'url': window.location.href,
      'usesJquery': !!window.jQuery
    })`,
    null,
    (result) => {
      const div = document.createElement("div");
      div.innerText = `${result.url} uses jQuery: ${result.
      usesJquery}`;
      document.body.appendChild(div);
```

```
    }
  );
});
```

Load this extension and open the devtools on `jquery.com`, which has a `jQuery` global object, and `wikipedia.org`, which does not (Figure 10-9). Clicking the button on each site will accurately record inside the devtools panel whether or not the site uses jQuery.

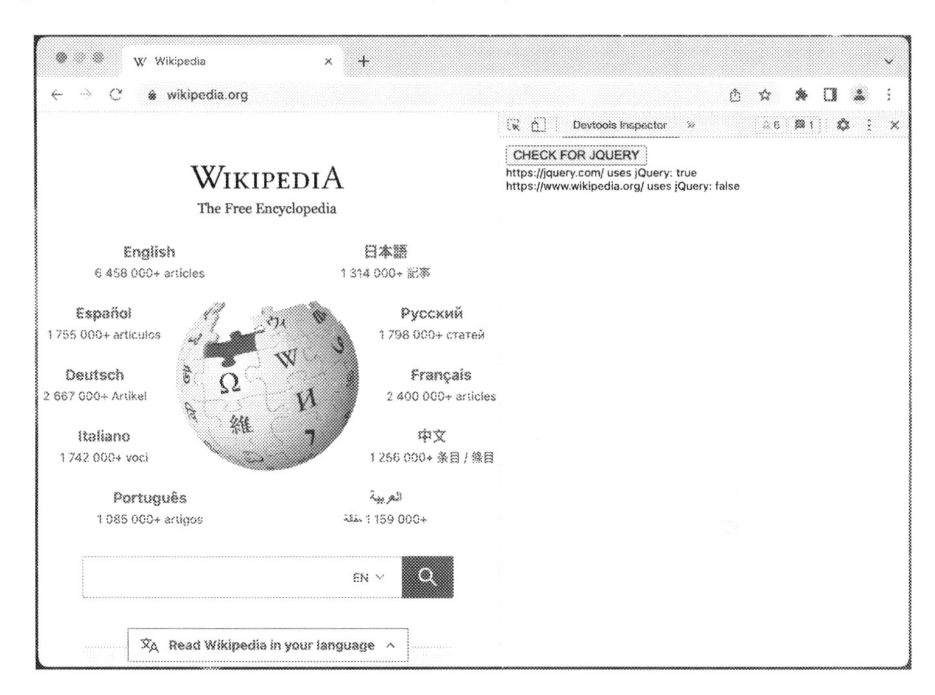

***Figure 10-9.** Inspecting the host page's JavaScript state*

For complicated expressions, you can use an instantaneously invoked function expression (IIFE) that returns a value. The previous expression could be refactored to use an IIFE:

```
chrome.devtools.inspectedWindow.eval(
  `(() => {
    const url = window.location.href;
```

```
      const usesJquery = !!window.jQuery;
      return { url, usesJquery };
    })()`,
  ...
)
```

JavaScript expressions passed to `eval()` also have access to the browser's console API, so special console values and methods such as `$0` and `inspect()` can be used. These are especially useful when used in a sidebar that extends the Elements interface because direct integration with the Element panel's DOM tree explorer is possible. The following example does exactly this:

Example 10-6a. manifest.json

```
{
  "name": "MVX",
  "version": "0.0.1",
  "manifest_version": 3,
  "devtools_page": "devtools.html"
}
```

Example 10-6b. devtools.html

```
<!DOCTYPE html>
<html>
  <body>
    <script src="devtools.js"></script>
  </body>
</html>
```

Example 10-6c. devtools.js

```
chrome.devtools.panels.elements.createSidebarPane(
  "Devtools Inspector",
  (sidebar) => {
    sidebar.setPage("inspect_panel.html");
  }
);
```

Example 10-6d. inspect_panel.html

```
<!DOCTYPE html>
<html>
  <head>
    <script src="inspect_panel.js" defer></script>
  </head>
  <body>
    <button id="inspect">INSPECT IMG</button>
    <button id="tagname">ACTIVE TAG NAME</button>
  </body>
</html>
```

Example 10-6e. inspect_panel.js

```
document.querySelector("#inspect").
addEventListener("click", () => {
  chrome.devtools.inspectedWindow.eval(
    `inspect(document.querySelector('img'))`
  );
});

document.querySelector("#tagname").addEventListener("click",
  () => {
    chrome.devtools.inspectedWindow.eval(
```

```
      `$0?.tagName`,
      null,
      (result) => {
        const div = document.createElement("div");
        div.innerText = result;
        document.body.appendChild(div);
      });
  }
);
```

Load this extension, open the developer tools, select the Elements tab, and open the Devtools Inspector sidebar.

In this example, the “INSPECT IMG” button is calling `inspect()` on the first image to appear in the document. Because this is called from a sidebar inside the Elements panel, you will see this immediately reflected in the native browser’s DOM inspector (Figure 10-10).

***Figure 10-10.** Programmatically inspecting the page's image*

Clicking the ACTIVE TAG NAME button will use the $0 token to reference whichever DOM inspector node was last inspected and print its tag name (Figure 10-11).

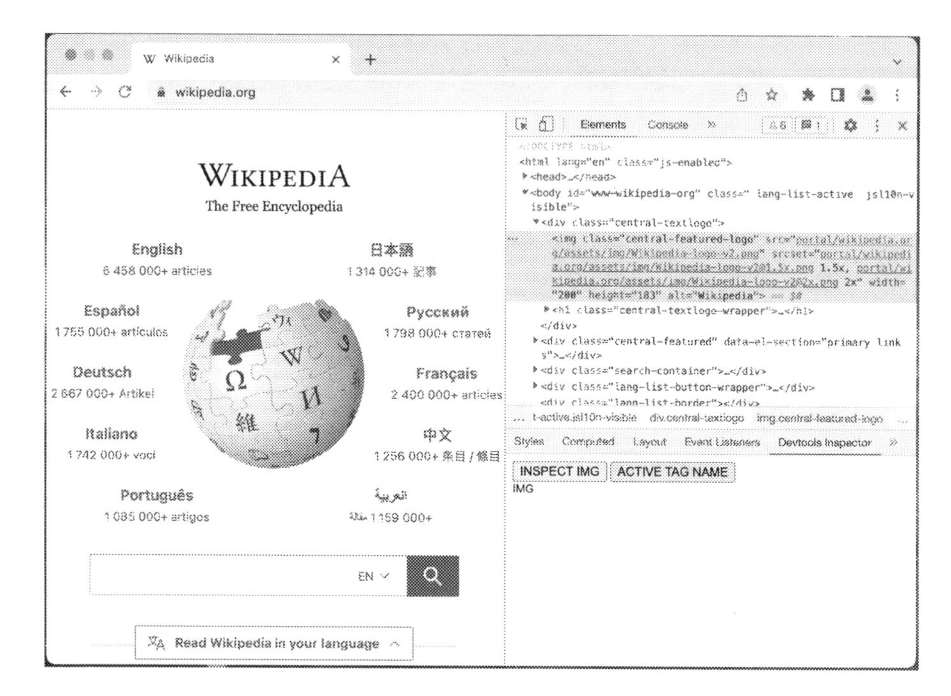

Figure 10-11. *Accessing the selected DOM node's tag name*

This bi-directional integration with the native browser allows you to build sophisticated devtools pages that can quickly direct the user around the page.

Content Scripts and Devtools Messaging

Typically, devtools pages are most useful when they can coordinate with content scripts injected into the page. Each component has its own responsibilities: the devtools pages are responsible for interacting with the Devtools API, the content scripts are responsible for managing page overlays and similar widgets, and the two can coordinate via messaging. The problems with this strategy are twofold:

- Although the Devtools API can access the host page's tab ID via `chrome.devtools.inspectedWindow.tabId`, it cannot use `chrome.tabs.sendMessage()` to dispatch a message to that specific tab.
- When sending messages from the content script to devtools, you must account for scenarios where there are multiple developer tools interfaces open simultaneously. Content scripts have no direct way of dispatching a message to only that page's devtools panel.

There are a handful of clever strategies to solve these issues:

- `runtime.sendMessage()` can solve the problem of the devtools page messaging the content script. The devtools page can include the tabID, and the content script can filter by the page's tab ID. The content script can then respond directly to that message, which will only be seen by the original devtools. To establish a pseudo-bidirectional channel, the content script can queue up messages, and the devtools page can intermittently poll.
- The devtools page establishes a long-lived connection with the background page. The background page manages a map of tab IDs to connections, so it can route each message to the correct connection.
- The devtools page combines an injected script with a content script that acts as an intermediary. It then uses `window.postMessage()` to pass messages to the content script.

Tip The Google Chrome team has an excellent writeup on this here: `https://developer.chrome.com/docs/extensions/mv3/devtools/#solutions`.

Other Devtools API Features

In addition to the examples shown in this chapter, the Devtools API includes some other interesting features:

- Devtools pages can evaluate `eval()` expressions as an extension content script using the `useContentScriptContext` option. This is useful to exchange data with the content script as well as access the WebExtensions API in the context of the page.
- Devtools pages are able to inspect which resources (documents, stylesheets, scripts, images, etc.) the page is currently using via `chrome.devtools.inspectedWindow.getResources()`, as well as listen for changes in those resources via the `onResourceAdded` and `onResourceContentCommitted` events.
- Devtools pages are able to force the page to reload with `chrome.devtools.inspectedWindow.reload()`. This `reload()` method also allows you to ignore the browser cache, inject custom scripts upon the next load, and spoof the user agent.

- Devtools pages can define a plugin to export Recorder data via `chrome.devtools.recorder.registerRecorderExtensionPlugin()`. For more information on the Recorder panel, see here: `https://developer.chrome.com/docs/devtools/recorder/`

Summary

In this chapter, you learned about how an extension can extend the browser's native developer tools interface. We went through the unusual way that an extension injects user interfaces into the developer tools, as well as all the major features of the Devtools API that only devtools pages have access to.

In the next chapter, we will cover all the major WebExtensions APIs and how they can be used.

CHAPTER 11

Extension and Browser APIs

The WebExtensions API is the secret sauce of browser extensions. It allows them to reach into the web page and the browser to make changes, inspect and modify network traffic, and control aspects of the native browser's user interface.

Global API Namespace

All extensions are accessible from inside the global API namespace. This is either available via the `chrome.*` namespace, or the `browser.*` namespace.

- Chromium browsers and Safari favor the `chrome.*` namespace
- Firefox favors the `browser.*` namespace

All browsers support the `chrome.*` namespace, so prefer to use that in all extensions.

M. Frisbie, *Building Browser Extensions*, https://doi.org/10.1007/978-1-4842-8725-5_11

Promises vs. Callbacks

The WebExtensions API was written before async/await was an industry standard. The initial API implementation used callbacks to support asynchronous code execution. For example, the following snippet executes a callback after a message response is received:

```
chrome.runtime.sendMessage("msg", (response) => {
  console.log("Received a response!", response);
});
```

To align with modern coding conventions, most browsers have retrofitted their API methods to support both callbacks and promises. The above snippet can be refactored to use async/await:

```
const response = await chrome.runtime.sendMessage("msg");
console.log("Received a response!", response);
```

There are some things to know about making this change:

- Not all API methods have been adapted to support promises. Check your browser's documentation to see if it is supported. Callbacks will always work.
- For each method call, only use a callback or a promise, never both.
- Mozilla's webextension-polyfill (https://github.com/mozilla/webextension-polyfill) can be used to augment the WebExtensions API methods to be promise-based irrespective of the host browser's implementation.

Error Handling

Errors thrown from WebExtensions API methods must be handled differently based on your usage. If you use callbacks, when the method fails the `chrome.runtime.lastError` property will be defined only inside the callback handler:

```
chrome.tabs.executeScript(tabId, details, () => {
  if (chrome.runtime.lastError) {
    // Error handling here
  }
})
```

If you use `async/await`, the error can be caught with a `.catch()` or `try/catch` block:

```
chrome.tabs.executeScript(tabId, details).catch((e) => {
  // Error handling here
})

// or

try {
  await chrome.tabs.executeScript(tabId, details);
} catch(e) {
  // Error handling here
}
```

Context-restricted APIs

Not all APIs can be used everywhere:

- Some APIs such as `tabCapture` and `fileSystem` are restricted to the foreground, meaning they cannot be accessed from a background service worker.

- The Devtools API can only be used in a devtools context.

Events API

The "Events API" refers to the general pattern of how you can add event listeners to events fired in browser extensions. Most WebExtensions APIs utilize this format.

Format

Each event type has an interface to add, remove, and inspect listeners. For example, the `chrome.runtime.onMessage` interface has the following methods:

- `chrome.runtime.onMessage.addListener()`
- `chrome.runtime.onMessage.dispatch()`
- `chrome.runtime.onMessage.hasListener()`
- `chrome.runtime.onMessage.hasListeners()`
- `chrome.runtime.onMessage.removeListener()`

Warning `dispatch()` can be used to forcibly dispatch an event, but it is not documented and therefore should not be relied upon.

These methods are shared by all event interfaces. `addListener()` is used to attach a handler function to run when an event is fired, and `hasListener()`, `hasListeners()`, and `removeListener()` are used to view and remove that same function.

The following example uses several of these methods to handle toolbar icon button clicks:

Example 11-1a. manifest.json

```
{
  "name": "MVX",
  "version": "0.0.1",
  "manifest_version": 3,
  "background": {
    "service_worker": "background.js",
    "type": "module"
  },
  "action": {},
  "permissions": []
}
```

Example 11-1b. background.js

```
let count = 0;

function handler() {
  console.log("Handler executed!");

  if (++count > 4) {
    chrome.action.onClicked.removeListener(handler);
  }
}

// false
console.log(chrome.action.onClicked.hasListener(handler));

chrome.action.onClicked.addListener(handler);

// true
console.log(chrome.action.onClicked.hasListener(handler));
```

This example sets a listener for onClicked events, listens for five events, and then de-registers itself.

Event Filtering

If you wished to restrict an event handler to a certain domain, you would need to perform filtering inside the handler:

```
chrome.webNavigation.onCommitted.addListener((event) => {
  if (!event.url.match(/^https:\/\/*.wikipedia\.org/)) {
    return;
  }

  // Handle filtered event
});
```

Instead, you can instruct the browser to declaratively filter events that match certain URLs. The browser natively performing this filtering will give a considerable performance boost. The above code can be refactored as follows:

```
chrome.webNavigation.onCommitted.addListener((event) => {
  // Handle filtered event
}, {
  url: [
    { hostSuffix: "wikipedia.org" }
  ]
});
```

WebExtensions API Quick Reference

This section is a comprehensive list of extension APIs. Each API includes a short snippet demonstrating common usage and links to the full documentation.

Tip The companion extension to this book, *Browser Extension Explorer*, has interactive demos and source code for most of these APIs. Get it here: https://buildbrowserextensions.com/b2x

---

Permissions

- Permissions API - Chrome Developers: https://developer.chrome.com/docs/extensions/reference/permissions/
- Permissions API - MDN: https://developer.mozilla.org/en-US/docs/Web/API/Permissions_API

The chrome.permissions API allows you to inspect current permissions and add or remove permissions. You can also add handlers that fire when permissions are added or removed.

```
chrome.action.onClicked.addListener(() => {
  // Can only request permissions after user action
  const permissionsGranted =
    await chrome.permissions.request({
      permissions: ['tabs']
    });
});
```

```
const hasPermissions = await chrome.permissions.contains({
  permissions: ['tabs']
};
```

Messaging

- Chrome Messaging Overview – Chrome Developers: `https://developer.chrome.com/docs/extensions/mv3/messaging/`
- `runtime` API – Chrome Developers: `https://developer.chrome.com/docs/extensions/reference/runtime/`
- `runtime` API – MDN: `https://developer.mozilla.org/en-US/docs/Mozilla/Add-ons/WebExtensions/API/runtime/`
- `tabs` API – Chrome Developers: `https://developer.chrome.com/docs/extensions/reference/tabs/`
- `tabs` API – MDN: `https://developer.mozilla.org/en-US/docs/Mozilla/Add-ons/WebExtensions/API/tabs/`

The extension messaging API is used to send messages between parts of the extension, or between the extension and an outside entity (such as another extension, the active web page, or an outside program).

One-off Messages

The `chrome.runtime.sendMessage()` method can be used to send single messages between extension components. It can only be used to send messages *from* a content script. Listeners can send a message back inside the message handler.

```
// Sender
chrome.runtime.sendMessage(msg, (response) => {
  // Handle response
});
```

```
// Receiver
chrome.runtime.onMessage.addListener((msg, sender,
sendResponse) => {
  // Handle initial message from sender
  sendResponse(responseMsg);
});
```

To send a one-off message to a specific content script, you must instead use `chrome.tabs.sendMessage()` and specify the `tabId`:

```
// Sender
chrome.tabs.sendMessage(tabId, msg, (response) => {
  // Handle response
});

// Receiver (content script)
chrome.runtime.onMessage.addListener((msg, sender,
sendResponse) => {
  // Handle initial message from sender
  sendResponse(responseMsg);
});
```

Opening Message Ports

Persistent message ports can be opened to connect two extension components that will be sending a large volume of message back and forth. It can only be used to connect a port *from* a content script.

```
// Endpoint 1
const port1 = chrome.runtime.connect({name: "portName"});
// Outgoing
port1.postMessage(msg);
// Incoming
port1.onMessage.addListener((msg) => {});
```

```
// Endpoint 2
let port2 = null;
chrome.runtime.onConnect.addListener((p) => {
  port2 = p;
});
// Outgoing
port2.postMessage(msg);
// Incoming
port2.onMessage.addListener((msg) => {});
```

To connect a port to specific content script, you must instead use `chrome.tabs.connect()` and specify the `tabId`:

```
// Endpoint 1
const port1 = chrome.tabs.connect(tabId, {name: "portName"});
// Outgoing
port1.postMessage(msg);
// Incoming
port1.onMessage.addListener((msg) => {});

// Endpoint 2 (content script)
let port2 = null;
chrome.runtime.onConnect.addListener((p) => {
  port2 = p;
});
// Outgoing
port2.postMessage(msg);
// Incoming
port2.onMessage.addListener((msg) => {});
```

Messaging Native Applications

Extensions can exchange messages with native applications. If the name of the native application is known (e.g., `com.my_company.my_application`), the extension can target it in a similar way to content scripts:

```
chrome.runtime.sendNativeMessage(
  applicationName, msg, (response) => {});
```

```
chrome.tabs.connectNative(
  applicationName, {name: "portName"});
```

An example of this is shown in the *Cross-Browser Extensions* chapter. Safari extensions use native messaging to connect the extension to the native iOS or macOS app.

Messaging Other Extensions

To send a one-off message to another extension, you can pass the extension's ID to `chrome.runtime.sendMessage()`:

```
// Sender
chrome.runtime.sendMessage(extensionId, msg, (response) => {
  // Handle response
});
```

```
// Receiver (foreign extension)
chrome.runtime.onMessageExternal.addListener((msg, sender,
sendResponse) => {
  // Handle initial message from sender
  sendResponse(responseMsg);
});
```

To connect a port to another extension, you can use `chrome.runtime.connect()` and specify the `extensionId`:

```
// Extension 1
const port1 = chrome.runtime.connect(extensionId, {name:
"portName"});
// Outgoing
port1.postMessage(msg);
// Incoming
port1.onMessage.addListener((msg) => {});

// Extension2
let port2 = null;
chrome.runtime.onConnectExternal.addListener((p) => {
  port2 = p;
});
// Outgoing
port2.postMessage(msg);
// Incoming
port2.onMessage.addListener((msg) => {});
```

This method also allows for regular web pages (not content scripts) to send messages to your extension in the exact same way. The API is exposed in the web page's JavaScript runtime, and your extension can receive messages if the following conditions are true:

- The host page knows the ID of your extension and passes it to `runtime.connect()` or `runtime.sendMessage()`
- Your extension whitelists the web page URL under the manifest's `externally_connectable` field

Storage

- storage API – Chrome Developers: https://developer.chrome.com/docs/extensions/reference/storage/
- storage API – MDN: https://developer.mozilla.org/en-US/docs/Mozilla/Add-ons/WebExtensions/API/storage

The extension storage API is a simple but powerful key/value storage. There are four main storage options you can use:

- `storage.local` stores values only on the local browser
- `storage.sync` stores values that are shared between the authenticated browser session
- `storage.session` stores values in memory that will be discarded when the browser closes
- `storage.managed` is a read-only store intended for enterprise users

`local`, `sync`, and `session` all share the following:

- With only the `storage` permission, default maximum storage size for each is 5 MB. This limit can be removed with the additional `unlimitedStorage` permission.
- Each features only a `get()` and `set()` method. These methods are asynchronous, and both can read and write in parallel.
- You can listen for changes to each by setting an `onChanged` handler.
- Plain JavaScript objects can be stored and retrieved as-is, there is no need to serialize/deserialize.

The following example shows a parallelized get/set and onChanged handler:

```
chrome.storage.onChanged.addListener(console.log);

await chrome.storage.local.set({ foo: "tmp" });
// { foo: { newValue "tmp" } }

await chrome.storage.local.set({ foo: "bar", baz: "qux" });
// {
//   foo: { oldValue: "tmp", newValue "bar" }
//   baz: { newValue "qux" }
// }

console.log(await chrome.storage.local.get(["foo", "baz"]));
// { foo: "bar", baz: "qux" }
```

Authentication

- identity API – Chrome Developers: https://developer.chrome.com/docs/extensions/reference/identity/
- identity API – MDN: https://developer.mozilla.org/en-US/docs/Mozilla/Add-ons/WebExtensions/API/identity

The chrome.identity API is used to manage authentication state and OAuth flows. Google Chrome supports extra methods that allow for native authentication inside the browser. All browsers support the use of launchWebAuthFlow for generic OAuth flows.

```
// Native browser OAuth
chrome.identity.getAuthToken(
  { interactive: true },
```

```
  (token) => {
    if (token) {
      const info = await chrome.identity.getProfileUserInfo(
        { accountStatus: "ANY" }
      );
    }
  }
);

// Supports generic OAuth
chrome.identity.launchWebAuthFlow(
  {
    url: authUrl,
    interactive: true,
  },
  (redirectUrl) => {
    if (redirectUrl) {
    }
  }
}
```

Note This API is covered in depth in the *Networking* chapter.

Network Requests

- declarativeNetRequest API – Chrome Developers: https://developer.chrome.com/docs/extensions/reference/declarativeNetRequest/

- `webRequest` API – Chrome Developers: `https://developer.chrome.com/docs/extensions/reference/webRequest/`
- `webRequest` API – MDN: `https://developer.mozilla.org/en-US/docs/Mozilla/Add-ons/WebExtensions/API/webRequest`
- `webNavigation` API – Chrome Developers: `https://developer.chrome.com/docs/extensions/reference/webNavigation/`
- `webNavigation` API – MDN: `https://developer.mozilla.org/en-US/docs/Mozilla/Add-ons/WebExtensions/API/webNavigation`

The network request APIs include `declarativeNetRequest`, `webRequest`, and `webNavigation`:

- `declarativeNetRequest` is used to declaratively instruct the browser to manage page traffic according to a set of rules defined by the extension.
- `webRequest` is used to imperatively control page traffic with JavaScript handlers
- `webNavigation` is used to inspect tab-level navigation events

```
// Using DNR to block traffic to wikipedia.org
chrome.declarativeNetRequest.updateDynamicRules({
  addRules: [{
    id: 1,
    priority: 1,
    action: {
      type: "block"
```

```
    },
    condition: {
      urlFilter: "https://www.wikpedia.org",
    },
  }]
});

// Using webRequest to block traffic to wikipedia.org
chrome.webRequest.onBeforeRequest.addListener(
  (details) => {
    return {
      cancel: true
    };
  },
  { urls: ["*://www.wikipedia.org/*"] },
  ["blocking"]
);

// Log all tab traffic with webNavigation
chrome.webNavigation.onCompleted.addListener((details) => {
  console.log(details.url);
});
```

Note These APIs are covered in depth in the *Networking* chapter.

Internationalization

- i18n API - Chrome Developers: https://developer.chrome.com/docs/extensions/reference/i18n/

- i18n API – MDN: https://developer.mozilla.org/en-US/docs/Mozilla/Add-ons/WebExtensions/API/i18n

The chrome.i18n API allows you to determine system languages as well as read messages out of your _locales/_code_/messages.json files. The following example reads the active system language and retrieves a message from that language:

```
chrome.i18n.getUILanguage();

chrome.i18n.getMessage("foo_message");
```

Browser and System Control

The WebExtensions API offers a number of methods for inspecting and controlling the host system or UI.

Power

- power API – Chrome Developers: https://developer.chrome.com/docs/extensions/reference/power/

The chrome.power API allows the extension to prevent the host system from going to sleep.

```
// Keeps the system active,
// but allows the screen to be dimmed or turned off.
chrome.power.requestKeepAwake("system");

// Keeps the screen and system active
chrome.power.requestKeepAwake("display");

// Allows the host to behave normally
chrome.power.releaseKeepAwake();
```

Omnibox

- omnibox API – Chrome Developers: https://developer.chrome.com/docs/extensions/reference/omnibox/
- omnibox API – MDN: https://developer.mozilla.org/en-US/docs/Mozilla/Add-ons/WebExtensions/API/omnibox

The chrome.omnibox API allows you to embed a special search interface into the browser's URL bar (Figure 11-1). You can control the keywork that triggers the interface, which results appear, how the results are presented, and what happens when a result is selected.

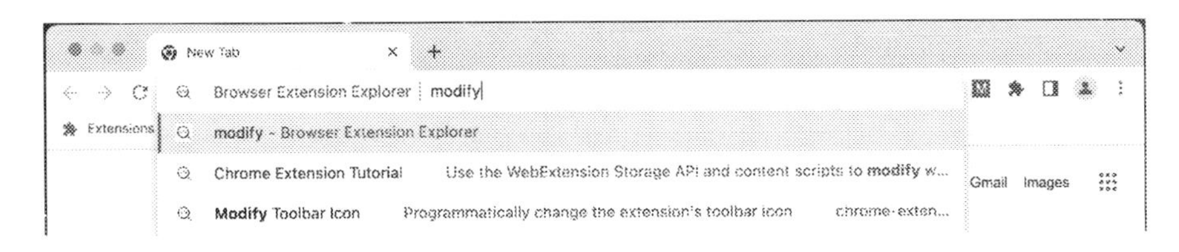

Figure 11-1. *Example omnibox results*

The following example populates the omnibar with a suggestion list, filtered by text match. If one is selected, it navigates to the URL.

```
const suggestions = [
  {
    content: url1,
    description: `
      ${title1}
      <dim>${subtitle1}</dim>
      <url>${url1}</url>`,
  },
  {
```

```
    content: url2,
    description: `
      ${title2}
      <dim>${subtitle2}</dim>
      <url>${url2}</url>`,
  }
];

chrome.omnibox.onInputChanged.addListener(
  (text, suggest) => {
    suggest(suggestions.filter(s => s.content.includes(text))
  }
);

chrome.omnibox.onInputEntered.addListener(
  (text, disposition) => {
    // Navigate to selected url
    chrome.tabs.update(activeTabId, { url: text });
  });
```

Action

- action API – Chrome Developers: `https://developer.chrome.com/docs/extensions/reference/action/`
- action API – MDN: `https://developer.mozilla.org/en-US/docs/Mozilla/Add-ons/WebExtensions/API/action`

The `chrome.action` API allows you to control the extension toolbar icon, including appearance, title text, badge content, badge color, popup page, and click handlers (Figure 11-2).

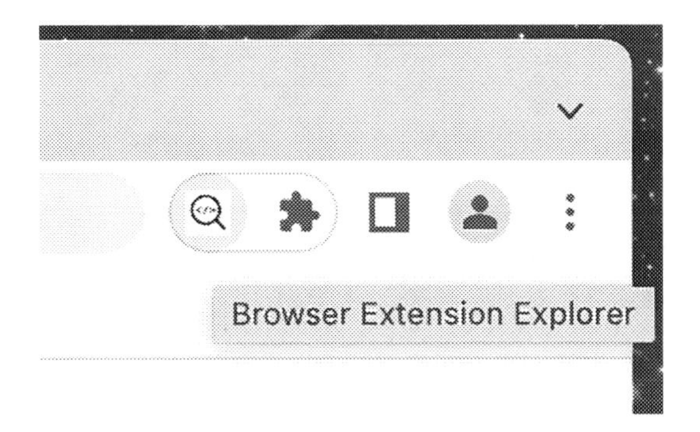

Figure 11-2. The toolbar icon button showing the title text

```
chrome.action.onClicked.addListener(() => {})
```

```
chrome.action.setTitle({ title: "foo"});
```

```
chrome.action.setBadgeText({ title: "bar"});
```

```
chrome.action.setPopup({
  popup: chrome.runtime.getURL("new_popup.html")
});
```

Notifications

- `notifications` API – Chrome Developers: `https://developer.chrome.com/docs/extensions/reference/notifications/`
- `notifications` API – MDN: `https://developer.mozilla.org/en-US/docs/Mozilla/Add-ons/WebExtensions/API/notifications`

The `chrome.notification` API allows an extension to display rich notifications to the user using the host operating system's notification mechanism (Figure 11-3).

Figure 11-3. *An example extension notification*

```
chrome.notifications.create(
  "NOTIFICATION_ID",
  {
    type: "basic",
    iconUrl: "/img.png",
    title: "My notification!",
    message: "This is the message",
    priority: 2
  }
);
```

Context Menu

- `contextMenus` API – Chrome Developers: `https://developer.chrome.com/docs/extensions/reference/contextMenus/`
- `menus` API – MDN: `https://developer.mozilla.org/en-US/docs/Mozilla/Add-ons/WebExtensions/API/menus`

The `chrome.contextMenus` API allows an extension to add interactive options to right click and context menus throughout the browser (Figure 11-4).

***Figure 11-4.** An expanded extension context menu*

```
chrome.contextMenus.create({
  id: "demo-radio",
  title: "Select a radio button...",
  contexts: ["all"],
});

for (let i of [1, 2, 3, 4, 5]) {
  chrome.contextMenus.create({
    id: `demo-radio-${i}`,
    parentId: "demo-radio",
    title: `Radio ${i}`,
    contexts: ["all"],
    type: "radio",
  });
}
```

```
chrome.contextMenus.create({
  id: "demo-media",
  title: "You right clicked a media element",
  contexts: ["image", "video", "audio"],
});

chrome.contextMenus.onClicked.addListener((info, tab) => {});
```

Page and Screen Capture

- pageCapture API – Chrome Developers: https://developer.chrome.com/docs/extensions/reference/pageCapture/
- tabCapture API – Chrome Developers: https://developer.chrome.com/docs/extensions/reference/tabCapture/
- tabCapture API – MDN: https://developer.mozilla.org/en-US/docs/Mozilla/Add-ons/WebExtensions/API/tabs/captureTab
- desktopCapture API – Chrome Developers: https://developer.chrome.com/docs/extensions/reference/desktopCapture/
- captureVisibleTab API – Chrome Developers: https://developer.chrome.com/docs/extensions/reference/tabs/#method-captureVisibleTab
- captureVisibleTab API – MDN: https://developer.mozilla.org/en-US/docs/Mozilla/Add-ons/WebExtensions/API/tabs/captureVisibleTab

Extensions are able to capture the system's current state in a handful of different ways: by saving the HTML, taking images of the active tab, or capturing media from the current desktop.

```
// Save a specific tab as MHTML
chrome.pageCapture.saveAsMHTML(
  {
    tabId: 123
  }
)

// Captures the visible area of the currently active tab.
chrome.action.onClicked.addListener(() => {
  chrome.tabCapture.capture(
    { video: true },
    (stream) => {}
  );
});

// Captures content of screen, individual windows or tabs.
chrome.desktopCapture.chooseDesktopMedia(
  sources: ["screen"],
  (streamId, options) => {}
);

// Captures the visible area of the currently active tab
// in the specified window.
chrome.tabs.captureVisibleTab(
  (dataUrl) =>{}
);
```

Proxy

- proxy API - Chrome Developers: `https://developer.chrome.com/docs/extensions/reference/proxy/`
- proxy API - MDN: `https://developer.mozilla.org/en-US/docs/Mozilla/Add-ons/WebExtensions/API/proxy`

Use the `chrome.proxy` API to manage the browser's proxy settings.

Note Per MDN: *Google Chrome provides an extension API also called "proxy" which is functionally similar to this API, in that extensions can use it to implement a proxying policy. However, the design of the Chrome API is completely different to this API. Because this API is incompatible with the Chrome proxy API, this API is only available through the browser namespace.*

```
chrome.proxy.settings.set(
  {
    value: {
      mode: "fixed_servers",
      rules: {
        proxyForHttp: {
          scheme: "socks5",
          host: "192.168.1.2",
        },
        bypassList: ["wikipedia.org"],
      },
    },
    scope: "regular",
```

```
  },
  () => {}
);
```

Browser State Management

The WebExtensions API gives you a broad set of tools for managing the state of the user's browser.

Font Settings

- fontSettings API – Chrome Developers: https://developer.chrome.com/docs/extensions/reference/fontSettings/

The API allows an extension to manage for some font settings to depend on certain generic font families and language scripts.

```
chrome.fontSettings.getFont(
  { genericFamily: 'standard', script: 'Egyp' },
  (details) => {}
);

chrome.fontSettings.setFont(
  { genericFamily: 'serif', script: 'Jpan',
    fontId: 'Comic Sans' }
);
```

Content Settings

- contentSettings API – Chrome Developers: https://developer.chrome.com/docs/extensions/reference/contentSettings/

This API allows you to customize the browser's behavior on a per-site basis instead of globally: enabling or disabling cookies, JavaScript, and plugins. Each of the following properties has a `get()`, `set()`, and `clear()` method:

- `automaticDownloads`
- `camera`
- `cookies`
- `fullscreen`
- `images`
- `javascript`
- `location`
- `microphone`
- `mouselock`
- `notifications`
- `plugins`
- `popups`
- `unsandboxedPlugins`

Cookies

- cookies API – Chrome Developers: `https://developer.chrome.com/docs/extensions/reference/cookies/`
- cookies API – MDN: `https://developer.mozilla.org/en-US/docs/Mozilla/Add-ons/WebExtensions/API/cookies`

The chrome.cookies API is a create/read/update/destroy interface for the browser's cookies.

```
const cookies = await chrome.cookies.getAll();

chrome.cookies.set({
    "name": "foo",
    "url": "https://www.wikipedia.org",
    "value": "bar"
});

chrome.cookies.remove(
    "name": "foo",
    "url": "https://www.wikipedia.org"
});

chrome.cookies.onChanged.addListener(() => {});
```

Bookmarks

- bookmarks API – Chrome Developers: https://developer.chrome.com/docs/extensions/reference/bookmarks/
- bookmarks API – MDN: https://developer.mozilla.org/en-US/docs/Mozilla/Add-ons/WebExtensions/API/bookmarks

The chrome.bookmarks API is a create/read/update/destroy interface for the browser's bookmarks. It includes methods to manage the hierarchical nature of bookmarks.

```
chrome.bookmarks.create(
  {'title': 'Wikipedia', 'url': 'https://www.wikipedia.org'}
);
```

```
const allBookmarks = await chrome.bookmarks.getTree();

const matchingNodes =
  await chrome.bookmarks.search({ query: 'wikipedia' });
```

History

- history API – Chrome Developers: https://developer.chrome.com/docs/extensions/reference/history/
- history API – MDN: https://developer.mozilla.org/en-US/docs/Mozilla/Add-ons/WebExtensions/API/history

The chrome.history API is a create/read/update/destroy interface for the browser's browsing history.

```
chrome.history.deleteAll();

const allPages = await chrome.history.search();

// Wikipedia pages in last 30 minutes
const pages = await chrome.history.search({
  text: 'wikipedia',
  startTime: Date.now() - (30 * 60 * 1E3)
});
```

Downloads

- downloads API – Chrome Developers: https://developer.chrome.com/docs/extensions/reference/downloads/

- downloads API – MDN: https://developer.mozilla.org/en-US/docs/Mozilla/Add-ons/WebExtensions/API/downloads

The chrome.downloads API is a create/read/update/destroy interface for the browser's downloads. "Creating" a download means forcing the browser to download from a specified URL.

```
// Start a download
chrome.downloads.download({
  url: "https://www.wikipedia.org/portal/wikipedia.org/assets/
  img/Wikipedia-logo-v2@2x.png",
});

const allDownloads = await chrome.downloads.search({});
```

Top Sites

- topSites API – Chrome Developers: https://developer.chrome.com/docs/extensions/reference/topSites/
- topSites API – MDN: https://developer.mozilla.org/en-US/docs/Mozilla/Add-ons/WebExtensions/API/topSites

This API allows an extension to read the "top sites" (most visited sites) displayed on the new tab page.

```
const topSites = await chrome.topSites.get();
```

Browsing Data

- browsingData API – Chrome Developers: https://developer.chrome.com/docs/extensions/reference/browsingData/

- browsingData API – MDN: https://developer.mozilla.org/en-US/docs/Mozilla/Add-ons/WebExtensions/API/browsingData

This API allows an extension to programmatically remove browsing data, which encompasses a considerable number of categories.

```
chrome.browsingData.remove({
  // Last 24 hours
  "since": (Date.now() - 24 * 60 * 60 * 1E3)
}, {
  "appcache": true,
  "cache": true,
  "cacheStorage": true,
  "cookies": true,
  "downloads": true,
  "fileSystems": true,
  "formData": true,
  "history": true,
  "indexedDB": true,
  "localStorage": true,
  "passwords": true,
  "serviceWorkers": true,
  "webSQL": true
});
```

Sessions

- sessions API – Chrome Developers: https://developer.chrome.com/docs/extensions/reference/sessions/

- sessions API – MDN: https://developer.mozilla.org/en-US/docs/Mozilla/Add-ons/WebExtensions/API/sessions

This API allows an extension to programmatically inspect and reopen recently closed tabs.

```
const recentlyClosed =
  await chrome.sessions.getRecentlyClosed();

// Restores the most recently closed tab
chrome.sessions.restore();
```

Tabs and Windows

- tabs API – Chrome Developers: https://developer.chrome.com/docs/extensions/reference/tabs/
- tabs API – MDN: https://developer.mozilla.org/en-US/docs/Mozilla/Add-ons/WebExtensions/API/tabs
- windows API – Chrome Developers: https://developer.chrome.com/docs/extensions/reference/windows/
- windows API – MDN: https://developer.mozilla.org/en-US/docs/Mozilla/Add-ons/WebExtensions/API/windows
- tabGroups API – Chrome Developers: https://developer.chrome.com/docs/extensions/reference/tabGroups/

These APIs allow a browser to totally control the tabs and windows that appear inside a browser. It can perform tasks such as create, remove, inspect, modify, rearrange, pin, and mute.

```
const [activeTab] = await chrome.tabs.query({
  active: true,
  currentWindow: true
});

chrome.tabs.create({
  active: false,
  url: "https://www.wikipedia.org",
});

// Close a tab
chrome.tabs.remove(tabId);

// Reload a tab
chrome.tabs.reload(tabId);

// Create a new window
chrome.windows.create({
  focused: true,
  url: "https://www.wikipedia.org ",
});

// Close a window
chrome.windows.remove(tabId);

const allTabGroups = await chrome.tabGroups.query();

// Update a tab group
chrome.tabGroups.update(
  groupId,
  { title: "foo" }
);
```

Debugger

- debugger API – Chrome Developers: https://developer.chrome.com/docs/extensions/reference/debugger/

The chrome.debugger API allows you to programmatically control the browser's debugger. With it, you can do almost anything that the Devtools API is capable of, including querying the response body, if the browser's developer tools interface is not open.

```
chrome.debugger.attach(
  tabId,
  "1.0",
  () => {}
);

chrome.debugger.sendCommand(
  tabId,
  "Debugger.enable"
);

chrome.debugger.sendCommand(
  tabId,
  "Debugger.setBreakpointByUrl",
  {
    lineNumber: 10,
    url: 'https://www.wikipedia.org/script.js'
  });
```

Search

- search API – Chrome Developers: https://developer.chrome.com/docs/extensions/reference/search/

This API allows you to programmatically execute searches in the browser's default search provider.

```
chrome.search.query(
  { disposition: "NEW_TAB", text: "wikipedia" });
```

Alarms

- alarms API - Chrome Developers: https://developer.chrome.com/docs/extensions/reference/alarms/
- alarms API - MDN: https://developer.mozilla.org/en-US/docs/Mozilla/Add-ons/WebExtensions/API/alarms

This API is used to schedule code to run in the future. It is similar in concept to `setTimeout()` and `setInterval()`, but it is able to wake a service worker.

```
// Fire alarm event in 1 minute
chrome.alarms.create({ delayInMinutes: 1 });

// Fire alarm event every 5 minutes
chrome.alarms.create({ periodInMinutes: 5 });

// Fire alarm event in 90 seconds
chrome.alarms.create({ when: (Date.now() + 90 * 1E3) });

chrome.alarms.onAlarm.addListener((alarm) => {})
```

Scripting

- scripting API - Chrome Developers: https://developer.chrome.com/docs/extensions/reference/scripting/

- scripting API – MDN: https://developer.mozilla.org/en-US/docs/Mozilla/Add-ons/WebExtensions/API/scripting

This API is used to programmatically inject JavaScript or CSS into the page.

```
function fooScript() {}

// Inject a function
chrome.scripting.executeScript({
  target: { tabId: 123 },
  function: fooScript
});

// Inject a script file
chrome.scripting.executeScript({
  target: { tabId: 123 },
  files: ['script.js']
});

// Inject CSS string
chrome.scripting.insertCSS({
  target: { tabId: 123 },
  css: 'body { background-color: red; }'
});

// Inject CSS file
chrome.scripting.insertCSS({
  target: { tabId: 123 },
  files: ['styles.css']
});
```

DOM

- dom API – Chrome Developers: https://developer.chrome.com/docs/extensions/reference/dom/

The dom API has a single method, openOrClosedShadowRoot(), used to get the open shadow root or the closed shadow root hosted by the specified element.

```
chrome.dom.openOrClosedShadowRoot(el);
```

Text to Speech

- tts API – Chrome Developers: https://developer.chrome.com/docs/extensions/reference/tts

The tts API allows you to instruct your browser to speak text aloud using it's native text-to-speech engine.

```
// Browser will speak the text aloud
chrome.tts.speak('Foo', {'lang': 'en-US', 'rate': 2.0});

// Waits for previous speech to finish
chrome.tts.speak('Bar', {'enqueue': true});

// Stops the speech immediately
chrome.tts.stop();
```

Privacy

- privacy API – Chrome Developers: https://developer.chrome.com/docs/extensions/reference/privacy/

This API allows an extension to get and set a user's privacy controls.

```
chrome.privacy.services.searchSuggestEnabled.get(
  {},
  (details) => {
    if (details.levelOfControl ===
        'controllable_by_this_extension') {
      chrome.privacy.services.searchSuggestEnabled.set({
        value: true }
      );
    }
  });
```

Idle

- idle API – Chrome Developers: `https://developer.chrome.com/docs/extensions/reference/idle/`

This API indicates when the host system has gone idle.

```
// Check system state every 30 seconds
chrome.idle.queryState(30);

chrome.idle.onStateChanged.addListener(() => {})
```

Devtools

- Devtools API – Chrome Developers: `https://developer.chrome.com/docs/extensions/mv3/devtools/`
- Devtools API – MDN: `https://developer.mozilla.org/en-US/docs/Mozilla/Add-ons/WebExtensions/Extending_the_developer_tools`

The Devtools API allows you to add custom interfaces to the browser's developer tools interface. These interfaces are granted special access to APIs only accessible from inside the developer tools.

```
// Create a devtools panel
chrome.devtools.panels.create(
  "Panel title",
  "path/to/icon.png",
  "panel.html"
);

// Sniff active page traffic
chrome.devtools.network.onNavigated.addListener((url) => {
});
```

Note This topic is covered in the *Devtools Pages* chapter.

Extension Introspection

- `extension` API – Chrome Developers: `https://developer.chrome.com/docs/extensions/reference/extension/`
- `extension` API – MDN: `https://developer.mozilla.org/en-US/docs/Mozilla/Add-ons/WebExtensions/API/extension`

This API is a collection of utilities. Many of the methods can be used to inspect the internal configuration of the running extension.

```
const popupUrl = chrome.extension.getURL("popup.html");

const allViews = chrome.extension.getViews();

const popups = chrome.extension.getViews({ type: "popup" });
```

Extension Management

- management API – Chrome Developers: https://developer.chrome.com/docs/extensions/reference/management/
- runtime API – Chrome Developers: https://developer.chrome.com/docs/extensions/reference/runtime/

Extensions are able to control the fundamentals of own operation, including reloading the extension, checking for updates, self-uninstalling, and setting the uninstall URL.

```
const selfInfo = chrome.management.getSelf();

// Uninstalls the running extension
chrome.management.uninstallSelf();

const manifest = chrome.runtime.getManifest();

// Reloads the extension
chrome.runtime.reload();

// Specifies the URL to direct the user to
// after uninstall
chrome.runtime.setUninstallURL(
  "https://www.wikipedia.org");
```

System State

- system APIs – Chrome Developers:
    - https://developer.chrome.com/docs/extensions/reference/system_cpu/

- `https://developer.chrome.com/docs/extensions/reference/system_display/`
- `https://developer.chrome.com/docs/extensions/reference/system_memory/`
- `https://developer.chrome.com/docs/extensions/reference/system_storage/`

The system API allows you to inspect certain details about the host operating system. The `cpu`, `display`, `memory`, and `storage` properties are all getters that return a JavaScript object filled with whatever the host system provides.

Enterprise Only

The following APIs are only usable by extensions force-installed by enterprise policy and are not covered in this chapter:

- `enterprise.deviceAttributes`
- `enterprise.hardwarePlatform`
- `enterprise.networkingAttributes`
- `enterprise.platformKeys`

Firefox Only

The following APIs are only usable on Firefox and are not covered in this chapter:

- `captivePortal`
- `contextualIdentites`
- `dns`

- `find`
- `menus`
- `pcks11`
- `sidebarAction`
- `theme`
- `userScripts`

Chrome OS Only

The following APIs are only usable on ChromeOS and are not covered in this chapter:

- `accesibilityFeatures`
- `audio`
- `certificateProvider`
- `fileBrowserHandler`
- `fileSystemProvider`
- `input.ime`
- `loginState`
- `platformKeys`
- `printing`
- `printingMetrics`
- `restart`
- `restartAfterDelay`
- `vpnProvider`

Deprecated

The following APIs are deprecated and should not be used:

- `instanceID`
- `gcm`

Summary

In this chapter, we covered all the various idiosyncrasies of the WebExtensions API, including promises and callbacks, error handling, and the events API. Finally, we went through each of the APIs, learning a bit about what they are for and seeing a code snippet for each.

In the next chapter, we will discuss the permissions that are required to enable these APIs as well as the best ways to manage permissions in an extension.

CHAPTER 12

Permissions

Browser extension permissions are conceptually identical to mobile app permissions. Both software platforms have the ability to access very powerful APIs, but to protect the end user permission to access these APIs must be explicitly requested on a piecewise basis. For both apps and extensions, permissions are declared by the developer in the codebase – for extensions, this is the extension manifest. In both cases, requesting access to trivial permissions will not require explicit user permission, but very powerful permissions will require the user to explicitly grant access. Furthermore, adding additional permissions in a subsequent update will typically require the user to explicitly accept this change in scope.

When building browser extensions, choosing permissions carefully is critically important. It has implications on how the marketplace listing will appear, the install and update flow for your extension, and how your extension will be reviewed by the marketplace.

Permissions Basics

To understand the basics of adding permissions, let's examine a very basic scenario that requires permissions. Begin with the following extension:

M. Frisbie, *Building Browser Extensions*, https://doi.org/10.1007/978-1-4842-8725-5_12

Example 12-1a. manifest.json

```
{
  "name": "MVX",
  "version": "0.0.1",
  "manifest_version": 3,
  "options_ui": {
    "open_in_tab": true,
    "page": "options.html"
  }
}
```

Example 12-1b. options.html

```
<!DOCTYPE html>
<html>
  <body>
    <script src="options.js"></script>
  </body>
</html>
```

Example 12-1c. options.js

```
chrome.storage.sync.set({ foo: "bar" });
```

This very simple extension consists of an options page that, when opened, attempts to write a dummy value to the browser storage.

Note This example uses an options page for two reasons: 1) because it is easier to access the console and reload the script, and 2) because when an error is thrown in the background page in the first turn of the event loop, the browser will mark the service worker as permanently idle and refuse to open the background worker developer tools.

After loading this extension and opening the options page, you will see this in the browser console (Figure 12-1).

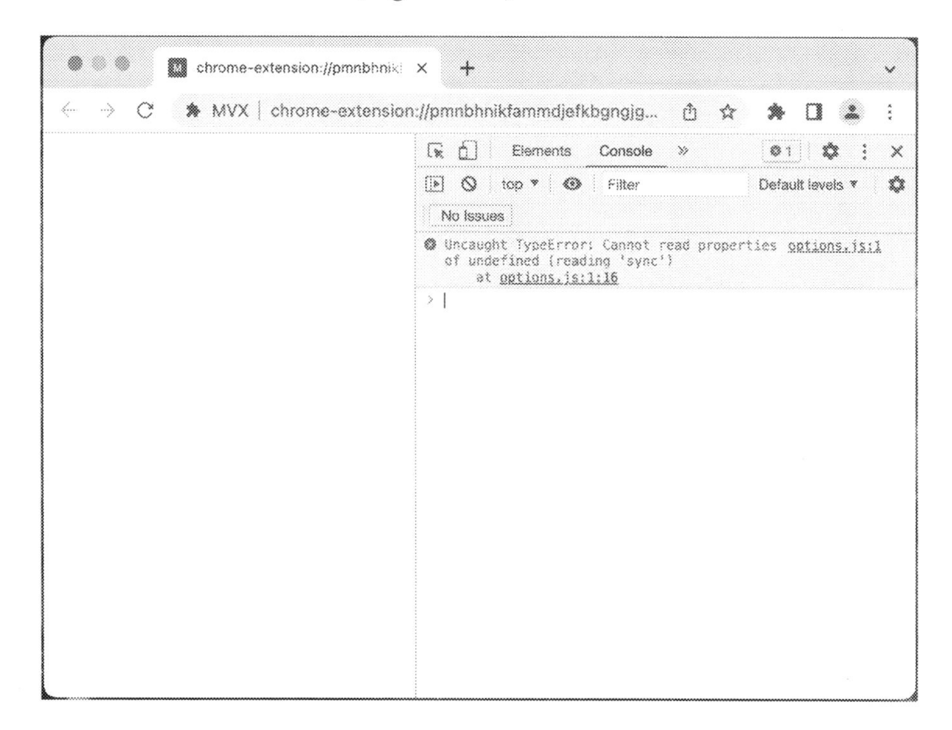

***Figure 12-1.** Error shown when attempting to set value in storage*

The reason for this error is that the `chrome.storage` API requires the `storage` permission. Because the permission was not requested, the browser simply does not define the `storage` property on the `chrome` global object, and the attempted `sync()` call throws the above error.

This might surprise you, as the entire extension was loaded without issue. It is important to understand that the browser makes no assumptions about what permissions might be needed when loading the extension, or if a requested permission will be needed in the codebase at all. All permissions handling occurs at runtime.

To fix this example, all you must to is add the `storage` permission as shown below:

Example 12-2. manifest.json with `storage` permissions added

```
{
  "name": "MVX",
  "version": "0.0.1",
  "manifest_version": 3,
  "options_ui": {
    "open_in_tab": true,
    "page": "options.html"
  },
  "permissions": ["storage"]
}
```

After reloading the extension, the options page will no longer throw the error. This is because you have successfully added the needed permissions to use the `chrome.storage` API.

Checking Permissions

You can programmatically read all the permissions the current execution context has access to via the `chrome.permissions.getAll()` method. Update the `options.js` script from above to log the extension's permissions:

Example 12-3. options.js

```
chrome.storage.sync.set({ foo: "bar" });

chrome.permissions.getAll().then(console.log);
```

Reload the extension, and reload the options page to yield as in Figure 12-2.

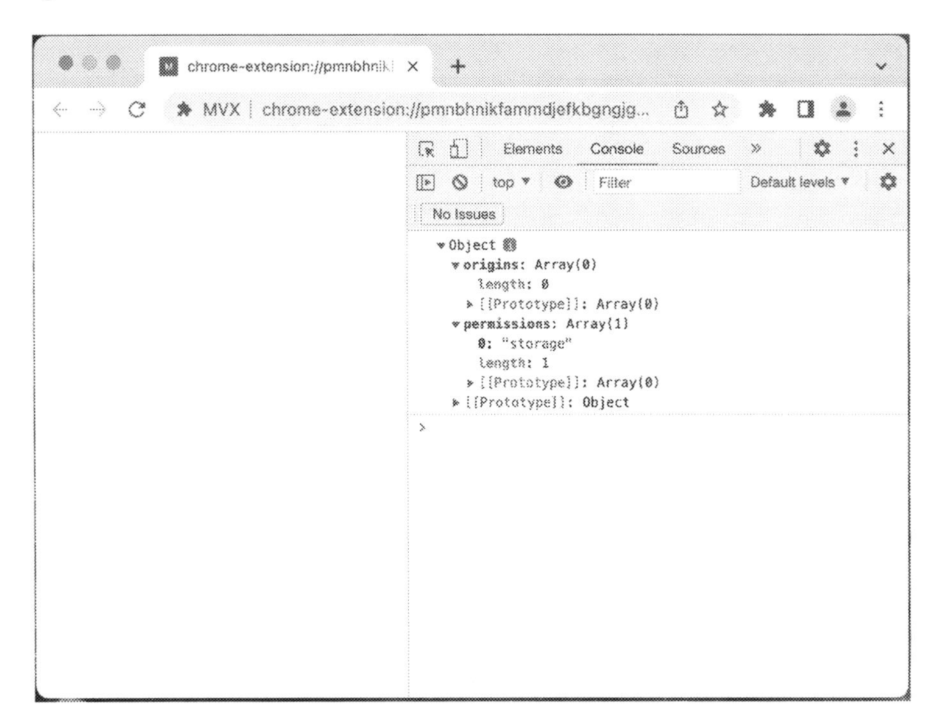

Figure 12-2. *Logging the extension's current permissions*

Note Once granted, optional permissions (covered in upcoming sections) are no different than required permissions, so `chrome.permissions.getAll()` computes a merged list of all the required *and* optional permissions.

Using Optional Permissions

As the name indicates, optional permissions are permissions that can be optionally requested from the user. Optional permissions serve two primary use cases:

- Permissions that will be requested right when the extension first loads, but that are not critical for the extension to operate properly. This is analogous to a mobile app requesting access to your location right when you open it for the first time.
- Permissions that will be requested only after the user performs some action that triggers the request, such as clicking a "connect to foobar.com" button. This is analogous to a mobile app requesting access to your device's photos only after you click a "share image" button.

Some examples of situations where optional permissions are useful

- You wish to allow users more control over the extension by allowing them to turn off some permissions, but still use some features of the extension
- You've already launched an extension but want to add more permissions without forcing the user to re-enable the extension
- You want to reduce the number of extension warnings that are displayed to the user after an install

Granting Permissions Declaratively vs. Imperatively

Whereas regular web browser permissions can be acquired *declaratively*, optional extension permissions must be acquired *imperatively*. Consider the following example of regular JavaScript running in a web page:

```
navigator.geolocation.getCurrentPosition(() => {})
```

The web browser geolocation API is not accessible by default, the user must grant access. However, the API is structured that simply calling this method will prompt the user with a dialog to grant permission; if the user grants permission, the script can proceed with execution as if the permission was granted all along.

Contrast this with extension example from the beginning of the chapter: calling a method without permissions will simply throw an error with no recourse. When using API methods requiring optional permissions, you must use the permissions API to check if the extension has permissions, request permissions if they are not granted, and only then can you proceed with the permissioned API call. This is demonstrated in the following example:

Example 12-4a. manifest.json

```
{
  "name": "MVX",
  "version": "0.0.1",
  "manifest_version": 3,
  "options_ui": {
    "open_in_tab": true,
    "page": "options.html"
  },
  "optional_permissions": ["storage"]
}
```

Example 12-4b. options.html

```
<!DOCTYPE html>
<html>
  <body>
    <button id="save">Save</button>

    <script src="options.js"></script>
  </body>
</html>
```

Example 12-4c. options.js

```
const permissions = {
  permissions: ["storage"],
};

document.querySelector("#save").addEventListener(
  "click",
  async () => {
    if (!(await chrome.permissions.contains(permissions))) {
      await chrome.permissions.request(permissions);
    }
    chrome.storage.sync.set({ foo: "bar" });
  });
```

Permission Request Idempotence

The previous example can be simplified even further. Requesting permissions is idempotent, so you can simply call `request()` each time with no penalty:

```
document.querySelector("#save").addEventListener(
  "click",
  async () => {
```

```
    await chrome.permissions.request(permissions);
    chrome.storage.sync.set({ foo: "bar" });
  });
```

Host Permissions

Beginning in manifest v3, `permissions` and `host_permissions` were split out into separate fields, with a mirrored split between `optional_permissions` and `optional_host_permissions`. Conceptually, the difference is straightforward: `permissions` are the APIs you need access to, and `host_permissions` are the origins you need to use the APIs in. As discussed in the *Extension Manifest* chapter, the host permissions list effectively creates a whitelist of domains with extra privileges.

According to MDN, an origin matching the whitelist grants access to the following:

- `XMLHttpRequest` and `fetch` access to those origins without cross-origin restrictions (even for requests made from content scripts)
- The ability to read tab-specific metadata without the `tabs` permission, such as the `url`, `title`, and `favIconUrl` properties of `Tab` objects
- The ability to inject scripts programmatically using `tabs.executeScript()` into pages served from those origins
- The ability to access cookies for that host using the cookies API, as long as the `cookies` API permission is also included

- The ability to bypass tracking protection for extension pages where a host is specified as a full domain or with wildcards. Content scripts, however, can only bypass tracking protection for hosts specified with a full domain

The only difference between checking and requesting `optional_permissions` vs. `optional_host_permissions` is the use of the `origins` property instead of `permissions` property. For example, checking for `google.com` origins would be done in the following way:

```
chrome.permissions.contains({ origins: ["*://*.google.com"] })
```

Permissions Lifetime

Once a permission is granted, the extension has that permission for the entire lifetime of the extension. However, it is possible that the user can explicitly revoke that permission via the browser's extension management page. If the extension is uninstalled and then reinstalled, all the optional permissions that were formerly granted are lost.

Permissions Warnings

For permissions such as `alarms` and `storage`, the APIs they enable are of little consequence to the user and therefore they can be accessed silently. Conversely, some permissions are sufficiently powerful and therefore require the user to explicitly grant access to the extension. This takes the form of a dialog box with a description of what the permissions entail. For example, the following is what displays in Google Chrome when requesting the `tabs` permission (Figure 12-3).

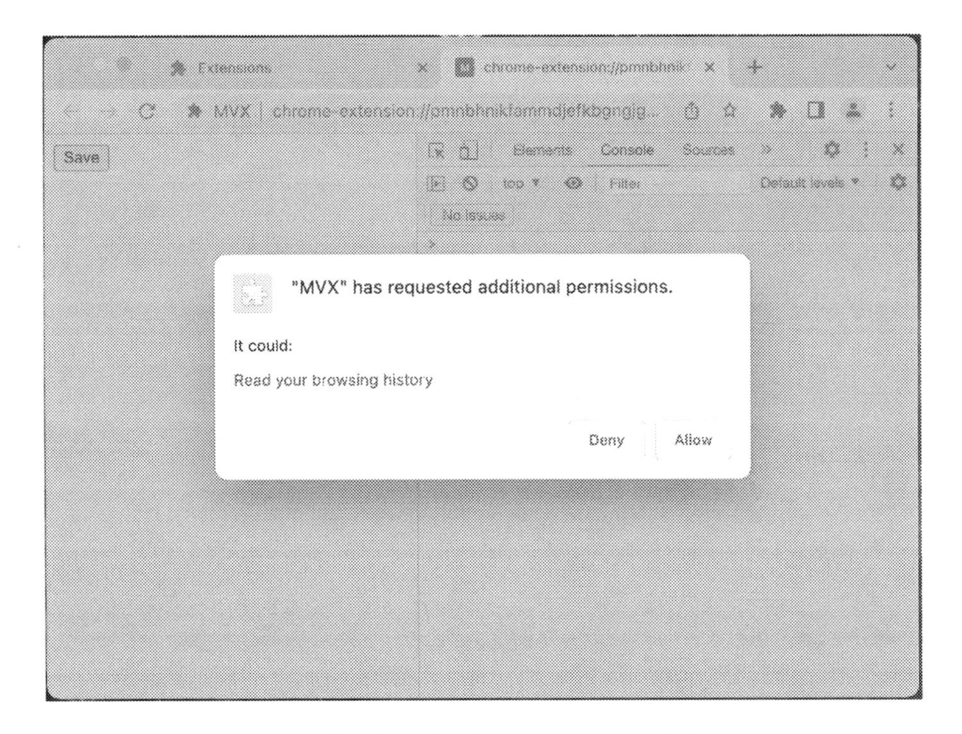

Figure 12-3. *Prompt displayed after requesting* `tabs` *permission*

For the `permissions` and `host_permissions` lists, the warning dialog will be displayed immediately after installing, and before the extension has an opportunity to execute any code. If the permission is denied, the extension will not be installed.

For `optional_permissions` and `optional_host_permissions`, the warning will only display when the extension makes the request for those permissions. If the permission is denied, the extension will continue to operate as it did before without the additional permissions.

Note Unlike HTML5 permissions, the extension will be able to make another request for the optional permission if it is initially denied.

Testing Permissions Warnings

When developing your extension, you will notice that loading an unpacked will not show the permission warning dialog when initially installing the extension. (Optional permissions will still show the warning dialog.) Of course, this is to avoid annoying the developer when they repeatedly reinstall their unfinished extension.

manfest.json - Trivial one-file browser extension used to generate permission warning dialog

```
{
  "name": "MVX",
  "version": "0.0.1",
  "manifest_version": 3,
  "permissions": ["tabs"]
}
```

To see the install-time permission warning dialog, you will need to pack the extension into a `.crx` file and then load that into your browser.

- Click "Pack extension" from the extension management page (Figure 12-4)
- Select the extension folder (the same folder you would select when loading unpacked) (Figure 12-5)
- Leave the `.pem` field blank
- The browser will generate two files, a `.crx` and a `.pem`.
- Drag and drop the `.crx` file into the extension management page to install it. If you did this correctly, the browser will prompt you with the permission warning dialog. (Figures 12-6 and 12-7)
- Delete the two created files, they have no further use.

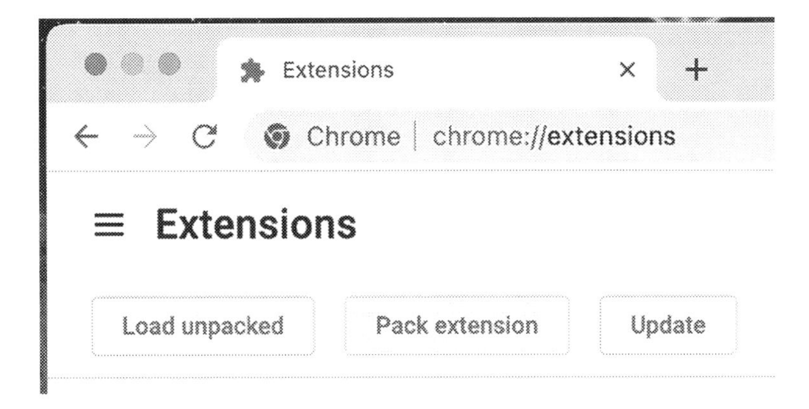

***Figure 12-4.** The "Pack extension" button on the extension management page*

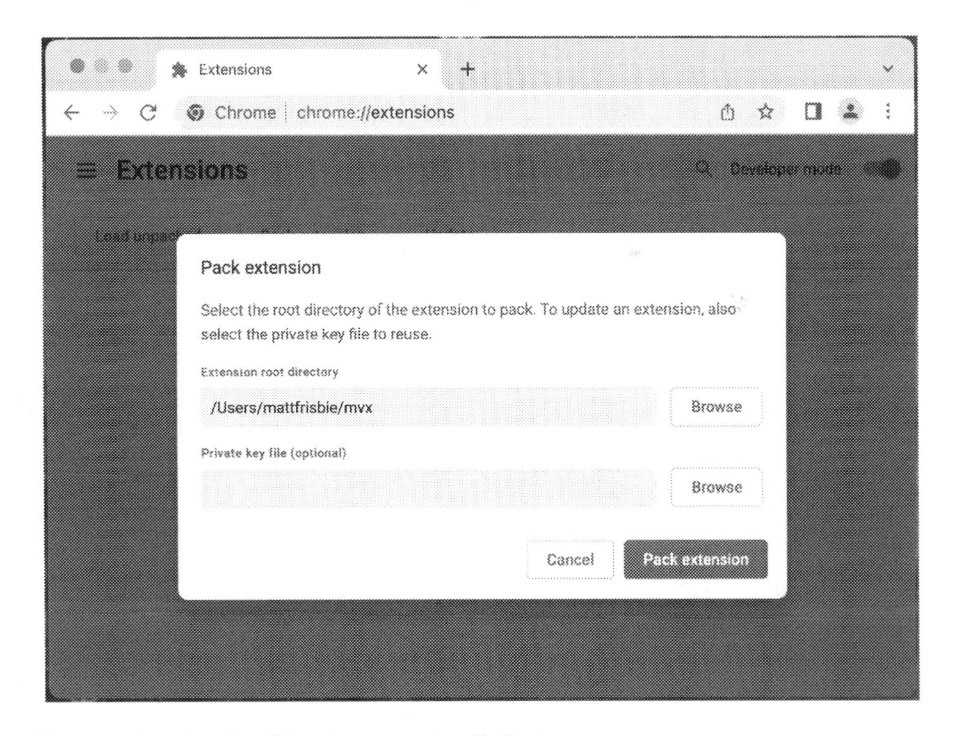

***Figure 12-5.** The "Pack extension" dialog*

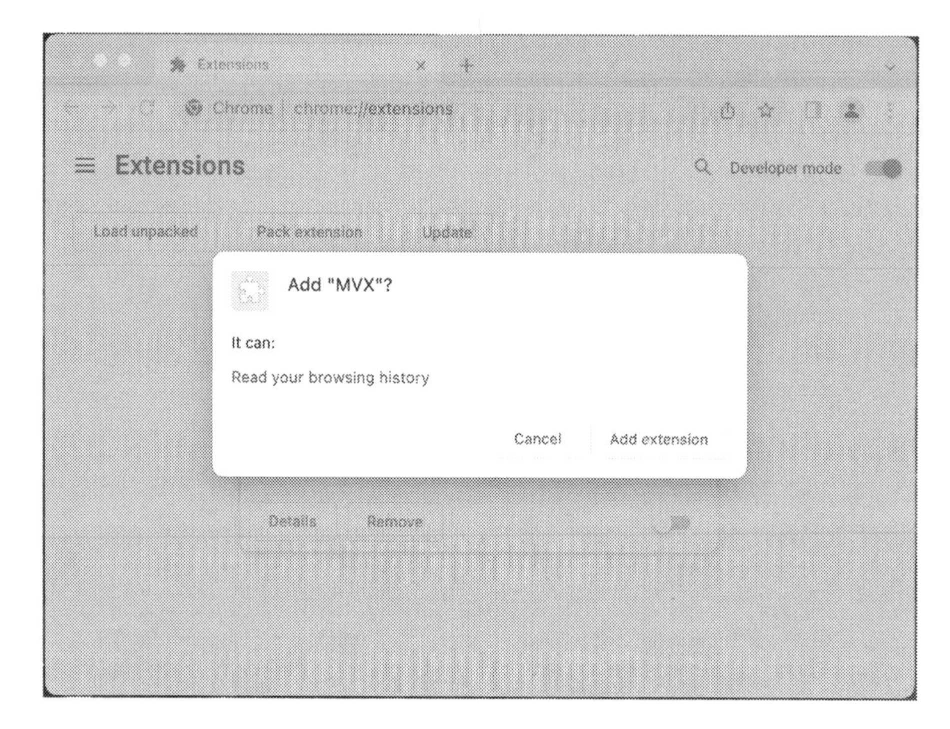

***Figure 12-6.** The install-time permissions warning dialog*

Note It used to be possible to install and use an extension with a `.crx` file – this is no longer the case. It can still be used to test warnings as shown here, but as you will see the extension will be permanently disabled by Chrome.

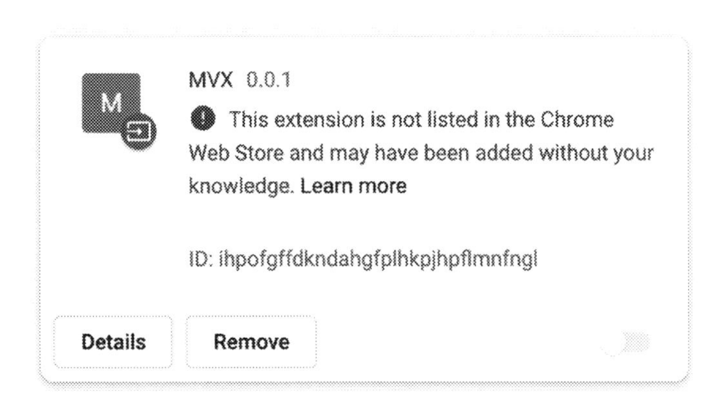

Figure 12-7. *The disabled* `.crx` *extension*

Considerations for Published Extensions

When publishing your extension to a marketplace, the permissions you select can have implications outside of your codebase.

Triggering the Slow Review Queue

When building an extension, you will probably not have any discretion for selecting which permissions are needed. After all, the needs of the extension are absolute, and the permissions needed to make it function will flow from there. However, if the speed of review for your extension is important, then it is important to understand that requiring some permissions such as `<all_urls>` will cause your extension to be placed in a slower review queue.

> **Tip** I have found in my experience that this queue will increase your extension review time from less than 24 hours to a few days.

Auto-Disable Updates

One critically important consideration is what happens when required permissions that will show warnings are added to an extension in an update. The browser silently updates extensions in the background, so it won't show the warning dialog as soon as the update is installed. Instead, it will silently disable the extension and add a small notification to the browser toolbar, indicating action is required. To re-enable the extension, the user must open this notification and accept the new permissions (Figures 12-8 and 12-9). This flow is shown in the following.

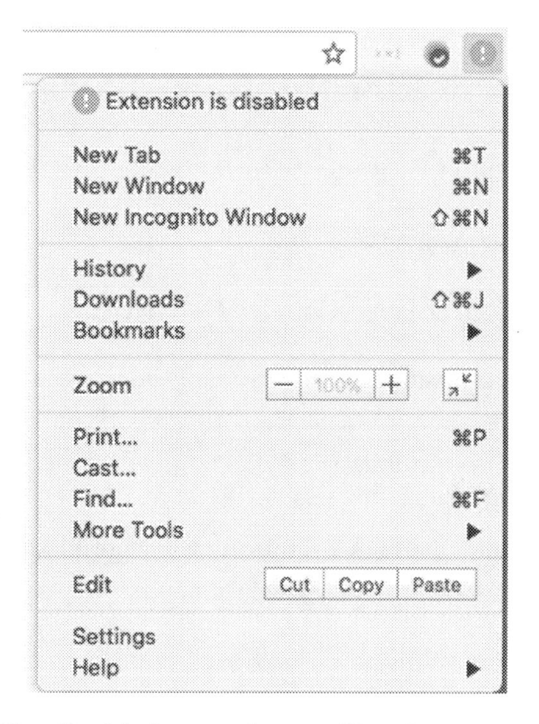

Figure 12-8. *The disabled extension notification*

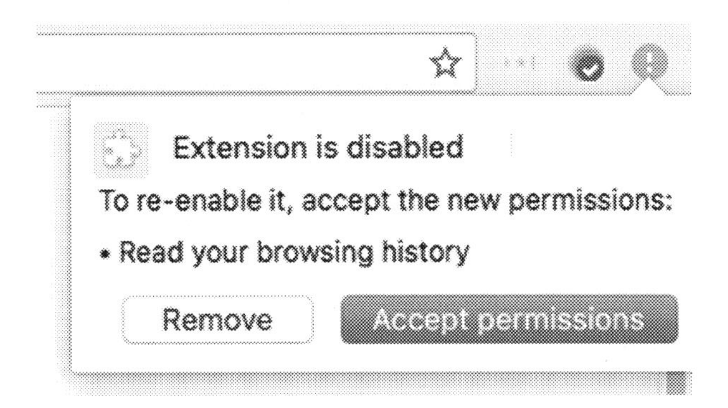

Figure 12-9. *The permissions dialog to re-enable the extension*

Permissions List

The following is a list of all permissions, what they enable, and the warning message they will incur (if any).

Note This permissions list includes values from different browser vendors and different manifest versions. Some permissions may be deprecated.

Note For consistency, the APIs are displayed inside the chrome namespace. This namespace is valid in all Chromium and Firefox browsers.

---

activeTab

The `activeTab` permission is commonly misunderstood – largely in part to its name. Extension developers were experiencing the following issues:

- Extensions only needed access to the "active tab," meaning the tab which was currently focused by the browser.

- Extensions needed access to the active tab irrespective of its domain, but did not want to incur the off-putting "Read and change all your data on the websites you visit" warning message.
- Extensions only needed temporary access to the active tab.

From this, the `activeTab` permission was born. This permission does not allow access to anything new: requesting the `<all_urls>` permission would make the `activeTab` permission pointless. However, by requesting `activeTab` instead of `<all_urls>`, the extension is granted extra permissions only after a limited set of user interactions without showing any warning to the user.

The allowed user interactions are:

- Executing an action
- Executing a context menu item
- Executing a keyboard shortcut command
- Accepting a suggestion from the Omnibox API

Once one of these user interactions occurs, the extension is temporarily granted the following extra permissions for that tab:

- Call `scripting.executeScript()` or `scripting.insertCSS()` on the active tab.
- Get the URL, title, and favicon for that tab via an API that returns a `tabs.Tab` object (essentially the same as the `tabs` permission).
- Intercept network requests in the tab to the tab's main frame origin using the `webRequest` API. The extension temporarily gets host permissions for the tab's main frame origin.

These extra permissions only last until the tab is navigated or is closed. This permission is available in Chromium browsers and Firefox.

alarms

- Gives your extension access to the `chrome.alarms` API
- Available for Chromium browsers and Firefox

background

- Makes Chrome start up early and shut down late, so that extensions can have a longer life
- Available for Chromium browsers and Firefox

When any installed extension has background permission, Chrome runs as a background process as soon as the user logs into their computer and before the user launches Chrome. The background permission also makes Chrome continue running after its last window is closed until the user explicitly quits Chrome.

The intended use of the `background` permission is to enable background scripts to perform useful work without being bound to the lifetime of the browser window.

bookmarks

- Grants your extension access to the `chrome.bookmarks` API
- Available for Chromium browsers and Firefox
- Chrome warning message: "Read and change your bookmarks"
- Firefox warning message: "Read and modify bookmarks"

browserSettings

- Enables an extension to modify certain global browser settings. Each property of this API is a `BrowserSetting` object, providing the ability to modify a particular setting
- Available for Firefox
- Firefox warning message: "Read and modify browser settings"

browsingData

- Gives your extension access to the `chrome.browsingData` API
- Available for Chromium browsers and Firefox
- Firefox warning message: "Clear recent browsing history, cookies, and related data"

captivePortal

- Determine the captive portal state of the user's connection. A captive portal is a web page displayed when a user first connects to a Wi-Fi network
- Available for Firefox

certificateProvider

- Gives your extension access to the `chrome.certificateProvider` API
- Available for Chromium browsers

clipboardRead

- Required if the extension uses `document.execCommand('paste')`
- Available for Chromium browsers and Firefox
- Chrome warning message: "Read data you copy and paste"
- Firefox warning message: "Get data from the clipboard"

clipboardWrite

- Indicates the extension uses `document.execCommand('copy')` or `document.execCommand('cut')`
- Available for Chromium browsers and Firefox
- Chrome warning message: "Modify data you copy and paste"
- Firefox warning message: "Input data to the clipboard"

contentSettings

- Grants your extension access to the `chrome.contentSettings` API.
- Available for Chromium browsers and Firefox
- Chrome warning message: "Change your settings that control websites' access to features such as cookies, JavaScript, plugins, geolocation, microphone, camera etc."

contextMenus

- Gives your extension access to the `chrome.contextMenus` API
- Available for Chromium browsers and Firefox

contextualIdentities

- List, create, remove, and update contextual identities, more commonly known as "containers"
- Available for Firefox

cookies

- Gives your extension access to the `chrome.cookies` API
- Available for Chromium browsers and Firefox

debugger

- Grants your extension access to the `chrome.debugger` API
- Available for Chromium browsers and Firefox
- Multiple Chrome warning messages:
    - "Access the page debugger backend"
    - "Read and change all your data on the websites you visit"

declarativeContent

- Gives your extension access to the `chrome.declarativeContent` API
- Available for Chromium browsers

declarativeNetRequest

- Grants your extension access to the `chrome.declarativeNetRequest` API
- Available for Chromium browsers
- Chrome warning message: "Block page content"

declarativeNetRequestFeedback

- Grants the extension access to events and methods within the `chrome.declarativeNetRequest` API which return information on declarative rules matched
- Available for Chromium browsers

declarativeWebRequest

- Gives your extension access to the `chrome.declarativeWebRequest` API
- Available for Chromium browsers

desktopCapture

- Grants your extension access to the `chrome.desktopCapture` API
- Available for Chromium browsers
- Chrome warning message: "Capture content of your screen"

Devtools page

- Technically not a permission, this is an extra warning that displays in Firefox when `devtools_page` is used in the manifest
- Firefox warning message: "Extend developer tools to access your data in open tabs"

dns

- Enables an extension to resolve domain names using the `dns` API
- Available for Firefox

documentScan

- Gives your extension access to the `chrome.documentScan` API
- Available for Chromium browsers

downloads

- Grants your extension access to the `chrome.downloads` API
- Available for Chromium browsers and Firefox
- Chrome warning message: "Manage your downloads"
- Firefox warning message: "Download files and read and modify the browser's download history"

downloads.open

- Grants your extension access to only the `chrome.downloads.open` API
- Chrome warning message: "Open downloaded files"
- Firefox warning message: "Open files downloaded to your computer"

enterprise.deviceAttributes

- Gives your extension access to the `chrome.enterprise.deviceAttributes` API
- Available for Chromium browsers

enterprise.hardwarePlatform

- Gives your extension access to the `chrome.enterprise.hardwarePlatform` API
- Available for Chromium browsers

enterprise.networkingAttributes

- Gives your extension access to the `chrome.enterprise.networkingAttributes` API
- Available for Chromium browsers

enterprise.platformKeys

- Gives your extension access to the `chrome.enterprise.platformKeys` API
- Available for Chromium browsers

experimental

- Required if the extension uses any `chrome.experimental.*` APIs
- Available for Chromium browsers

fileBrowserHandler

- Gives your extension access to the `chrome.fileBrowserHandler` API
- Available for Chromium browsers

fileSystemProvider

- Gives your extension access to the `chrome.fileSystemProvider` API
- Available for Chromium browsers

find

- Enable the extension to find text in a web page and highlight matches with the `find` API
- Available for Firefox
- Firefox warning message: "Read the text of all open tabs"

fontSettings

- Gives your extension access to the `chrome.fontSettings` API
- Available for Chromium browsers

gcm

- Gives your extension access to the `chrome.gcm` API
- Available for Chromium browsers

geolocation

- Allows the extension to use the HTML5 geolocation API without prompting the user for permission
- Available for Chromium browsers and Firefox
- Chrome warning message: "Detect your physical location"
- Firefox warning message: "Access your location"

history

- Grants your extension access to the `chrome.history` API
- Available for Chromium browsers and Firefox
- Chrome warning message: "Read and change your browsing history"
- Firefox warning message: "Access browsing history"

Host Permissions

Host permissions can either be requested globally, or for only a subset of hosts. These permissions can be requested on all browsers, and the warning message displayed may appear in several different ways.

Note It may be possible to avoid declaring any host permissions by using the `activeTab` permission.

Global Host Permission

Global host permission means the extension has access to every host with a permitted protocol. This is appropriate for extensions that need to manage all the browser's pages and traffic all the time. There are several different ways to request this, but they all have the same effect:

- `http://*/*`
- `https://*/*`
- `*://*/*`
- `<all_urls>`

This will show the following warning messages:

- Chrome warning message: "Read and change all your data on the websites you visit"
- Firefox warning message: "Access your data for all websites"

Tip If your extension uses this permission, your extension will be placed in the manual review queue when submitting to extension marketplaces. As a result, it will take significantly longer to be approved.

Partial Host Permission

Partial host permission means the extension has access to only hosts that match one or more matchers. This is appropriate for extensions that know ahead of time the set of hosts that it will need to manage or communicate with.

Note Refer to the Extension Manifest chapter for coverage on how matchers work.

The warning displayed will vary based on how many hosts are covered. A simple single host matcher for `foobar.com` will display the following warnings:

- Chrome warning message: "Read and change your data on `foobar.com`"
- Firefox warning message: "Grants the extension access to `https://foobar.com`"

If more than one host is covered, the browser will adjust the warning message based on how many hosts are covered. For example, Firefox also will show the following messages:

- Access your data for sites in the [named] domain
- Access your data in # other domains
- Access your data for [named site]
- Access your data on # other sites

identity

- Gives your extension access to the `chrome.identity` API
- Available in Chromium browsers and Firefox

idle

- Gives your extension access to the `chrome.idle` API
- Available for Chromium browsers and Firefox

loginState

- Gives your extension access to the `chrome.loginState` API
- Available in Chromium browsers

management

- Grants the extension access to the `chrome.management` API
- Available for Chromium browsers and Firefox

- Chrome warning message: "Manage your apps, extensions, and themes"
- Firefox warning message: "Monitor extension usage and manage themes"

menus

- Add items to the browser's menu system with the `menus` API
- Available for Firefox

Note This API is modeled on Chrome's `contextMenus` API, which enables Chrome extensions to add items to the browser's context menu. The `menus` API adds a few features to Chrome's API.

---

menus.overrideContext

- Hide all default Firefox menu items in favor of providing a custom context menu UI
- Available for Firefox

nativeMessaging

- Gives the extension access to the native messaging API
- Available for Chromium browsers and Firefox
- Chrome warning message: "Communicate with cooperating native applications"
- Firefox warning message: "Exchange messages with programs other than Firefox"

notifications

- Grants your extension access to the `chrome.notifications` API
- Available for Chromium browsers and Firefox
- Chrome warning message: "Display notifications"
- Firefox warning message: "Display notifications to you"

pageCapture

- Grants the extension access to the `chrome.pageCapture` API
- Available for Chromium browsers and Firefox
- Chrome warning message: "Read and change all your data on the websites you visit"

pkcs11

- The pkcs11 API enables an extension to enumerate PKCS #11 security modules and to make them accessible to the browser as sources of keys and certificates
- Available for Firefox
- Firefox warning message: "Provide cryptographic authentication services"

Per Wikipedia:

> *Most commercial certificate authority (CA) software uses PKCS #11 to access the CA signing key or to enroll user certificates. Cross-platform software that needs to use smart cards uses PKCS #11, such as Mozilla Firefox and OpenSSL (using an extension).*

platformKeys

- Gives your extension access to the `chrome.platformKeys` API
- Available in Chromium browsers

power

- Gives your extension access to the `chrome.power` API
- Available for Chromium browsers

printerProvider

- Gives your extension access to the `chrome.printerProvider` API
- Available for Chromium browsers

printing

- Gives your extension access to the `chrome.printing` API
- Available for Chromium browsers

printingMetrics

- Gives your extension access to the `chrome.printingMetrics` API
- Available for Chromium browsers

privacy

- Gives the extension access to the `chrome.privacy` API
- Available for Chromium browsers and Firefox
- Chrome warning message: "Change your privacy-related settings"
- Firefox warning message: "Read and modify privacy settings"

processes

- Gives your extension access to the `chrome.processes` API
- Available for Chromium browsers

proxy

- Grants the extension access to the `chrome.proxy` API
- Available for Chromium browsers and Firefox
- Chrome warning message: "Read and change all your data on the websites you visit"
- Firefox warning message: "Control browser proxy settings"

scripting

- Gives your extension access to the `chrome.scripting` API
- Available for Chromium browsers and Firefox

search

- Gives your extension access to the `chrome.search` API
- Available for Chromium browsers and Firefox

sessions

- Gives your extension access to the `chrome.sessions` API
- Available for Chromium browsers and Firefox
- Firefox warning message: "Access recently closed tabs"

signedInDevices

- Gives your extension access to the `chrome.signedInDevices` API
- Available for Chromium browsers

storage

- Gives your extension access to the `chrome.storage` API
- Available for Chromium browsers and Firefox

system.cpu

- Gives your extension access to the `chrome.system.cpu` API
- Available for Chromium browsers

system.display

- Gives your extension access to the `chrome.system.display` API
- Available for Chromium browsers

system.memory

- Gives your extension access to the `chrome.system.memory` API
- Available for Chromium browsers

system.storage

- Grants the extension access to the `chrome.system.storage` API
- Available for Chromium browsers
- Chrome warning message: "Identify and eject storage devices"

tabCapture

- Grants the extensions access to the `chrome.tabCapture` API

- Available for Chromium browsers
- Chrome warning message: "Read and change all your data on the websites you visit"

tabGroups

- Gives your extension access to the `chrome.tabGroups` API
- Available for Chromium browsers

tabHide

- Allows the extension to use the `tabs.hide()` API
- Available for Firefox

tabs

- Grants the extension access to privileged fields of the Tab objects used by several APIs including `chrome.tabs` and `chrome.windows`
- Available for Chromium browsers and Firefox
- Chrome warning message: "Read your browsing history"
- Firefox warning message: "Access browser tabs"

Note In many circumstances the extension will not need to declare the `tabs` permission to make use of these APIs.

---

theme

- Enables browser extensions to update the browser theme
- Available for Firefox

topSites

- Grants the extension access to the `chrome.topSites` API
- Available for Chromium browsers and Firefox
- Chrome warning message: "Read a list of your most frequently visited websites"
- Firefox warning message: "Access browsing history"

tts

- Gives your extension access to the `chrome.tts` API
- Available for Chromium browsers

ttsEngine

- Grants the extension access to the `chrome.ttsEngine` API
- Available for Chromium browsers
- Chrome warning message: "Read all text spoken using synthesized speech"

unlimitedStorage

- Provides an unlimited quota for storing client-side data, such as databases and local storage files. Without this permission, the extension is limited to 5 MB of local storage
- Available for Chromium browsers and Firefox
- Firefox warning message: "Store unlimited amount of client-side data"

Note This permission applies only to Web SQL Database and application cache. Also, it doesn't currently work with wildcard subdomains such as http://*.example.com.

---

vpnProvider

- Gives your extension access to the `chrome.vpnProvider` API
- Available for Chromium browsers

wallpaper

- Gives your extension access to the `chrome.wallpaper` API
- Available for Chromium browsers

webNavigation

- Grants the extension access to the `chrome.webNavigation` API

- Available for Chromium browsers and Firefox
- Chrome warning message: "Read your browsing history"
- Firefox warning message: "Access browser activity during navigation"

webRequest

- Gives your extension access to the `chrome.webRequest` API
- Available in Chromium browsers and Firefox

webRequestBlocking

- Required if the extension uses the `chrome.webRequest` API in a blocking fashion
- Available in Chromium browsers and Firefox

Summary

In this chapter, you learned about what permissions are, what they do, and how to declare them. The chapter also covered the difference between required, optional, and host permissions. It also explained all the tricky implications with selecting and changing permissions.

In the next chapter, we will cover all the different aspects of how extensions can use and modify the browser's network capabilities, as well as how it can creatively use content scripts to act as an agent of the authenticated user. This chapter also covers the important differences between `webRequest` and `declarativeNetRequest`.

CHAPTER 13

Networking

As you wade deeper into browser extension development, you will quickly realize that there are some interesting idiosyncrasies when it comes to sending network requests. Although browser extensions and web pages use the same APIs and network layers to send requests, there are fundamental differences that you will need to surmount when building a well-formed browser extension. This chapter will cover some core areas of extension networking: dispatching network requests, authentication, and browser extension networking APIs.

Comparing Websites and Extensions

To begin this chapter, let's set the stage by comparing a traditional website and a browser extension.

Category	Websites	Browser Extensions (MV3)
Origin	A website has a predictable origin and a user-provided domain.	Browser extensions are automatically assigned an origin via the extension ID.
APIs	Websites can use `XMLHttpRequest` or `fetch()` anywhere.	Background scripts can only use `fetch()`.

(continued)

M. Frisbie, *Building Browser Extensions*, https://doi.org/10.1007/978-1-4842-8725-5_13

Category	Websites	Browser Extensions (MV3)
Remote assets	Remote assets can be served from the same origin without configuring a cross-origin policy.	Remote assets must be loaded with a cross-origin policy correctly configured. Scripts cannot be executed from remote origins.
Page types	All web pages on a website can send requests and authenticate in consistent fashion.	Popup/options pages, content scripts, and background scripts all have different restrictions for sending requests, for example, content scripts are subject to the host page's cross-origin restrictions, but popups are not.
Server requests	The website can send same-origin requests to the backend.	If a browser extension uses a backend server, the requests will *always* be cross-origin.
Authentication	No restrictions: the website can use cookie auth, JWT auth, or OAuth anywhere.	Not all forms of authentication work everywhere, for example, service workers can't use cookie authentication.
Long-running requests	Any long-running requests will stay alive while a tab is open.	Long-running requests in background service workers, popups, and content scripts may all be unexpectedly terminated, for example, a popup is closed or a service worker is terminated.
Cross-browser	The website origin remains consistent across browsers.	The browser extension origin is different across browsers: `chrome-extension://extensionID` vs. `moz-extension://uuid`.

Networking Architecture

When it comes to sending network requests, different components of browser extensions are better than others for certain tasks. How you dispatch your network requests will depend on the nature of your browser extension. This section will cover some things to consider when designing your extension.

Options Pages

Options pages are nearly identical to a traditional website, and therefore they are a natural choice for many developers when building a browser extension. If your entire user interface is built inside options pages, you will not have any problem using any form of authentication, be it cookie auth, JSON Web Token (JWT) auth, or OAuth. Unless the options page is rendered as a modal (`open_in_tab=false`), it will enjoy the same lifecycle as a browser tab, so long-running requests can be safely dispatched from an options page without risk of early termination.

The options page is a good option as a supplement for browser extensions that wish to rely heavily on a background script, but also wish to execute long-running requests. The background script can kick open an options tab as a vehicle for the long-running requests.

Popup and Devtools Pages

Popup and devtools pages are nearly identical in nature to options pages, but with one primary difference: they are expected to be closed early and often. Thus, they are not a good vehicle for long-running network requests. Otherwise, they are good choices for authentication and general-purpose network request.

Content Scripts

Content scripts are a particularly interesting tool for sending network requests. Because they are running on the host page, they are subject to the same cross origin restrictions. This means talking to your own server will likely require delegating that request to the background script. However, because content script requests are treated as host page requests, they can use the host page's cookies – meaning you can send requests as the authenticated user.

Authenticating inside the content script is tricky, as the host page can see anything placed into the DOM or in a shared API. Furthermore, long-running network requests are obviously dependent on the host page remaining open; if the tab closes or the user navigates away, the request or websocket will be abruptly terminated.

Tip The authentication spoofing ability is incredibly powerful! It usually requires some reverse engineering of the host page, but it allows you to automate authenticated actions that the host page is allowed to perform. For example, suppose some web page shows an authenticated user's shopping cart with 100 items in it. Each item has a "remove item" button that triggers a network request to `/cart/remove` with a JSON payload like `{"item_id": 123}`, and you wish to empty the cart. Instead of automating 100 button clicks, you can instead extract the required `item_id` values and the content script can send those 100 authenticated requests directly.

Background Scripts

The transition from manifest v2 to manifest v3 was especially challenging for background scripts, as the network request paradigm changed in substantial and breaking ways. Previously, the background script existed as a persistent headless web page, meaning that cookie auth, long-running requests, and auth dialog windows were allowed. Now, all these things have materially changed:

- Cookie authentication is still technically possible, but the cookies need to be passed in from a rendered HTML page and manually provided, which is very annoying and impractical - or impossible, in the case of HttpOnly cookies.
- The browser does not consider inflight requests when determining if a service worker is idle, so long-running requests are subject to early termination.
- Auth dialog windows cannot make use of `window.open()`, they must use the identity API.

Background scripts are still an excellent and very capable tool, but with manifest v3 they are certainly more limited. Extensions that use JWT or OAuth authentication and do not rely on long-running requests will be able to seamlessly utilize background service worker networking without issue.

Pinning an Extension ID

In the context of extension networking, it is useful to be able to predict and control the origin of a browser extension. When developing locally, the browser will assign your extension an ID automatically; when uploading to the Chrome web store, it will assign your extension an entirely different ID. For developers that wish to have a consistent ID, this is problematic.

Fortunately, it is possible to pin your extension's ID ahead of time to make it consistent and predictable. Doing so involves the following steps:

1. **Upload the initial version of your extension to the Chrome Web Store.** The store will generate a public key for your extension, which in turn is used to generate the extension ID. Your local browser will generate the same extension ID if it is provided that public key (Figure 13-1).

2. **Retrieve the public key from the web store (Figure 13-2)**.

3. **Add the public key to your manifest under the "key" property**. Strip out the BEGIN/END lines and all the whitespace and pass it in as one big string (Figure 13-3).

4. **Load the extension locally**. Your local browser should generate an identical extension ID to the Chrome Web Store (Figure 13-4).

Caution Keep in mind that the production extension and the local extension having the same ID means the browser will consider them to be the same. To prevent collision conflicts, ensure you only have the production or local extension installed at any given time.

This process is shown below:

Figure 13-1. *The Chrome Web Store package page including the public key link. Note the ID beginning with "jnof"*

Figure 13-2. *The revealed public key*

```
{} manifest.json ×
{} manifest.json > ...
1 ∨ {
2     "manifest_version": 3,
3     "version": "1.0.5",
4     "key": "MIIBIjANBgkqhkiG9w0BAQEFAAOCAQ8AMIIBCgKCAQEA...
```

***Figure 13-3.** The flattened public key passed to the manifest*

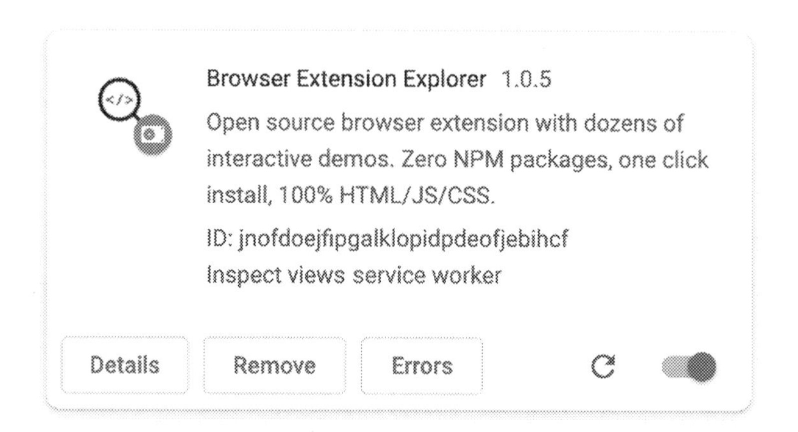

***Figure 13-4.** The extension loaded locally. Note the ID beginning with "jnof"*

Authentication Styles

The web wouldn't have gotten far without the ability to authenticate. Browser extensions can use the same foundational technologies as websites to authenticate. However, due to the innate architecture of extensions, the way you go about authenticating must be carefully considered. This section discusses different modalities of authentication.

No Authentication

Browser extensions don't necessarily need to authenticate. Often, a clever application of a small portion of the WebExtensions API is all that is needed to make an extension useful. What's more, when a content script interacts with the raw DOM, the browser extension's ability to interact with authenticated sessions is totally disjoint from any concept of a logged in state. In other words, the host website can do the heavy lifting of logging in the user, the browser extension can wait for a logged in state, and then the content script can read from and write to the DOM.

Some APIs allow you to take advantage of native browser identity separation without managing authentication. For example, the storage API allows you to use `chrome.storage.sync`, which is attached to the user's browser account and will be synced to their account, or `chrome.storage.local`, which is localized to the current browser instance.

Content Script Spoofing

As mentioned earlier in the chapter, network requests from a content script are treated the same as network requests from a host page script. Therefore, if a website uses HttpOnly cookie authentication, a content script will be able to piggyback on that authenticated state and send requests that will automatically include those cookies.

Of course, a well-built website will also include a CSRF token, but since the CSRF token is usually provided in a consistent location such as inside a `<form>`, a content script can inspect the DOM, extract the CSRF token, and pass that along with the outgoing request.

Cookie Authentication

Cookie authentication is technically possible for browser extension user interfaces, but I don't recommend it. This style of authentication works best when the web page is rendered directly by a server, and for browser extensions this is never the case. Furthermore, a cookie-based authenticated state can't be directly accessed by the background service worker. Overall, because it involves so much unnecessary overhead to implement, I recommend you avoid cookie authentication unless you have a particularly compelling reason to do so.

Json Web Token Authentication

Token-style authentication works well for app-based authentication where cookies aren't practical. For browser extensions, token authentication schemes like JWT (JSON Web Token) are ideal. Popups, options pages, devtools pages, and background scripts can all directly authenticate with a server and share the authentication token between extension components without issue. Content scripts are able to use JWTs, but the host page's cross-origin policy will likely block requests to the server, so sending requests indirectly via the background service worker is the preferred workaround.

OAuth and OpenID

With the `chrome.identity` API, browser extensions have first-class support for OAuth and OpenID. This API is not supported inside content scripts, but it can be effectively deployed anywhere else in a browser extension. For developers that do not wish to implement a backend server, authorization and authentication via OAuth or OpenID is extremely practical.

The `chrome.identity` API is spearheaded by Google Chrome, but it enjoys at least partial support in all chromium browsers and Firefox. In Google Chrome, browser extensions enjoy additional identity API methods including a streamlined OAuth authorization flow (more on this later in the chapter).

Note Safari currently has no support for the identity API.

OAuth, OpenID, and the Identity API

Note This section assumes you have basic knowledge of how the OAuth2 protocol works. For an introduction to OAuth2, Auth0 has an excellent writeup on it: `https://auth0.com/intro-to-iam/what-is-oauth-2/`.

The ability to delegate authentication and authorization to a third-party platform is incredibly useful, but implementing this in browser extensions is tricky. Consider some of the challenges involved:

- Delegating a login to a third-party platform requires the ability to open a trusted interface to collect the credentials. Background service workers cannot utilize `window.open()`.
- Configuring a platform to support OAuth requires knowledge of the extension ID ahead of time.
- OAuth and OpenID utilize the same underlying protocol, which includes a redirect URL. Browser extensions can only render inside private URLs with an extension protocol.

Fortunately, the identity API solves all these problems by providing a flexible set of tools for implementing delegated authentication and authorization.

OAuth API Methods

There are two ways of using OAuth in an extension:

- `chrome.identity.getAuthToken()` allows you to natively authenticate. This method allows you to skip providing a redirect URL and making the authorization token request. Instead, you simply provide the required values inside the `oauth2` manifest property and call this method. The browser will kick open the OAuth dialog and the method's callback will be passed the OAuth token. This is *by far* the simplest way of implementing OAuth in an extension, but it is only available inside Google Chrome. **This requires a "Chrome app" client ID.**
- `chrome.identity.launchWebAuthFlow()` is the more generalized method for using OAuth2. It is cross-browser (works on Firefox, Edge, etc.) and cross-platform (supports OAuth2 with Facebook, Github, etc.). It is much more labor intensive, as it requires you to manually implement each of the OAuth2 steps.

OAuth Redirect URLs

To solve the OAuth redirect URL problem, the browser supports a special URL that will direct the auth flow back to the extension. To access this URL, you can use the `chrome.identity.getRedirectURL()` method. The Chrome documentation describes its behavior:

> *This method enables auth flows with non-Google identity providers by launching a web view and navigating it to the first URL in the provider's auth flow. When the provider redirects to a URL matching the pattern https://<app-id>.chromiumapp.org/*, the window will close, and the final redirect URL will be passed to the callback function.*

In other words, the browser gives this URL special treatment in order to support authentication in the context of browser extensions. All chromium browsers and Firefox support this method.

Tip You can see this special URL handling logic in the chromium source code: `https://chromium.googlesource.com/chromium/chromium/+/master/chrome/browser/extensions/api/identity/web_auth_flow.cc`.

Configuring the Authorization Platform

The first step in setting up OAuth for a chrome extension is to configure the authorization platform to provide access to the extension. This involves configuring the OAuth consent screen and generating a client id (Figures 13-5, 13-6, 13-7, 13-8, and 13-9). The consent screen is what will be shown in the popup when the user begins the OAuth authentication flow; the client ID is the string that uniquely identifies the extension and allows it to engage with the authorization platform (Figure 13-10).

Note This process will be slightly different for various authorization platforms and OAuth flows, but it will always provide you with a client ID.

The following screenshots demonstrate some of these steps when configuring Google OAuth.

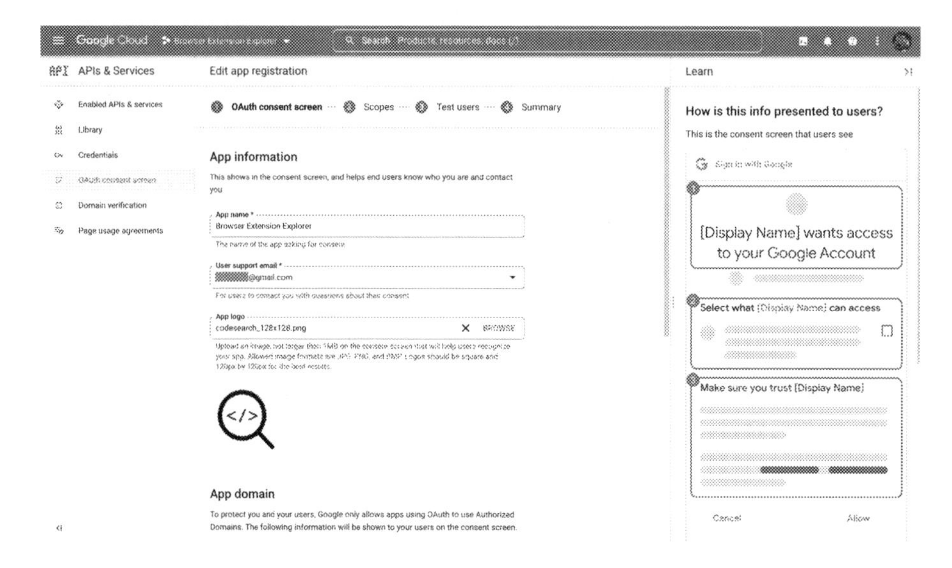

***Figure 13-5.** Configuring the OAuth consent screen in the Google Cloud dashboard*

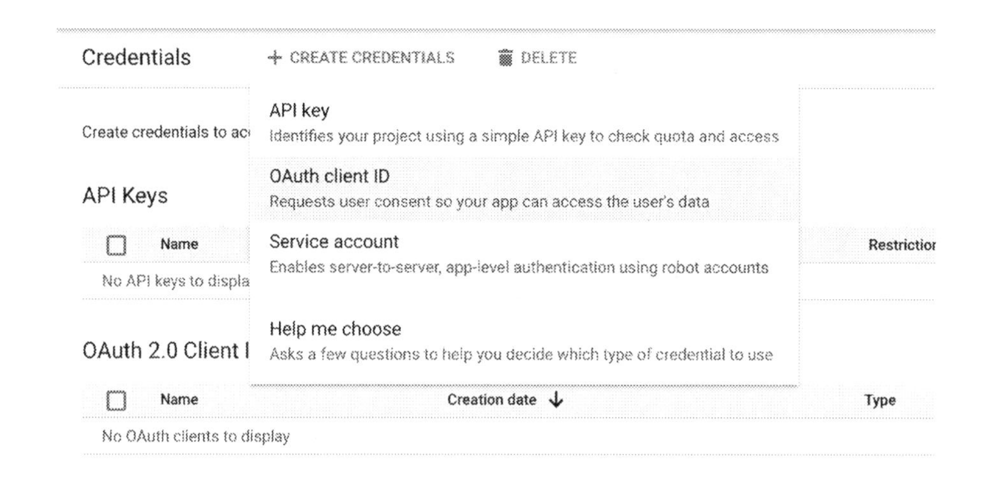

***Figure 13-6.** Creating OAuth client ID credentials for a browser extension in the Google Cloud dashboard*

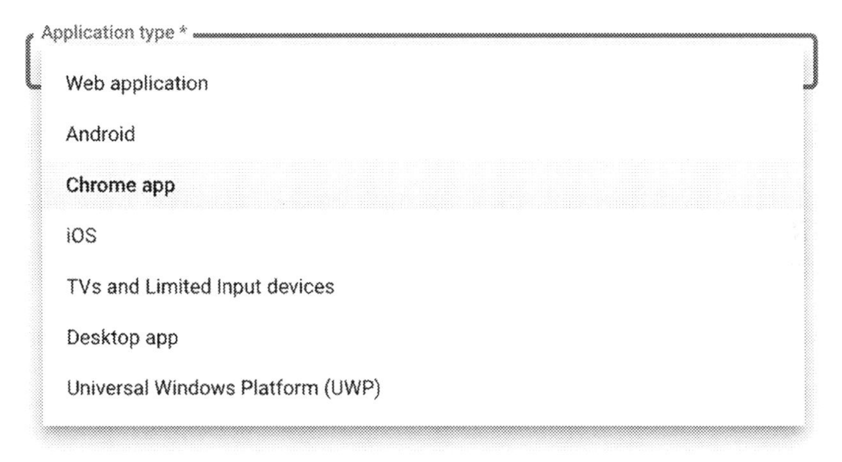

Figure 13-7. *Google's options for an OAuth client ID*

Not all platforms will support this distinction. In the case of Google OAuth, both "Chrome app" and "Web application" can be used for browser extensions.

- **Chrome app** means you are using the manifest `oauth2` manifest field and the `getAuthToken()` method. This will also authenticate the user in the active Google Chrome browser profile, which may not be desirable.
- **Web application** means you are using the `launchWebAuthFlow()` method. This allows you to authenticate separately from the Google Chrome browser profile.

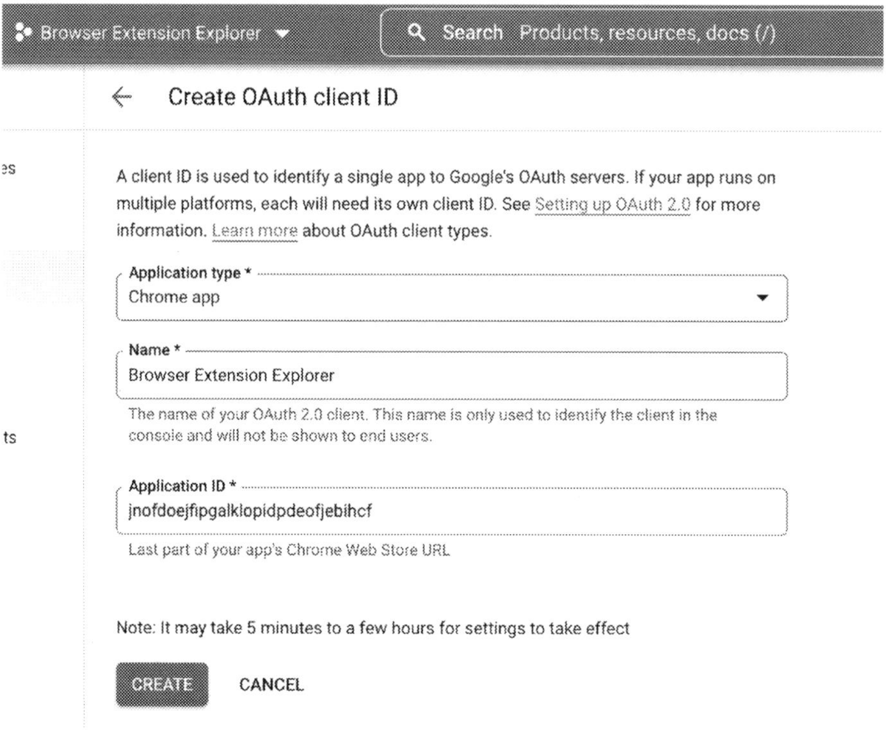

Figure 13-8. Configuring a Chrome app OAuth client ID

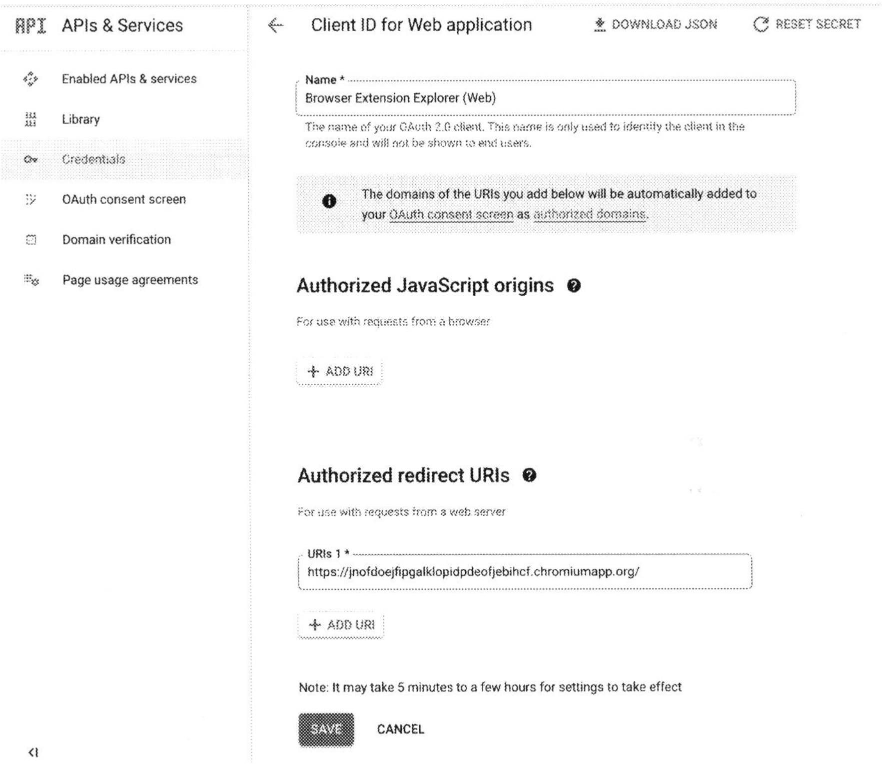

API APIs & Services

Enabled APIs & services

Library

Credentials

OAuth consent screen

Domain verification

Page usage agreements

Client ID for Web application

DOWNLOAD JSON

RESET SECRET

Name *

Browser Extension Explorer (Web)

The domains of the URIs you add below will be automatically added to your OAuth consent screen as authorized domains.

Authorized JavaScript origins

For use with requests from a browser

+ ADD URI

Authorized redirect URIs

For use with requests from a web server

URIs 1 *

https://jnofdoejfipgalklopidpdeofjebihcf.chromiumapp.org/

+ ADD URI

Note: It may take 5 minutes to a few hours for settings to take effect

SAVE CANCEL

Figure 13-9. *Configuring a Web application client ID*

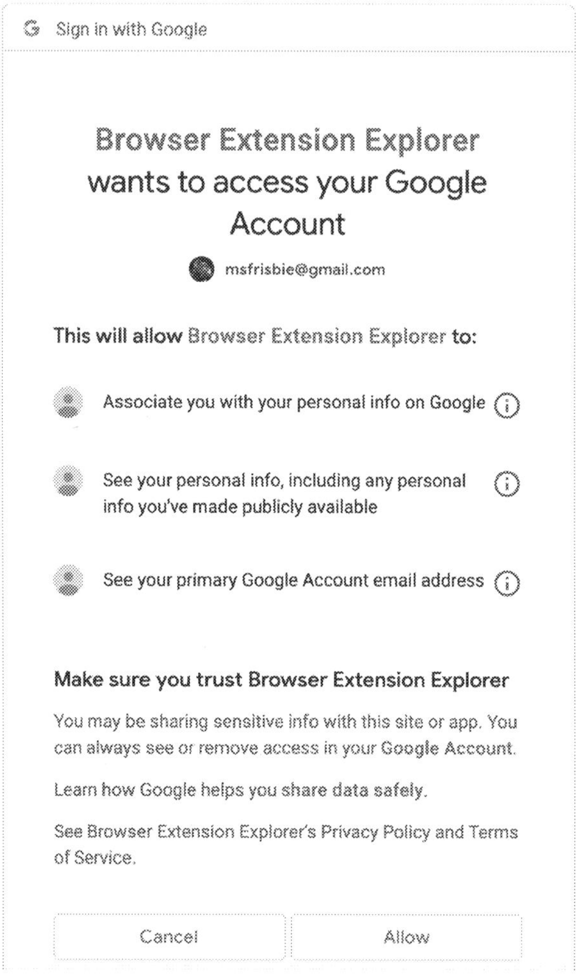

Figure 13-10. *The working OAuth consent screen*

Google will eventually provide you with your client ID in a downloadable JSON. A dummy example is shown here:

client_secret.json

```
{
  "installed": {
    "client_id": "<some_id>.apps.googleusercontent.com",
```

```
    "project_id": "browser-extension-explorer",
    "auth_uri": "https://accounts.google.com/o/oauth2/auth",
    "token_uri": "https://oauth2.googleapis.com/token",
    "auth_provider_x509_cert_url": "https://www.googleapis.com/
    oauth2/v1/certs"
  }
}
```

Other platforms will provide you the client ID in a different fashion and format, but ultimately this is what must make it into your browser extension to enable OAuth authentication.

Additional Help

Setting up OAuth is extremely confusing. I've hand-selected some links that walk you through setting it up in various ways:

- `https://developer.chrome.com/docs/extensions/mv3/tut_oauth/`
- `https://blog.plasmo.com/p/firebase-chrome-extension`

OAuth and OpenID Examples

When it comes to OAuth for extensions, there really isn't a good substitute for getting your hands dirty with actual working code. The following examples demonstrate slightly different ways of configuring and triggering an OAuth flow. **These examples are provided in source code, but they will not work without some legwork on your end. You will need to configure your own OAuth provider information such as client IDs to make them work correctly.**

Tip The book's companion extension, *Browser Extension Explorer*, includes three working OAuth examples. Visit `buildingbrowserextensions.com` to install it.

Google OAuth with getAuthToken()

This example uses Google Chrome's native OAuth faculties to authenticate the user. Clicking the toolbar icon triggers the OAuth flow, and a successful authentication will log some basic fields. Some things to note:

- The permissions requested include `identity`, which gives access to the identity API, and `identity.email`, which allows the extension to easily access the email and Gaia ID of the user account signed into the current profile via `chrome.identity.getProfileUserInfo()`.
- `getAuthToken()` is idempotent. After the user authenticates, it will cache the OAuth token. If called a when the user is authenticated, no OAuth dialog will appear: the method will retrieve the token from the cache and pass it to the callback. The `interactive` option controls whether it will attempt to launch the OAuth dialog if the user is *not* authenticated. If `false`, it will exit and throw an error if not authenticated. Otherwise, the OAuth dialog will open.
- Note that nowhere in this flow are any URLs other than what is provided in the manifest. The redirect URL and OAuth endpoints are all automatically handled by the browser!

Example 13-1a. manifest.json

```
{
  "name": "MVX",
  "version": "0.0.1",
  "manifest_version": 3,
  "action": {},
  "background": {
    "service_worker": "background.js",
    "type": "module"
  },
  "permissions": ["identity", "identity.email"],
  "oauth2": {
    "client_id": "YOUR_CLIENT_ID",
    "scopes": [
      "https://www.googleapis.com/auth/userinfo.email",
      "https://www.googleapis.com/auth/userinfo.profile"
    ]
  }
}
```

Example 13-1b. background.js

```
chrome.action.onClicked.addListener(() => {
  chrome.identity.getAuthToken(
    {
      interactive: true,
    },
    (token) => {
      if (token) {
        chrome.identity.getProfileUserInfo(
          { accountStatus: "ANY" },
          (info) => console.log(info)
```

```
        );
      }
    }
  );
});

// Console output:
// { "email": <google_email>, "id": <google_gaia_id> }
```

Google OpenID with launchWebAuthFlow( )

Note This section assumes you have basic knowledge of how the OpenID Connect protocol works. For an introduction to OpenID, Auth0 has an excellent writeup on it: `https://auth0.com/intro-to-iam/what-is-openid-connect-oidc/`.

This example implements a Google OpenID Connect flow to authenticate the user using `launchWebAuthFlow()`. Clicking the toolbar icon triggers the OpenID flow, and a successful authentication will log the OpenID payload. Some things to note

- Compared to the previous example, we no longer have a need for the `identity.email` permission since we are not using the `getProfileUserInfo()` method.
- Note that the client ID is being passed inside JavaScript rather than provided in the manifest.
- With `launchWebAuthFlow()`, you must now manually provide the redirect URL that the browser will use to redirect back into your extension's callback.
- `launchWebAuthFlow()` has an `interactive` control which behaves identically to that of `getAuthToken()`.

- OpenID requires specific query string parameters in the initial URL and returns a JSON web token (JWT). This example unpacks the JWT so you can see the data packaged inside.

Example 13-2a. manifest.json

```
{
  "name": "MVX",
  "version": "0.0.1",
  "manifest_version": 3,
  "action": {},
  "background": {
    "service_worker": "background.js",
    "type": "module"
  },
  "permissions": ["identity"]
}
```

Example 13-2b. background.js

```
chrome.action.onClicked.addListener(() => {
  const clientId = "YOUR_CLIENT_ID";
  const extensionRedirectUri = chrome.identity.
  getRedirectURL();
  const nonce = Math.random().toString(36).substring(2, 15);

  const authUrl = new URL("https://accounts.google.com/o/
  oauth2/v2/auth");

  // Define fields for OpenID
  authUrl.searchParams.set("client_id", clientId);
  authUrl.searchParams.set("response_type", "id_token");
  authUrl.searchParams.set("redirect_uri", extensionRedirectUri);
```

```
  authUrl.searchParams.set("scope", "openid profile email");
  authUrl.searchParams.set("nonce", nonce);
  authUrl.searchParams.set("prompt", "consent");

  chrome.identity.launchWebAuthFlow(
    {
      url: authUrl.href,
      interactive: true,
    },
    (redirectUrl) => {
      if (redirectUrl) {
        // The ID token is in the URL hash
        const urlHash = redirectUrl.split("#")[1];
        const params = new URLSearchParams(urlHash);
        const jwt = params.get("id_token");

        // Parse the JSON Web Token
        const base64Url = jwt.split(".")[1];
        const base64 = base64Url.replace("-", "+").
        replace("_", "/");
        const token = JSON.parse(atob(base64));

        console.log(token);
      }
    }
  );
});

// Console output:
// {
//     "iss": "https://accounts.google.com",
//     "azp": "...",
```

```
//     "aud": "...",
//     "sub": "...",
//     "email": "XXXXX@gmail.com",
//     "email_verified": true,
//     "nonce": "...",
//     "name": "Matt Frisbie",
//     "picture": "...",
//     "given_name": "Matt",
//     "family_name": "Frisbie",
//     "locale": "en",
//     "iat": ...,
//     "exp": ...,
//     "jti": "..."
// }
```

Manual Github OAuth with launchWebAuthFlow()

This example implements a Github OAuth2 flow to authenticate the user using `launchWebAuthFlow()`. Clicking the toolbar icon triggers the Github OAuth2 flow, and a successful authentication will log the Github profile payload. Some things to note

- This example does all the legwork of a full OAuth flow: launching the authentication dialog, collecting the authorization code, using that to fetch the access token, and finally performing an OAuth-authenticated request.
- The Github OAuth dialog passes the initial authorization code by appending it to the redirect URL, which here is plucked out inside the callback.

- Github's OAuth provides you with a client secret that must be included with the request to fetch the access token.

Example 13-3a. manifest.json

```
{
  "name": "MVX",
  "version": "0.0.1",
  "manifest_version": 3,
  "action": {},
  "background": {
    "service_worker": "background.js",
    "type": "module"
  },
  "permissions": ["identity"]
}
```

Example 13-3b. background.js

```
chrome.action.onClicked.addListener(() => {
  const clientId = "YOUR_CLIENT_ID";
  const extensionRedirectUri = chrome.identity.getRedirectURL();

  const authUrl = new URL("https://github.com/login/oauth/
  authorize");

  authUrl.searchParams.set("client_id", clientId);
  authUrl.searchParams.set("redirect_uri", extensionRedirectUri);

  chrome.identity.launchWebAuthFlow(
    {
      url: authUrl.href,
      interactive: true,
    },
```

```
async (redirectUrl) => {
  if (redirectUrl) {
    const queryString = new URL(redirectUrl).search;
    const params = new URLSearchParams(queryString);
    const code = params.get("code");

    const authUrl = new URL("https://github.com/login/
    oauth/access_token");
    authUrl.searchParams.append("client_id", clientId);
    authUrl.searchParams.append("redirect_uri",
    extensionRedirectUri);
    authUrl.searchParams.append(
      "client_secret",
      "YOUR_CLIENT_SECRET"
    );
    authUrl.searchParams.append("code", code);

    const response = await fetch(authUrl, {
      method: "POST",
      headers: {
        Accept: "application/json",
      },
    });

    const accessTokenData = await response.json();

    const r = await fetch("https://api.github.com/user", {
      headers: {
        Authorization: "Bearer " + accessTokenData.
        access_token,
      },
    });

    console.log(await r.json());
```

```
      }
    }
  );
});

// Console output:
// {
//     "login": "msfrisbie",
//     "id": ...,
//     "node_id": "...",
//     "avatar_url": "...",
//     "name": " Matt Frisbie",
//     "blog": "https://www.mattfriz.com",
//     "location": "Chicago, IL",
//     "bio": "Software engineer, bestselling author",
//     "twitter_username": "mattfriz",
//     "url": "https://api.github.com/users/msfrisbie",
//     ...
//   }}
```

Networking APIs

Browser extensions are granted access to some powerful APIs that can be used to inspect and modify traffic flow inside the browser. These methods are the reason ad blocking extensions are so effective. This section will examine three APIs:

- The `webNavigation` API allows you to observe top-level browser navigation events in very granular detail.
- The `webRequest` API allows you to intercept and modify traffic in a blocking fashion, meaning that for any network request, the extension can inject a JavaScript

function that may or may not modify or cancel the request entirely. The "blocking" designator indicates that the network request will wait for the JavaScript function to return before continuing.

- The `declarativeNetRequest` API allows you to build rulesets that instruct the browser how it should natively handle network requests. These rules may tell the browser to modify or block a request. This API is the successor to the `webRequest` API and is considerably less powerful in several ways. This API is only available in manifest v3.

Note In manifest v3, support for `webRequest` is fragmented. For example, Firefox will continue to support this API, whereas Chromium browsers are removing support.

The webNavigation API

The `webNavigation` API allows an extension to see navigation events from the browser. The API allows an extension to add event handler for the following navigation lifecycle events:

- onBeforeNavigate
- onCommitted
- onCompleted
- onCreatedNavigationTarget
- onDOMContentLoaded
- onErrorOccurred

- onHistoryStateUpdated
- onReferenceFragmentUpdated
- onTabReplaced

Figure 13-11 shows the flow of events.

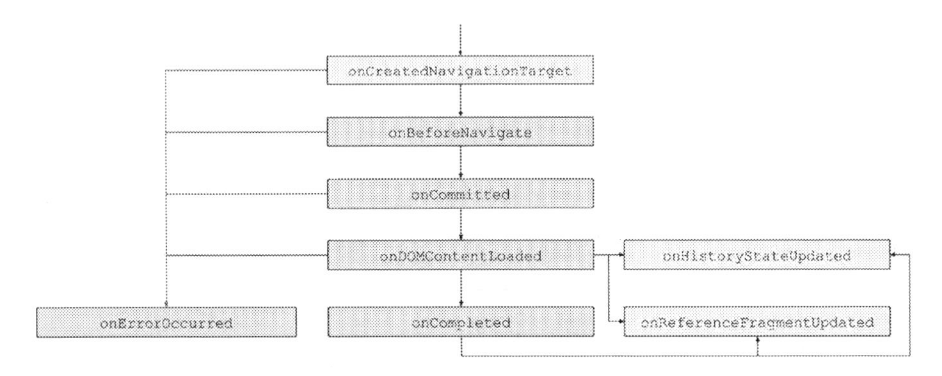

Figure 13-11. *The `webNavigation` event flow*

Note Details of each of these events can be found in the MDN documentation: `https://developer.mozilla.org/en-US/docs/Mozilla/Add-ons/WebExtensions/API/webNavigation`.

Most of the time, extensions will only care to set handlers for the primary lifecycle events fired by normal browser navigation:

1. onBeforeNavigate
2. onCommitted
3. onDOMContentLoaded
4. onCompleted

The following simple extension will log to the extension console any time a tab in the browser visits a new URL. Load the extension, open a new tab, and navigate to any website to see navigation events in real time.

Example 13-4a. manifest.json

```
{
  "name": "MVX",
  "version": "0.0.1",
  "manifest_version": 3,
  "background": {
    "service_worker": "background.js",
    "type": "module"
  },
  "permissions": ["webNavigation"]
}
```

Example 13-4b. background.js

```
chrome.webNavigation.onCompleted.addListener((details) => {
  console.log(details);
});

// Example console log:
// {
//     "documentId": "7D0F7EBBCB0020C74DA89F2D36C461B4",
//     "documentLifecycle": "active",
//     "frameId": 0,
//     "frameType": "outermost_frame",
//     "parentFrameId": -1,
//     "processId": 1040,
//     "tabId": 173953269,
//     "timeStamp": 1661549345594.7412,
```

```
//      "url": "https://en.wikipedia.org/wiki/Main_Page"
// }
```

The webRequest API

The `webRequest` API allows browser extensions to inspect and modify network requests events from a web page. The API allows an extension to add event handler for the following request lifecycle events:

- onActionIgnored
- onAuthRequired
- onBeforeRedirect
- onBeforeRequest
- onBeforeSendHeaders
- onCompleted
- onErrorOccurred
- onHeadersReceived
- onResponseStarted
- onSendHeaders

Figure 13-12 shows the flow of events.

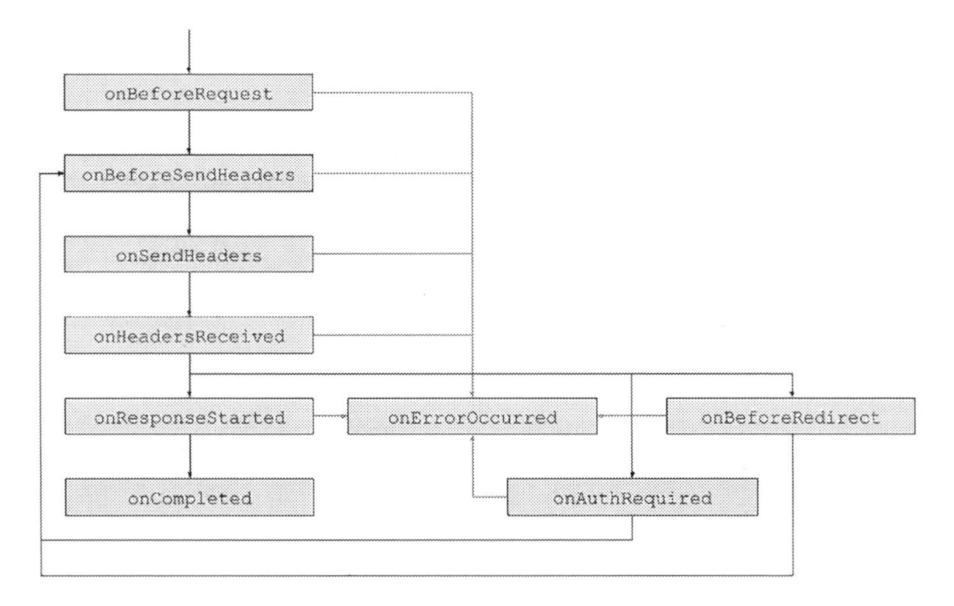

Figure 13-12. *The* `webRequest` *event flow*

Note Details of each of these events can be found in the MDN documentation: `https://developer.mozilla.org/en-US/docs/Mozilla/Add-ons/WebExtensions/API/webRequest`.

Modifying Requests

If you merely wish to inspect the request lifecycle event data, only the `webRequest` permission is needed. If, however, you wish to potentially modify these requests, you will need an additional `webRequestBlocking` permission. This grants you the ability to perform the following tasks:

- The extension can **cancel a request** inside the `onBeforeRequest`, `onBeforeSendHeaders`, or `onAuthRequired` blocking handler.

- The extension can **redirect the request** inside the onBeforeRequest or onHeadersReceived blocking handler.
- The extension can **modify the request headers** inside the onBeforeSendHeaders blocking handler.
- The extension can **modify the response headers** in the onHeadersReceived blocking handler.
- The extension can **modify the request's authentication credentials** in the onAuthRequired blocking handler.

The following simple example will block all image requests on Wikipedia. Keep in mind that you must also request URL permissions if you want to inspect or modify requests on that origin.

Note The webRequest API and manifest v3 lack support in Google Chrome, so this example is written in manifest v2. I recommend testing it out in Firefox.

Example 13-5a. manifest.json

```
{
  "name": "MVX",
  "version": "0.0.1",
  "manifest_version": 2,
  "background": {
    "scripts": ["background.js"]
  },
  "permissions": [
    "webRequest",
```

```
    "webRequestBlocking",
    "<all_urls>"
  ]
}
```

Example 13-5b. background.js

```
chrome.webRequest.onBeforeRequest.addListener(
  () => {
    return {
      cancel: true,
    };
  },
  {
    urls: [
     "*://www.wikipedia.org/portal/wikipedia.org/assets/img/*"
    ],
  },
  ["blocking"]
);
```

Fragmentation

The browser extension space is headed in a bizarre direction. At the time this book was written, it appears that Chromium browsers have decided to end support for `webRequest` in manifest v3, but Firefox may continue to support the API in manifest v3. It is unclear where the space will end up, but at the moment I would not recommend building an extension that relies directly upon this API.

The declarativeNetRequest API

The `declarativeNetRequest` API (DNR) is billed as the successor to the `webRequest` API. The motivation for this shift was to eliminate the blocking JavaScript handlers in favor of a more efficient declarative model that is implemented by the browser. Now, instead of performing modifications inside a JavaScript function, you will supply the "instructions" for each matching request as a JSON config object.

For most extensions, DNR is an effective replacement for `webRequest`. However, ad blocker quality will suffer for two primary reasons:

- Browsers enforce a global cap on the number of rules that extensions can define for `declarativeNetRequest`. Modern ad blockers define on the order of 100,000+ rules, and ad blocker extensions are undoubtedly going to run into this cap limit quickly.
- Modern ad blockers rely on sophisticated logic inside the blocking `webRequest` handlers. Not all of this logic can be translated into the comparatively simplistic `declarativeNetRequest` rules, so ad blocker extensions will not be as effective at fighting ads.

Permissions

The `declarativeNetRequest` API can be used with three different permissions:

- The `declarativeNetRequest` permission allows your extension to define DNR rules, but you will still need to request host permissions to apply rules on specific origins.

- The `declarativeNetRequestWithHostAccess` permission can be used instead of the `declarativeNetRequest` permission. It allows you to block or upgrade requests on any origin without requesting host permissions. Redirects or header modification will still require specific host permissions.
- The `declarativeNetRequestFeedback` permission can be added as a supplement to the previous two. With it, your extension can access functions and events which return information on rules matched.

Rule and Ruleset Structure

All DNR rules take the form of a JSON object. Only one rule will ever be applied per request, per extension. Each rule object is structured as follows:

- The `id` must be a unique positive integer.
- The `priority` is an optional integer that can be used to control which rule is applied in scenarios where multiple rules match a request.
- The `condition` is an object that describes when this rule should be applied. With it, you can include or exclude domains, domain types, tab IDs, and resource types.
- The `action` is an object that describes what this rule does. It includes a `type`, which can be `block`, `redirect`, `allow`, `upgradeScheme`, `modifyHeaders`, or `allowAllRequests`, and various properties which configure how the rule should behave.

DNR rules are defined in one of two ways:

- **Static rulesets** are arrays of rule objects in JSON files. Ruleset files can be provided in the manifest or added programmatically. They can also be enabled or disabled on demand. Static rulesets can only ever exist as immutable files packaged with the extension. The total number of static rules is limited by the browser.
- **Dynamic rules** are rule objects that are exclusively programmatically created. They can be added, removed, modified, and enabled or disabled. A subset of dynamic rule are **session rules**, which are dynamic rules that are not persisted across browsers. The total number of dynamic rules is limited by the browser.

Whether static or dynamic, a DNR rule is treated the same by the browser.

Note The `declarativeNetRequest` API has quite a bit of depth to it. Refer to the Google Chrome documentation for details on all its features: `https://developer.chrome.com/docs/extensions/reference/declarativeNetRequest`.

Static Rulesets

Let's examine static rulesets by examining the following simple extension that can block images on Wikipedia:

Example 13-6a. manifest.json

```
{
  "name": "MVX",
  "version": "0.0.1",
```

```
  "manifest_version": 3,
  "background": {
    "service_worker": "background.js",
    "type": "module"
  },
  "declarative_net_request": {
    "rule_resources": [
      {
        "id": "ruleset_1",
        "enabled": true,
        "path": "rules_1.json"
      }
    ]
  },
  "action": {},
  "permissions": ["declarativeNetRequest"],
  "host_permissions": [
    "*://*.wikipedia.org/*",
    "*://*.wikimedia.org/*"
  ]
}
```

Example 13-6b. background.js

```
const RULESET_ID = "ruleset_1";

chrome.action.onClicked.addListener(async () => {
  const enabled_rulesets =
    await chrome.declarativeNetRequest.getEnabledRulesets();

  if (enabled_rulesets.includes(RULESET_ID)) {
    chrome.declarativeNetRequest.updateEnabledRulesets({
      disableRulesetIds: [RULESET_ID],
```

```
    });
  } else {
    chrome.declarativeNetRequest.updateEnabledRulesets({
      enableRulesetIds: [RULESET_ID],
    });
  }

  console.log("Toggled ruleset");
});
```

Example 13-6c. rules_1.json

```
[
  {
    "id": 1,
    "priority": 1,
    "action": {
      "type": "block"
    },
    "condition": {
      "domains": ["wikipedia.org", "wikimedia.org"],
      "resourceTypes": ["image"]
    }
  }
]
```

Load this extension and navigate to `wikipedia.org`. The initial extension state will enable the ruleset. You will notice that images do not load. Click the extension's toolbar button to toggle the ruleset. When you reload Wikipedia again, images should load normally.

You may notice that a new `_metadata` directory has appeared inside your local development folder (Figure 13-13). As the name suggests, the binary file inside the directory is how the browser keeps track of active rulesets. Feel free to ignore it but ensure you do not commit it to version control or add it to a production build.

Figure 13-13. *Automatically generated indexed ruleset binary*

Dynamic Rules

Dynamic rules are very similar to static rulesets. In similar fashion, they can be queried, added, and removed on demand. In this example, let's instead write a dynamic redirect rule:

Example 13-7a. manifest.json

```
{
  "name": "MVX",
  "version": "0.0.1",
  "manifest_version": 3,
  "background": {
    "service_worker": "background.js",
    "type": "module"
  },
  "action": {},
  "permissions": ["declarativeNetRequest"],
```

```
  "host_permissions": ["*://*.wikipedia.org/*", "*://*.
  wikimedia.org/*"]
}
```

Example 13-7b. background.js

```
const RULE_ID = 1;

const RULE_1 = {
  id: RULE_ID,
  priority: 1,
  action: {
    type: "redirect",
    redirect: {
      url: "https://upload.wikimedia.org/wikipedia/commons/
      thumb/b/b1/Hot_dog_with_mustard.png/1920px-Hot_dog_with_
      mustard.png",
    },
  },
  condition: {
    domains: ["wikipedia.org", "wikimedia.org"],
    resourceTypes: ["image"],
  },
};

chrome.action.onClicked.addListener(async () => {
  const dynamic_rules = await
    chrome.declarativeNetRequest.getDynamicRules();

  if (dynamic_rules.find((rule) => rule.id === 1)) {
    chrome.declarativeNetRequest.updateDynamicRules({
      removeRuleIds: RULE_ID,
    });
```

```
  } else {
    chrome.declarativeNetRequest.updateDynamicRules({
      addRules: [RULE_1],
    });
  }

  console.log("Toggled rule");
});
```

Load this extension and navigate to `wikipedia.org`. You will notice that images load normally. Click the extension's toolbar button and reload Wikipedia again. All images on Wikipedia should now be a hot dog.

Summary

In this chapter, we explored a variety of modalities in which browser extensions can send network requests. We reviewed all the different components and how they can and should send network requests. Next, we discussed authentication strategies, including in-depth coverage on how to implement OAuth in browser extensions. Finally, we discussed how to use the major WebExtensions APIs that can inspect and manipulate traffic in the browser.

In the next chapter, we will cover how to develop an extension locally, publish it on extension marketplaces, and deploy updates.

CHAPTER 14

Extension Development and Deployment

The process of developing, testing, and publishing a browser extension is significantly different from developing a traditional website. The steps involved more closely resemble that of a mobile app than a web technology. Gaining a better understanding of how to effectively develop, publish, and distribute your extension is critical to mastery of the subject.

Note This chapter will be Google Chrome-centric, but all major browsers (with the exception of Safari) offer nearly identical facilities when developing locally and when publishing to a marketplace.

Local Development

You'll spend quite a lot of time developing your extension locally, so it's worth getting familiar with how all the parts fit together. In this section, we'll explore how a locally loaded extension works and all the different ways you can look under the hood.

M. Frisbie, *Building Browser Extensions*, https://doi.org/10.1007/978-1-4842-8725-5_14

Tip For developers new to extension development, the *Browser Extension Crash Course* chapter demonstrates the basic process of loading a local extension into your browser for development purposes.

Inspecting Your Extension

Begin by installing this dummy extension:

Example 14-1a. manifest.json

```
{
  "name": "MVX",
  "version": "0.0.1",
  "manifest_version": 3,
  "background": {
    "service_worker": "background.js",
    "type": "module"
  },
  "options_ui": {
    "open_in_tab": true,
    "page": "options.html"
  },
  "content_scripts": [
    {
      "matches": ["<all_urls>"],
      "css": [],
      "js": ["content-script.js"]
    }
  ],
```

```
  "permissions": [
    "scripting",
    "declarativeNetRequest",
    "tabs"
   ],
  "host_permissions": ["<all_urls>"]
}
```

Example 14-1b. options.html

```
<!DOCTYPE html>
<html>
  <body>
    <h1>Options</h1>

    <script src="options.js"></script>
  </body>
</html>
```

Example 14-1c. options.js

```
console.log("Initialized options!");
```

Example 14-1d. background.js

```
console.log("Initialized background!");
```

Example 14-1e. content-script.js

```
console.log("Content script initialized!");
```

Once this extension is loaded locally, your browser will add a card inside the browser extension management view. In Google Chrome, the URL for this page is `chrome://extensions`. An example card is shown in Figure 14-1.

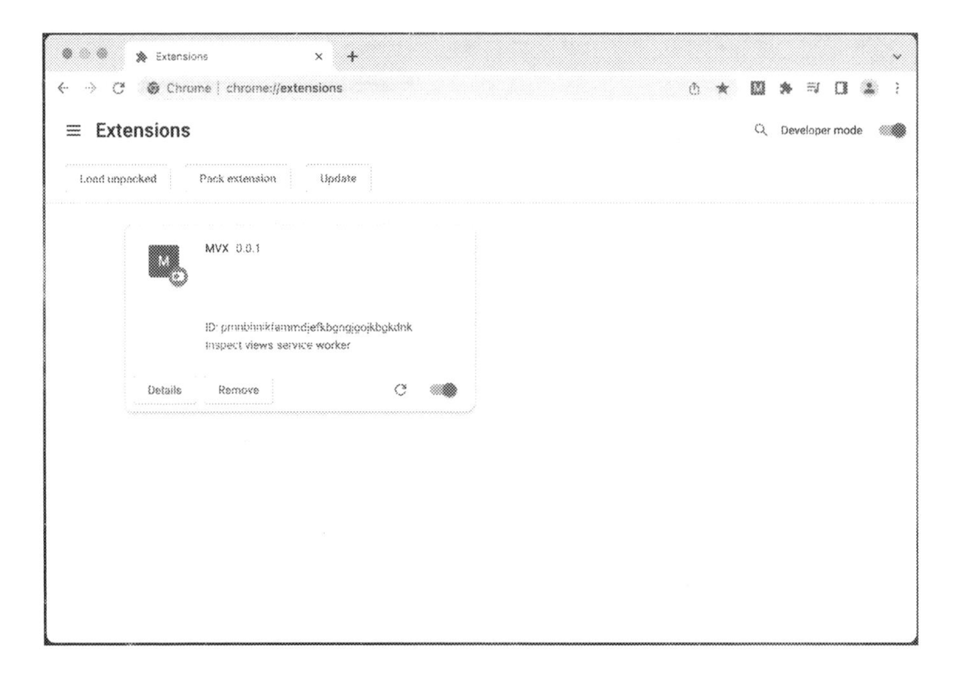

Figure 14-1. *An example extension card in the extension management page view*

From this card, you're able to view the details page, uninstall or disable the extension, view the extension's errors page, and reload the extension.

Note Details about reloading an extension are covered later in this chapter.

Clicking to open the details page will reveal something like Figure 14-2.

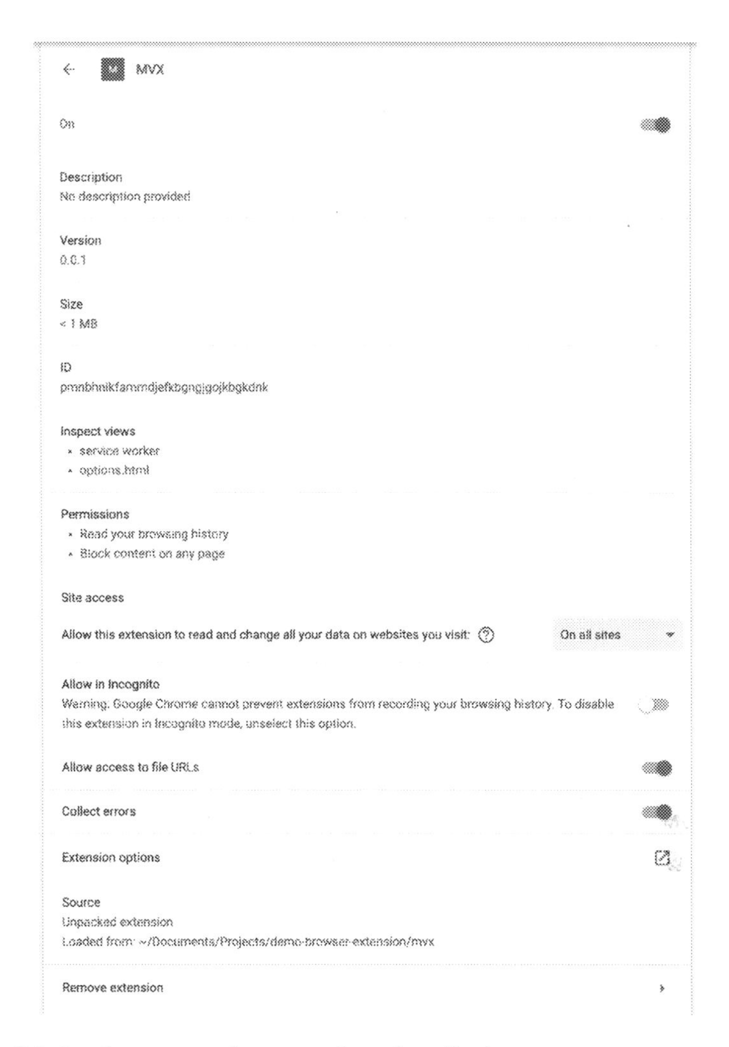

Figure 14-2. *An example extension detail view*

There are a few things to note in this view:

- **This view is a snapshot.** Values listed inside are not real-time and will not update unless the page reloads.

- **Inspect views** contains a list of links paired to each extension view that is currently active. This list is analogous to the values returned from `chrome.extension.getViews()`. Each link will open a developer tools window targeted at that particular extension view. (The "views" name can be confusing, as this tool also allows you to inspect the background service worker, which has no user interface.)
- **Permissions** displays the list of permissions prompts that the extension would have to explicitly request if it were loaded in production. Because this extension is loaded in development mode, the permissions dialog is silenced.
- **Source** indicates where in the current OS's filesystem it is loading the extension files from.

Inspecting an Extension View

Clicking the "options" link under *Inspect Views* will open the corresponding developer tools interfaces (Figure 14-3).

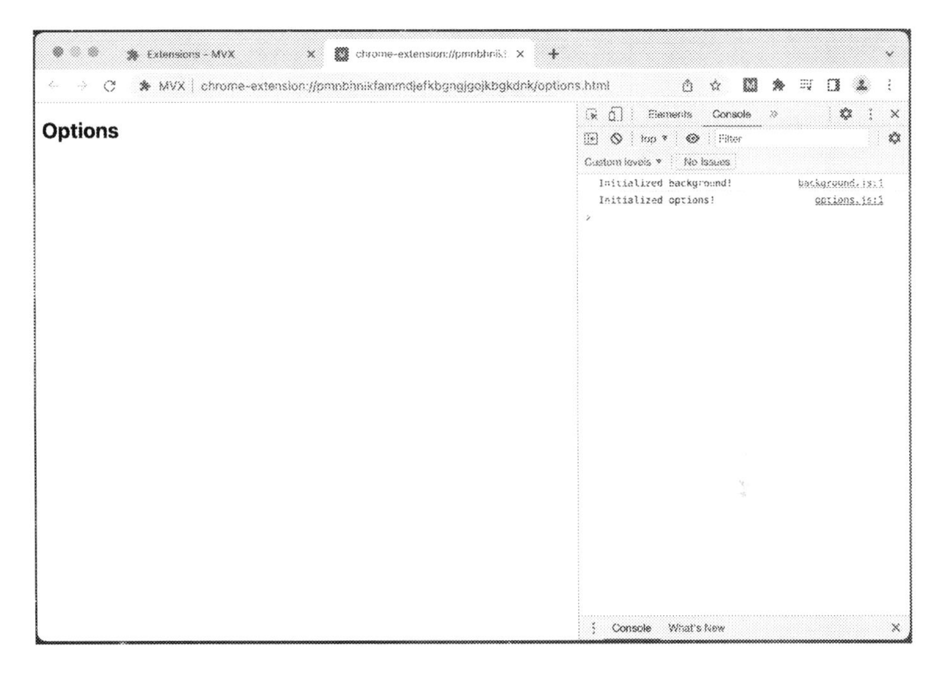

Figure 14-3. The options page inspect view

Note here that the console is showing log output for both the current tab console output and the background service worker. If you wish to split out console outputs, the developer console allows you to select specific sources (Figure 14-4).

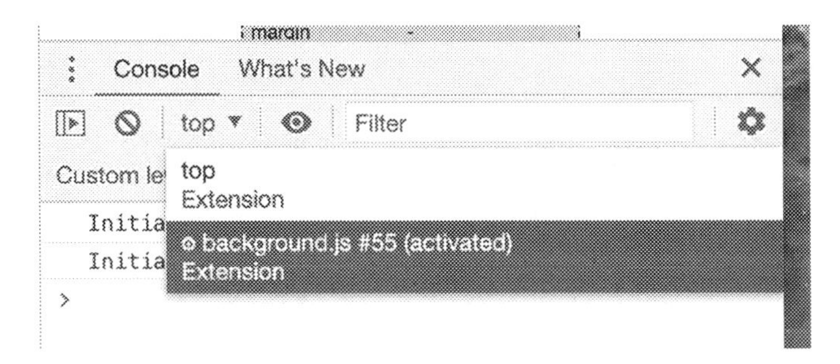

Figure 14-4. Selecting a logging source in developer tools

Inspecting a Background Service Worker

It's also possible to directly inspect a background service worker. Clicking the *Inspect view* link will reveal something like the following (Figure 14-5).

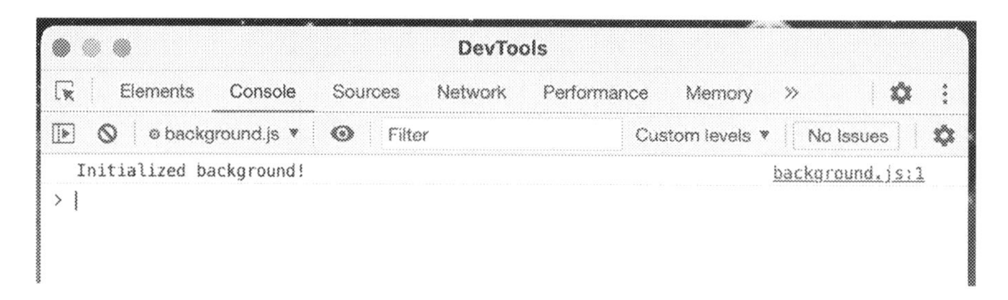

Figure 14-5. *Inspecting the background service worker*

Warning One *extremely* important thing to keep in mind is that this background service worker will interfere with the lifecycle of the service worker. It will prevent the service worker from going idle. It will also prolong the lifespan of a service worker past reloads, causing bizarre behavior when debugging an extension. **When you are done with a service worker developer tools window, close it immediately**. Leaving it open in the background will change the behavior of your local extension in unpredictable ways and make it much harder to debug.

Chrome offers a real-time view of your service worker status and log output at `chrome://serviceworker-internals/` (Figure 14-6). This page will not interfere with how your service workers behave, allowing them to go idle.

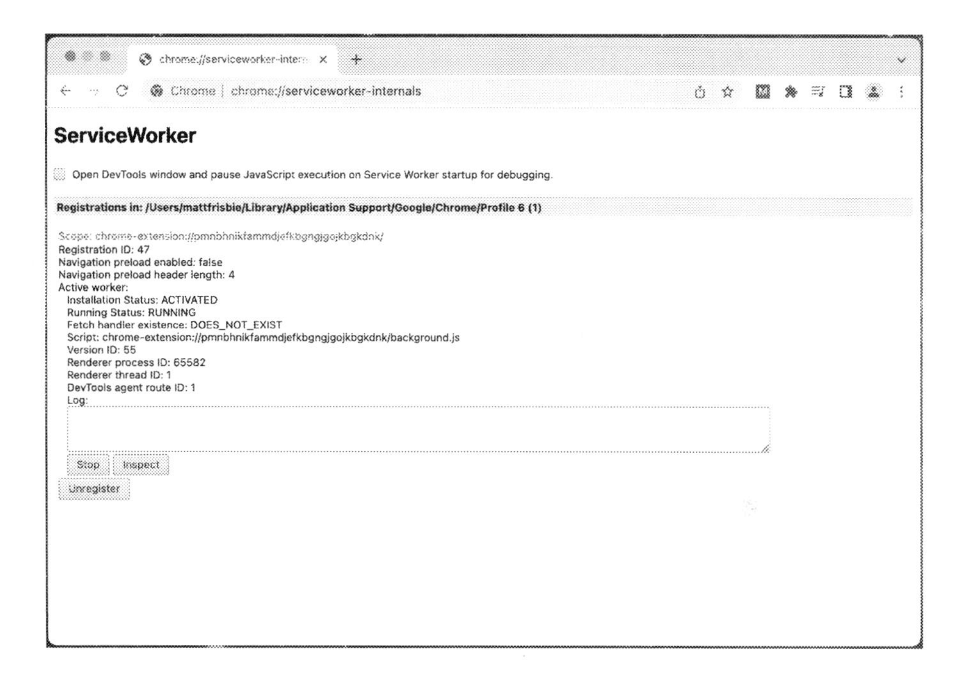

Figure 14-6. *Google Chrome's service worker internals page*

Inspecting a Content Script

Inspecting the console for web pages with content scripts will mix the console output for the web page and the content script together (Figure 14-7).

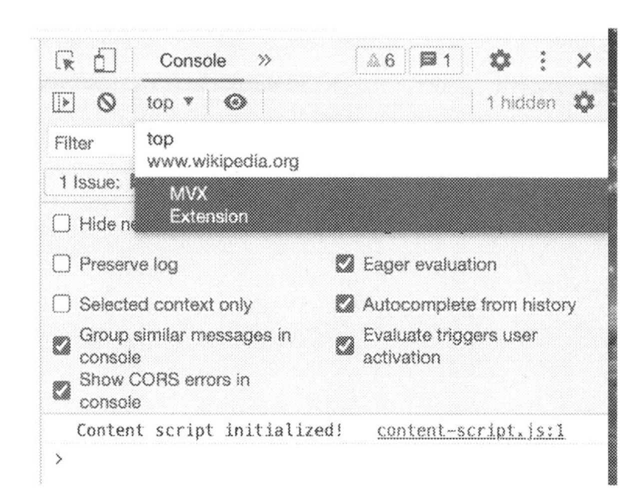

***Figure 14-7.** Example console output for Wikipedia.org*

As with background service workers and options pages, it is possible to filter for only the content script console output.

File Changes

In the extension detail view shown above, it indicates where in the filesystem the extension was loaded from. This is because the extension is serving files directly from that directory! Any changes you make to the source files will be immediately reflected the next time the extension loads them via network request. For example, a modification to `popup.html` will show the very next time the popup is opened. This does *not* apply to files that the extension uses only on install such as `manifest.json`. Updates to these files will only be reflected upon a formal extension reload.

Error Monitoring

Monitoring errors during development can be tricky. For views that have HTML interfaces, errors thrown in the page can be monitored via the normal developer tools console. All errors thrown in an extension, no matter where they are thrown, will appear in the extension error view (Figures 14-8, 14-9 and 14-10).

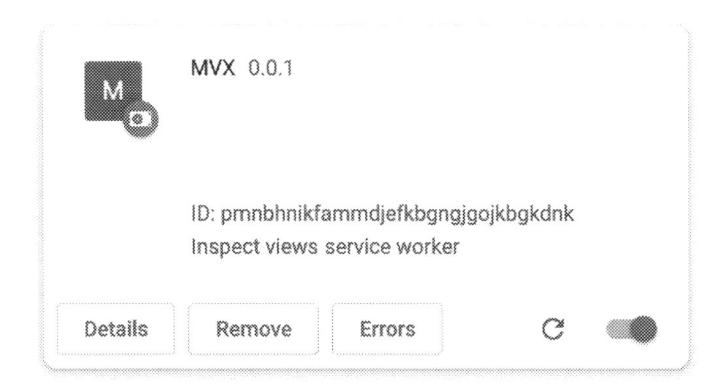

***Figure 14-8.** The Errors button will only appear when the extension throws its first error. This button will open the extensions error view*

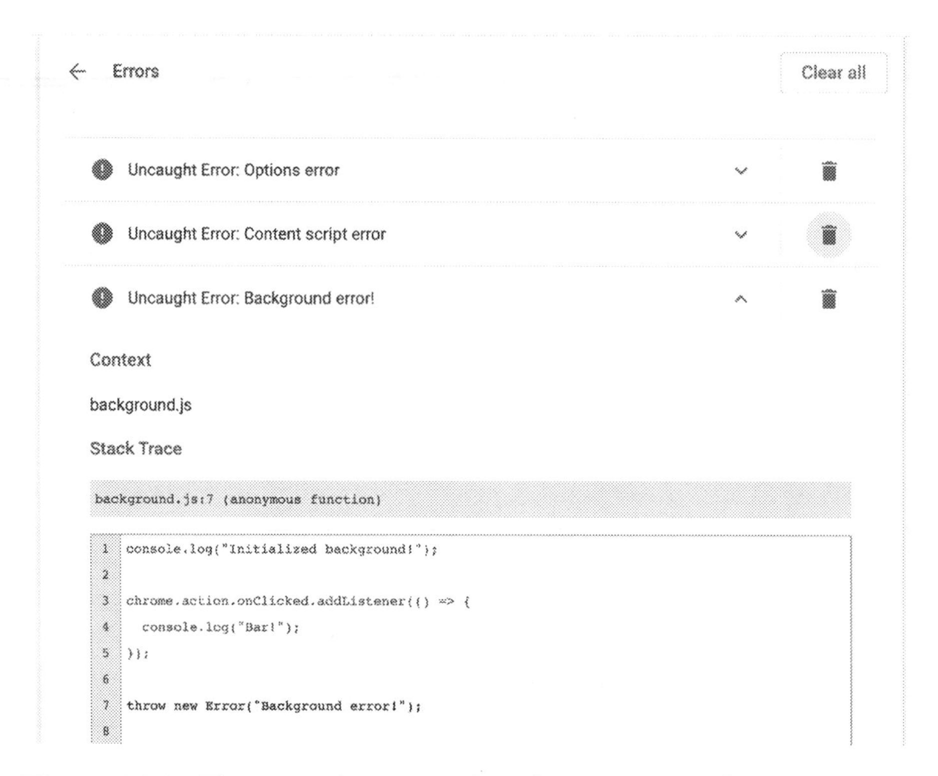

***Figure 14-9.** The extension error view showing errors from multiple sources*

Warning If a service worker throws an error in the first turn of the event loop, it will fail to register. This is important, as any event handlers that it sets will never execute.

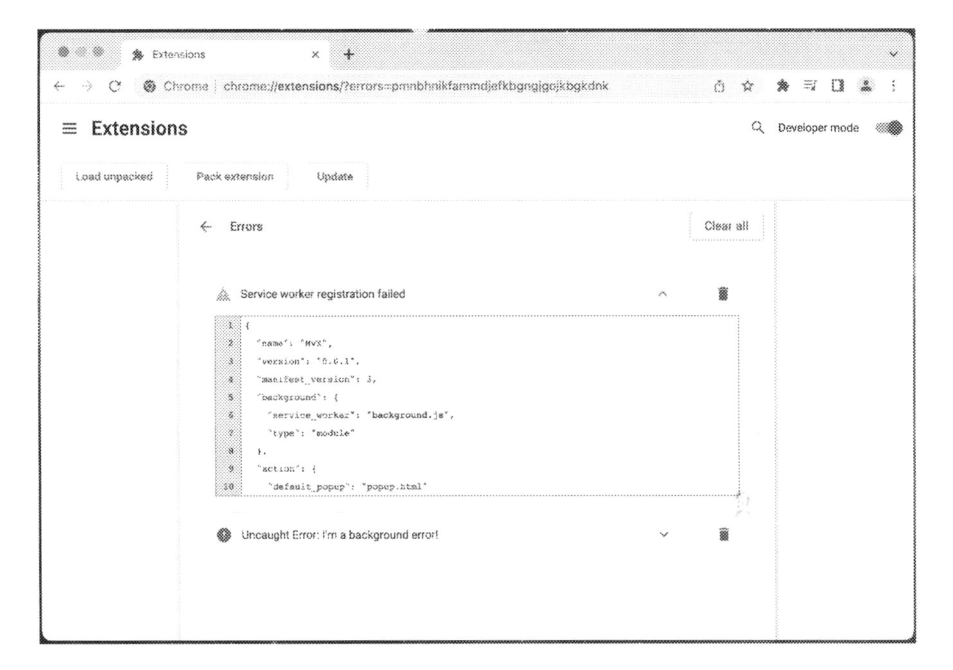

Figure 14-10. *A service worker fails to register after an error thrown during initialization*

Extension Reloads

There are several different points at which portions of the extension are reloaded:

- An **extension reload** obtains a new copy of `manifest.json`, updates the background service worker, and closes any stale popups and options pages that are open. This is required when the `manifest.json` changes.
- An **extension page reload** is a page refresh of any page that uses the extension protocol `chrome-extension://`. This is required to reflect changes in HTML, JS, CSS, and images in popup and options pages.

- A **web page reload** is a page refresh of any web page that has content scripts injected. This is required to reflect changes in the injected content scripts.
- A **devtools reload** is closing and opening the browser's developer tools interface. This is required to reflect changes in devtools pages.

There are three ways to force an extension reload:

- Uninstall and reinstall the extension
- Click the reload icon ↻ in the corresponding card on the Chrome Extensions page
- Programmatically reload the extension using `chrome.runtime.reload()` or `chrome.management.setEnabled()`

Automated Extension Tests

Because the components of browser extensions are built from web technologies, testing them is not too different from testing web pages. Popular tools such as Jest and Puppeteer can be configured to power automated tests for your extension. Some idiomatic aspects of browser extensions such as popups and content scripts can't be directly tested, but with some clever workarounds you will still be able to compose a robust and effective test suite.

Note This section assumes you are familiar with JavaScript automated testing. If not, the Jest documentation has a good tutorial geared for beginners: `https://jestjs.io/docs/tutorial-react`

Unit Tests

Because unit tests don't rely on extension components rendering inside their native browser containers, these tests can be written in a nearly identical fashion to regular web page unit tests. To stub out the chrome extension APIs, the `sinon-chrome` package is excellent: `https://github.com/acvetkov/sinon-chrome`. This package allows you to stub out the callback values for extension APIs in a very clean manner.

A popular unit test setup for extensions is to use Parcel as the main build tool, React as the framework, and Jest as the test runner. The following example sets up a very simple extension with a popup that reads from the chrome storage API. The example includes some unit tests that make sure the popup renders as expected:

Example 14-2a. manifest.json

```
{
  "name": "MVX",
  "version": "0.0.1",
  "manifest_version": 3,
  "action": {
    "default_popup": "index.html"
  },
  "permissions": ["storage"]
}
```

Example 14-2b. package.json

```
{
  "scripts": {
    "start": "parcel watch manifest.json -host localhost",
    "build": "parcel build manifest.json",
    "test": "jest -watch"
  },
```

```
  "dependencies": {
    "@types/chrome": "^0.0.196",
    "react": "^18.2.0",
    "react-dom": "^18.2.0"
  },
  "devDependencies": {
    "@babel/preset-env": "^7.18.10",
    "@babel/preset-react": "^7.18.6",
    "@parcel/config-webextension": "^2.7.0",
    "@testing-library/jest-dom": "^5.16.5",
    "@testing-library/react": "^13.4.0",
    "jest": "^29.0.2",
    "jest-environment-jsdom": "^29.0.2",
    "parcel": "^2.7.0",
    "process": "^0.11.10",
    "sinon-chrome": "^3.0.1"
  },
  "jest": {
    "testEnvironment": "jsdom"
  }
}
```

Example 14-2c. index.html

```
<!DOCTYPE html>
<html>
  <body>
    <div id="app"></div>
    <script type="module" src="index.tsx"></script>
  </body>
</html>
```

Example 14-2d. index.tsx

```
import React from "react";
import { createRoot } from "react-dom/client";
import { Popup } from "./Popup";

const rootElement = document.getElementById("app");
const root = createRoot(rootElement);

root.render(<Popup />);
```

Example 14-2e. .parcelrc

```
{
  "extends": "@parcel/config-webextension",
  "transformers": {
    "*.{js,mjs,jsx,cjs,ts,tsx}": [
      "@parcel/transformer-js",
      "@parcel/transformer-react-refresh-wrap"
    ]
  }
}
```

Example 14-2f. .babelrc

```
{
  "presets": [
    ["@babel/preset-env", { "targets": { "node":
"current" } }],
    "@babel/preset-react"
  ]
}
```

Example 14-2g. Popup.tsx

```
import React, { useEffect, useState } from "react";

export function Popup() {
  const [count, setCount] = useState(null);

  useEffect(() => {
    chrome.storage.sync.get(["count"], (result) => {
      if (typeof result.count !== "number") {
        result.count = 0;
      }
      setCount(result.count);
    });
  }, []);

  if (count != null) {
    return <h1>Popup count: {count}</h1>;
  }
}
```

Example 14-2h. Popup.test.js

```
import { render, screen } from "@testing-library/react";
import React from "react";
import { Popup } from "./Popup";
import chrome from "sinon-chrome";

describe("Popup", () => {
  beforeAll(() => {
    global.chrome = chrome;
  });

  test("Reads from the storage api", () => {
    render(<Popup />);
```

```
    expect(chrome.storage.sync.get.withArgs(["count"]).
    calledOnce).toBe(true);
  });

  test("Renders a default value", () => {
    chrome.storage.sync.get.withArgs(["count"]).yields({ count:
    undefined });

    render(<Popup />);

    expect(screen.queryByText("Popup count: 0")).not.
    toBeNull();
  });

  test("Renders the storage API value", () => {
    chrome.storage.sync.get.withArgs(["count"]).yields({
    count: 3 });

    render(<Popup />);

    expect(screen.queryByText("Popup count: 3")).not.
    toBeNull();
  });

  afterAll(() => {
    chrome.flush();
  });
});
```

Tip If you are setting this example up from scratch, running `yarn install` should get this setup working.

For developers already familiar with how typical React unit testing looks, most of this should not surprise you. Some things to note about this implementation

- Most of this example is typical unit test boilerplate. The parts that are unique to browser extension unit testing are shown in bold.
- Parcel does not need Babel to compile, but Jest does. The extra values in `.parcelrc` are to conditionally use Babel as a compiler only for unit tests.
- The `sinon-chrome` package is being used to detect calls to the storage API, but also is able to stub out the values that are returned in the API's callback.

With all the packages installed, you should find that `npm run start` will start up a Parcel development build, and `npm test` will run your unit test suite (Figure 14-11).

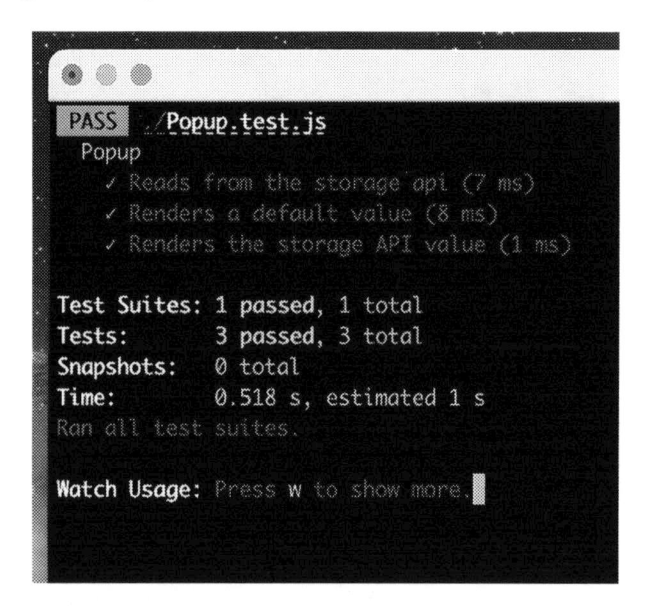

Figure 14-11. *A passing unit test run*

Integration Tests

Integration testing browser extension is made possible via Puppeteer (`https://pptr.dev/`). It allows you to programmatically control a Chromium browser, including navigating to URLs and dispatching user events. It cannot perfectly replicate all the different ways that a browser extension will render its views, but it is by far the best tool available to power an integration test suite.

Puppeteer can be configured to load an extension via the `--load-extension` flag. This flag should be pointed to a local directory on your machine that contains your extension code. You will also need to disable headless mode, as extension cannot be loaded in a headless browser:

```
const path = `path/to/your/extension`;

const browser = await puppeteer.launch({
  // Disable headless mode
  headless: false,
  args: [
    `--disable-extensions-except=${path}`,
    `--load-extension=${path}`
  ]
});
```

This will boot up a Chromium browser, but you'll need to direct the browser to a URL for your extension. Of course, you will need to know ahead of time what the extension's ID is. A good strategy for this is to control the extension ID via the manifest's `key` field:

```
const page = await browser.newPage();
await page.goto(
  'chrome-extension://<extensionID>/popup.html');
// Now you can run test code
```

Because all extension views, including popup pages, can be loaded via direct extension URL, all your extension pages can be tested in this way. Puppeteer can be used to run any Chromium browser, so an integration test suite can target browsers like Google Chrome, Microsoft Edge, or Opera.

Note Setting up a full working integration test with puppeteer is outside the scope of this book. Some full examples are listed in the *Additional Reading* section below.

Additional Reading

Setting up automated testing is tricky, and frankly, annoying. The following are some links to blog posts and documentation about various extension testing setups:

- `https://www.streaver.com/blog/posts/testing-web-extensions`
- `https://github.com/clarkbw/jest-webextension-mock`
- `https://www.npmjs.com/package/jest-chrome`
- `https://medium.com/information-and-technology/unit-testing-browser-extensions-bdd4e60a4f3d`
- `https://medium.com/information-and-technology/integration-testing-browser-extensions-with-jest-676b4e9940ca`
- `https://gokatz.me/blog/automate-chrome-extension-testing/`

- `https://tweak-extension.com/blog/complete-guide-test-chrome-extension-puppeteer/`
- `https://pptr.dev/#working-with-chrome-extensions`

Publishing Extensions

To publish an extension to the Chrome Web Store, you'll first need to pay the one-time $5 fee for a developer account. Once this account is set up, you're ready to submit. Extensions are always uploaded as a zip file of your extension's files and assets.

Store Listing

To publish an extension, you'll need to specify how it should appear to users in the Chrome Web Store. Some items are automatically extracted from the manifest:

- Extension title
- Extension summary
- Icon

Everything else, you'll need to supply yourself:

- Description
- Extension Category
- Assets (including videos and screenshots)
- URLs (main website, support URL, privacy policy URL)

Note These fields can be changed later, but each change will make the entire extension undergo a slow manual review – even if the code was not changed.

Privacy Practices

In the Chrome Web Store, you will need to provide a high-level description of what this extension is doing, as well as a justification for each permission category that is considered sensitive (identity, scripting, etc.). You will also need to indicate if and how you are tracking your users, and in what way.

Review Process

Your extension will undergo manual review the first time it is submitted to ensure it meets Chrome Web Store standards. Once it's approved, it will be available for anyone to install!

Updating Extensions

Once your extension is published, the process of updating it is more or less identical to the initial publishing process. You'll upload a zip file with an updated version number in the manifest. Any additional permissions will require additional justification.

Update Considerations

Once you have an existing userbase and want to push out an update, there are some things you should keep in mind.

Update Delays

Updates are not rolled out immediately. Once you submit an update, it must be reviewed and approved before a user's browser will be able to install it. The user's browser will periodically send out update checks every few hours and download the update if there is one available. However, the browser will lazily apply that update if the extension is active, so there is sometimes a considerable delay between when an update is published and when it is installed. This delay can be between a few minutes and upwards of a week.

Auto-Disabling

Suppose you have a collection of users with your extension installed. If a new version is published that requires a new permission that needs explicit user approval, your extension will be disabled until the user grants that permission. The browser will not pop up a dialog when the extension is disabled, only a small icon will appear. This means that you may suffer unintentional user attrition when adding addition permissions. Using optional permissions can solve this problem.

Note Details of this are covered in detail in the *Permissions* chapter.

Cancelling Updates

When this book was written, it was unfortunately still not possible to cancel an update once it is submitted for review. Be very careful when submitting for review, as a mistake may mean you must wait days before a fix can be submitted.

Automated Update Publishing

Instead of manually uploading zip files to a web page, it is possible to automatically submit your update to the Chrome Web Store via a REST API. To do this, you will first need to acquire credentials to authenticate your API requests. Details of this process can be found here:

https://developer.chrome.com/docs/webstore/using_webstore_api/

Once you have the required credentials, you can manage a significant portion of your extension via API, documented here:

https://developer.chrome.com/docs/webstore/api_index/

Interacting with the API via command line is clunky. Instead, use an NPM package to push your updates:

https://github.com/simov/chrome-webstore

Tip The Plasmo platform has a terrific automatic submission tool called Browser Platform Publisher. Refer to the *Tooling and Frameworks* chapter for details.

Tracking User Activity

Once you have people installing and using your extension, you will certainly want to know how many of them there are and what they are doing.

Dashboard Metrics

The Chrome Developer Dashboard shows you several important metrics about your extension, including:

- Users/day
- Impressions/day
- Installs/day
- Uninstalls/day

Note The number of weekly users you see in the Chrome Web Store is the amount of users whose Chrome browser has checked for an update of your app within the last week. It is not the number of people who have installed your item.

Analytics Libraries

Tracking user activity in a browser extension is mostly the same as tracking web page activity. There are a few wrinkles to consider:

- **Events in a content script should be tracked in a background service worker.** Outgoing network requests to send analytics data are subject to adblockers and cross-origin restrictions.
- **Events in a background script will not have a page URL.**
- **You must preload your analytics library scripts in manifest v3.** Many analytics libraries such as Google Analytics give the option to dynamically load an analytics script - this is no longer allowed.

Tip Adblockers will be unable to block requests sent from extension pages or background scripts. Therefore, unlike web pages (where a large fraction of analytics traffic gets blocked), you can expect to have near-perfect analytics fidelity with browser extensions.

Setting Up Google Analytics

Many extension developers wish to use Google Analytics (GA) for their browser extension. GA4 makes this a bit trickier, but with some configuration, this is certainly possible.

Set Up ga.js

For a manifest v3 extension, you will need to download the `ga.js` script (`https://www.googletagmanager.com/gtag/js?id=GA_TRACKING_ID`) and save it as a local script inside your extension.

Google Analytics checks the URL protocol of the active page before deciding to send analytics pings. If it isn't `http` or `https`, it will decline to send. When using the GA3 script, it was possible to override this behavior via `checkProtocolTask`:

```
ga('set', 'checkProtocolTask', null);
```

However, it appears that in GA4, there is currently no ability to override this behavior. If you wish to use GA4 with an extension, you will need to disable this protocol check. Find the following line in your `ga.js` and remove it or comment it out:

```
"http:" != c && "https:" != c && (N(29), a.abort());
```

After doing this, you should be able to set up Google Analytics as follows:

```
const script = document.createElement("script");
```

```
script.async = true;
script.src = "/ga.js";
document.body.appendChild(script);

window.dataLayer = window.dataLayer || [];
function gtag() {
  dataLayer.push(arguments);
}

const GA_ID = "GA_TRACKING_ID";


gtag("js", new Date());
// Disable automatic pageview reporting
gtag("config", GA_ID, {
  send_page_view: false,
});
// Manually send the pageview event
gtag("event", "page_view", {
  page_path: window.location.path,
});
```

This is a bit of a hack, but at the time this book was published it is the only known way of getting the GA4 script to work nicely with browser extensions.

Install and Uninstall Events

You are able to perform special tasks when the user installs and uninstalls an extension. For example, the background script can perform a task only when the user newly installs an extension:

background.js

```
chrome.runtime.onInstalled.addListener((details) => {
```

```
    if (details.reason === chrome.runtime.OnInstalledReason.
    INSTALL) {
      // Anything in here will only execute on first install
      openWelcomePage();
    }
});
```

You won't be able to execute code on an uninstall, but you are able to direct the user to a URL of your choosing with `chrome.runtime.setUninstallURL`:

```
chrome.runtime.setUninstallURL("https://foobar.com/survey");
```

There are no restrictions on this URL, I recommend using it to collect analytics data, give a survey, display contact information for troubleshooting, or offer some helpful tips that might get them to reinstall.

Summary

In this chapter, we discussed a number of topics involved with building and publishing an extension. We discussed a range of tactics that can be used to better understanding what is going on inside your local extension. Next, we went through the different testing formats that work well for browser extensions. We went through all the important parts involved with publishing and updating extensions in the Chrome Web Store. Finally, we discussed how analytics tools can be effectively folded into your browser extension.

In the next chapter, we will cover all the details involved with building a browser extension that targets more than one browser.

CHAPTER 15

Cross-Browser Extensions

When it comes to supporting multiple platforms, browser extensions exist somewhere in between websites and mobile apps. One end of the spectrum is the website, which enjoys a "write-once-run-anywhere" developer experience. On the other end of the spectrum is the mobile app, which is written in a proprietary language and will only work on a specific operating system and a subset of device types. In this chapter, we will discuss what challenges and tradeoffs are involved when supporting an extension on multiple browsers.

Introduction to Cross-Browser Support

Website code enjoys a consistent host environment. You can write a website once, load it on any OS or device or browser, and expect that it will work correctly. There are some corner cases where browsers diverge, but these are relatively rare. All browser vendors spend lots of time ensuring that their product conforms to the W3C standards and will render a web page more or less in the same way as any other browser.

M. Frisbie, *Building Browser Extensions*, https://doi.org/10.1007/978-1-4842-8725-5_15

Mobile apps run in a proprietary host environment. If you want to have a mobile app run on multiple operating systems, code written for Android is nearly useless when it comes to building for iOS. Apps are distributed in different places, written in different languages, built for different devices, and utilize completely different SDKs.

Browser extensions borrow a little bit from each of these modalities. Extensions use an API that is standardized across browsers, but not all browsers support the full API. Extensions all are built with HTML, JavaScript, and CSS, but the manifest support between browsers has certain idiosyncrasies and incompatibilities. Extensions are distributed in browser-specific app stores, but a majority of web browsers are built atop Chromium – meaning they all can install apps distributed by the Chrome Web Store.

Browser Coverage Tradeoffs

When choosing if and to what extent you will support multiple browsers, you should begin by asking yourself who your target user is. For a majority of extensions, the answer to this question will be, "as many people as possible"! Supporting all major browsers is certainly possible, but depending on your extension, this may be overkill. Variable API support, multiple app stores, and idiomatic JS/CSS engines can ensnare a developer's time.

Browser Share

Fortunately, for extensions that are just getting started, you can very easily support a majority of users with a single codebase. Consider the following metrics for desktop browser share in 2022 (Figure 15-1).

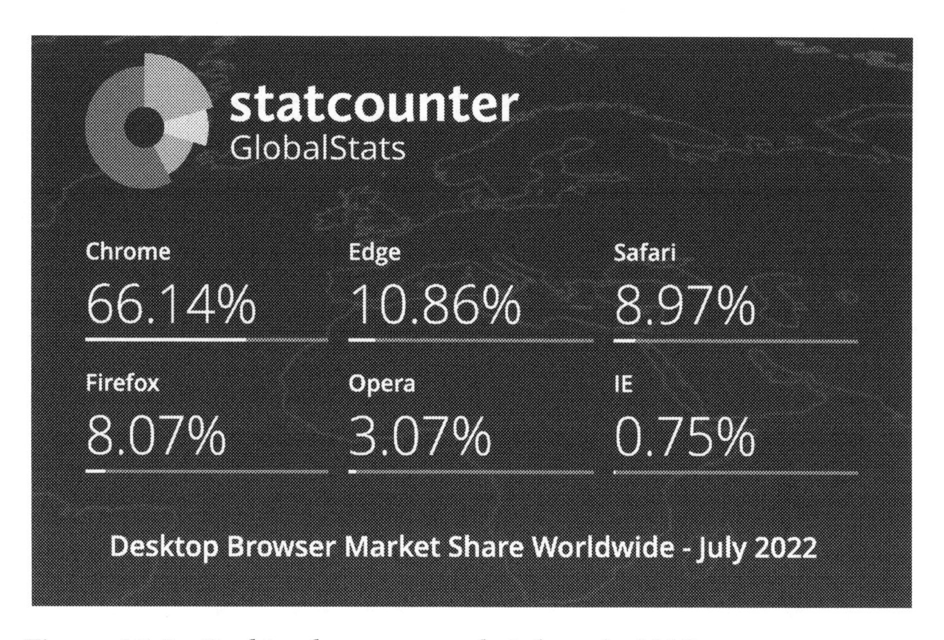

Figure 15-1. *Desktop browser market share in 2022*

Google Chrome dominates the market at 66%. If you were to deploy your extension to just the Chrome Web Store, you are automatically covering 2/3 of the market.

Chromium Browser Extension Sharing

Fortunately, the modern browser landscape is working to your advantage. Many major browsers such as Edge, Opera, Vivaldi, and Brave are all build upon the open-source Chromium browser. As a result, all these browsers feature nearly perfect compatibility with extensions built for Google Chrome. Each of these browsers can either directly install from, or be configured to install from, the Chrome Web Store. Therefore, an extension published only to the Chrome Web Store can in fact be installed by Chrome, Edge, and Opera: ***over 80%*** of desktop traffic!

Note There are minor differences between Google Chrome and other Chromium browsers, such as the identity API. Nevertheless, the overall API parity between all Chromium browsers is nearly seamless.

Adapting Your Codebase

Depending on how broad you want your extension support to be, organizing your codebase may require some finesse. In this section, we'll cover a few simple principles that can be used.

API Probing

Not all browsers support the full WebExtensions API. If a particular method is critical to your extension, and a browser does not support it, then there is little you can do. In situations like these, it is probably best to *not* support the browser, and encourage the user to use a supported browser.

If, however, the API you wish to use is not critical, and the extension can function without it (even in a degraded state), then you can safely probe for an API or a method to check if it is available. For example:

```
if (chrome.storage.session) {
  // API is available, proceed normally
} else {
  // API is not available. UX options:
  // - Fall back to similar API
  // - Disable or hide buttons
  // - Notify user
  // - Silently degrade
}
```

Differential Manifests

When working in development mode, you will find that most browsers are relatively permissive when it comes to manifest structure. However, when deploying to a marketplace, you may run into a situation where there are strict incompatibilities between what two different marketplaces allow or disallow.

To address this, you will need to generate differential manifests for each deployment bundle. A common pattern is to maintain a single "master" manifest, and then perform ad-hoc modifications specific to each marketplace when generating the deployment bundles.

Tip Differential manifest generation can be quite tedious. Extension development platforms such as Plasmo (`https://www.plasmo.com/`) can automate this process for you.

Manifest v2/v3

At the time this book was published, extension developers are stuck in an unenviable position where some marketplaces like the Chrome Web Store are only accepting manifest v3, and others like the Firefox Addon marketplace are only accepting manifest v2. It seems very likely that this status quo is transitory, and soon all major marketplaces will coalesce around manifest v3. I would not recommend splitting support between manifest v2 and v3, the chasm between how the two behave is not worth bridging; you should target support for manifest v3.

Extension Marketplaces

Just as mobile apps must be installed from an app store, extensions must be installed from an extension marketplace. All major browsers maintain their own extension store.

Marketplace Similarities

The following is a list of features that are consistent between extension marketplaces:

- **A developer account is required.** No marketplace allows you to publish a browser extension anonymously. You can always create a separate developer account that does not identify you personally.
- **All new extensions and extension updates undergo review.** Every extension version submitted will undergo some kind of review process before it is approved. Some reviews will be automated, and some will be manual. The permissions you request in your extension manifest may change how closely your extension is scrutinized.
- **All extensions require some copy and assets for the listing.** Icons, titles, descriptions, promotional images, and links to host websites are just a few of the things you can provide when publishing an extension. Some marketplaces will automatically draw a portion of this content from the manifest automatically. Additionally, different marketplaces will require a different content.

- **All marketplaces support manual publishing (except Safari).** This involves uploading a zip file containing all the assets and files for the extension. The store will perform an automated analysis of this zip file to check if it is valid, and if it is, add it to the review queue.
- **All marketplaces support automated publishing.** This is covered in the *Extension Development and Deployment* chapter.

Marketplace Differences

The following is a list of features that are different between extension marketplaces:

- **Marketplaces have different automated file checking processes.** Linting, filetype checks, file sizes, and manifest validation are just a few of the categories that each marketplace will implement slightly differently.
- **Marketplaces will review submissions at different speeds.** The Chrome Web Store typically takes a few days to approve submissions, whereas the Mozilla Add-ons marketplace approves submissions almost instantly.

Chrome Web Store

`https://chrome.google.com/webstore`

The Chrome Web Store is by far the largest and most popular marketplace for browser extensions (Figure 15-2). It has 180,000 Google Chrome extensions available, which is roughly 10% of the Apple App Store's 1.8 million mobile apps. As mentioned earlier in the chapter, all

Chromium browsers are capable of installing extensions directly from this marketplace. To publish an extension, you will need a Chrome Web Store developer account. It requires a one-time $5 registration fee.

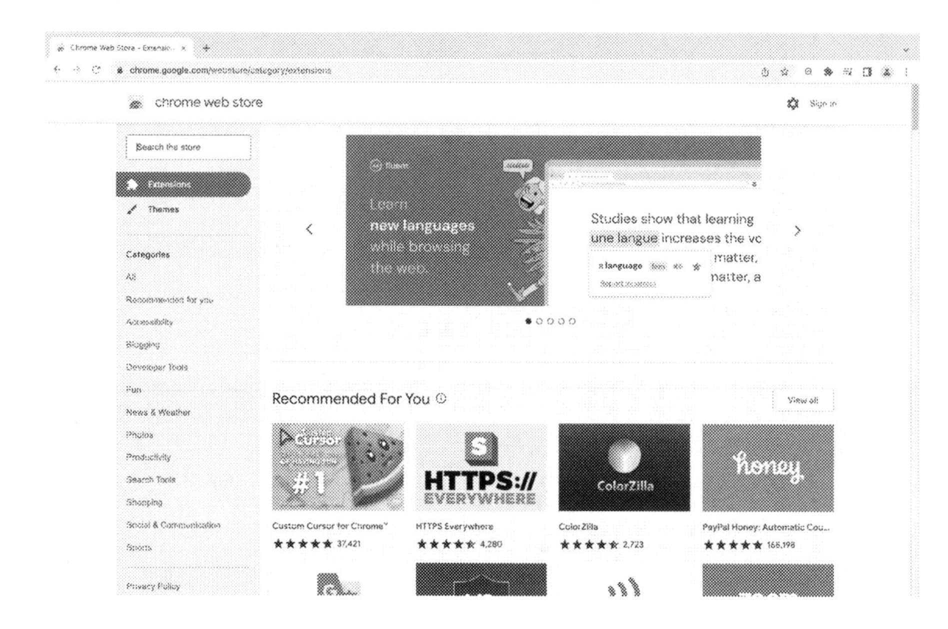

Figure 15-2. *The Chrome Web Store web page*

Add-ons for Firefox

`https://addons.mozilla.org/`

It is free to publish extensions to the Firefox extensions marketplace (Figure 15-3).

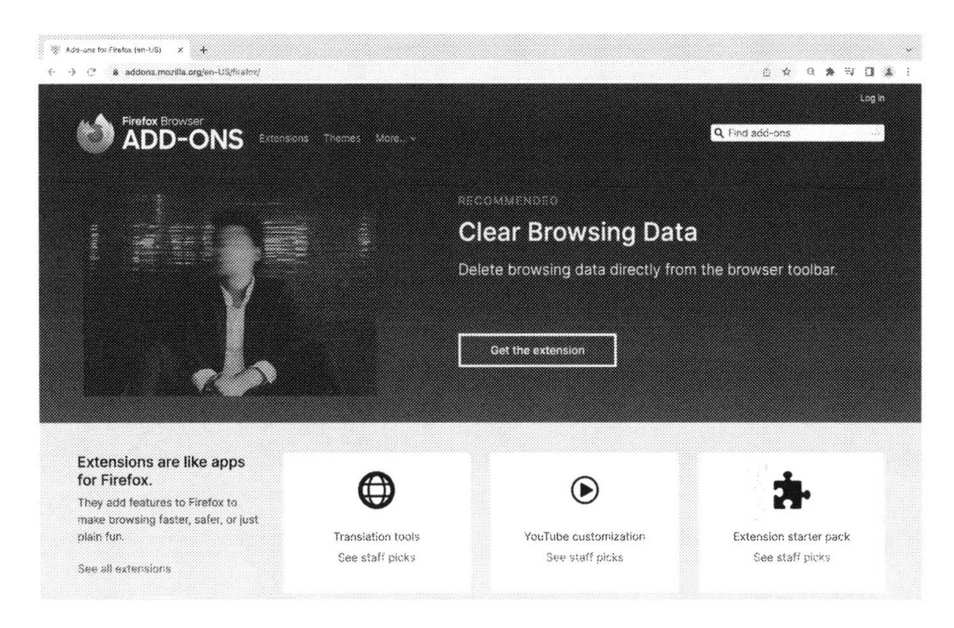

Figure 15-3. *The Firefox Add-ons web page*

Microsoft Edge Add-ons

`https://microsoftedge.microsoft.com/addons/Microsoft-Edge-Extensions-Home`

It is free to publish extensions to the Microsoft Edge extensions marketplace (Figure 15-4).

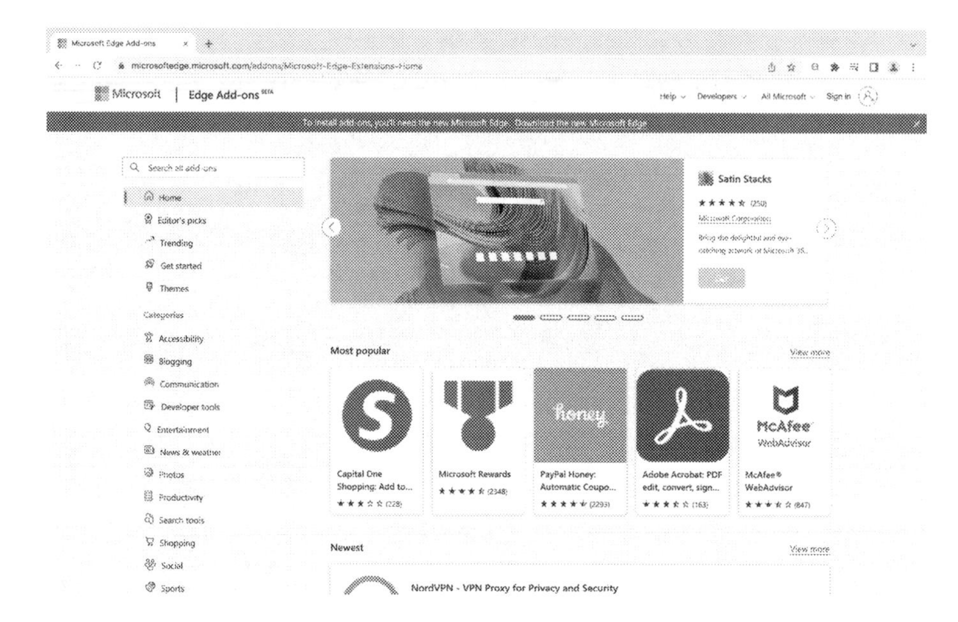

__Figure 15-4.__ The Microsoft Edge Add-ons web page

Safari Extensions App Store

The Safari Extension Store is only accessible through the Safari browser (Figure 15-5). Publishing an extension to the App Store requires an Apple Developer Account, which is $99/year. You will also need Xcode installed to build the extension and deploy it to the app store.

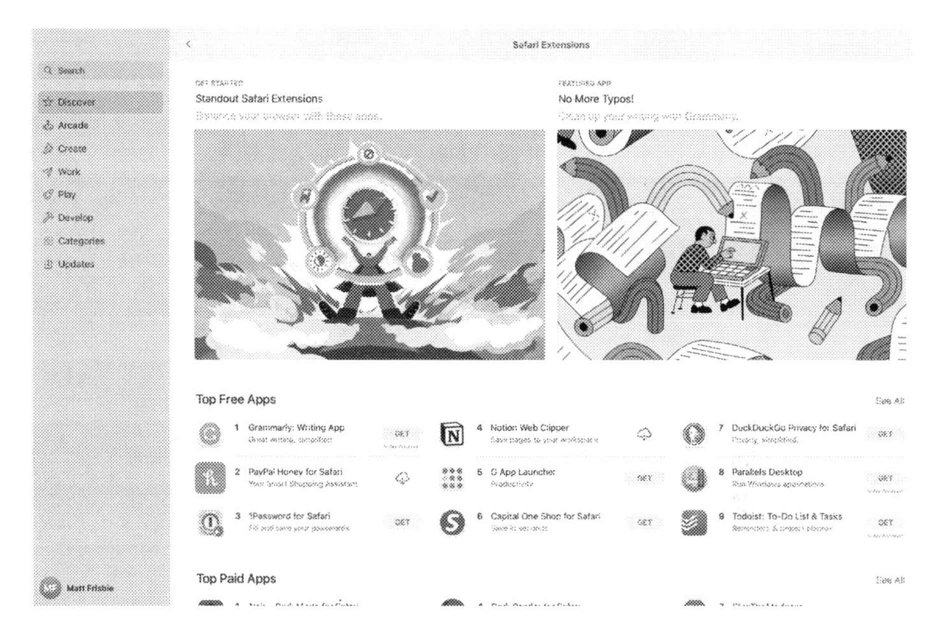

Figure 15-5. *The Apple Safari Extensions App Store*

Opera Addons

`https://addons.opera.com/`

It is free to publish extensions to the Opera extensions marketplace (Figure 15-6).

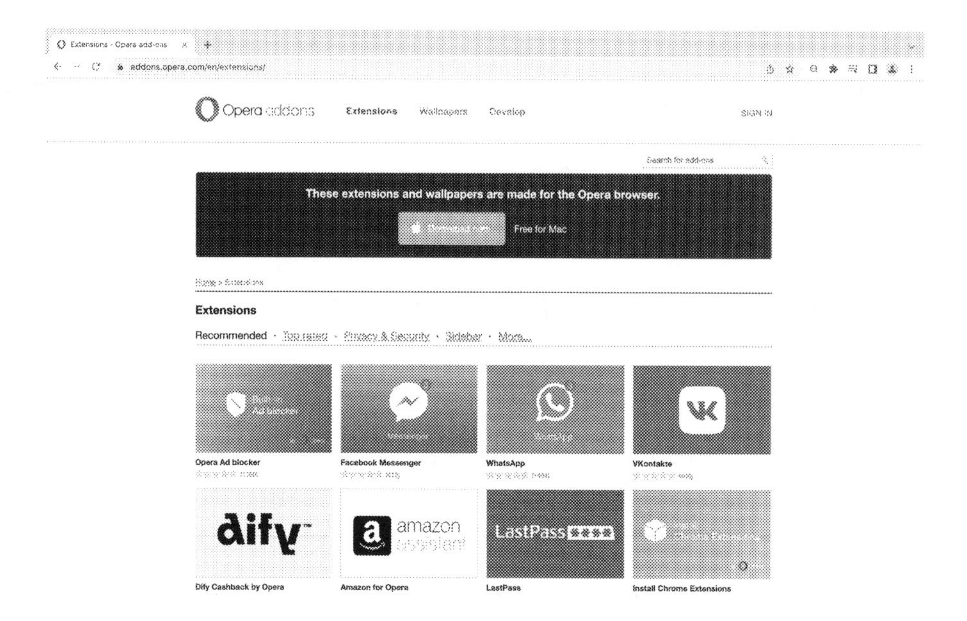

Figure 15-6. *The Opera Add-ons web page*

Mobile Extensions

Support for extensions is limited on mobile devices. Major browsers like Google Chrome do not support it on any OS, and Apple forbids non-Safari browsers from installing third-party extensions on iOS. However, on both Android and iOS devices it is still possible to install browser extensions if you are using the appropriate browser. API support is mixed on mobile devices.

Mobile Extension User Interfaces

With respect to WebExtensions API support, mobile browsers that allow extensions generally have parity with their desktop equivalents. Popups, options pages, content scripts, and background pages all will still run and render. However, due to the mobile form factor, there are some UX differences to consider:

- The toolbar action button used to open the popup are accessible through the browser's menu button.
- The options page is generally accessed through a "Settings" button in the extension's management view. This is fairly hard to find for the user, so do not expect this to be a common entrypoint.
- Safari extensions are packaged as apps. Therefore, they include an additional native app user interface. This is discussed later in the chapter.
- On mobile devices, the popup page will typically render either as a standalone web page (Firefox, Kiwi) or as a native modal (Safari).
- The options page will always render as stand-alone web page.

Kiwi Browser

If you're looking to install Chrome extensions on an Android device, the best solution is to use the Kiwi Browser (Figure 15-7). The browser is based on Webkit and Chromium, and you can directly install extensions from the Chrome Web Store. Using extensions in the Kiwi browser is only possible on Android.

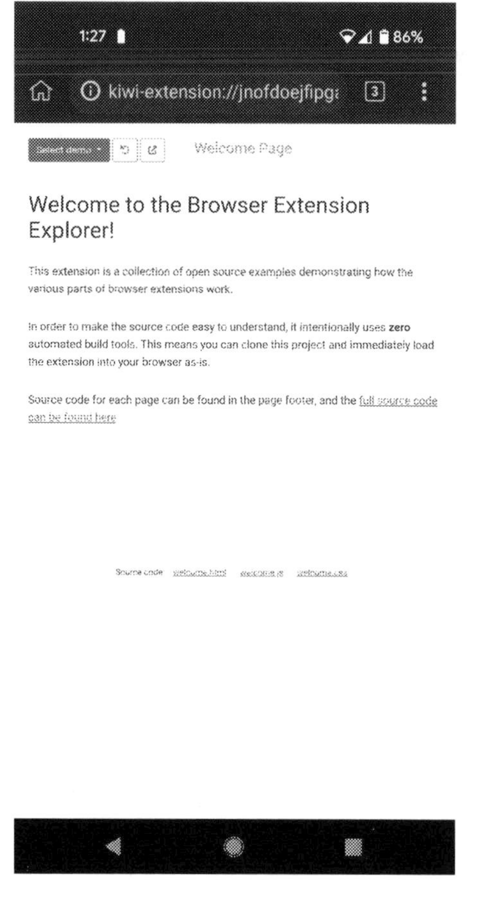

Figure 15-7. *The Kiwi Browser showing an extension page*

Firefox Mobile

Extensions published on the Firefox marketplace can choose to be installable for Firefox mobile (Figures 15-8 and 15-9). You can directly install extensions from the Firefox Add-ons marketplace. Extensions on the Firefox Mobile browser are only possible on Android.

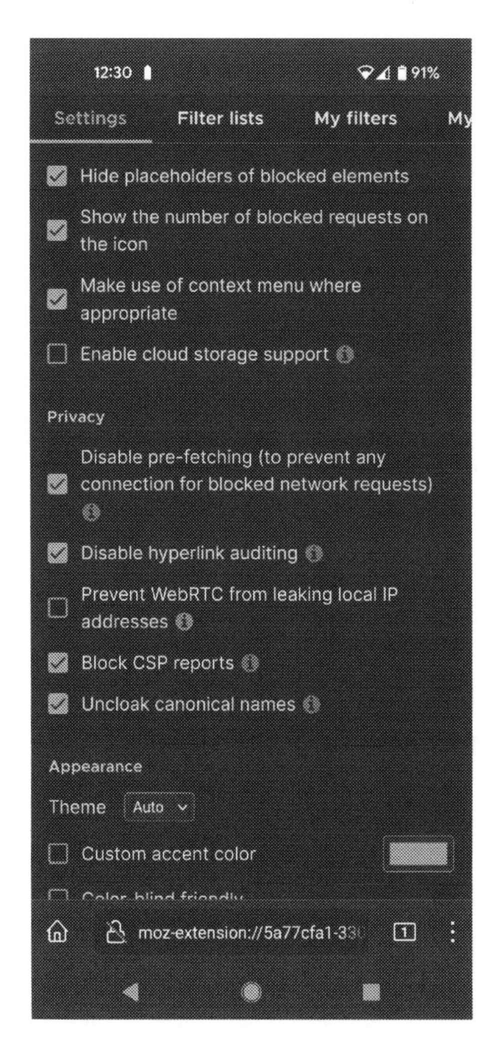

***Figure 15-8.** The uBlock Origin options page in Firefox Mobile*

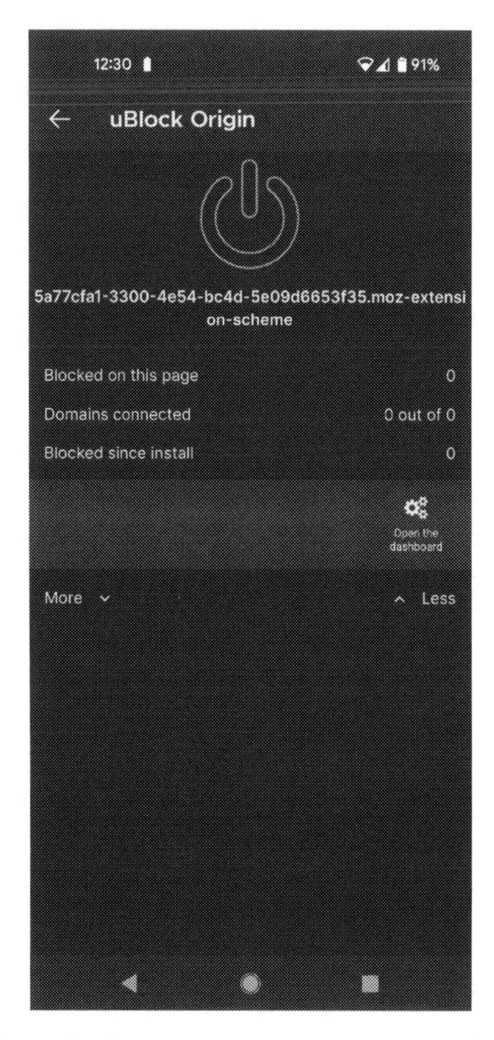

Figure 15-9. *The uBlock Origin popup page in Firefox Mobile*

iOS Safari

Safari extensions can be installed on iOS devices through the App Store. These are structured differently than other mobile extensions. Publishing a Safari extension for iOS involves a considerable amount of extra effort, but at its core it still includes the same web architecture as other desktop extensions (Figures 15-10 and 15-11).

Note Safari app development is covered in depth later in the chapter.

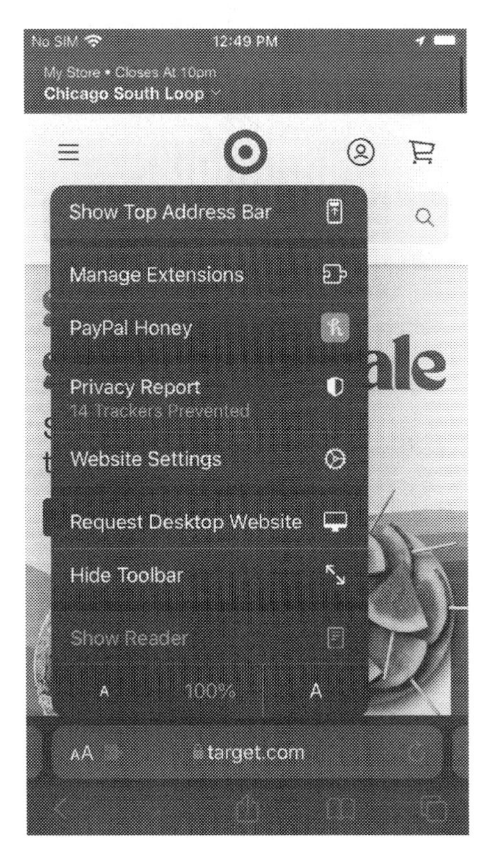

***Figure 15-10.** The Safari browser menu showing the options for an installed Extension*

***Figure 15-11.** An extension popup page showing in the iOS Safari browser*

Automated Deployment

As of 2022, all major extension marketplaces support automated deployment. The details of deploying to each store are out of the scope of this book, but you can find links to the documentation for each marketplace:

- **Chrome Web Store:** `https://developer.chrome.com/docs/webstore/api_index/`

- **Microsoft Edge Add-ons Marketplace:** `https://docs.microsoft.com/en-us/microsoft-edge/extensions-chromium/publish/api/using-addons-api`
- **Firefox Add-ons Marketplace:** `https://addons-server.readthedocs.io/en/latest/topics/api/signing.html`
- **Apple App Store:** `https://developer.apple.com/documentation/appstoreconnectapi`

Tip Some extension development platforms such as Plasmo (`https://www.plasmo.com/`) can automate deployment of your extension to these marketplaces.

WebExtensions API Support

Not all browsers fully support the WebExtensions API, and some have support for non-standardized API features. These are changing all the time, so this book will only link to the following pages that catalog each browser's API support:

- **MDN table showing support across all browsers:** `https://developer.mozilla.org/en-US/docs/Mozilla/Add-ons/WebExtensions/Browser_support_for_JavaScript_APIs`
- **Google Chrome API reference:** `https://developer.chrome.com/docs/extensions/reference/`
- **Microsoft Edge API support:** `https://docs.microsoft.com/en-us/microsoft-edge/extensions-chromium/developer-guide/api-support`

- **Safari WebExtensions API compatibility:** https://developer.apple.com/documentation/safariservices/safari_web_extensions/assessing_your_safari_web_extension_s_browser_compatibility
- **Opera API support:** https://dev.opera.com/extensions/apis/

Safari Extension Development

Non-Safari browser extensions are just raw HTML, JS, and CSS, and they can be loaded into the browser directly. Safari's browser extension implementation allows you to use a HTML/JS/CSS codebase, but running that codebase inside an Apple device requires a healthy amount of extra work. This section will cover the extra steps required to build a browser extension for Safari.

Note This section assumes you are either building a Safari extension from scratch, or porting a non-Safari HTML/JS/CSS extension codebase over to Safari.

Prerequisites

Safari browser extensions are developed and installed as apps and published to the App Store. Therefore, they must be built on Apple's app development infrastructure. You will need the following to develop and publish a Safari extension:

- A Mac computer with Xcode installed for development
- A developer certificate to sign your code ($99/year)

Architecture

According to the Safari developer documentation:

> *A Safari web extension consists of three parts that operate independently in their own sandboxed environments:*
>
> - *A macOS or iOS app that can have a user interface*
> - *JavaScript code and web files that work in the browser*
> - *A native app extension that mediates between the macOS or iOS app and the JavaScript code*

This may sound confusing at first. To better understand how each of these parts works together, let's generate a new Xcode extension project, install it on an Apple device, and analyze each piece.

Creating an Extension Project

In Xcode, create a new project using the "Safari Extension App" template. For your first project, let's choose Swift as the language (Figures 15-12, 15-13, and 15-14).

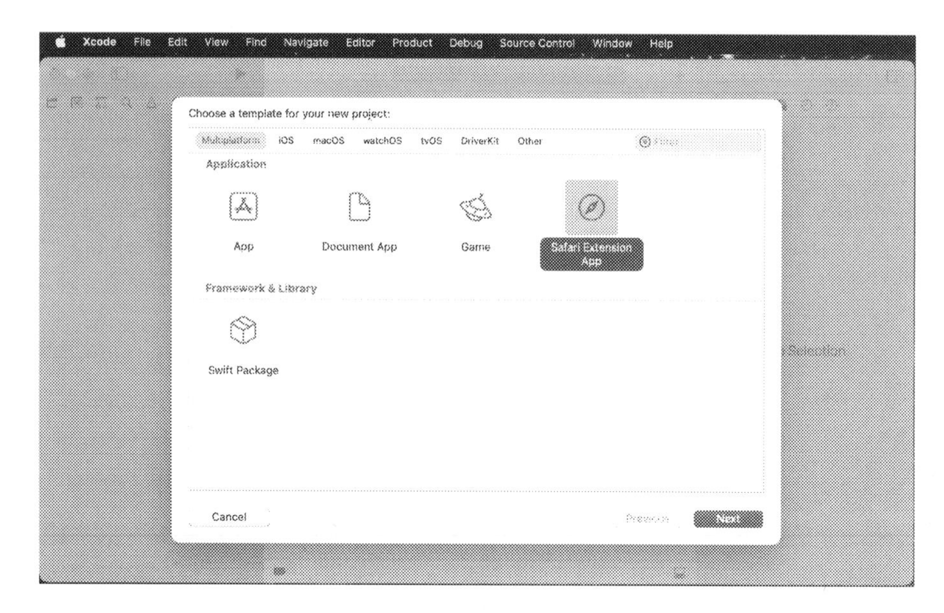

Figure 15-12. *The Xcode Safari Extension App template*

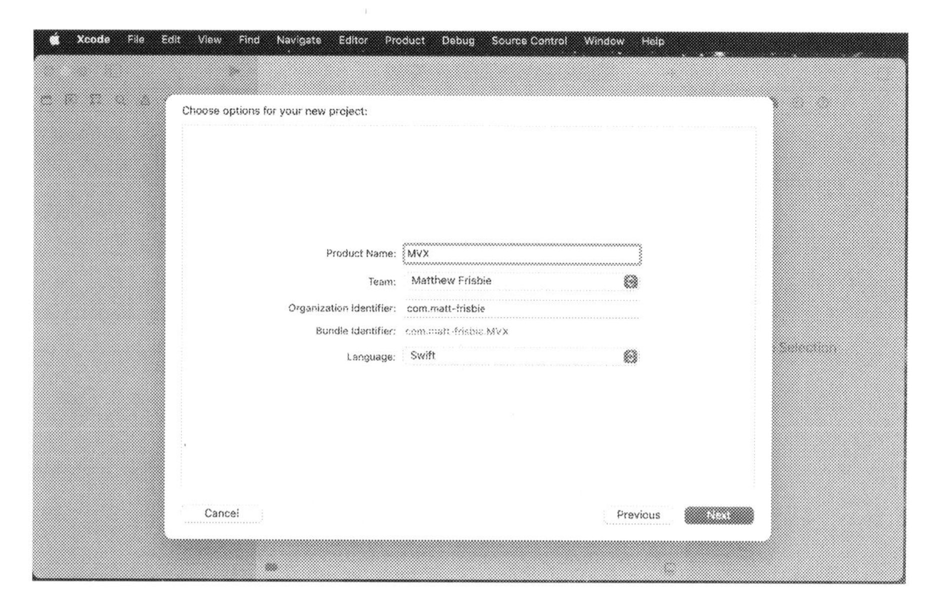

Figure 15-13. *Setting options for the new project*

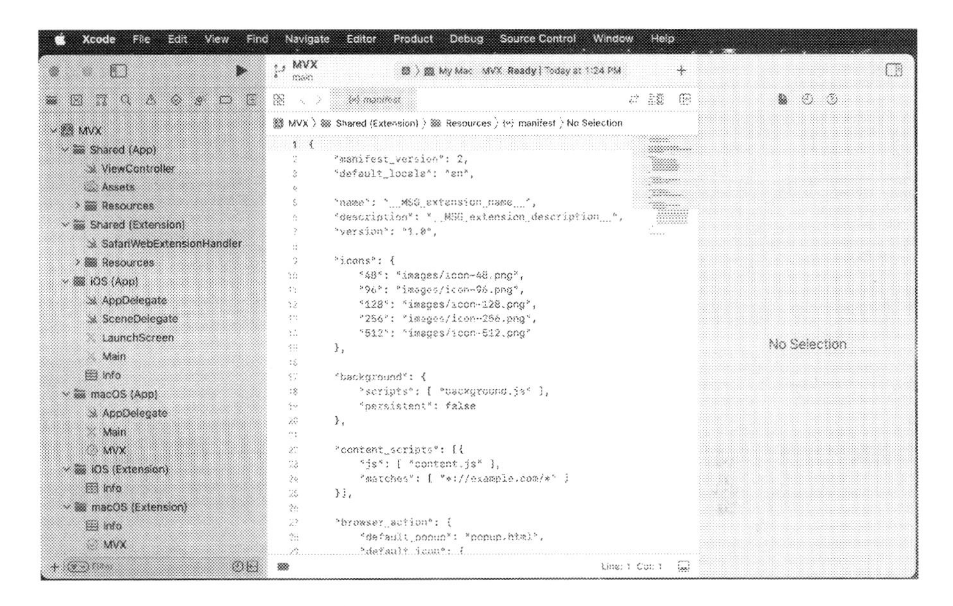

Figure 15-14. The new extension project's code

Note The Xcode template generates a manifest v2 extension, but Safari also supports manifest v3. We can ignore this difference for now.

Let's go through what each of these generated folders is:

- **iOS (App)** and **macOS (App)** are the formal apps that the OS will install. On iOS, this will show up as an app tile on the home screen. The generated version of these apps is just a simple web view.
- **Shared (App)** is the web view content. The generated version is just the default icon, some text, and a button.

- **iOS (Extension)** and **macOS (Extension)** are the native app extensions that mediate between the JS and the native app.
- **Shared (Extension)** is the formal extension code: manifest.json and JS/CSS/HTML, assets, locales, etc. This directory also includes an ExtensionHandler swift file that is used to handle messaging sent between the JS and the native app.

Note Xcode has separate build targets for iOS and macOS. This should make sense; although these apps share code, you are developing two entirely separate apps for two separate platforms.

Writing the App

The generated extension doesn't do much out of the box. Let's modify it to do the following:

- Use manifest v3
- Exchange message between the popup, background, and content script
- Show an options page
- Send messages to the native app

Update the XCode project files to match the following code:

manifest.json

```
{
  "manifest_version": 3,
  "default_locale": "en",
```

```
"name": "__MSG_extension_name__",
"description": "__MSG_extension_description__",
"version": "1.0",
"icons": {
    "48": "images/icon-48.png",
    "96": "images/icon-96.png",
    "128": "images/icon-128.png",
    "256": "images/icon-256.png",
    "512": "images/icon-512.png"
},
"options_ui": {
  "page": "options.html"
},
"background": {
    "service_worker": "background.js"
},
"content_scripts": [{
    "js": [ "content.js" ],
    "matches": [ "<all_urls>" ]
}],
"action": {
    "default_popup": "popup.html",
    "default_icon": {
        "16": "images/toolbar-icon-16.png",
        "19": "images/toolbar-icon-19.png",
        "32": "images/toolbar-icon-32.png",
        "38": "images/toolbar-icon-38.png",
        "48": "images/toolbar-icon-48.png",
        "72": "images/toolbar-icon-72.png"
    }
},
```

```
    "permissions": ["tabs", "nativeMessaging"],
    "host_permissions": ["<all_urls>"]
}
```

options.html

```
<!DOCTYPE html>
<html>
<head>
    <meta name="viewport" content="width=device-width">
    <meta charset="UTF-8">
</head>
<body>
    <h1>I'm the options page!</h1>
</body>
</html>
```

popup.html

```
<!DOCTYPE html>
<html>
<head>
    <meta charset="UTF-8">
    <link rel="stylesheet" href="popup.css">
    <script type="module" src="popup.js"></script>
</head>
<body>
    <h1>I'm the popup page!</h1>

    <button id="set-bg-color">Change background color</button>
    <button id="send-native-message">Send native
    message</button>
</body>
</html>
```

popup.js

```
document.querySelector("#set-bg-color").
addEventListener("click", () => {
  const randomColor = "#" + Math.floor(Math.random()*(2 **
  24 - 1)).toString(16);

  chrome.tabs.query({
    active: true,
    currentWindow: true
  }, (tabs) => {
    chrome.tabs.sendMessage(
      tabs[0].id,
      { backgroundColor: randomColor },
      (response) => console.log(response)
    );
  });
});

document.querySelector("#send-native-message").
addEventListener("click", () => {
  chrome.runtime.sendNativeMessage(
    "com.matt-frisbie.MVX",
    {msg: "foobar"},
    (response) => console.log(response)
  );
});
```

content.js

```
console.log('Content script initialized!');

chrome.runtime.sendMessage({ greeting: "hello"
}).then((response) => {
```

```
  console.log("Content script received response: ", response);
});

chrome.runtime.onMessage.addListener((request, sender,
sendResponse) => {
  console.log("Content script received request: ", request);
  console.log("Sender: ", sender);

  if (request.backgroundColor) {
    document.body.style.backgroundColor = request.
    backgroundColor;
  }
});
```

background.js

```
chrome.runtime.onMessage.addListener((request, sender,
sendResponse) => {
  console.log("Background received request: ", request);
  console.log("Sender: ", sender);

  if (request.greeting === "hello") {
    return sendResponse({ farewell: "goodbye" });
  }
});
```

Example 15-1. *SafariWebExtensionHandler.swift*

```
import SafariServices
import os.log

let SFExtensionMessageKey = "message"

class SafariWebExtensionHandler: NSObject,
NSExtensionRequestHandling {
```

```
    func beginRequest(with context: NSExtensionContext) {
        let item = context.inputItems[0] as! NSExtensionItem
        let message = item.userInfo?[SFExtensionMessageKey]
        os_log(.info, "MVX App received: %{public}@",
        message as! CVarArg)

        let response = NSExtensionItem()
        response.userInfo = [ SFExtensionMessageKey:
        [ "App response to": message ] ]

        context.completeRequest(returningItems: [response],
        completionHandler: nil)
    }
}
```

Most of this code should match what you've seen elsewhere in this book. For the most part, this is a conventional background/popup/options/content script setup for an extension. Bolded in the code are the portions needed to send messages from the extension JavaScript code to the native app Swift code. Some things to note here:

- The special permission `nativeMessaging` is needed to dispatch native messages.
- The `chrome.runtime.sendNativeMessage` is used to dispatch a native message.
- To target a native app, you must use the native app's name. For Safari extensions, this is the App Bundle Identifier. In this example, the identifier is `com.matt-frisbie.MVX`

Testing on macOS

Note If you wish to develop Safari extensions without signing the app, you will need to enable Safari to load unsigned extensions. To do so, choose Safari ➤ Preferences, click Advanced, then select "Show Develop menu in menu bar." Next, open the Develop menu and check "Allow unsigned extensions."

Let's first test this on desktop Safari. In Xcode, build the app for macOS (Figure 15-15).

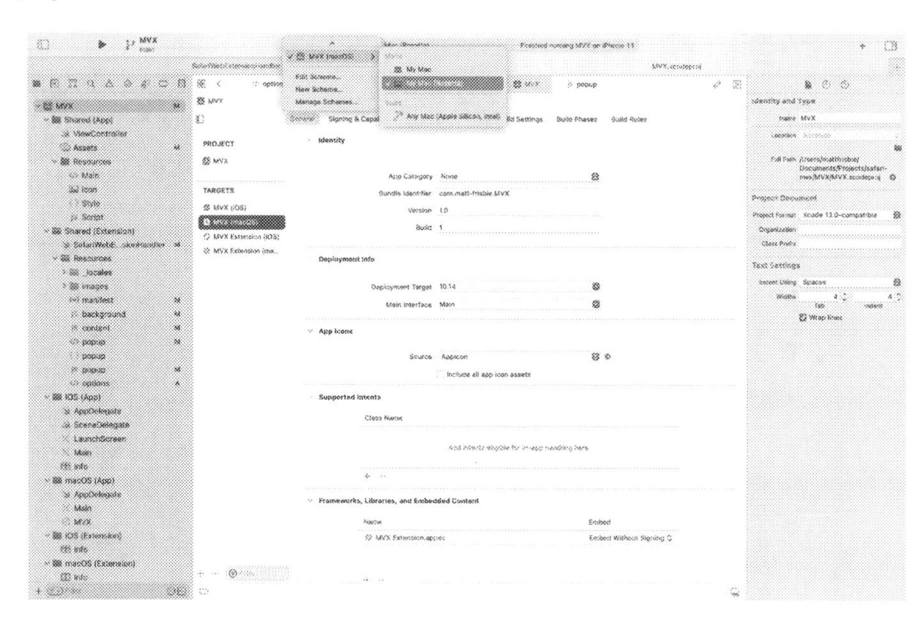

Figure 15-15. *Building the extension for macOS*

When the build finishes, you will see the extension app open (Figure 15-16).

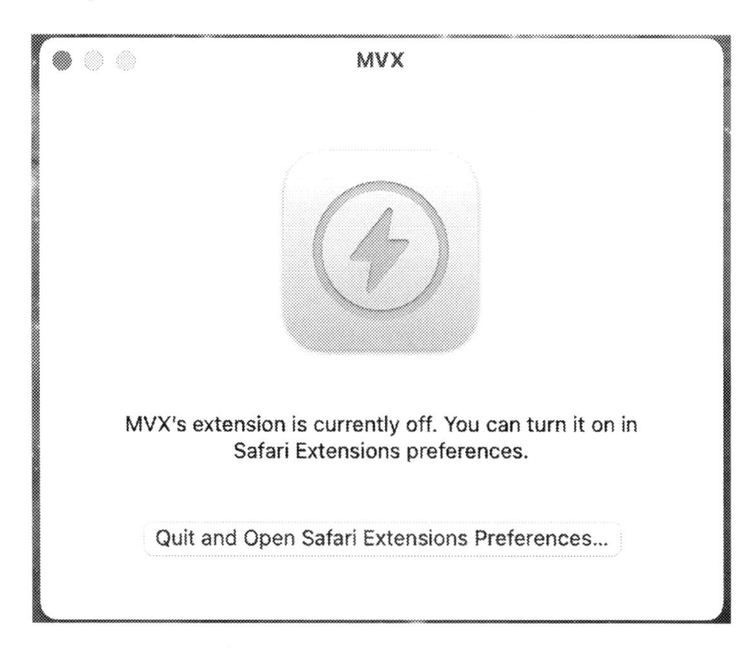

Figure 15-16. *The macOS extension app*

The view you are seeing is the native OS app displaying a web view. Xcode will have automatically installed the extension for Safari, so click this "Quit and Open..." button to open the browser's preferences. Check the box next to "MVX" to enable the extension (Figure 15-17).

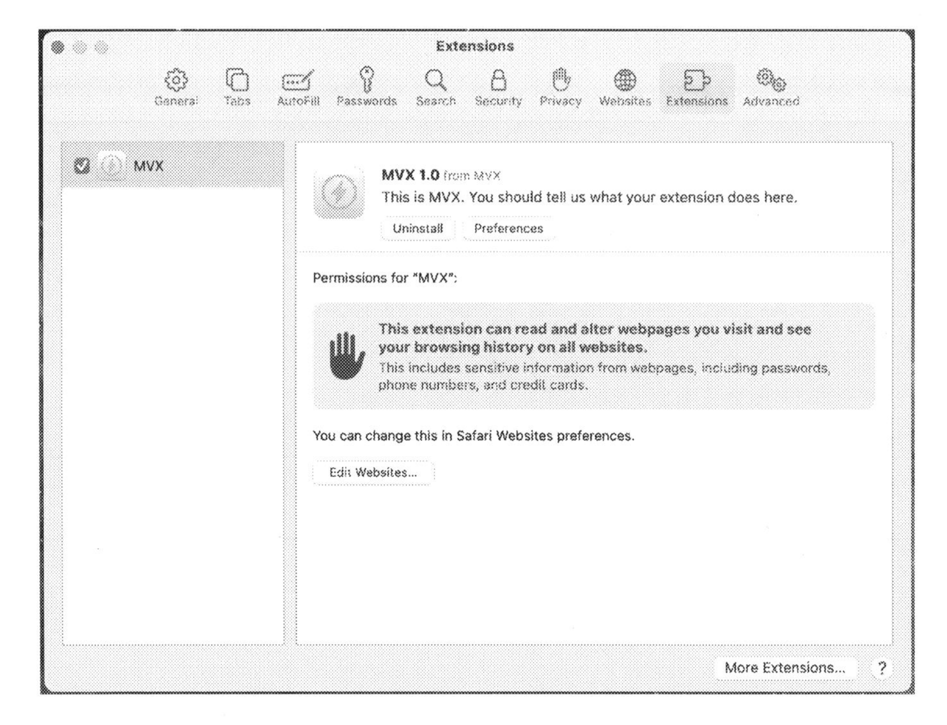

***Figure 15-17.** The enabled Safari extension*

Note This app is requesting the `<all_urls>` host permission, so Safari will ask you to confirm the permission before enabling the extension.

Click the "Preferences" button, and your options page will open (Figure 15-18).

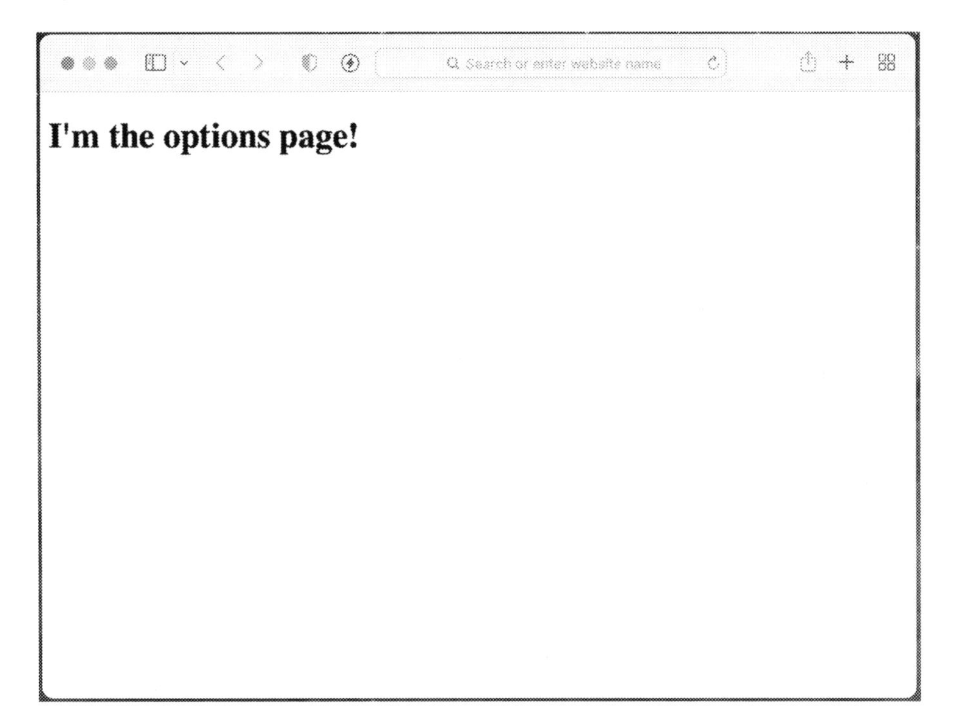

Figure 15-18. *The options page*

Next, navigate to a valid web page like wikipedia.org. Open the console to verify the content script is completing the message handshake with the background script (Figure 15-19).

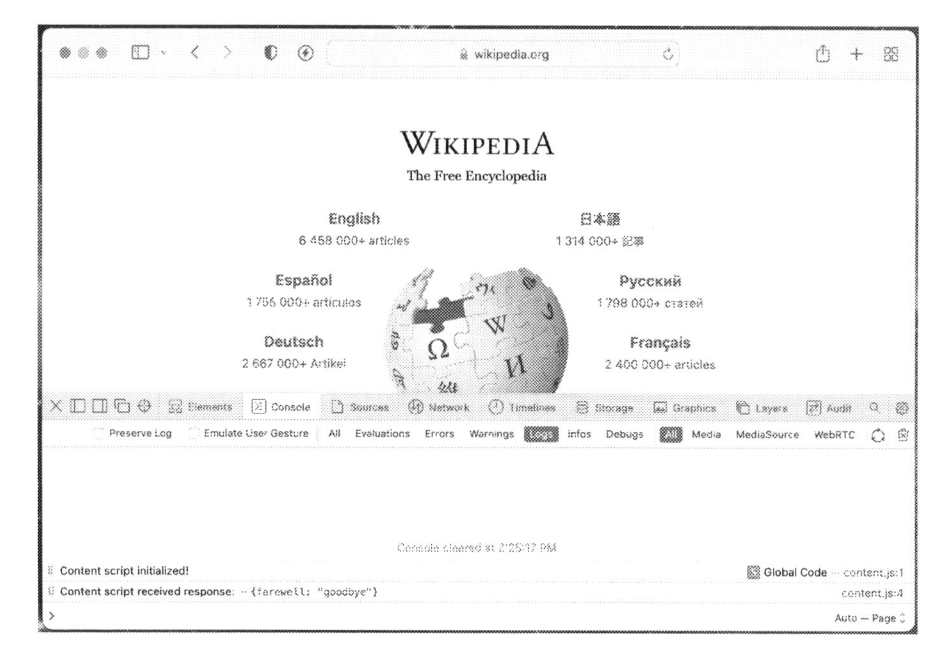

Figure 15-19. *The content script logs*

The default extension icon is the encircled lightning bolt, click it to open the popup page. Click the "Change background color" to set the background to a random color. You should see the content script log the message it received (Figure 15-20).

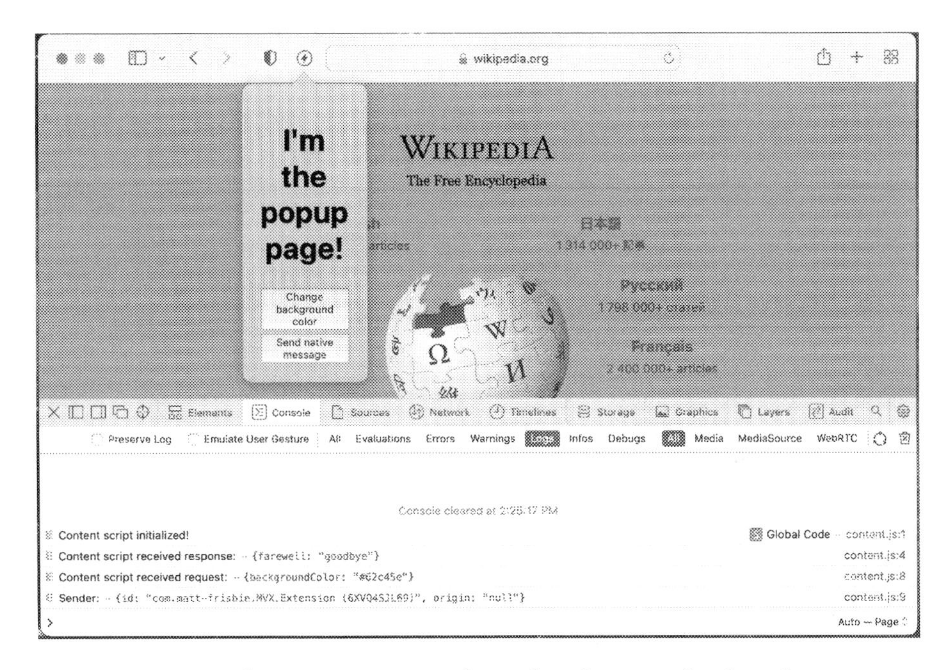

***Figure 15-20.** The popup page after a background color change*

The second popup button will send a message to the background app. To check the logs for the background app, you will need to open the macOS Console app and filter for messages from the extension. Filter for messages from the MVX process, and for messages containing our dummy "foobar" message. The following screenshot shows the log output you should expect to see after clicking "Send native message" (Figure 15-21).

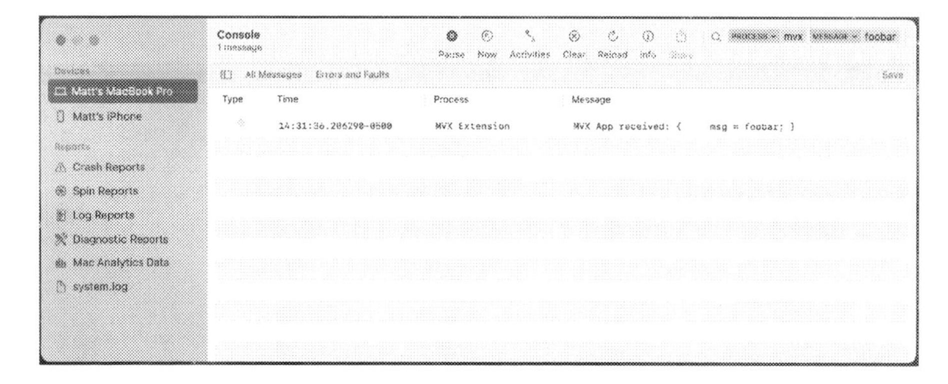

Figure 15-21. *The os_log output from the macOS extension's native app*

Testing on iOS

In Xcode, build the app for iOS, and use a simulator (Figure 15-22).

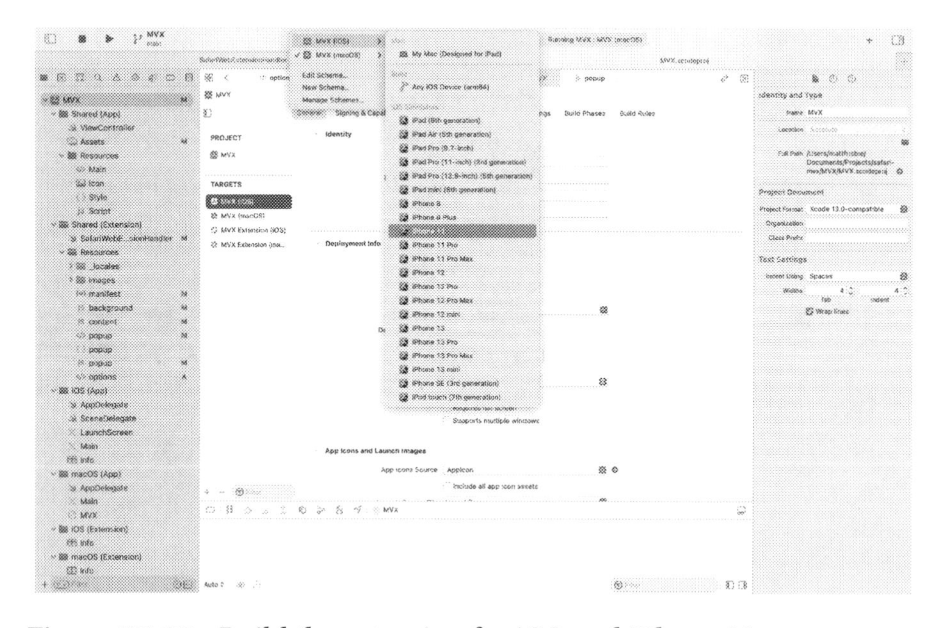

Figure 15-22. *Build the extension for iOS and iPhone 11*

The simulator will dump you right into the native app (Figure 15-23). The view you are seeing is the native OS app displaying a web view.

Figure 15-23. *The native iOS app*

Xcode will have automatically installed the extension. You can see this app by viewing the home screen (Figure 15-24).

***Figure 15-24.** The extension app on the home screen*

Safari extension apps can be managed by opening the Safari settings and selecting "Extensions" (Figures 15-25 and 15-26).

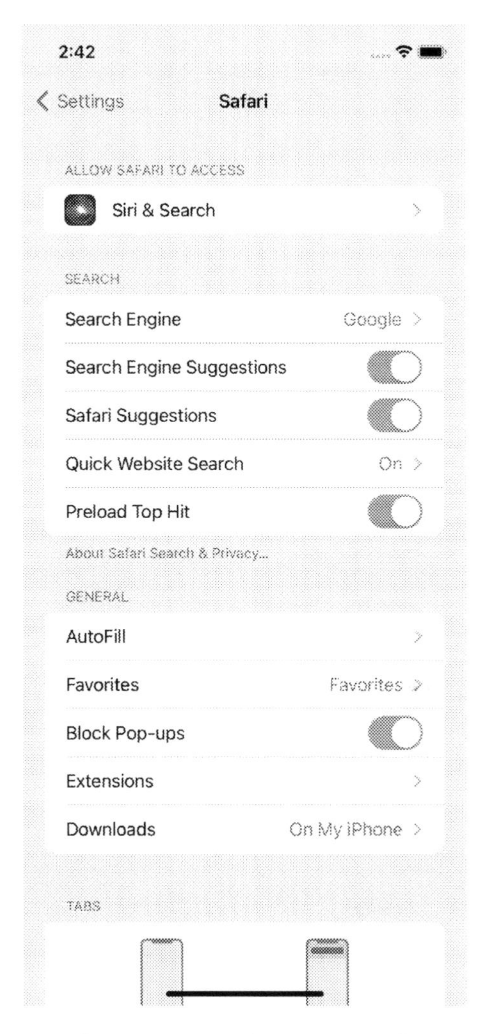

Figure 15-25. *iOS Safari settings showing an "Extensions" option*

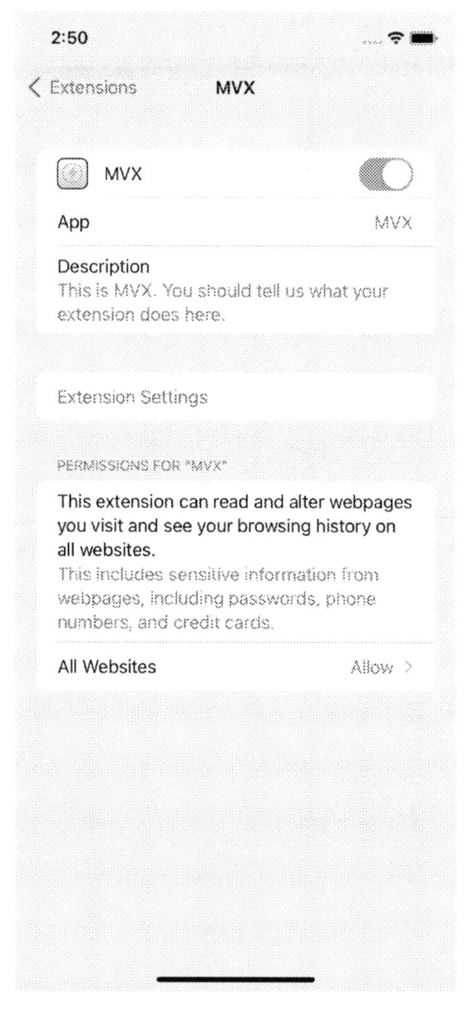

***Figure 15-26.** The MVX extension detail page on iOS*

Clicking "Extension Settings" will open the options page (Figure 15-27).

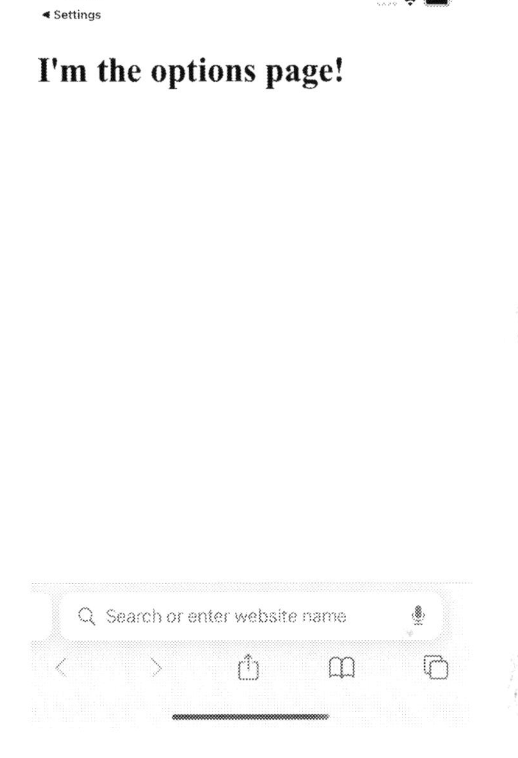

Figure 15-27. *The options page on iOS Safari*

Next, navigate to a valid web page like wikipedia.org. When iOS Safari has extensions installed, the URL bar will display a puzzle piece. Click this to reveal the menu, which should contain an MVX extension option (Figure 15-28).

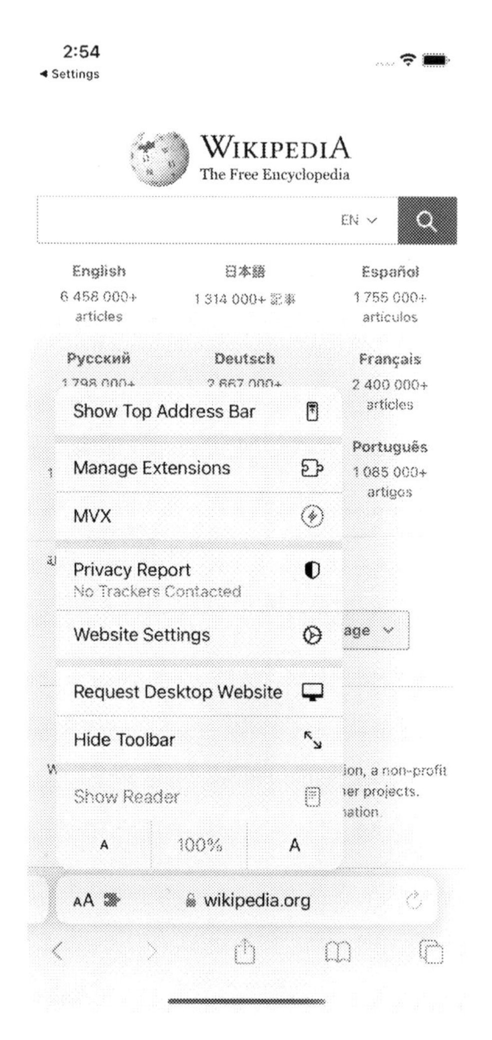

Figure 15-28. *The iOS Safari extension menu options*

This MVX option functions as the toolbar button, and selecting it will open the extension's popup page. Click the "Change background color" button to test that the content script is functioning (Figure 15-29).

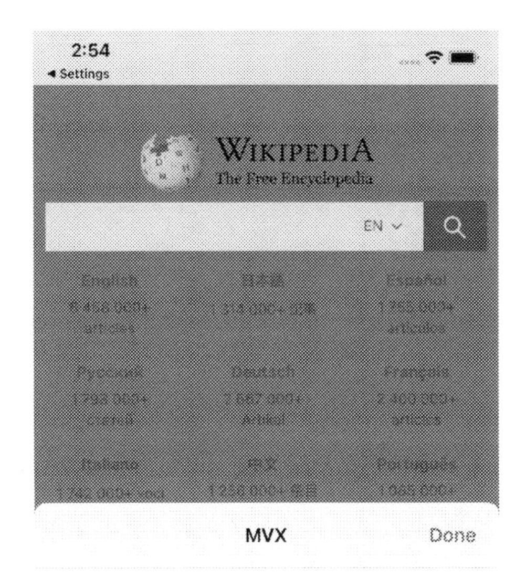

***Figure 15-29.** The popup page modifies the web page's background color*

You can track the log messages created by clicking the "Send native message" button through the Console app in the same way as macOS Safari (Figure 15-30).

Figure 15-30. *The os_log output from the iOS extension's native app*

Deploying to the App Store

You will need to deploy separate apps for iOS and macOS. The deployment process is no different than publishing regular iOS or macOS apps. At a high level, you'll need to perform the following steps:

1. Create a project archive
2. Build and sign the bundle
3. Validate the bundle
4. Push to the App Store to begin the approval process

An example macOS deploy flow is shown in Figures 15-31, 15-32, and 15-33.

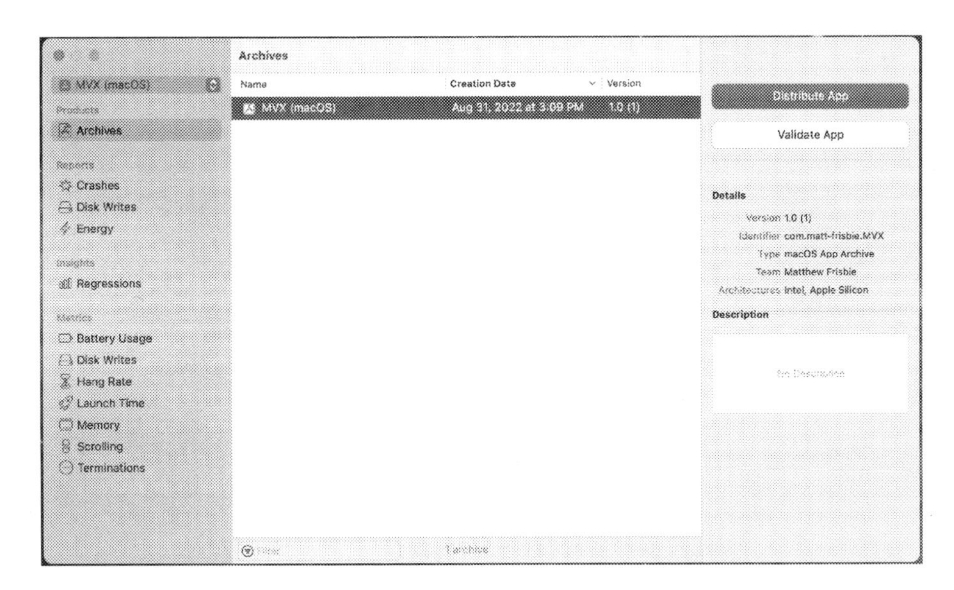

***Figure 15-31.** The generated project archive used for publishing*

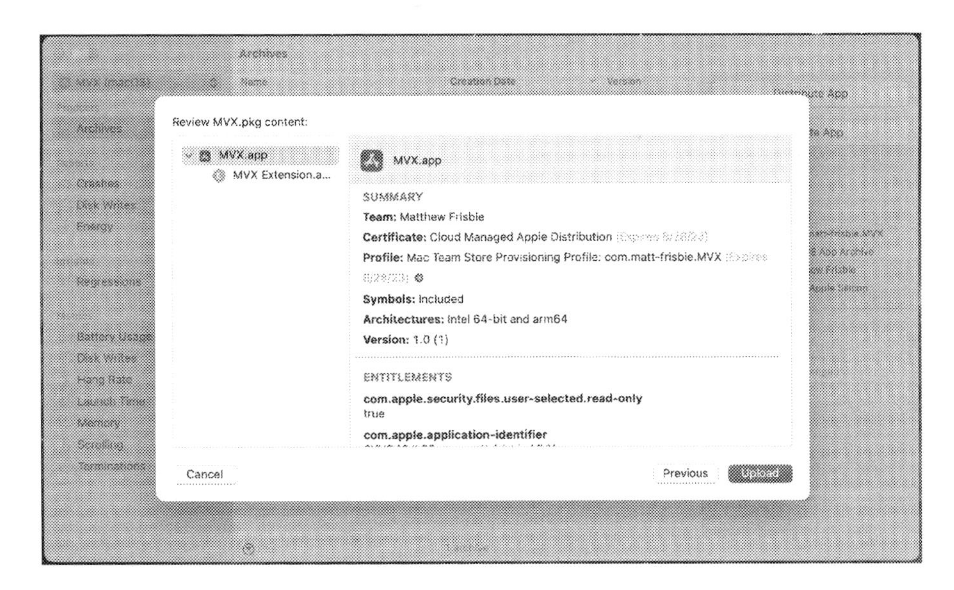

***Figure 15-32.** The packaged project ready to be published*

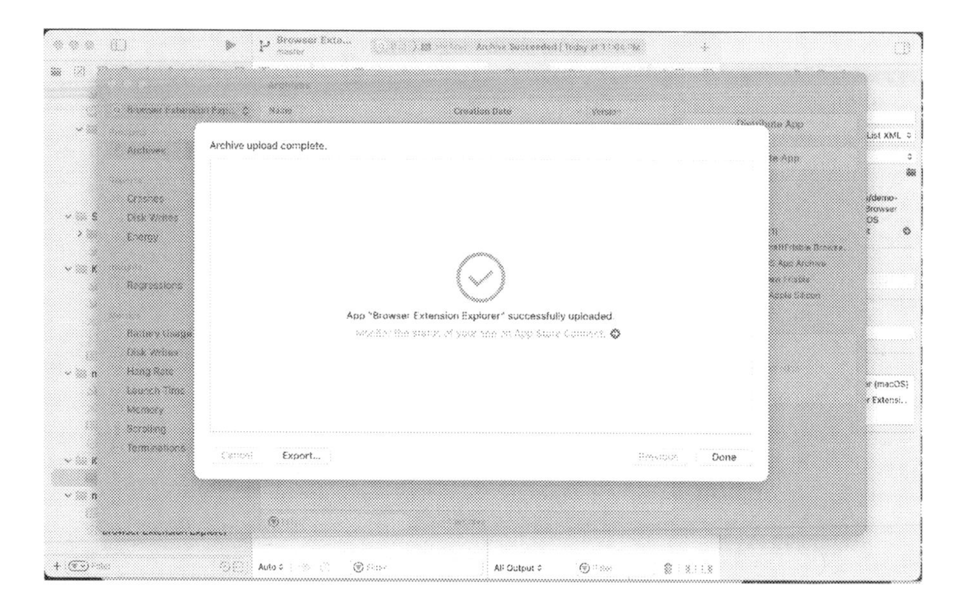

***Figure 15-33.** An example success screen when your project is successfully published*

Converting an Existing Extension

Xcode has a command line utility built-in which will automatically convert an existing browser extension codebase into a Safari extension. The following command will generate an Xcode extension project including your existing files:

```
xcrun safari-web-extension-converter /path/to/extension
```

Tip More details on this CLI tool can be found here: `https://developer.apple.com/documentation/safariservices/safari_web_extensions/converting_a_web_extension_for_safari`.

Firefox Idiosyncrasies

Other than Safari, which is covered thoroughly in the previous extension, the Firefox addon ecosystem has some notable differences that you should be aware of when developing for it.

Manifest Versions

At the time this book was written, Firefox is in a transitional period. The organization is attempting to soften the messy transition from manifest v2 to v3 by extending support for APIs like `webRequestBlocking` that developers wish to cling to. This state of things will likely not persist for far into the future, but for the time being, keep the following things in mind:

- Currently, Firefox is the only major browser that does not allow you to load manifest v3 extensions by default. It can be enabled, but its support is spotty.
- Currently, Firefox is currently the only major webstore that does not accept manifest v3 extensions.
- Firefox indicated that it will adopt manifest v3, but also preserve features that developers still need and use. What this ultimately will look like is unclear.

Additionally, when manifest v3 is eventually supported, you will need an add-on ID in your manifest. The MDN documentation includes the following:

> *All Manifest V3 extensions need an add-on ID in their manifest.json when submitted to AMO. Contrary to Manifest V2 extensions, AMO will not accept Manifest V3 extensions without an ID and it will not automatically embed this ID in the signed packaged extension.*

The add-on ID is declared under browser_specific_settings.gecko.id. For example:

manifest.json

```
{
  ...
  "browser_specific_settings": {
    "gecko": {
      "id": "browserextensionexplorer@
buildingbrowserextensions.com"
    }
  },
  ...
}
```

Note Read the Mozilla announcement here: https://blog.mozilla.org/addons/2022/05/18/manifest-v3-in-firefox-recap-next-steps/.

Sidebars

Firefox sidebars are extension-controlled containers that are defined similarly to popups. They are declared in the manifest under the sidebar_action key and appear alongside the active web page on either side (Figure 15-34).

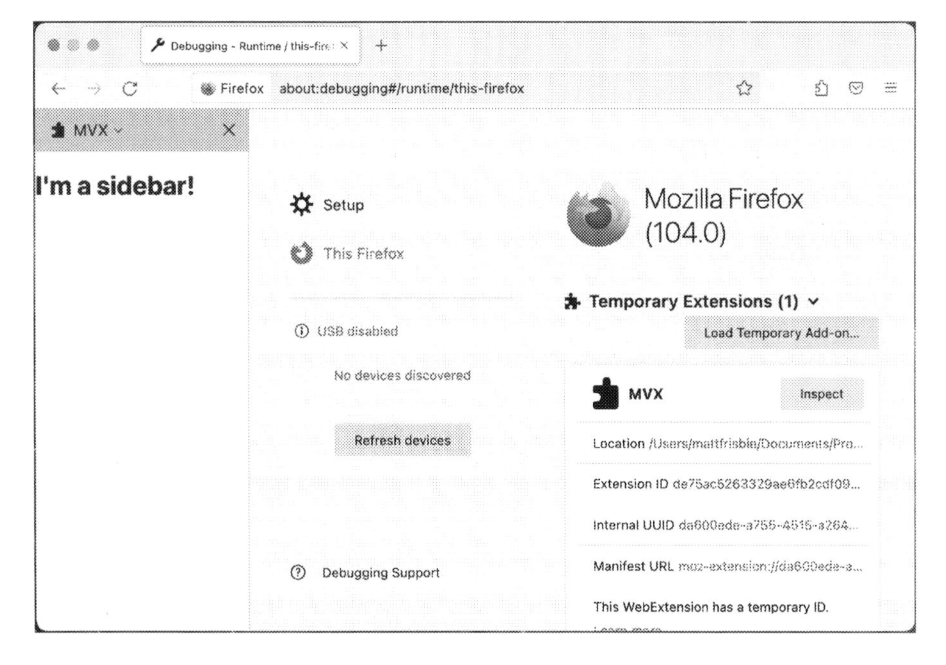

Figure 15-34. *A Mozilla Firefox sidebar*

API Additions

Firefox is unlike other browsers in that it adds a significant number of APIs to the extension API namespace:

- `captivePortal`
- `contextualIdentites`
- `dns`
- `find`
- `menus`
- `pcks11`

- `sidebarAction`
- `theme`
- `userScripts`

Tip For a summary of these API differences, refer to this link: `https://developer.mozilla.org/en-US/docs/Mozilla/Add-ons/WebExtensions/Firefox_differentiators`.

Summary

In this chapter, we covered all the complicated aspects of creating an extension that supports multiple browsers. We discussed how an extension built on the Chrome Web Store can support a vast majority of desktop browsers that are based off the Chromium project. We also discussed all the different places you can deploy a browser extension as well as different ways extensions can be used on mobile.

This chapter also covered various browser idiosyncrasies. It described in detail how to develop and publish extensions for Safari on iOS and macOS, as well as all the unique aspects of developing for Firefox.

In the next chapter, we will cover all the different tools, platforms, and frameworks that you can use to make extension development and deployment easier.

CHAPTER 16

Tooling and Frameworks

Modern browser extensions are rarely written from scratch. There is a wealth of developer tools at your disposal that allow you to efficiently build and test extensions in your chosen JavaScript framework and seamlessly publish them to multiple extension marketplaces.

Building Extensions with React

For developers who wish to build a browser extension with a JavaScript framework, the most common choice is React. How you ultimately fold React into your extension will largely depend on the scope and complexity of your application. Some things to consider:

- **Does your extension have one or many entrypoints?** Here, "entrypoint" can mean either an HTML file that will be loaded (popup.html or options.html), or a UI rendered via a content script. A single HTML entrypoint will greatly simplify the architecture of your extension.
- **Does your extension UI need to share state between different views?** Extensions only have an asynchronous shared storage mechanism, which makes using tools like Redux more complicated.

M. Frisbie, *Building Browser Extensions*, https://doi.org/10.1007/978-1-4842-8725-5_16

- **Does your extension require a React UI inside a content script?** Mounting a single page application in the page is different than rendering it inside a controlled HTML file.
- **How will your single page application use routing?** Content scripts, options pages, and popup pages all have different routing considerations that may affect how you roll out your React app.

Single Entrypoint React Extensions

If your extension only requires a single entrypoint (such as popup or options), then reaching for an app generated by `create-react-app` (CRA) can be a good option. In this section, we'll discuss how to create a very simple extension with CRA, and we'll also cover some of the drawbacks with using this strategy. Let's begin by generating a CRA application with TypeScript:

```
$ npx create-react-app mvx-react --template typescript
```

This will churn out a basic application structure that is designed for the web. We will need to customize it to make it usable in an extension. Begin by adding the type definitions for the WebExtensions API:

```
$ yarn add @types/chrome -D
```

The CRA generates a `manifest.json` intended for a progressive web application. It's already in the `public` directory, so it's perfect for you to repurpose for an extension manifest. Update the file with the following:

manifest.json

```
{
  "name": "MVX React",
  "description": "Minimum Viable Extension - React",
  "version": "0.0.1",
  "manifest_version": 3,
  "action": {
    "default_popup": "index.html"
  },
  "icons": {
    "16": "logo192.png",
    "48": "logo192.png",
    "128": "logo192.png"
  }
}
```

One final change is a minor CSS tweak. Since this is rendering inside the popup container, we need to enforce minimum dimensions – otherwise the browser will collapse the container to the size of the content. Add the following rules to `index.css`:

index.css

```
body {
  ...
  width: 400px;
  min-height: 400px;
}
```

This isn't ready to run yet. When building your application, CRA will try to place JavaScript inline in the page. Manifest v3 extensions explicitly disallow this, so you will need to configure the CRA build process to only load scripts from a URL. You can prevent CRA from inlining scripts by setting the environment variable INLINE_RUNTIME_CHUNK to false. There's a handful of ways to do this, but the simplest is to just prefix the assignment to the package.json commands:

package.json

```
{

  "scripts": {
    "start": "INLINE_RUNTIME_CHUNK=false react-scripts start",
    "build": "INLINE_RUNTIME_CHUNK=false react-scripts build",
    "test": "react-scripts test",
    "eject": "react-scripts eject"
  },
  ...
}
```

The app is ready to be installed as an extension. If we were running this as a website, we would execute npm run start to boot up a development server. However, because manifest v3 forbids loading code from remote sources – specifically, a server running on localhost:3000 – this will not work. Instead, you will need to execute npm run build and load the build directory into the browser. When the build succeeds, load the extension into the browser and open the popup. You should see the CRA default page (Figure 16-1).

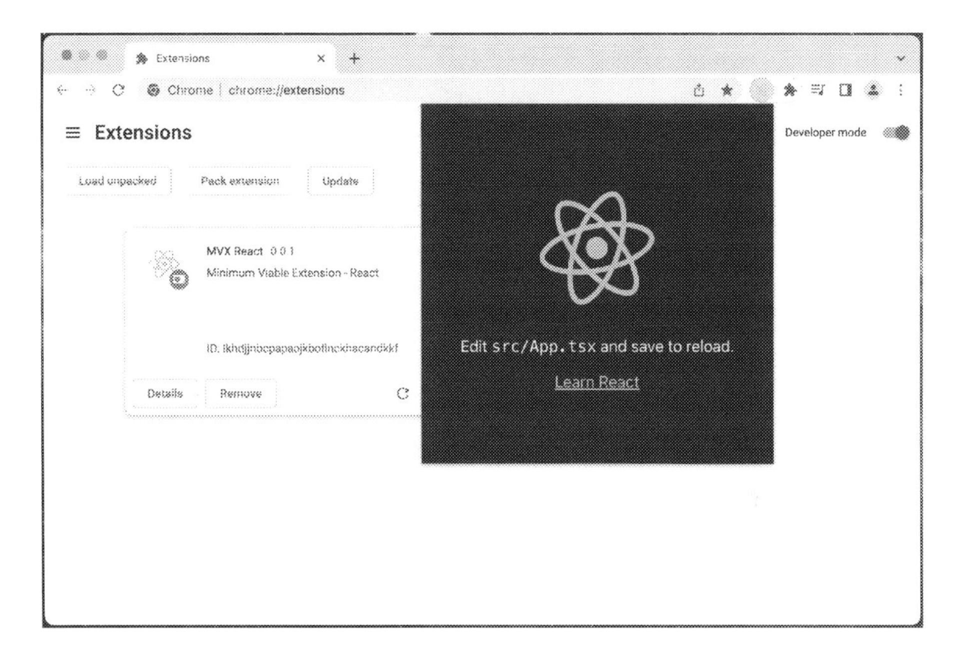

Figure 16-1. *The Create React App index.html rendered in a popup*

Tip Using `npm run build` is a suitable workaround for smaller projects, but it is not a scalable solution. Read on in the chapter for better build tools.

Multiple Entrypoint React Extensions

If your app has more than one entrypoint, then `create-react-app` is probably not a good solution for you. You will need a development configuration that supports multiple independent entrypoints, including independent JS and CSS bundles. Read on in the chapter for several excellent solutions.

Reactive State Management

When managing state for a complex single page application, most developers will reach for a reactive state management container such as Redux. It is often advantageous to persist and rehydrate state, allowing for the application to remain consistent across reloads. There are two primary challenges in the context of browser extensions:

- The typical storage APIs that we would use such as `localStorage` or `IndexedDB` are not shared between extension pieces. For example, a popup writing to `localStorage` will be isolated from a content script writing to `localStorage` because their scripts are running on different origins!
- The only shared storage mechanism, `chrome.storage`, is asynchronous.

Often, you may only need to share a small piece of state, such as authentication data, between multiple extension views. Things like route state, server-loaded data, and other view-centric information are likely bound to a specific extension view, and therefore persisting it in something like `localStorage` may be acceptable. For example, a popup that loads a user's preferences from the server is safe to store that data locally if it will not be displayed anywhere else.

In situations where state must be shared between components, it is possible to configure Redux to use `chrome.storage` as an asynchronous store. The `chrome.storage.onChanged` event means that each view can react to other views mutating the store. There are two popular GitHub repositories that implement this:

- `https://github.com/ssorallen/redux-persist-webextension-storage`
- `https://github.com/robinmalburn/redux-persist-chrome-storage`

Tip If you're not familiar with Redux, read up on the React Redux library here: `https://react-redux.js.org/`.

Routing

When managing view state for a complex single page application, most developers will reach for a routing solution such as React Router. There are two primary challenges in the context of browser extensions:

- In views such as popups and options pages, the browser is loading an HTML file directly, so using an out-of-the-box routing solution will lead to invalid paths such as `index.html/foo/bar` that will break on reload.
- In views rendered via content scripts, you should not modify the host page URL whatsoever. Assume the host page will use the URL hash or query string fully, which can break any routing values you append to it.

Fortunately, both of these problems have straightforward solutions.

Extension Views and HashRouter

Across all browsers, extension views have a URL structure similar to the following:

```
extension-protocol://path/to/file.html
```

All major single page application routers support some form of URL hash routing, which will not interfere with the extension path and can survive page reloads:

```
extension-protocol://path/to/file.html#/your/app/route
```

For example, React Router can implement this routing strategy using `HashRouter`.

Tip Documentation on `HashRouter` can be found here: `https://v5.reactrouter.com/web/api/HashRouter`.

If you want the popup to always open the most recent URL, you can dynamically update your popup URL via `chrome.action.setPopup()` and include the hash route.

Content Scripts and MemoryRouter

For views that render via a content script, you may have a complicated user interface that can benefit from routing, but modifying the page URL bar is not an option. All major single page application routers support some form of in-memory routing. These routers are often intended for native applications that do not have a URL, but they work equally well for extension content script views. React Router can implement this routing strategy using `MemoryRouter`.

If you need your router state to survive page reloads, you can persist your router state in your app state. Be aware that you may need to account for multiple route states across different tabs.

Tip Documentation on `MemoryRouter` can be found here: `https://v5.reactrouter.com/web/api/MemoryRouter`

Mozilla Tools

Mozilla maintains a suite of tools geared for developing browser extensions. To a certain extent they are geared toward developing for Firefox, but in general they can be effectively used to develop for any browser.

web-ext

`https://github.com/mozilla/web-ext`

The `web-ext` project is a suite of CLI tools for developing and publishing browser extensions. It features these commands:

- `web-ext build` creates an extension package from source
- `web-ext sign` signs the extension so it can be installed in Firefox
- `web-ext run` runs the extension
- `web-ext lint` validates the extension source
- `web-ext docs` opens the web-ext documentation in a browser

There is also a Webpack plugin that wraps `web-ext` (not maintained by Mozilla):

`https://github.com/hiikezoe/web-ext-webpack-plugin`

Running `webpack` by itself will build the extension, effectively running `web-ext` build on the output of your Webpack build.

webextension-polyfill

`https://github.com/mozilla/webextension-polyfill`

Browsers are gradually moving the WebExtensions API over to an async/await friendly format, but the transition is not yet complete. Mozilla maintains this polyfill library to make the entire API return promises, eliminating the need for callbacks.

Bundlers and CLI Tools

When developing browser extensions, I strongly recommend using some form of software to assist in building and packaging the extension – especially if you are using a JavaScript framework like React, or have an extension with multiple entrypoints. Because the extension and framework space is currently undergoing a seismic shift, there are a lot of tools and repositories out there that are outdated: either they target only manifest v2, or don't support newer versions of frameworks. In this selection, I've hand-selected some projects that are actively maintained and can support development of browser extensions.

Warning A major feature of bundlers is Hot Module Replacement (HMR), the ability to hot swap out portions of an application as the developer updates the source files. For manifest v3 extension development, due to script restrictions, this is strictly incompatible; you will need to disable conventional HMR. Some bundlers rework HMR by altering it to programmatically reload the extension.

Parcel

https://parceljs.org/

If you are choosing an open-source tool for browser extension development, Parcel is by far my top choice. It has excellent support for manifest v3, multiple entrypoints, TypeScript, React, Vue, and Sass.

For developers coming from the world of Webpack, Parcel may be a bit disorienting at first. Whereas Webpack uses a dense configuration file to organize how it will build an application, Parcel is configuration-free. In lieu of a verbose configuration file, it uses pre-configured NPM packages that enable Parcel to implicitly understand how to build and bundle an application.

You can install the `@parcel/config-webextension` NPM package (`https://parceljs.org/recipes/web-extension/`) to enable Parcel to build your web extension. Using this recipe, Parcel can parse your `manifest.json` file for entrypoints. It will then parse those HTML files to understand how it should build the JS and CSS bundles for each separate entrypoint.

Translation from uncompiled file extensions such as TypeScript (.ts), React (.jsx/.tsx), Vue (.vue), and Sass (.scss) files is automatic, meaning you can directly use these files in the manifest and HTML entrypoints and Parcel will handle the compilation and file path replacement for you. Some examples:

manifest.json

```
{
  ...
  "content_scripts": [
    {
      "matches": ["<all_urls>"],
      "js": ["content-script.tsx"],
```

```
      "css": ["content-script.scss"]
    }
  ],
  ...
}
```

popup.html

```
<!DOCTYPE html>
<html lang="en">
  <head>
    <meta charset="UTF-8" />
    <meta name="viewport" content="width=device-width, initial-
    scale=1.0" />
    <link href="popup.scss" rel="stylesheet" />
  </head>

  <body>
    <div id="app"></div>
    <script type="module" src="popup.tsx"></script>
  </body>
</html>
```

Note Refer to the Parcel documentation for instructions on how to set up a new browser extension project, as well as coverage of other features: `https://parceljs.org/recipes/web-extension/`.

Webpack

`https://webpack.js.org/`

Webpack is often the go-to choices for website development, and it certainly continues to be a sensible choice for browser extension development. Unlike Parcel, Webpack favors explicitly defining behavior inside a config file. For particularly complicated extensions, it may be advantageous for you to have the ability to explicitly dictate how Webpack should compile and bundle your extension files. Webpack also has a significantly larger community behind it, which may be an important consideration for long-term support.

For developers who wish to begin with a Webpack config file geared for building manifest v3 browser extensions, I would recommend one of the following two repositories:

- `https://github.com/lxieyang/chrome-extension-boilerplate-react`
- `https://github.com/sszczep/chrome-extension-webpack`

Warning There is a relatively large number of GitHub repositories containing outdated Webpack browser extension templates. These target older versions of Webpack or are strictly limited to manifest v2. Be careful when choosing a starter repository, it can often be very painful to move off of it.

Plasmo

`https://www.plasmo.com/`

Plasmo's website says it best:

> *Plasmo is a platform for developing browser extensions. Shipping extensions like shipping websites – FAST.*

There are many aspects of the browser extension development and deployment process that are painful, and Plasmo is designed to hide all of the unpleasantness under the hood. As you will see in this section, it has a robust set of features that hide all the nastiness of generating multiple manifest versions, supporting different browsers, and deploying to all the extension marketplaces.

Tip For its ease of use, engaged maintainers, active developer community, and powerful featureset, I would recommend using Plasmo over anything else to develop a browser extension.

High-level Overview

The Plasmo framework builds opinionated abstractions on top of Parcel that considerably improves the extension development experience. Like Parcel, Plasmo features a convention-over-configuration design philosophy. For example, if you want to add an options page to your extension, you can just create an `options.tsx` React component in the project's root directory, and Plasmo will do the rest: automatically compile that file into JS/CSS/HTML assets, generate a new `manifest.json` with the new HTML file as the options page, and reload the extension.

Tip Plasmo is incredibly easy to start using right away. Check out their *Getting Started* guide here: `https://docs.plasmo.com/#getting-started`

JavaScript Frameworks

Plasmo is unopinionated when it comes to JavaScript frameworks. It supports React, Vue, and Svelte. By default, the CLI `init` command will generate a React application, but switching over to a different framework is trivial:

- To use Vue, install the `vue` package and change your files to use `.vue` extensions (e.g., `popup.vue`).
- To use Svelte, install `svelte` and `svelte-preprocess`, initialize your `svelte.config.js` file, and change your files to use `.svelte` extensions (e.g., `popup.svelte`).

Documentation and Examples

Bad documentation has long been a thorn in the side of extension development. Manifest versions are inconsistent, API coverage is spotty or unclear, and examples are inconsistent. Plasmo features *very* robust and complete documentation:

`https://docs.plasmo.com/`

Plasmo's docs also include a collection of "quickstarts," which are detailed instructions on how to incorporate popular libraries. This is especially useful for developers like me, because the first two things I do in a new project is install and set up Tailwind and Redux.

`https://docs.plasmo.com/quickstarts`

For developers who prefer to learn by example, the Plasmo GitHub account features a wide collection of examples explaining how to accomplish common tasks:

`https://github.com/PlasmoHQ/examples`

Differential Build Outputs

Plasmo has some very useful CLI features for generating application builds. It is capable of generating both manifest v2 and manifest v3 outputs with a command line flag, like so:

```
# Generates build/chrome-dev-mv3/ directory
pnpm dev --target=chrome-mv3

# Generates build/firefox-dev-mv2/ directory
pnpm dev --target=firefox-mv2

# Generates build/chrome-prod-mv3/ directory
pnpm build --target=chrome-mv3

# Generates build/firefox-prod-mv2/ directory
pnpm build --target=firefox-mv2
```

Note `chrome-mv3` is the default target

Furthermore, Plasmo can create a zip of these builds that can be directly handed off to the extension marketplaces. This is done with the `--zip` flag:

```
# Generates build/chrome-prod-mv3.zip
pnpm build --zip

# Generates build/firefox-prod-mv2.zip
pnpm build --target=firefox-mv2 --zip
```

Automatic Manifest Generation

Instead of writing a `manifest.json` file yourself, Plasmo generates the manifest based on your source files and configurations you export from your code – similar to how Next.js abstracts page routing and SSG with the file system and page components.

Values in your project's `package.json` will typically be redundant with the corresponding values in your extension manifest. Plasmo will automatically copy over values from `package.json` into your `manifest.json`:

- `packageJson.version -> manifest.version`
- `packageJson.displayName -> manifest.name`
- `packageJson.description -> manifest.description`
- `packageJson.author -> manifest.author`
- `packageJson.homepage -> manifest.homepage_url`

Icon Generation

Browser extensions display its icon throughout the browser, and the icons must be tediously listed in multiple places inside the manifest. As shown below, Plasmo will take a single source 512x512 icon in the `assets/` directory, generate multiple resized icons, and automatically include them in the manifest wherever needed (Figure 16-2).

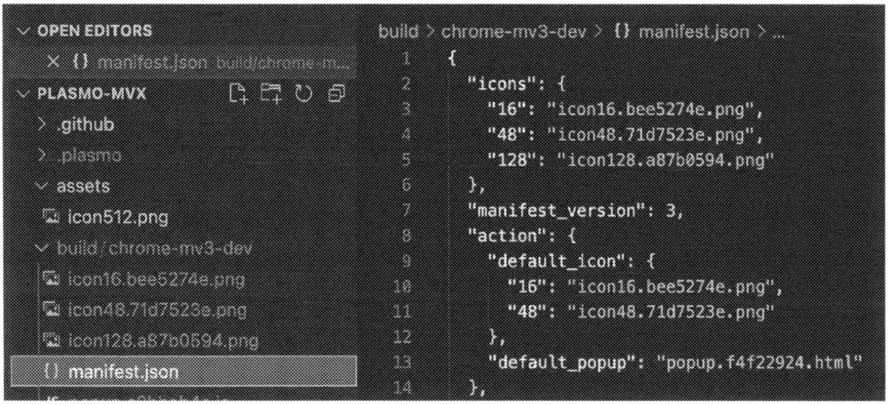

Figure 16-2. *Dynamic icon generation from single asset image*

Bundling Remote Code

In manifest v3, loading and executing remote code is strictly forbidden. To solve this problem, Plasmo will parse your `import` statements for remotely hosted assets, fetch them, and bundle them inside the extension. In the following screenshot, we can see that `popup.tsx` is importing the remote Google Tag Manager JavaScript, and the file is automatically included in the `build/chrome-mv3-dev/` directory (Figure 16-3).

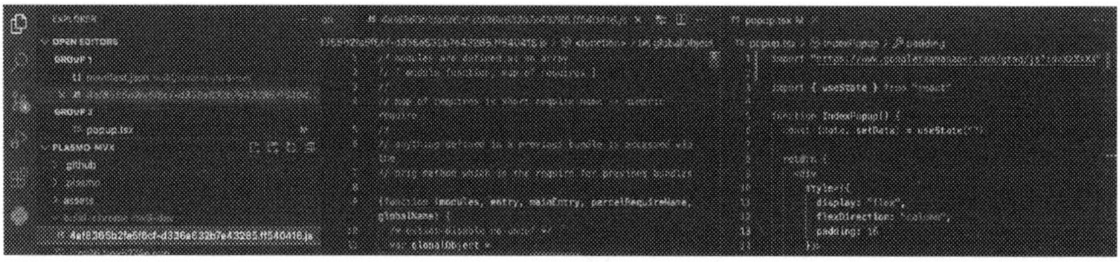

***Figure 16-3.** Plasmo automatically bundles the gtag.js into the extension*

Environment Variables

Plasmo features an intuitive solution for environment variables based on the `dotenv` NPM package. Environment variables can be placed in a `.env` file in the root directory of your project, and they will become available:

- In JavaScript via the `process.env` namespace
- In `import` URLs
- In `package.json` manifest overrides

The following snippets demonstrate each of these:

.env

```
PLASMO_PUBLIC_FOO=foo
PLASMO_PUBLIC_GTAG_ID=123456789
PLASMO_PUBLIC_CRX_PUBLIC_KEY=asdf-1234-asdf-1234
```

popup.tsx

```
import " https://www.googletagmanager.com/gtag/js?id=$PLASMO_
PUBLIC_GTAG_ID"

function IndexPopup() {
  return <div>{process.env.PLASMO_PUBLIC_FOO}</div>;
}

export default IndexPopup
```

manifest.json

```
{
  "key": "$CRX_PUBLIC_KEY"
}
```

Note Plasmo mirrors the Next.js `.env` file convention with `.local`, `.production`, and `.development` suffix rules. Read more here: `https://docs.plasmo.com/workflows/env.`

Content Script Mounting

Injecting a user interface in a content script usually requires some bootstrapping, and Plasmo does all this for you as a Content Script UI. You can define your component in a `content.*` file with a `PlasmoContentScript` definition. Plasmo will automatically add a corresponding `content_scripts` entry in your manifest. The following is an example of this:

content.tsx

```
import type { PlasmoContentScript } from "plasmo"

const config: PlasmoContentScript = {
  matches: ["<all_urls>"]
}

function IndexContentUI() {
  return (
    <h1
      style={{
        backgroundColor: "blue",
        color: "white",
        padding: "12rem"
      }}>
      I'm the content script widget!
    </h1>
  )
}

export default IndexContentUI
```

This widget will be injected on every web page. Note below that Plasmo is injecting the component inside a Shadow DOM container to prevent CSS interference (Figure 16-4).

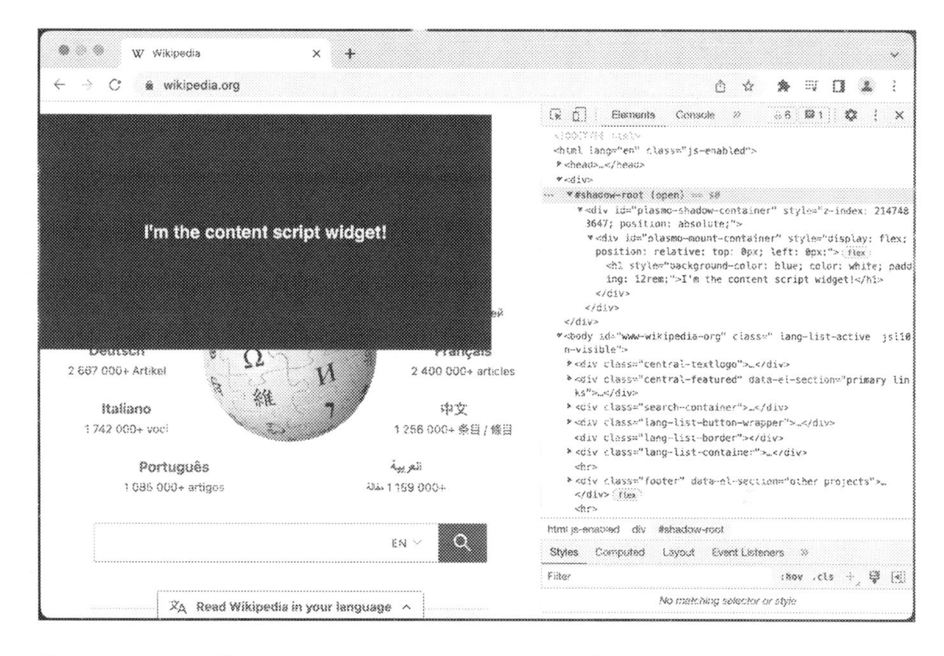

Figure 16-4. *The injected content script widget inside a Shadow DOM*

Extension-friendly Hot Module Replacement

Manifest v3 disallows traditional HMR, but Plasmo offers something similar. When developing your extension, Plasmo injects a web socket listener into the development build of the extension. Whenever a bundle change happens, Plasmo sends the refresh message and it either executes `chrome.runtime.reload()` or `location.reload()` depending on the context. While this isn't strictly the same as HMR, it still allows you to see code updates in real time.

Automated Deployment with Browser Platform Publish

Plasmo ships with a GitHub action called Browser Platform Publish (BPP) that will automatically publish your extension updates to all supported browser extension marketplaces. Setting up BPP involves the following steps:

1. **Perform the initial publish of your extension to each marketplace.** You'll need an existing extension on each marketplace before you can use BPP to publish updates.
2. **Generate credentials for each marketplace.** Extension marketplaces allow you to generate authentication tokens to automatically sign and publish updates. You will need to do this for each marketplace.
3. **Provide the credentials to BPP.** Once you've acquired your credentials for each marketplace, you'll provide it to the BPP GitHub action as an encrypted repository secret.

Once this one-time setup is performed, you will be able to seamlessly push updates to all the extension marketplaces simultaneously. The following links provide more details on context on how to set up and use BPP:

- Details on retrieving credentials: `https://github.com/PlasmoHQ/bms/blob/main/tokens.md`
- GitHub action page for BPP: `https://github.com/marketplace/actions/browser-platform-publisher`

- BPP GitHub repository: `https://github.com/PlasmoHQ/bpp`
- Introduction to using BPP: `https://docs.plasmo.com/workflows/submit`

Useful Sites

- `https://buildingbrowserextensions.com` is the companion website of this book. It includes a link to the Browser Extension Explorer, a Chrome extension that consists of open source demos for each extension API.
- `https://developer.chrome.com/` is Chrome's official site to help you build Extensions, publish on the Chrome Web Store, optimize your website, and more.
- `https://extensionworkshop.com/` helps with creating and publishing Firefox add-ons that make browsing smarter, safer, and faster. You'll find the resources you need, whether you're getting started with extension development, preparing to launch your innovation, or developing a custom enterprise solution.
- `https://webext.eu/` quickly generates browser extension templates with just a few clicks. It is maintained by Mozilla. It is very handy for quickly prototyping extensions.

Summary

In this chapter, we discussed a wide variety of automated tools that you can use to speed up and simplify extension development. First, we discussed how React can be configured to neatly fit into an extension project, as well as how to integrate some popular React libraries. Next, we covered a variety of popular open source build tools that can be used to manage the inherent complexity of browser extensions. Finally, we covered all the different features that the Plasmo platform has to offer.

Index

M. Frisbie, *Building Browser Extensions*, https://doi.org/10.1007/978-1-4842-8725-5

D

E

F

G

N

O

P, Q

R

S

T

U

V

W

X, Y, Z

Printed in the United States
by Baker & Taylor Publisher Services